Nathaniel M. Williams

The Gospel according to Matthew:

With notes: intended for Sabbath schools, families, and ministers

Nathaniel M. Williams

The Gospel according to Matthew:
With notes: intended for Sabbath schools, families, and ministers

ISBN/EAN: 9783337714376

Printed in Europe, USA, Canada, Australia, Japan

Cover: Foto ©ninafisch / pixelio.de

More available books at **www.hansebooks.com**

THE

GOSPEL ACCORDING TO MATTHEW;

WITH

NOTES:

INTENDED FOR

SABBATH SCHOOLS, FAMILIES, AND MINISTERS.

BY

NATHANIEL MARSHMAN WILLIAMS.

With Illustrations.

MEMPHIS, TENN.:
SOUTHERN BAPTIST PUBLICATION SOCIETY.

Entered according to Act of Congress, in the year 1870, by
GOULD AND LINCOLN,
In the Clerk's Office of the District Court for the District of Massachusetts.

The Memory

OF

HIS FATHER,

Rev. Nathaniel West Williams,

TO WHOSE

PRECEPTS AND EXAMPLE HE IS GREATLY INDEBTED,

THIS VOLUME IS INSCRIBED

BY

THE AUTHOR.

PREFACE.

The Christian public may ask why this Commentary was written. To such an inquiry it may be replied, that it was written to aid Sabbath-school teachers and scholars, and the people generally, as well as those ministers who may not be able to provide themselves with large and expensive Commentaries, in securing a more exact understanding of the word of God, so far as is possible through the author, by making available the results of the latest biblical scholarship. Since most of the other similar works were written, much advance has been made in knowledge of Palestine, ancient Egypt, and Assyria; one of the most valuable of all ancient manuscripts has been brought out from its concealment in the convent of St. Catherine, at the foot of Mount Sinai (hence called the Sinaitic Manuscript), by means of which, in part, a more accurate Greek text has been obtained; and juster principles of criticism have been reached.

In no instance has the author passed over a verse in silence to avoid its difficulties. It has been his purpose to bestow more attention upon difficult passages than upon others. When he has not been able to arrive at satisfactory conclusions, he has not hesitated to say so. In some cases, probability of meaning is all that he has felt justified in affirming. It is a source of pleasure to all sincere Christians, that, concerning much the greater part of the Scriptures, there can be no difference of opinion. There are, however, portions of the Gospel here examined, respecting which the author has felt compelled to differ from other commentators whose works are intended for the people. Those passages which teach, more or less directly, the conditions of membership in a Christian Church, and those which pertain to the two symbolic rites of Christianity, have been explained, by most expositors, it seems to the author, in a manner contrary to the principles of sound criticism, and to most of the best biblical scholarship of Christendom. Baptism, and the relation of the Lord's Supper to baptism, are considered at some length in the notes on the nineteenth and twentieth verses of the last chapter.

The thanks of the author are due to A. N. Arnold, D.D., Professor in the Theological Seminary of Chicago, formerly a resident missionary in Greece, for permission to examine and appropriate portions of a valuable manuscript on the practice of the Greek Church in respect to baptism; and to Rev. William F. Snow, the scholarly pastor of the Eliot Congregational Church in Lawrence, for permission to transfer the substance of an unpublished paper read before the Andover Association of Congregational ministers, on the very difficult twenty-fourth chapter. The view is unlike that usually taken.

The plan and arrangement of the notes differ from those of most other similar works.

1. This Gospel has been examined, for the most part, as if there were no other. Some reference to the others has been indispensable. If, in them, statements shall be met, which seem to be in conflict with the record already examined, or which present a more distinct view of our Lord, they will be carefully considered.

2. The notes are chiefly explanatory; yet the doctrinal, and the practical are not wanting. But, instead of grouping doctrinal and practical thoughts at the close of each chapter, in a sermon-like way, they are introduced at points where the text itself suggests them. It has been the aim to express practical thoughts in a condensed form. As to the explanatory parts, the author has endeavored, on the one hand, to avoid such brevity as to leave the inquirer with scarcely a thread upon which to lay hold in his search for truth; and, on the other hand, to avoid using so many words that no sharp and definite impression can be made. Most Sabbath-school teachers have so little time for the study of the lesson, that they are very justly impatient at being compelled to wander about through a bewildering forest of words. If one well-directed blow will open the nut, another blow does positive harm.

3. The testimony of many intelligent Sabbath-school teachers has led the author to adopt the plan of making the illustrative part of the work fuller than is usual, believing that illustrations from ancient customs and from sacred

geography should be sufficiently numerous to obviate the necessity of buying books in this department of knowledge.

In profound gratitude for the accumulated knowledge of past ages, it may be said that the means of giving to the people of the present day a conception of the will of God, as revealed in the Bible, are undoubtedly superior to those of any former period.

Should this volume prove acceptable, it may be followed by one or more on the other Gospels. If God should crown the present effort with his blessing, to him be all the praise.

N. M. W.

METHUEN, MASS., Jan., 1870.

CONTENTS.

CHAPTER I.
The Genealogy and Birth of Jesus 15

CHAPTER II.
Events Immediately Following the Birth 22

CHAPTER III.
The Baptism of Jesus by John the Baptist 39

CHAPTER IV.
Jesus Tempted; Begins his Ministry 47

CHAPTER V.
Sermon on the Mount. Illustrations; Class 1 . . 57

CHAPTER VI.
Sermon on the Mount. Illustrations; Class 2 . . . 81

CHAPTER VII.

Sermon on the Mount. 95

CHAPTER VIII.

A Series of Miracles 101

CHAPTER IX.

A Series of Miracles. 112

CHAPTER X.

Jesus Commissions and Sends the Twelve 122

CHAPTER XI.

A Message from John; The Lord's Opinion of John . . 138

CHAPTER XII.

The Disciples Plucking Ears of Grain; Jesus Healing a Withered Hand, and Falsely Accused by the Pharisees, etc. 147

CHAPTER XIII.

Jesus Illustrates the Founding and the Development of his Kingdom in Seven Parables. 162

    1 — The Sower 163
    2 — The Tares 168
    3 — The Mustard Seed 170

4 — THE LEAVEN 171
5 — THE HIDDEN TREASURE . . . 174
6 — THE PEARL MERCHANT . . . 175
7 — THE NET 176

CHAPTER XIV.

NEWS OF JOHN'S DEATH; FEEDING A GREAT MULTITUDE;
RESCUE OF PETER 179

CHAPTER XV.

DEBATE WITH PHARISEES FROM THE CAPITAL; HEALS A GENTILE
IN THE GENTILE WORLD; FEEDS FOUR THOUSAND . . 187

CHAPTER XVI.

A SIGN ASKED; PETER AND HIS FELLOW-DISCIPLES CONFESS
JESUS AS THE MESSIAH; JESUS FORETELLS HIS OWN
DEATH 194

CHAPTER XVII.

THE TRANSFIGURATION; A LUNATIC HEALED; HIS DEATH AGAIN
ANNOUNCED 202

CHAPTER XVIII.

JESUS DISCOURSES TO HIS DISCIPLES 209

CHAPTER XIX.

FINAL DEPARTURE FROM GALILEE; THE DIVORCE QUESTION;
THE RICH YOUNG MAN 215

CHAPTER XX.

PARABLE OF THE LABORERS; HIS DEATH ONCE MORE ANNOUNCED; SALOME'S REQUEST; TWO BLIND MEN CURED . 223

CHAPTER XXI.

THE TRIUMPHAL ENTRY INTO JERUSALEM; CLEANSES THE TEMPLE; CURSES THE FIG-TREE; UTTERS THE PARABLE OF THE TWO SONS, AND THE PARABLE OF THE WICKED HUSBANDMEN 229

CHAPTER XXII.

THE PARABLE OF THE MARRIAGE FESTIVAL: THE PHARISEES, THE HERODIANS, AND THE SADDUCEES AIM TO ENSNARE JESUS WITH PERPLEXING QUESTIONS 240

CHAPTER XXIII.

JESUS DENOUNCES THE SCRIBES AND PHARISEES 248

CHAPTER XXIV.

JESUS DISCOURSES TO HIS DISCIPLES 257

CHAPTER XXV.

THE DUTY OF WATCHING FOR THE FINAL COMING FURTHER ENFORCED; THE LAST JUDGMENT 270

CHAPTER XXVI.

THE INSTITUTION OF THE SUPPER; THE LORD'S PASSION; PETER'S
DENIAL 280

CHAPTER XXVII.

THE SUICIDE OF JUDAS; JESUS CRUCIFIED AND BURIED . . 801

CHAPTER XXVIII.

RESURRECTION OF JESUS; THE LAST COMMISSION . . . 819

List of Illustrations.

	Page
BETHLEHEM	23
JERUSALEM AS SEEN FROM OLIVET	26
PLAN OF JERUSALEM	29
RACHEL'S TOMB	36
NAZARETH	38
SANDALS	45
WINNOWING	46
FISHING-NET	54
ALTAR	71
WATER-SKINS	117
RUINS OF SAMARIA	127
NINEVEH	160
SHEKEL	208
WINE-PRESS	238
FRONTLETS	250
WOMEN GRINDING	268
COURT OF THE PALACE OF THE HIGH PRIEST	300
DIFFERENT FORMS OF CROSSES	312
GROUND PLAN OF SEPULCHRES	318

THE

GOSPEL ACCORDING TO MATTHEW.

THE TITLE. *The Gospel*—The good news of salvation by Jesus Christ, first as orally delivered, then as written. There are not, strictly speaking, four Gospels. There is but one, a "four-sided Gospel." *According to*—Matthew narrates the good news *after his manner*, Mark after his. The same may be said of Luke and John. Though all the evangelists were inspired by the Holy Spirit, and therefore wrote truthfully, yet all were left free to select such facts from the life of Jesus as they chose, to narrate the facts in the order in which they occurred, or not in that order, and to present the facts in such a style of language, in such a manner of thinking, and for such a specific purpose, as their habits of education and their mental characteristics might naturally lead them to adopt. Matthew presents the Gospel *as the fulfilment of the law*. This is the peculiarity of his view. In this respect Matthew resembles James. This characteristic of his Gospel accords with the purpose for which it was primarily written; namely, to teach Jewish converts that Jesus was the Messiah of whom their Sacred Scriptures speak. This explains the freedom with which Matthew quotes from those writings, and explains also his manifest desire to prove that Jesus was a descendant of David and Abraham. It is important to remember that he does not profess to relate the events of our Lord's life according to the order of time.

CHAPTER I.

THE book of the generation of Jesus Christ, the son of David, the son of Abraham.

2 Abraham begat Isaac; and Isaac begat Jacob; and Jacob begat Judas and his brethren; 3 And Judas begat Phares and Zara of Thamar; and Pha-

---

CHAPTER I.

THE GENEALOGY AND THE BIRTH OF JESUS.

1. *The book of the generation—*

The roll of the descent, or, the birth-roll. Not the entire book of Matthew is meant, but the first seventeen verses. As it had been foretold in the Old Testament that the Messiah would descend from Abraham, and

res begat Esrom; and Esrom begat Aram;

4 And Aram begat Aminadab; and Aminadab begat Naasson; and Naasson begat Salmon;

5 And Salmon begat Booz of Rachab; and Booz begat Obed of Ruth; and Obed begat Jesse;

6 And Jesse begat David the king; and David the king begat Solomon of her *that had been the wife* of Urias;

7 And Solomon begat Roboam; and Roboam begat Abia; and Abia begat Asa;

8 And Asa begat Josaphat; and Josaphat begat Joram; and Joram begat Ozias;

9 And Ozias begat Joatham; and Joatham begat Achaz; and Achaz begat Ezekias;

10 And Ezekias begat Manasses; and Manasses begat Amon; and Amon begat Josias;

11 And Josias begat Jechonias and his brethren, about the time they were carried away to Babylon:

12 And after they were brought to Babylon, Jechonias begat Salathiel; and Salathiel begat Zorobabel;

13 And Zorobabel begat Abiud; and Abiud begat Eliakim; and Eliakim begat Azor;

14 And Azor begat Sadoc; and Sadoc begat Achim; and Achim begat Eliud;

15 And Eliud begat Elea-

---

would be an heir to the throne of David, it was necessary to prove that Jesus was a legal heir to David's throne and was the seed of Abraham. *Jesus Christ*—Jesus means Saviour. Though the name was borne by others, it was peculiarly appropriate to our Lord, for (vs 21) he was to save his people from their sins. Christ means anointed. It is equivalent to Messiah, and this is the representative of the Hebrew word *Mashiah*, which so often occurs in the Old Testament. It is there applied to priests and to kings, but it is used with special reference to the great Deliverer whom the prophets taught the Jews to expect both for themselves and for the Gentiles. Jesus is the proper name, and Christ is the official title, though both came to be used as proper names. Both are applied by our Lord to himself in his intercessory prayer (John 17: 3). *The son*— This term was used with much more latitude by the Jews than by us. In some cases, as here, it means descendant, however remote. Bearing this in mind, we shall be saved from some serious mistakes in the interpretation of the Scriptures. Should the Jews accept as the Messiah of their own Sacred Writings some man that may hereafter arise claiming to be such, it would be impossible to prove him to be a descendant of Abraham, and a legal heir to the throne of David; for they have lost the genealogical tables by which alone it could be proved. *Of David*—Had he not the right, then, to the throne on which Herod was sitting? Regarding the question as merely a national one, it should undoubtedly be answered in the affirmative, but that is not the only light in which it should be considered. The Messiah was not to reign on the throne of David in the usual sense, but in a sense altogether peculiar.

12. *Jechonias begat Salathiel*—In Jeremiah 22: 30 is a prophecy that

CHAPTER I.

zar; and Eleazar begat Matthan; and Matthan begat Jacob;

16 And Jacob begat Joseph the husband of Mary, of whom was born Jesus, who is called Christ.

17 So all the generations from Abraham to David *are* fourteen generations; and from David until the carrying away into Babylon *are* fourteen generations; and from the carrying away into Babylon unto Christ *are* fourteen generations.

Jechonias (Coniah) should not have a successor on the throne, and Luke (3:27) says that Salathiel was the son of Neri. We accept, therefore, the suggestion of Lord Hervey in Smith's Dictionary of the Bible, "that St. Matthew gives the *succession*, not the strict birth." In other words, Matthew, in saying that Jechonias *begat* Salathiel, does not mean to affirm that Salathiel was literally the son of Jechonias, but only that Salathiel (the son of Neri) was Jechonias' *heir to the throne*. Thus is the discrepancy between Jeremiah and Matthew removed.

16. Notice how the evangelist arrests the order of the genealogy. Up to this point we have the natural succession. Now follows a case utterly unlike all that have preceded. Matthan begets Jacob, and Jacob begets Joseph, but does Joseph beget Jesus? Joseph, the husband of *Mary of whom was born Jesus*. Jesus, then, had a mother, but not a father.

17. *Fourteen generations*, etc.— Forty-two in all: but this seems to contradict the Old Testament. According to that, the number was greater. How may the discrepancy be removed? It has been shown "that it was a common practice with the Jews to distribute genealogies into divisions, each containing some favorite or mystical number, and that, in order to do this, generations were either repeated or left out." Jewish history from Abraham to Jesus Christ comprised three great periods; the first extending from Abraham to David, the second from David to the Captivity, and the third from the Captivity to Christ. It is possible that the classification was intended as an aid to the memory.

Observe that four women are included in the list. Thamar had been guilty of incest; Bathsheba of adultery. Neither Rachab nor Ruth was of Jewish extraction. "All sorts of men: kings, heroes, shepherds, mechanics, heathens, sinners, prophets, poets, sages, are among the ancestors of Christ, and become poorer and obscurer as they approach Christ." Being in the line from which the Messiah was to come did not necessarily make one righteous; nor was the character of Jesus in the least defiled by the gross depravity of some of his ancestors. Those who take pride in their ancestry should remember this.

We prefer the view which regards the genealogy of Matthew as intended to exhibit *the legal succession to the throne of David*, Christ being the last in the line, and Joseph, his reputed father, being his immediate predecessor. Luke's genealogy, which is so unlike this, is a record of Joseph's *natural* descent through private persons, not through kings. As Mary "was in all probability the daughter of Jacob, and first cousin to Joseph, her husband," Matthew's genealogy—and this is equally true of Luke's—is "in point of fact, though not of form," "as much hers as her husband's." The following pedigree, condensed from Lord Hervey's, gives both the royal line and the natural line:—

LUKE.
Adam.
|
Seth.
|
Enos, &c.
MATTHEW AND LUKE.
Abraham.
|
Isaac.
|
Jacob, &c.
David = Bathsheba.
|

MATTHEW.　　　　　　　　　　LUKE.
(Royal line.)　　　　　　　　　*(Natural line.)*
Solomon.　　　　　　　　　　　Nathan.
|　　　　　　　　　　　　　　　　|
Roboam, &c.　　　　　　　　　Mattatha, &c.
|　　　　　　　　　　　　　　　　|
Jechonias (i.e. Je-　　　　　　Addi.
hoiakim).　　　　　　　　　　　|
|　　　　　　　　　　　　　　　Melchi.
Jechonias (i.e. Jehoi-　　　　　|
achin), childless.　　　　　　　Neri.

MATTHEW AND LUKE.
|
$\left(\begin{array}{c}\textit{Royal heir of}\\ \textit{Jechonias.}\end{array}\right)$ = Salathiel = $\left(\begin{array}{c}\textit{Real son}\\ \textit{of Neri.}\end{array}\right)$
|
Zorobabel, &c.
|

MATTHEW.　　　　　　　　　　LUKE.
(Royal line.)　　　　　　　　　*(Natural line.)*
Eliakim.　　　　　　　　　　　　Joseph.
|　　　　　　　　　　　　　　　　|
Azor, &c.　　　　　　　　　　　Semei.
|　　　　　　　　　　　　　　　　|
Eleazar.　　　　　　　　　　　　Levi.

MATTHEW AND LUKE.
|
$\left(\begin{array}{c}\textit{Royal heir}\\ \textit{of Eleazar.}\end{array}\right)$ = Matthan or Matthat = $\left(\begin{array}{c}\textit{Real son}\\ \textit{of Levi.}\end{array}\right)$
|
Jacob.　　　　　　　　　　　　Heli.

MATTHEW AND LUKE.
|
Mary = $\left(\begin{array}{c}\textit{Royal heir}\\ \textit{of Jacob.}\end{array}\right)$　Joseph = $\left(\begin{array}{c}\textit{Real son}\\ \textit{of Heli.}\end{array}\right)$
|
JESUS CHRIST.

CHAPTER I.

19

18 ¶ Now the birth of Jesus Christ was on this wise: When as his mother Mary was espoused to Joseph, before they came together, she was found with child of the Holy Ghost.

19 Then Joseph her husband, being a just *man*, and not willing to make her a public example, was minded to put her away privily.

20 But while he thought on

---

749 U.C.[1] June, B.C. 5.[2]

18. *On this wise*—In the manner about to be narrated. *Was espoused*—Engaged to be married. *Before they came together*—Before they began to live together in the same house as husband and wife. Her state is the effect of supernatural agency. Thus facts did not allow the evangelist to continue the genealogy in the order of natural succession. That God should give a sinful being to save sinful beings is not credible. The Saviour of the world must therefore be begotten not by man, but by the Holy Spirit. Let us meditate often and reverently upon this "single event in the history of our race that bridges over the stupendous chasm between God and man." Considered with purity of intention, no fact recorded in the Bible has greater power to bring the soul near to its Maker. *Mary*—Enough that is false has been written concerning the mother of our Lord to fill many a volume; all that is known about her can be told in a few words. Nothing is known of her early life. There is nothing unreasonable in the supposition that Jacob was her father, but we *know* absolutely nothing concerning her parentage. The song to which she gave utterance in her visit to Elizabeth proves that she was remarkably familiar with her own Sacred Scriptures. Enough has been given us by the evangelists to show that she was a woman of great excellence; but they have not given us the least possible ground for supposing that

she was without actual sin,—an opinion that became very general about six hundred years ago,—or that she was conceived without sin ("Immaculate Conception"),—a notion which originated a little later, and was formally decreed in 1854 as an article of belief for the entire Roman Catholic world. That Mary has become an object of worship, as Protestants insist, will not be doubted by one who is acquainted with "The Path to Paradise; or, Catholic Christian's Manual," from which is taken the following: "Hail! holy Queen, Mother of mercy, our life, our sweetness, and our hope; to thee do we cry, poor banished sons of Eve; to thee do we send up our sighs, moaning and weeping in this valley of tears. Turn, then, most gracious advocate, thy eyes of mercy toward us; and after this our exile ended, show unto us the blessed fruit of thy womb, Jesus."

19. *A just man*—Not, as some say, humane, but righteous. Being such a man, he felt that the connection ought to be sundered. *A public example*—Possibly "to bring the case before the local Sanhedrim." Though he felt that the relation ought not to be continued, yet he could not decide to expose her to public punishment, which, by the law of Moses, would have been death by stoning, unless it could be shown that she was not voluntary in the act which he believed her to have committed. See Deut. 22: 23-26. *Was minded*—Inclined. He inclined to put her away privately; that is, to give her a bill of divorcement (Deut. 24: 1), which would be silent relative to the cause. Thus Mary, the mother of the world's

---

[1] From the building of Rome.
[2] See note on Chapter 2: 1, third paragraph.

these things, behold, the angel of the Lord appeared unto him in a dream, saying, Joseph, thou son of David, fear not to take unto thee Mary thy wife: for that which is conceived in her is of the Holy Ghost.

21 And she shall bring forth a son, and thou shalt call his name JESUS: for he shall save his people from their sins.

Saviour, lay for a time under the gravest suspicion. To what humiliation did the Son of God submit! Joseph is seen to be both virtuous and pious. If he misunderstands Mary, if he even believes her criminal, we should consider that he had no means of knowing her innocence except her own denial of guilt. *He loves her still*, and, therefore, cannot expose her to punishment; but he also loves the law of God. Surely we need not wonder that "the situation of the two betrothed descendants of David, at their first appearance in history," has been called "tragical." *Joseph, her husband*— "It was a maxim of the Jewish law that betrothal was of equal force with marriage."

20. *On these things*—On the many points involved in his relations to Mary,—her supposed infidelity, and what he ought to do in consequence. His inclination must be arrested. He would need more than Mary's word, and therefore God gives him more. *The angel*—An angel. The original meaning of this word is messenger. In the Revelation of John, the pastors of the seven churches of Asia Minor are called angels. The word generally denotes an order of moral beings higher than man. Angels were employed during the Mosaic dispensation, and in the earlier part of the Christian, as God's agents in accomplishing his will. They generally appeared to human beings in the form of a man. Though superior to men, they are far inferior to the Son of God (Heb. 1: 5-8). In what they do for those who shall be heirs of salvation, they are *ministering* spirits; that is, *servants*. They are *swift* in service, like winds and lightning (Heb. 1: 7). They have not all been proof against temptation (25: 41). Angels long since ceased to come to men in a visible form. Whether they now come in some invisible manner is a question concerning which nothing positive is known. That bad angels continue their influence over men is very clearly taught, 1 Peter 5: 8, and many other passages. *How* good angels serve God on behalf of his people is a subject on which it is not profitable to speculate. *In a dream*— That God used the dream, in earlier times, as one means of communicating his will, admits of no doubt; but, in accordance with the progressive nature of revelation, the dream became less used as the Christian era was opening. *Is conceived*—Is begotten. *The Holy Ghost*—See note on 12: 31, 32. God's means are various: an angel for Mary; a dream for Joseph. *Thy wife*—In Jewish law, though only betrothed. Mary sees the angel; Joseph dreams that he sees him. God's vindication of Mary's character should encourage those who are unjustly suspected.

21. *Sins*—Sin itself and the punishment which it deserves. *His people*—Not believing Jews only, which is probably all that Joseph understood by it, but all, in every age, whom God has purposed to save through faith, whether Jews or Gentiles. How early and how fully is the object of Christ's advent revealed! Let all imitate the angel in speaking of Jesus to others. Let Sabbath-school teachers keep in sympathy with Christ in respect to the object of his advent. Since en-

22 Now all this was done, that it might be fulfilled which was spoken of the Lord by the prophet, saying,

23 Behold, a virgin shall be with child, and shall bring forth a son, and they shall call his name Emmanuel, which being interpreted is, God with us.

24 Then Joseph, being raised from sleep, did as the angel of the Lord had bidden him, and took unto him his wife:

25 And knew her not till she had brought forth her firstborn son: and he called his name JESUS.

---

tire sinlessness is the rich gift which awaits the believer after death, with what faith should he expect the Saviour's help in the warfare of the present life!

22, 23. The prophecy referred to is in Isa. 7:14. Does it refer only to the birth of Jesus Christ; or, only to the birth of some child in the time of Isaiah; or, to the birth of both? What were the circumstances? In the time of Ahaz, king of Judah, Jerusalem was threatened by the united armies of Syria and Samaria. The prophet assures Ahaz that Jerusalem shall not be captured, and gives him a sign to prove the truth of his words. The sign is the birth of a child, who will be called Immanuel. Before the child will be old enough to refuse the evil and choose the good, Jerusalem will be delivered from its peril. In a short time, seven hundred years before the birth of Jesus, Isaiah's wife becomes mother of a child, to whom is given the name *Maher-shalal-hashbaz*, which means, He hasteth to the prey. The name was given, because the child, as foretold, was a sign to Ahaz that the invasion of Jerusalem should fail of success. Immanuel, as importing substantially the same thing, was the other name of the child. This seems to be the primary meaning of the prophecy. Has it any other meaning? *Now all this was done that*—It has been shown that in this case, and in a multitude of other similar cases, the word *that* expresses intention, not mere result. We conclude, therefore, that the Holy Spirit means to teach us through the evangelist that the prophecy has a secondary reference, which is the more important and the far grander of the two. As Isaiah's son was a sign to Ahaz that Jerusalem should be delivered from its enemies, so the son of Mary is a sign of the great spiritual deliverance which God will bring to men. "The application of this prophecy to Christ is not a mere accommodation, meaning that the words, originally used in one sense and in reference to one subject, might now be repeated in another sense and of another subject; for this does not satisfy the strong terms of the passage (*all this happened that it might be fulfilled*), nor would such a fanciful coincidence have been alleged with so much emphasis by Matthew, still less by the angel. The only sense that can be reasonably put upon the words is, that the miraculous conception of Messiah was predicted by Isaiah in the words here quoted."—*Alexander. Immanuel*—God with us.

25. The effort has been made to show, and it has been distinctly taught by the Roman Catholic Church, that this verse teaches the perpetual virginity of Mary. The opinion that the mother of our Lord may have had other sons is pronounced in the Douay version (Roman Catholic) as "most impiously inferred" from these words. It cannot indeed be conclusively proved

CHAPTER II.

NOW when Jesus was born in Bethlehem of Judea, in the days of Herod the king, behold, there came wise men from the east to Jerusalem,

---

by the word "first-born," that Mary had other sons; for it would have been in accordance with the Jewish law to apply the word to an *only* child. *Knew her not till*—Not even these words prove it. Paul says (1 Tim. 4 : 13), *Till I come* give attendance to reading, etc. Matthew says (12 : 20), A bruised reed shall he not break, and smoking flax shall he not quench, *till he send*, etc. Paul does not mean to intimate that Timothy may give himself to reading *only* till he come; and we are not to infer that Christ will avoid breaking a bruised **reed** *only* till he has sent forth judgment unto victory. Our interpretation of the passage should be independent of the perversion of it by Romanists. On the whole, the words are not decisive of the question relative to the perpetual virginity of Mary. See more, however, in the note upon 13 : 55, concerning "his brethren."

INFANT BAPTISM.—This chapter teaches nothing at all concerning it. Yet it has been said (Lange) that Anti-Pædobaptists overlook the mystery that through Abraham's faith the blessing has descended in his seed as an heir-loom; "otherwise they would see more meaning in the admission of infants into the visible church." Error lurks in all such statements. Through Abraham the blessing descends upon all who have Abraham's faith, and upon *no others*. All who die in infancy, we have reason to believe, are saved; but as infants have no faith, they are not entitled to membership in visible churches. Though the dogma that infants are entitled to church-membership has less hold upon men than formerly, yet it is still cherished by a very large majority of the Christian world. It has had a fearful influence in corrupting Christianity.

CHAPTER II.

EVENTS IMMEDIATELY FOLLOWING THE BIRTH.

750 U.C. Feb., B.C. 4.

1. *Bethlehem of Judea*—Judea was the southern of the three provinces into which Palestine was divided. The name is derived from the name of the tribe of Judah. "It embodied 'the original territories of the tribes of Judah and Benjamin, together with Dan and Simeon; being almost the same with the old kingdom of Judah, and about one hundred miles in length and sixty in breadth.'"

Bethlehem—Bread-house. The infidel Renan affirms, as if Matthew must have been less informed than himself, that Jesus was born in Galilee. There was another Bethlehem not far from the Sea of Galilee (Josh. 19 : 15), but the evangelist affirms that the birth occurred in Bethlehem of Judea. This was about six miles south of Jerusalem. A small village may give birth to great and good men. Boaz, David, and Jesus Christ were all born in Bethlehem. The modern town, Beit-lahm, has about three thousand inhabitants; Thomson says, "Not far from four thousand, and most of them belong to the Greek Church." The same writer speaks of them as a turbulent people, and as being "ever distinguished in the great feasts at Jerusalem by their fierce and lawless manners." Of the cave which very ancient tradition has marked as the place of the Saviour's birth, mention will be made in the note on Luke 2 : 7.

CHAPTER II.

2 Saying, Where is he that is born King of the Jews? for

When Jesus was born—Neither the day, nor the month, nor the year, is certainly known; yet by several distinct lines of reasoning the learned have been able to approximate the time. Little more can be done than to indicate the results. the birth of Jesus occurred, beyond all question, at least four years earlier than what is called the beginning of the Christian era. The time of reckoning our era is traceable to an erroneous calculation of Dionysius, a monk of the sixth century.

BETHLEHEM.

sults. It is certain, according to this chapter, that Jesus was born before the death of Herod. Herod died in the year of Rome 750, not far from the 1st of April. How much before Herod's death Jesus was born, is the point which we have not the means of determining. This may be said with very great probability, that it must have occurred between the year of Rome 747 and 750. The latter part of 749 has most to commend it. As to the month, January, April, June, May, and December have had their respective advocates. That December 25 was the day of the birth is incapable of being proved.

It should be borne in mind that *Herod the king*—The Herodian family was of a foreign race,—the Idumean or Edomite, which sprung from Esau, Jacob's twin brother. The Herods had become Jews, however, by adopting the Jewish religion, and were firm in their attachment to it, though having little of its spiritual life. It seems to have been their desire to establish an independent monarchy, but they never succeeded in attaining such a degree of power as to be able to throw off subjection to Rome. Herod the Great had been made king of Judea by the Senate, Rome being then mistress of Palestine. How remarkable that a descendant of Esau should now be ruling over the de-

we have seen his star in the east, and are come to worship him.

3 When Herod the king had heard *these things*, he was troubled, and all Jerusalem with him.

4 And when he had gath-

scendants of Jacob! Herod was a tyrant. He was surpassed in cruelty by few of the human race. He murdered his wife, Mariamne, Hyrcanus her grandfather, and his own sons, Alexander, Aristobulus, and Antipater. He burnt to death forty Jews, because, when it was rumored that he was dying, they had torn down a large gold eagle which he had set up over the gate of the temple. This tyrannical act occurred on the night of March 12–13, in the year of Rome 750. On that night, according to Josephus, there was an eclipse of the moon, and astronomy proves the statement correct. This is a fact of much value in determining the date of Herod's death, and this date is an important condition in determining the date of our Lord's birth. The following is a table of so much of the family as is necessary to include the **Herods of the New Testament:**—

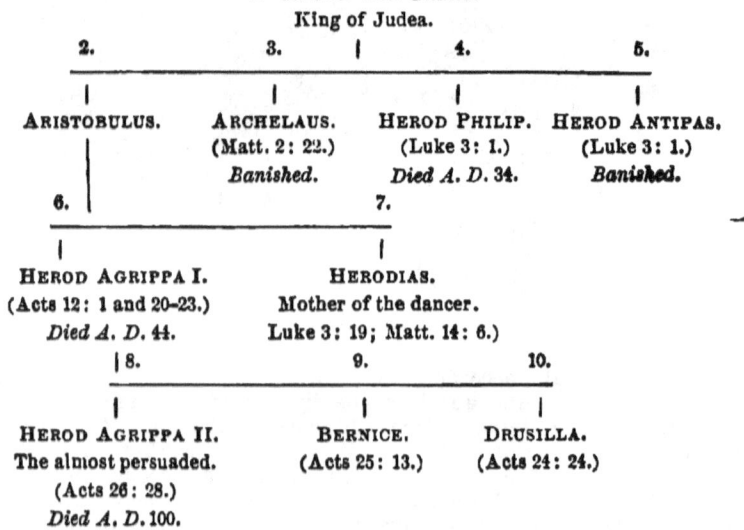

Wise men from the east—Eastern wise men. The original word is *magoi*. Hence our English words, *magic* and *magicians*. It is impossible to tell whether they came from Arabia, or from Mesopotamia, or, which is more probable, from Persia. "Magi formed among the Persians and Medes a much-respected priestly class; they employed themselves especially with the mysteries of nature, astrology, and medicine. There was also among the Babylonians (Jer. 39: 3), at the time of the Chaldean dynasty, such an order, at the head of which was Daniel. Dan. 2: 48. The name Magian was then in general transferred to all without distinction of country, commonly wandering orientals, who

JERUSALEM, AS SEEN FROM OLIVET.

CHAPTER II. 27

ered all the chief priests and scribes of the people together, had dedicated themselves to those sciences." Philo, a Jew, "mentions Magi with warm praise as men who gave themselves to the study of nature and the contemplation of the divine perfections." Many, however, who bore the general name of Magi, were bad men—impostors, deceivers; for example, Simon Magus (Acts 8:9), and Elymas the sorcerer (Acts 13:8). By some of the earlier writers of the Christian church, it was hastily judged that the wise men who went to Bethlehem were mere sorcerers. We have no reason to doubt that the men were sincere seekers of truth, "without any conscious fraud." They were probably Gentiles. They came from afar to find the King of the Jews, while the Jews themselves, living at the centre of the Jewish theocracy, with light shining upon them from the prophecies, had not yet begun to inquire whether such a person has made his appearance. It is a very saddening thought that one may live near the spot where Jesus is, yet make no effort to find him.

The number of the wise men is not given. Men have shown their desire to be "wise above what is written" by affirming that there were three; that they were kings; and that their names were Gaspar, Melchior, and Balthazar; that Gaspar presented the gold, Melchior the frankincense, and Balthazar the myrrh! In the Greek Church is the utterly baseless tradition that the Magi had "a retinue of one thousand men, having left behind them, on the further bank of the Euphrates, an army of seven thousand."

But why did the men associate with the appearance of a star the idea that one had been born who was destined to be King of the Jews? 1. Jews having been dispersed through eastern countries, the Magi could not have failed to learn something he demanded of them where Christ should be born.

of the expectation which they had so warmly cherished relative to the coming of a great Deliverer. 2. It is well known that the opinion had obtained great currency through a considerable part of the East, that not far from that time some one would appear among the Jews who would effect a great change in the world. 3. The Magi may have been specially illuminated from heaven; for, after they had found the object of their search, they were warned by God in a dream concerning their return. 4. There seems to be nothing unreasonable in the supposition that they were acquainted with Balaam's prophecy: *There shall come a Star out of Jacob*, and a Sceptre shall rise out of Israel, and shall smite the corners of Moab, and destroy all the children of Sheth. Num. 24:17.

Jerusalem—Sight of peace, inheritance of peace, foundation of peace, are the three principal meanings which have been given to this word. It is a compound, and the uncertainty pertains to the first two syllables. It has been supposed to be the same city as Salem, of which Melchizedek was king, but the identity of the two places is not certain. It stands in latitude 31 deg. 46 min. 35 sec. north, which makes it about as near the equator as the southern towns of Mississippi and Alabama, in the United States. It lies thirty-two miles east of the Mediterranean Sea, and eighteen west of the Jordan. During a long period, Jerusalem was the religious centre of the earth, and in some later ages it was held to be the physical centre. A map of the world of the fourteenth century so represents it. The location of the city gives it much natural strength; for it "occupies the southern termination of a table-land, which is cut off from the country round it on the west, south, and east sides, by ravines more than usu-

5 And they said unto him, In Bethlehem of Judea: for thus it is written by the prophet,

6 And thou Bethlehem, *in* the land of Juda, art not the least among the princes of Ju-

---

ally deep and precipitous." The one of these ravines, the eastern, is called the Valley of Jehosaphat; the other, running first south and then east till it meets the former, the Valley of Hinnom. "How sudden is their descent may be gathered from the fact, that the level at the point of junction—about a mile and a quarter from the starting-point of each—is more than six hundred feet below that of the upper plateau from which they commenced their descent." Between these two valleys is another, running nearly south till it meets the other two at the point of their junction, and dividing the city "into two unequal portions." This is called the Valley of the Tyropoeon. On the western side of the Tyropoeon is Mount Zion; on the eastern Mount Moriah, on which the temple stood. In the time of our Saviour, a stone bridge connected the eastern side with the western. The bridge is described by Josephus. It rested upon an arch now known as "Robinson's Arch." "One of the most remarkable of the recent discoveries at Jerusalem is the disinterring of the opposite buttress or pier of the bridge on the *western* side of the valley, and of the stones of the pavement which formed the floor of this causeway." Fifty-five feet below the surface has been found "a mass of masonry, constructed of fine bevelled stones of great size, and evidently remaining in their original position." The span of the arch was forty-one feet six inches, and some of the stones, which "may now be seen in the excavated cavern," weigh "at least twenty tons." "The apostles must have very often passed over it while yet the arch remained entire; and so also must their Master and ours often have passed over it with them."

The fortunes of Jerusalem have been more various, perhaps, than those of any other city in the known world. As a punishment to the Jews, it was delivered into the hands of Nebuchadnezzar, B. C. 586, its walls were razed, and its temple was burnt. In the reign of Cyrus and of Darius the temple was rebuilt, and in the reign of Artaxerxes the building of the walls and the city was brought to completion. A little more than three hundred years before Christ, the city was taken by Ptolemy on the Sabbath, *when the Jews were unwilling to fight*, and many of the inhabitants were carried to Egypt. It came under the dominion of Antiochus the Great, B. C. 203, between whom and the kings of Egypt there were many wars. It suffered much at the hands of Antiochus Epiphanes, its walls again being razed, a statue of Jupiter set up in the temple, and the ceremonies of the Jewish religion forbidden. "Jerusalem was deserted by priests and people, and the daily sacrifice of the altar was discontinued." The Maccabees, father and sons, succeeded, after the most patriotic and valorous exertions, in recovering the city and restoring the temple-services. "The sacrifices were recommenced exactly three years after the temple had been dedicated to Jupiter Olympus." In the year 63 B. C., the temple was taken by the Roman general, Pompey, and twelve thousand Jews were massacred. The city fell into the hands of the Parthians, B. C. 40, but was retaken by Herod the Great, B. C. 37. The temple was rebuilt by Herod on a scale of great splendor. Jerusalem was at last taken by Titus, the Roman general, A. D. 70. "For more than fifty years after its destruction by Titus, Jerusalem disappears from

CHAPTER II.

history." It reappears in the reign of the Emperor Hadrian, but the emperor gave the new city the name of Ælia Capitolina. It was not till the lapse of several hundred years that the old name came again into use. The city was taken by the Persians A. D. 614. It had long been inhabited chiefly by Christians. In 637 A. D. it fell into the hands of

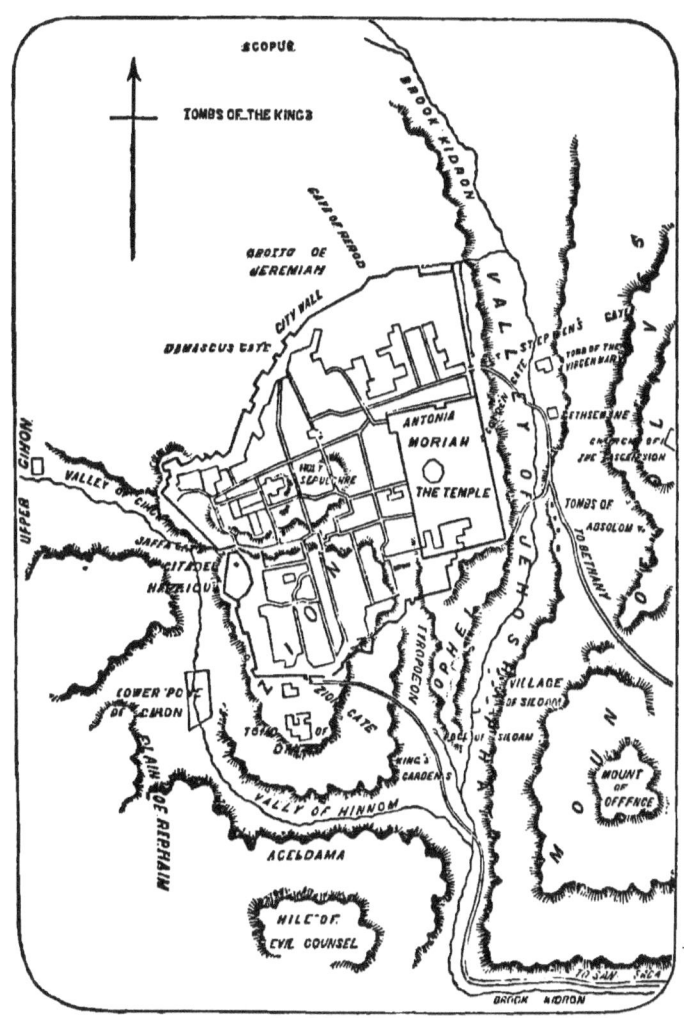

PLAN OF JERUSALEM.

the Arabs, Saracens or eastern people, under Khalif Omar. It was captured from the Saracens, A. D. 1099, by the Crusaders; but the Christians lost it in 1187, it being retaken by Saladin. With the exception of a brief period in 1243, it has remained in the hands of Muhammedans to the present day. Such have been the fortunes of the

CHAPTER II.

da: for out of thee shall come a Governor, that shall rule my people Israel.

7 Then Herod, when he had privily called the wise men, inquired of them diligently what time the star appeared.

8 And he sent them to Beth-

---

city to which the wise men went in their search for the new-born "King of the Jews."

2. *His star in the east*—His; the star that speaks of him. In former times the star was held by some to be a comet, by others a meteor,—opinions which have nothing in their favor. The common Christian mind deems it to have been a supernatural appearance; and not till a comparatively recent period have biblical scholars been in possession of facts that even seemed to point in any other direction. The facts referred to are these: Distinguished astronomers have affirmed that a conjunction of the planets Jupiter and Saturn occurred in the year of Rome 747, May 20, and was repeated Oct. 27, and Nov. 12. On May 20, the Magi, it has been said, would have seen the stars in their *united brightness in the east*. If they then began their journey, and arrived in Jerusalem about Oct. 27, the November conjunction would have appeared south of Jerusalem; that is, in the direction of Bethlehem. The distinguished English commentator Alford, Lange, Nast, and Alexander, regard these facts as a sufficient explanation of the inspired statement respecting the star. They therefore reject the interpretation that the appearance was miraculous. But since the publication of their Commentaries, more light has been thrown upon the question by the careful calculations of Rev. Charles Pritchard, Hon. Secretary of the Royal Astronomical Society of Great Britain. Mr. Pritchard's investigations, as he himself tells us in Smith's Dictionary of the Bible, confirmed the fact of the conjunctions in the year B. C. 7, though the dates were found to be different. The last of the conjunctions is proved to have occurred not in November, but Dec. 4. Starting at that time, the Magi "would first see Jupiter and his dull and somewhat distant companion . . . decidedly to the east of Bethlehem. By the time they came to Rachel's tomb the planets would be due south of them, on the meridian, and no longer over the hill of Bethlehem. . . The planets would soon be on their right hands, and a little *behind* them: the star, therefore, ceased altogether to go before them as a guide. Arrived on the hill and in the village, it became physically impossible for the star to stand over any house whatever close to them, seeing that it was now visible far away beyond the hill to the west, and far off in the heavens at an altitude of 57 deg. As they advanced, the star would of necessity recede, and under no circumstances could it be said to stand 'over' any house, unless at the distance of miles from the place where they were. . . . Thus the beautiful phantasm of Kepler and Ideler, which has fascinated so many writers, vanishes before the more perfect daylight of investigation." The result of Mr. Pritchard's investigations is an instructive illustration of the necessity of care in the use of alleged facts of science by interpreters of the Bible. The star must be regarded as miraculous.

To worship him—Not to adore him as a divine being, but, in accordance with oriental custom, *to do him homage*.

3. *Was troubled*—Herod is now seventy years old. He is covered with the guilt of infamous crimes, his body is corrupt through vice, and his temper is more irascible than ever. He is suspected in Rome and

lehem, and said, Go, and search diligently for the young child; and when ye have found *him*, bring me word again, that I

hated in Jerusalem. His throne is tottering. Is it surprising that such a man trembles at the words, Where is he that is born King of the Jews? The new king is an infant, it is true, but a party may soon gather around him which will make Herod's throne still more insecure. *All Jerusalem*—In fear of the civil commotions that may arise and of the consequent outburst of Herod's wrath. The people have been expecting the Messiah, but now that he has come, they are filled with fear. *All* must not be pressed too far. There were a few who were waiting in such spirituality and faith for the kingdom of God, that they could not have participated in the general alarm. Even old and very profligate sinners are not proof against fear.

4. *The chief priests and scribes*—This was probably a meeting, a special one, of the Sanhedrim, the highest judicial body among the Jews. The Sanhedrim consisted of the chief priests, scribes, and elders. The third class is not here mentioned. The chief priests probably included the high priest, ex-high priests, and the heads of the twenty-four courses into which the priests were divided. See 1 Chron. 24: 3-19. The scribes were the writers and interpreters of the law. See a fuller description of them in the note on 5: 20. The number of the Sanhedrim is variously stated as seventy, seventy-one, and seventy-two. The last is the least probable. The Magi had asked, *Where?* with desire to bow before him; Herod asks, *Where?* lest he shall be compelled to bow. A question may breathe life or death, according to the spirit from which it comes. *Should be born*—That is, according to the Jewish Scriptures.

5, 6. The decision of the Sanhedrim, which was reached, probably, without discussion, is, that the Messiah is to be born in Bethlehem. Whether the infant whom the Magi believe to have appeared is the Messiah, is another question, but that Bethlehem is the place where the true Messiah is to be born they have no doubt; for this is what one of their own prophets has declared. In its application of the remarkable words of Micah (5: 2) to the Messiah, how much more candid is even this Sanhedrim than later Jews, who, to weaken the evidence that Jesus was the Messiah, have denied that the prophet intends to make any reference whatever to the expected Deliverer.

The prophecy is not quoted with verbal exactness; but there is no perversion of its meaning. Micah says, Among the *thousands* of Judah; Matthew, Among the *princes* of Juda,—both meaning the same thing. The tribes of Israel were divided into *families*, or *chiliads*, or *thousands*, each having a *prince* or *governor*, who resided in some central town. Bethlehem was a small, insignificant village: In itself it might be considered as one of the least of all; but in fact thou Bethlehem art not the least, for out of thee shall come, since in thee shall be born, a *governor* that shall. etc. *Shall rule*—Shall feed, shall be a shepherd unto. *My people Israel*—All, whether Jews or Gentiles, that have Abraham's faith. How much higher does Bethlehem stand to-day than Jerusalem! The theocratic metropolis is ever sinking more deeply under the appalling crime of attempting to crush out the life which Bethlehem gave to the world. Eternal honor may crown what the world holds in contempt. If providence lead to Bethlehem, we should not be unwilling to turn the back upon Jerusalem.

7. *Privily*—Under the circumstances, this shows the working of

CHAPTER II.

may come and worship him also.

9 When they had heard the king, they departed; and, lo, the star, which they saw in the east, went before them, till it came and stood over where the young child was.

10 When they saw the star, they rejoiced with exceeding great joy.

11 ¶ And when they were come into the house, they saw the young child with Mary his mother, and fell down and worshipped him: and when they

---

a bad purpose. *Inquired diligently*—Made accurate inquiry, that he might learn exactly. Accurate investigation for a *good* end is a duty. Sharpness of intellect in a bad cause cuts back.

8. *Worship him also*—As in vs. 2, to do him homage. Hypocrisy, which sought Jesus in Bethlehem, rested not till it brought him to Jerusalem and nailed him to the cross.

9, 10. *Went before . . and stood over*—On the false interpretation of these expressions suggested by certain astronomical calculations, see note on vs. 2. They saw the star, for they went in the night, not an uncommon time for journeying in the East. *When they saw* does not imply that the star had ceased to shine, and has again become visible, though such may have been the fact. Notice the great strength of the expression used to indicate their joy. The star leads to the word, and the word leads back to the star. The principal of an academy was led to the word through the study of that wonderful fact in chemistry,—Definite Proportions. Imbued with love of the word, he applied himself with fresh zeal to the study of God's works. Sometimes the order is the reverse. The word leads to the star, and the star leads back to the word. Many have no interest in God's works till they have received his word. The star and the word may combine to lead to Christ.

11. *The house*—According to Luke, Jesus was not *born* in a house; but it would appear that before the arrival of the Magi he had been removed to a house. This is no proof that the family had taken up its *abode* in Bethlehem. "The star always rests over the house where Christ is." Joseph is not mentioned. He may have been absent; or, as in the omission of *elders* in vs. 4, it may be regarded as a brief form of statement. Compare Luke 2: 16, where he *is* mentioned in connection with Mary and the babe. Joseph, however, soon sinks wholly out of sight, while Mary, whom he had inclined *to put away privily*, comes occasionally before us throughout the Gospel, though with none of the prominence given her by Romanists. The King is found! While the learned doctors of the metropolis are wrapped in indifference, these "travel-stained" Gentiles are upon their faces doing homage to the son of David, and, we cannot but think, with some clearer perception than they first had, of the spirituality of his nature, though with none. probably, of his deity. *Treasures*—Boxes or chests. *Gold*—The first instalment of what the Gentiles will give for the advancement of Christianity in coming ages. *Frankincense*—"A vegetable resin, brittle, glittering, and of a bitter taste. It is obtained by successive incisions in the bark of a tree. The Hebrews imported their frankincense from Arabia, and more particularly from Saba. It may be that the finest kind was always procured from India. The olibanum, or frankincense used by the Jews in the temple services, is not to be confounded with the frankincense of commerce, which is a spontaneous

had opened their treasures, they presented unto him gifts; gold, and frankincense, and myrrh.

12 And being warned of God in a dream that they should not return to Herod, they departed into their own country another way.

13 And when they were departed, behold, the angel of the Lord appeareth to Joseph in a dream, saying, Arise, and take the young child and his mother, and flee into Egypt, and be thou there until I bring thee word: for Herod will seek the young child to destroy him.

14 When he arose, he took the young child and his mother by night, and departed into Egypt:

15 And was there until the death of Herod: that it might be fulfilled which was spoken of the Lord by the prophet, saying, Out of Egypt have I called my son.

---

exudation of the Norway spruce fir, and resembles, in its nature and uses, the Burgundy pitch, which is obtained from the same tree." *Myrrh*—Found in Arabia Felix, and exuding as "a white liquid, which thickens and becomes a gum," from "a thorny tree like an acacia." See Isa. 60: 6;—All they from Sheba shall come: they shall bring gold and incense. All the treasures of the earth belong to Christ.

Some give money to Christianity without bowing the knee to Christ. Some find Christ in the word, but give him no worship. He that finds Christ must worship him; he that worships him must give him treasures.

12. *Warned*—The warning must have dispelled whatever confidence they had in Herod's sincerity. The way of return through Jerusalem would doubtless have been the commonly travelled route. The less public way should be cheerfully chosen if pointed out by our divine guide. *Another way*—God has various ways, in either of which he may direct his people to walk.

13, 14. *Flee*—Not as in vs. 20, *go*. The case required immediate action. The morning light might bring ruffians from Herod. *Into Egypt*—The distance was not great, not more than sixty or eighty miles, but Egypt was beyond Herod's jurisdiction. The Egyptian government was tolerant toward Jews, many of whom lived there. "The paintings and sculptures on the monuments indicate a very high degree of personal safety, showing us that the people of all ranks commonly went unarmed, and without military protection." *When he arose*—And he arose. It is not meant that he did not depart till the usual time of rising. He arose immediately. He started in the night. Behold the babe that has come into the world as the light of men, borne away in the night from the land of the ancient Shekinah to heathen Egypt for safety! "Egypt the land of *tombs*, the *cradle* of God's people."

15. *Until the death of Herod*—Till about April 1, 750 of the building of Rome. The time of the sojourn in Egypt cannot be positively determined, but the writer prefers the supposition that it was three or four months. *That it might be*—Purpose, not mere result. *The prophet*—Hosea 11:1. The words have primary reference to the call of Israel out of Egypt by Moses; secondary, to the call of God's only begotten Son out of Egypt. Such an application to Jesus of the words of the Old Testament *is sanctioned by the Holy Spirit*. It cannot,

CHAPTER II.

16 ¶ Then Herod, when he saw that he was mocked of the wise men, was exceeding wroth, and sent forth, and slew all the children that were in Bethlehem, and in all the coasts thereof, from two years old and under, according to the time which he had diligently inquired of the wise men.

17 Then was fulfilled that which was spoken by Jeremy the prophet, saying,

18 In Rama there was a voice heard, lamentation, and weeping, and great mourning,

---

therefore, be a misapplication. The Old Testament is full of Christ; hence the wonderful unity of the Old and the New.

16. *Mocked*—Matthew is not here attributing a bad spirit to the Magi, but is stating, in part, the spirit attributed to them by the king, and, in part, the tyrant's writhing under the disappointment of his plans. Herod feels mortified and incensed, for he knows that he has been outwitted. *Children*—Only the males, for the original word is in the masculine gender. *From two years old and under*—The Magi could not have arrived immediately after the birth, but we need not infer that it was just two years since the star first appeared. Resolved to secure at all hazards the destruction of the child, Herod would be likely to give the executioners a wide margin.

The events recorded in this narrative have been regarded by infidels and sceptics as entirely improbable. It has been especially objected that the massacre has not been reported by Josephus. But Josephus, if he had ever heard of it, would not have regarded the massacre of so small a number of infants—the number must have been small in so small a village—as demanding notice amid the great number of terrible crimes of which Herod had been guilty. As to the improbability that so atrocious an act could have been ordered, it is sufficient to remark that it sinks into insignificance when considered by the side of a crime which the monster planned almost in the act of dying. Causing all the principal men of Jerusalem to be shut up in the Hippodrome, he requested his sister Salome and her husband to give orders to put them to death immediately after his decease, that he might have "the honor of a memorable mourning." His character had been so hateful to the Jews that he feared they would give him no "such mourning as men usually expect at a king's death."—*Josephus*.

It has been affirmed that sin must lose its power as life advances. This is confuted by the case of Herod. The death of the infants of Bethlehem sent sorrow through the little village and its borders; the death of the infant Jesus would have made everlasting the sorrows of a world. In attempting to save one's crown, one may crown himself with infamy.

17, 18. *Jeremy the prophet*—31: 15. The words allude to the captives which were carried to Babylon by Nebuzaradan over the road that passed by Ramah. Rachel, the wife of Jacob, was buried near Bethlehem, and is represented by the prophet as rising from her grave to mourn over the fate of her descendants. Matthew applies the prophecy to the slaughter of the infants in Bethlehem. Rachel, regarded by the evangelist as "a type of the mothers in Bethlehem," is represented as again rising from her tomb and weeping over the death of the infants. Notice the *analogy* between the events that took place under Nebuzaradan and those that occurred under Herod. "It is through the evangelists that the Holy Spirit has afforded us a true insight

Rachel weeping *for* her children, and would not be comforted, because they are not.

19 ¶ But when Herod was dead, behold, an angel of the Lord appeareth in a dream to Joseph in Egypt,

20 Saying, Arise, and take the young child and his mother, and go into the land of Israel: for they are dead which sought the young child's life.

21 And he arose, and took the young child and his mother, and came into the land of Israel.

22 But when he heard that Archelaus did reign in Judea

---

into the inner meaning of the prophets, who were the *historians* of the elder dispensation, as in the epistles he has set forth the antitypes of the ancient law. That is surely a meagre theology and unscholar-like criticism which finds nothing more than a fanciful adaptation in the Scriptures quoted in the opening chapter of St. Matthew."—*Westcott*. *Ramah*—It was situated about six miles north of Jerusalem, within the limits of the tribe of Benjamin. It has been thought by some, unnecessarily, that there must have been a Ramah on the southern side, *nearer to Rachel's sepulchre*. Dr. Robinson has identified

RACHEL'S TOMB.

the Ramah of Matthew with the modern village Er-ram. Rachel was the daughter of Laban. She became the wife of Jacob. She died not far from Bethlehem in giving birth to a son, who received from her while she was dying the name Ben-oni, meaning *son of my sorrow*. The name was changed by the father to Benjamin, the meaning of which is doubtful. It is an interesting fact that the site of Rachel's tomb "has never been questioned." It is about five miles south of Jerusalem, and one-half mile north of Bethlehem.

20. *Into the land of Israel*—He is not told to what town he should go, but the child must not be trained in Egypt for his great life-work. His youth must be spent where its perfect purity shall be better known by his countrymen. He must go to his own, though it is certain that his own will not receive him. Would God there were none now living who seek Jesus to destroy him! Theodore Parker declares that Christianity is but one religion among many, and, like Buddhism and Muhammedanism, is destined to perish. Rationalism would do what Herod was prevented from doing.

21. *He arose, and took*—Joseph, who, as Lange says, is "the model of all foster-fathers." One reason why the Messiah was not born of a virgin *unmarried and unbetrothed* may have been, that the infant and the mother needed that peculiarly watchful and delicate protection, in the persecution and flight, which they could receive from a husband and foster-father.

22. *Archelaus*—See genealogical table in note upon vs. 1. At the death of his father, Archelaus received one half of the kingdom, consisting of Idumea, Judea, Samaria, and the cities on the coast. *Did reign*—According to his father's will he was king, and for a time he

CHAPTER II.

in the room of his father Herod, he was afraid to go thither: notwithstanding, being warned of God in a dream, he turned aside into the parts of Galilee:

23 And he came and dwelt

---

was popularly so regarded, but the Emperor of Rome, Augustus, never sanctioned the title. He ruled under the title of ethnarch, which, strictly speaking, meant ruler of a nation, but the word was used indefinitely for ruler of part of a nation. Like his father, he was tyrannical; and, the Jews complaining, he was banished to Vienne, in Gaul. His tyranny made Joseph *afraid to go to Judea. Notwithstanding* does not truly represent the original. *And* is the true rendering. It seems to have been Joseph's intention to dwell in Bethlehem or Jerusalem. The capital or its vicinity might seem to him and Mary to yield better advantages for educating the child in the knowledge of God. The divine warning points, however, to Galilee, now governed by Herod Antipas, who had become tetrarch of Galilee and Perea. Antipas was not so much "milder" than Archelaus as to create any special encouragement that on that ground Galilee would be a place of greater safety than Judea. "He was unscrupulous (Luke 3: 19), tyrannical (Luke 13: 3), and weak (Matt. 14: 9)." *Galilee*—Palestine was divided into Galilee, Samaria, and Judea. Galilee consisted of Upper Galilee and Lower Galilee. "It is a remarkable fact that the first three Gospels are chiefly taken up with our Lord's ministrations in this province, while the Gospel of John dwells more upon those in Judea... The apostles were all Galileans by either birth or residence (Acts 1: 11)." Not all bad fathers have bad sons; not all good fathers have good sons. Ahaz was a bad man; Hezekiah, his son, was a good man; Manasseh, Hezekiah's son, was a bad man. A bad man, however, will far more probably have a bad son, if he have any at all, and a good man will be much more likely to have a good son. The phrase, "children of the covenant," is often used with too great latitude. Properly speaking, "children of the covenant" are those, and only those, who have faith. The salvation of infants through the atonement is wholly another subject. The doctrine that there is any spiritual connection between believers and their infants is not found in the Bible. All who have Abraham's faith are Abraham's children. Unbelieving children cannot be children of the covenant.

23. *Nazareth*—This had been the home of Joseph and Mary before the birth of Jesus; for Luke (2: 39) says, They returned into Galilee, to *their own city*, Nazareth. The "city," which was nothing but a little village, stood in a "green basin of table-land." "Fifteen gently rounded hills 'seem as if they had met to form an enclosure' for this peaceful basin,—'they rise round it like the edge of a shell to guard it from intrusion. It is a rich and beautiful field, in the midst of these green hills,—abounding in gay flowers, in fig-trees, small gardens, hedges of the prickly pear; and the dense rich grass affords an abundant pasture. The village stands on the steep slope of the south-western side of the valley; its chief object, the great Franciscan Convent of the Annunciation, with its white campanile and brown enclosure." The prospect from one of the neighboring hills is pronounced by Dr. Hackett as "unquestionably one of the most beautiful and sublime spectacles which earth has to show." Nazareth was so situated as to be "hidden from view till you look down upon it from the adjacent heights." It was a place in itself of no importance,

4

in a city called Nazareth: that it might be fulfilled which was spoken by the prophets, He shall be called a Nazarene.

---

and was little known beyond its immediate vicinity. In this secluded and obscure village, Jesus spent nearly all his life before entering

NAZARETH.

upon his public work. Residence there rather than in or near Jerusalem was most in accordance with the great end in view.

He shall be called a Nazarene—These words are not in the Old Testament, though Matthew says that they were spoken by the prophets. Several of the solutions proposed are unsatisfactory. Prof. Day, of Yale College, in Smith's Dictionary of the Bible, prefers the explanation that the Messiah is described, in Isa. 11:1, as a *Netzer* (that is, a shoot, sprout, of Jesse), "the proper Hebrew name of Nazareth." Thus the Messiah was represented as "a humble, despised descendant of the decayed royal family." Another explanation is this: In many places of the Old Testament the Messiah is represented as *despised*. Nazareth was despised not only by inhabitants of Judea, but by many in Galilee itself where it was located; and therefore calling Jesus a *Nazarene* was equivalent to calling him *despised*. Which explanation, if either, is the correct one, the writer is unable to say.

In concluding our examination of this introductory part of the Gospel, consider the remarkable words in Isa. 53:2: For he shall grow up before him *as a tender plant, and as a root out of a dry ground:* he hath *no form nor comeliness;* and when we shall see him there is *no beauty* that we should desire him. Jesus, the son of Mary, answers to this description. His mother and his reputed father held an ordinary position in Jewish society, while from the whole line had passed away all of royalty but the name. *He is despised and rejected of men*, says the same prophet. How true was this of Jesus even in his infancy!

CHAPTER III.

IN those days came John the Baptist, preaching in the wilderness of Judea,

2 And saying, Repent ye: for the kingdom of heaven is at hand.

3 For this is he that was spoken of by the prophet Esai-

CHAPTER III.

THE BAPTISM OF JESUS BY JOHN THE BAPTIST.

780 U.C. Jan., A.D. 27.

1. *In those days*—In the latter part of Jesus' residence in Nazareth. John may have preached a few months before he began to baptize. *Came*—Publicly appeared. He was in the deserts till the day of his shewing unto Israel. Luke 1: 80. John was the son of Zacharias and Elisabeth. His father was a priest, and his mother was of the daughters of Aaron. His coming to herald the Messiah was foretold centuries before. Isa. 11: 3. He was remarkable for the spirituality of his character and for the pungency of his appeals. He will ever be regarded as among the foremost men of our race. *The Baptist*—Some, as Dr. Conant, regard this as a surname; others, as descriptive. The nature of the act which led to its application to John is considered in the notes on 28: 19.

Was John the first baptizer? Was this a new rite? or, had it been administered before? It has been affirmed that when a heathen became a proselyte to Judaism, he was initiated into the new faith by baptism. That we have *no direct proof*, however, that proselyte baptism was practised till many years after the death of John, is now generally conceded. Whether even "*a* baptism" was practised before John is not by any means certain, though the baptism of things, as cups, and pots, and brazen vessels (Mark 7: 4), would naturally suggest the baptism of sinners when they had been brought to repentance by such a reformer as John. Was John's baptism Christian baptism? Was John himself of the old dispensation, or of the new? He was neither wholly of the one, nor wholly of the other. The light, the life, the power of the old theocracy culminated in the son of Zacharias and Elisabeth, crowning him, though the last, yet the best, of the prophets. John was not regarded by our Lord as a member of the new dispensation. Luke 7: 28. Had his life not been prematurely cut off, he would have come at last wholly into the Messiah's kingdom, but only as a private man. In his official character, he stood between the two dispensations. From Acts 18: 25 and 19: 1-5, it must be inferred that there was some distinction between John's baptism and that of Christ's disciples. John's baptism, then, may be considered as not Christian in the sense that it was not baptism into the acknowledgment of *Jesus* as the Messiah, but only of the *Messiah as foretold*, the persons baptized not being aware that Jesus himself was the Messiah. If, however, any choose to take the opposite view, they need not be alarmed at the curse of the Council of Trent, as quoted by Dr. Hackett in his Commentary on the Acts: "If any shall say that the baptism of John and the baptism of Christ are identical, let him be accursed."

In the wilderness—Not a region of forests, nor a sandy desert. A region was called a wilderness if it was thinly inhabited and consisted of pasturage instead of tillage. The wilderness of Judea lay between Jerusalem and the Jordan, and along the western side of the Dead Sea. *Preached*—Not in the methodical

as, saying, The voice of one crying in the wilderness, Pre-

style of later times. What he preached is infinitely more important than how he preached.

2. *Repent*—The Greek word, even in classic authors, expresses not mere *reformation of conduct*, but an inward change, a change of views and feelings, including sorrow for wrong done. Here, and almost everywhere in the New Testament, it means sorrow for sin committed against God. with consequent change of life. It was not upon *the subject* of repentance that John preached, leaving one to apply it to one's self or not as one chose,—the favorite method of some preachers,—but *repenting as a duty that moment binding upon all present*. The Douay or Roman Catholic version says, *Do penance;* and a foot-note explains this as meaning not only "repentance and amendment of life, but also punishing past sins by fasting and such like penitential exercises,"—a fearful perversion of the word of God. It has been said that John's conception of repentance fell short of that which was afterwards entertained by the disciples of Jesus; but, in the words of Dr. Lange, "His idea of repentance exceeded the outward requirements of the Mosaic law as much as his rite of immersion that of sprinkling."

For the kingdom, etc.—The reason why the people should immediately repent. *Kingdom of heaven* —The same as *kingdom of God;* as in the parable of the prodigal son (Luke 15:21), I have sinned against *heaven*, is the same as, I have sinned against *God*. The conception of a kingdom of God is traceable to the times of Daniel (Dan. 2:44) and of Jeremiah (Jer. 23:5). But the conception was to be more fully realized in the times of the Messiah. Then the kingdom was to embrace not Jews only, but Jews and Gentiles, and it was to consist of these not as nations, not as states, not as state churches, but as persons regenerated by the Holy Spirit. This is the true ideal of the kingdom, but it has not even yet been fully realized. Hence we must still pray, Let thy kingdom come. Many regard kingdom of God and church as identical. See upon this important point 16:18, 19. Notice the word *church* in vs. 18 and *kingdom* in vs. 19. But the kingdom of God may be viewed as (1.) External; (2.) Internal; (3.) Beginning; (4.) Advancing; (5.) Completed. The second cannot be affirmed of the church, and therefore church and kingdom are not always and strictly the same. Jesus also preached, Repent, for the kingdom of heaven is at hand. Matt. 4:17. If the forerunner, without the example of Jesus, preached as Jesus did, those who come after are doubly criminal if they preach otherwise. Sabbath-school teacher, fail not to preach to your pupils as John and Jesus preached.

3. *For this is he*—The reason, given by the evangelist, not by John, why the Baptist has appeared. It had been foretold, Isa. 40:3. Barnes says that the language was spoken at first with reference to the return from the captivity at Babylon; but there is no evidence of this. As eastern kings were accustomed to be preceded by a company that should prepare the way for them, levelling hills, raising low places, making rough places smooth, so the Messiah is represented as having the way prepared for him by one running before him, proclaiming that he is coming, and bidding the people prepare by penitence to receive him. But why not have sent the Messiah without such heralding? Such a question differs not at all from one that may be asked concerning the entire Mosaic dispensation. As the entire Jewish economy was the necessary heralding of the entire Messianic kingdom for the purpose

CHAPTER III.

pare ye the way of the Lord, make his paths straight.

4 And the same John had his raiment of camel's hair, and a leathern girdle about his loins; and his meat was locusts and wild honey.

5 ¶ Then went out to him Jerusalem, and all Judea, and all the region round about Jordan,

6 And were baptized of him in Jordan, confessing their sins.

---

of discipline, it was necessary, as the heralding was drawing to a close, that it should be concentrated and intensified in a single voice for the purpose of arousing greater attention. It was the adaptation of infinite wisdom to the wants of the human mind, and innumerable analogies are found under the divine government. God is continually preparing men for greater events by less events. Some hear the herald's voice, but not him of whom it speaks. Few of the Pharisees and Sadducees that heard the voice of John gave attention to the voice of Jesus. Some, hearing not the herald's voice, are terrified when the chief voice speaks.

4. *Of camel's hair*—Not of the *skin* of the camel, as some have said, but of the coarser hair. The finer hair was made into garments for the wealthy. *Leathern girdle* —In the East, the girdle is necessary because the people dress in loose, flowing garments. But they are also used by some for ornament. Some wore girdles "of linen, embroidered with silk, and sometimes with gold and silver thread, and frequently studded with gold and precious stones or pearls." The poorer people wore *leathern* girdles. A girdle of silk and gold would not have been in harmony with John's character or with the object of his mission. *Meat*—The meaning of this word has changed. The original means food. *Locusts*—This word came from two Latin words, *locus* (place), and *ustus* (burnt). Locusts are so destructive that they make fields look as if burnt over. They prevail in Arabia, Egypt, Mesopotamia, and Persia. "Their numbers are so incredible that rivers have been blocked and many square miles covered by them, the stench of their decaying bodies infecting the air for hundreds of miles." Armies have been stopped in their course by locusts. Arabs say that it is written "in good Arabic on their wings that they are God's avengers." It was formerly asserted by some that the locusts which John ate were not insects, but the long, sweet pods of the locust-tree, "*St. John's Bread*." But the Mosaic law (Lev. 11 : 22) permitted locusts as an article of food. They are used for food at the present time, "the legs and wings being pulled off, the bodies fried in oil, and are considered a delicacy; they are sometimes dried in the sun, pounded up, and used as a flour for making bread. In many towns in Arabia there are shops where locusts are sold by measure." *Wild honey*— Not, as some say, honey which exuded from trees, but that which was made by wild, unhived bees, and stored in the crevices of rocks and in trees. Elijah is described (2 Kings 1 : 8) as a hairy man, and girt with a girdle of leather about his loins.

5, 6. *All*—Great multitudes. So many went out from Jerusalem that the city might be considered as almost emptied of its inhabitants. *Jordan*—In the original it is everywhere preceded by the definite article, and it ought to be preceded by it in an English translation. *The Jordan* means the river itself, which would be a very needless statement, were it not that Dr. Whedon (Meth-

7 ¶ But when he saw many of the Pharisees and Sadducees come to his baptism, he said unto them, O generation of vipers, who hath warned you to flee from the wrath to come?

---

odist), in his Commentary on Matthew, makes the unscholarly remark that a person could be in the Jordan on dry ground! How? By standing within the limits of the first terrace, to which the river may sometimes overflow! The Jordan is the only considerable river in Palestine. The name means Descender, the appropriateness of which appears from the fact that, "from its fountain-heads to the point where it is lost to nature, it rushes down one continuous inclined plane, only broken by a series of rapids or precipitous falls. Between the Lake of Tiberias and the Dead Sea, Lieutenant Lynch passed down twenty-seven rapids which he calls threatening; besides a great many more of lesser magnitude." The river is also remarkable for its sinuosity, often winding eastward and westward through a valley which is five or six miles broad. It has three or four fords, but in most of its course between the Sea of Tiberias and the Dead Sea it is several feet deep. Lieutenant Lynch, of the American Exploring Expedition, found the water, even where two travellers (Irby and Mangles) forded it on horseback, "between five and six feet deep." Dr. Shaw calculates the average breadth at thirty yards, and the depth at nine feet. Such is the river on the banks of which we find John and the multitudes.

Baptized of—Immersed by. That this is the meaning of the Greek word see proof in the notes on 28: 19. That the word means *to sprinkle*, no man of any pretensions to acquaintance with the literature of the Greek language would now affirm.

The spiritual import of baptism is well stated by Lange, though he is not a Baptist. "Immersion," he says, "was the usual mode of baptism and the *symbol of repentance*. . . . We must keep in view the idea of a symbolical descent into the grave, or the death of sin, although this view, as explained in Rom. 6, could not yet have been fully realized at the time." "Baptism implies a descent into the depths, 1. Of self-knowledge; 2. Of repentance; 3. Of renunciation of the world; 4. Of self-surrender to the grace of the Lord." *Confessing their sins*—The condition upon the fulfilment of which they were baptized. No confession no baptism, was John's principle.

7. *Pharisees and Sadducees*—These, with the Essenes, constituted the three principal religious parties among the Jews. *The Pharisees* held that, in addition to the written law, there was an unwritten, an oral, law delivered to Moses on Sinai, and by him delivered to Joshua, by Joshua to the elders, by the elders to the prophets, and by the prophets to the men of the Great Synagogue. This oral law and their explanations were regarded as of equal authority with the written law. It is to these that our Lord so often referred as *traditions*. The most terrible denunciations that ever fell from his lips were directed against the Pharisees on account of these perversions of the law of God. The orthodox Jews of our own times hold the same view. Besides the undisputed traditions, were many others which were not believed to be direct revelations from God, but were nevertheless regarded as peculiarly sacred. Upon this class of traditions the Pharisees themselves were divided into opposite schools, —the school of Hillel and the school of Shammai. Phariseeism was a system of intense self-righteousness

CHAPTER III. 43

8 Bring forth therefore fruits meet for repentance:

9 And think not to say within yourselves, We have Abra-

The Sadducees taunted the Pharisees with desiring to purify the sun itself.

It will be seen that likening Unitarianism to Phariseeism, as is done by a certain class of preachers, results from a misconception. The two systems may resemble each other in that they attribute to men a righteousness which has no foundation in fact; but in most respects they are unlike. Phariseeism is reproduced in modern ritualism, which Unitarianism has generally held in contempt; and this is seen in the intensest form in Romanism. It is now (1869) the greatest danger to which the evangelical churches of the United States are exposed.

Sadducees—They were so called, probably, either from a man named *Zadok*, or from a Hebrew word meaning *righteous*. They were the opponents of the Pharisees. *a*. They denied that God gave to Moses any other than the written law. *b*. They denied the resurrection and the existence of angel and spirit. Acts 23 : 8. *c*. They laid great stress upon the freedom of the will, while the Pharisees gave more prominence to the doctrine of providence. *d*. It was formerly held that they received only the five books of Moses; but this opinion is now rejected. *e*. The Sadducees, as a religious body, disappear from history after the first century. Should modern rationalism, including the later type of Unitarianism and Universalism, claim consanguinity with Sadduceeism, we need not scruple to admit the claim. The Pharisees were more popular; the Sadducees the more intellectual.

The *Essenes* are not mentioned in the Scriptures, but as a sect *seeming* to hold a position midway between the other two parties, some knowledge of it should be sought by students of the Bible. The origin of the name is doubtful. "As a sect they were distinguished by an aspiration after ideal purity rather than by any special code of doctrines. . . . From the cities they retired to the wilderness to realize the conceptions of religion which they had formed, but still on the whole they remained true to their ancient faith." Those who entered into full membership bound themselves by an oath "to observe piety, justice, obedience, honesty, and secrecy." Their doctrines were substantially like those of the Pharisees. Marriage, except in a few cases, was abjured. Property was held in common. They observed the Sabbath with great strictness. They aimed at the highest degree of spirituality, but missed the mark. They answer to the mystics of later times. *Christianity creates a style of character containing elements not found in the Pharisee, or the Sadducee, or the Essene, and marking it as divine.*

To his baptism—Not to see others baptized, but to be baptized themselves. *Generation*—Brood. *Vipers*—It expresses the poisonous, deceptive, destructive influence of the men. *Who hath warned you*—He suspects their motives. He cannot believe that they have yet been made to acknowledge their exposure. *The wrath to come*—God's anger, not merely in such national destruction as the prophets of old were accustomed to denounce, but the punishments of the future life. Threatened wrath should be preached, whatever the intellectual culture of the hearers.

8. *Fruits meet for repentance* are works of such a nature as to prove that one has repented. Here is none of the spirit of legality. Paul uses words conveying exactly the same sentiment:—That they should repent and turn to God, and *do works meet for repentance*

ham to *our* father: for I say unto you, that God is able of these stones to raise up children unto Abraham.

10 And now also the axe is laid unto the root of the trees: therefore every tree which bringeth not forth good fruit is hewn down, and cast into the fire.

11 I indeed baptize you with water unto repentance: but he

26: 20. Paul was far enough from teaching that works are a ground of justification. But John, standing in the twilight of Christianity, and Paul standing in the light of its full-orbed splendor, alike taught the necessity of evincing the genuineness of our repentance by bringing forth the fruits of holiness.

9. *Think not to say*—Do not even think of saying. That thought, Abraham is our father, we are in the covenant, we therefore need no repentance, was their imaginary life, their real death. *These stones*—Not, as some say, the Gentiles, but the stones on the ground. John does not say that God will do it, but he says that he can. God made Adam out of the dust of the earth. Of course he can raise up children to Abraham out of stones. "Children of the church" is an ambiguous phrase that may work much mischief in the heart of a child. Pious parentage can avail nothing by itself.

10. *The axe is laid unto*—Not, lies at or near the tree ready to be taken up, but *is laid to*, implying an impending stroke. Commentators, however, are not entirely agreed which is the meaning. The nation of Israel had passed through many crises, but through none like this. It is now on the verge of final ruin, and will perish unless it repent. As individuals, too, they have reached a crisis surpassing all that have preceded. *Is hewn down*—Observe that the verbs are in the present. Henceforth this is to be God's method of dealing with men. If it has always been his method, yet it is now far more distinctly and solemnly made known. Men are hereafter to understand that for the impenitent there is no possible escape from punishment. *Fire* stands for punishment as certainly as trees stand for men. Compare the words of Jesus himself; 7: 19. The question of future punishment is considered in the note on 25: 46.

11. *With water*—*In* water. *With the Holy Ghost*—*In* the Holy Ghost. The Greek preposition is *en*. That the meaning is here *in* is held by the following eminent Biblical scholars, not one of whom is in denominational relations with those who practise immersion:—*Lange:* "I indeed baptize you in (*en*) water (immersing you in the element of water)." "He shall baptize, or immerse, you in the Holy Ghost." *Dr. Nast:* "Literally in (*en*) the Holy Ghost and fire." *Alexander:* "He shall baptize in holy spirit or (the) Holy Spirit." *Dr. George Campbell:* "In water . . . in the Holy Spirit." *Bengel:* "*In.*" *Douay version* (Catholic): "I indeed baptize you in water. . . . he shall baptize you in the Holy Ghost." "So it was rendered," says Dr. Conant, "in the versions of Wiclif, Tyndale, Matthews (so called), the Bishops', and in the Rhemish version. The Genevan has '*with water*,' which was followed by King James' revisers, though the Bishops' Bible had given the correct rendering, 'in water.'" Notice vs. 6. Baptized of him *in* Jordan. There, of course, nearly all the commentators feel compelled to admit the idea of locality, for to say Baptized *with* the Jordan is simplicity indeed. Dr. John J. Owen, perceiving the "incongruity" of translating "with the Jordan," adopts the "circumlocu-

that cometh after me is mightier than I, whose shoes I am not worthy to bear: he shall baptize you with the Holy Ghost, and *with* fire:

12 Whose fan *is* in his hand,

tion," "*with water from Jordan*," —a rendering which Dr. Campbell long ago condemned, with noble and scholarly candor, as *a glaring deviation from the text*.

Unto repentance—Not, I baptize you for the purpose of *leading you to* repentance; for he refused to baptize many of the Pharisees and Sadducees because they had not repented. Nor is any distinction implied between baptism unto repentance and baptism unto regeneration. John, it is true, gave more prominence to what man ought to do than to what God does; but this is not proof that he had no conception of the new birth. The repentance which John required presupposed regeneration. Whence, then, the contrast between John and the Messiah? John was characterized for calling men to baptism on a profession of repentance; the Messiah's reign was to be characterized for the baptism of the Holy Spirit. *With the Holy Ghost and with fire*—Not, some of you in the Holy Ghost and some of you in fire, that is, regenerating some and punishing others. *With* before *fire* was unfortunately supplied by the translators. The Holy Ghost *and fire* ought to have been the rendering. But this makes the connection between Holy Ghost and fire so close that it is difficult to consider the one as referring to the righteous and the other to the wicked. That fire is used in the next verse and elsewhere for punishment is not conclusive. See Acts 2:3, 4. John does not mean to say that the very persons whom he had baptized in water unto repentance Jesus would baptize in the Holy Spirit and fire; but *you* is used in a general sense. He means to say that while he has baptized people in water, etc., Jesus will baptize people in the Holy Spirit and fire. As remarked above, this will be the characteristic of the Messiah. *Fire* —The purifying, dross-consuming influence of the Spirit. *Mightier*— Superior in rank, office, and work. So impressive was John's view of the superiority of Jesus that he puts himself lower than a slave; for a slave would not have been deemed unworthy to bear his master's shoes.

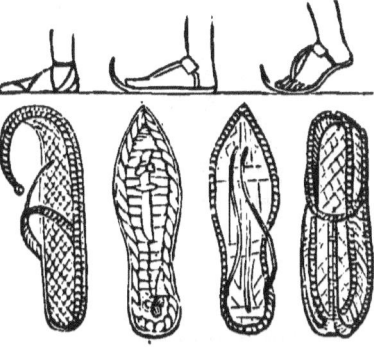

SANDALS.

Shoes—Sandals. Something worn *under the feet*, as the original means. In Palestine they were little else than a sole of leather, felt, cloth, or wood, bound to the bottom of the foot by thongs or straps. Humility and boldness in proclaiming unwelcome truths, are not opposite qualities. The former is a check upon the latter.

12. The thought expressed in vs. 10, that they have now arrived at a crisis, a judgment, is here expressed in a different and equally solemn manner, but with the additional thought that some will successfully pass the crisis. The representations of the Scriptures (Isa. 30:24; Jer. 4:11) relative to the ancient process of separating the chaff from the wheat have been strikingly confirmed by discoveries in Egypt.

MATTHEW.

and he will thoroughly purge his floor, and gather his wheat into the garner; but he will burn up the chaff with unquenchable fire.

13 ¶ Then cometh Jesus from Galilee to Jordan unto John, to be baptized of him.

14 But John forbade him, saying, I have need to be baptized of thee, and comest thou to me?

15 And Jesus, answering,

Monuments and tombs have revealed the entire process of ploughing, sowing, reaping, threshing, and winnowing. The grain was tossed up in the wind with shovels or with fans,—"their precise difference is very doubtful." *Purge*—Cleanse.

WINNOWING.

Floor—A plot of open, hard ground. *Garner*—The place for storing the grain. The fan *in the hand* corresponds with the axe *laid to* the root of the trees. *Unquenchable fire*— Punishment in the next world. See note on future punishment; 25: 46.

Fan, the truth as preached by Jesus Christ; the floor, at first Palestine, eventually the whole world; the wheat, believers; the chaff, unbelievers; the garner, protecting providences, the church, but especially heaven; the final winnowing time, the last judgment, but the process is continually, though imperceptibly, going on in this life. Every Christian congregation, Sunday school, and family is a threshing-floor. The minister, the teacher, the parent, are Christ's agents in winnowing.

13. *Cometh to . . . Jordan*—John (1: 28) says that the baptism took place in Bethabara beyond Jordan. This was the Bethany that was located on the east side of the river, nearly opposite Jericho.

14. *John forbade him*—Aimed to prevent, and was beginning to prevent him. *I have need*—Conscious of sin, and, by the revealing power of the Holy Spirit, perceiving the superiority of Jesus' character, he could see no propriety in doing the act requested. His knowledge of the Saviour was not, probably, the result of personal acquaintance; for John had lived in obscurity in one part of Palestine, and Jesus in obscurity in another part (John 1: 31).

15. *Suffer it now*—Just now. It implies not only time, but allusion to present circumstances. Suffer it under existing conditions as known to me. *To fulfil all righteousness*— Not, to fulfil every precept (this was a rite which the law did not require), but to do the will of God in this particular, though this is too general. "Whatever," says Dr. Conant, "may be the full depth of meaning in this language of our Lord, so much as this at least we are to understand by it, that had he omitted this act of obedience, he would have left incomplete that perfect righteousness which in our nature he has wrought out. If aught that it became him to fulfil had been left unfulfilled, something essential would have been wanting."

Observe that Jesus was willing to submit to a rite which had just been administered to penitent sinners. Ought penitent sinners, then, in later times, however high in culture

said unto him, Suffer *it to be so now*: for thus it becometh us to fulfil all righteousness. Then he suffered him.

16 And Jesus, when he was baptized, went up straightway out of the water: and, lo, the heavens were opened unto him, and he saw the Spirit of God descending like a dove, and lighting upon him:

17 And, lo, a voice from heaven, saying, This is my beloved Son, in whom I am well pleased.

CHAPTER IV.

THEN was Jesus led up of the Spirit into the wilderness, to be tempted of the devil.

---

and social position, to shrink from a rite to which the holy Redeemer submitted? Jesus *sought* baptism; so should all do who believe in him. Jesus was buried in the waters of baptism, so afterwards in suffering; in both cases as if sinful.

16. *Went up out of the water*—Here, strangely enough, the translators have given a rendering which is more in harmony with the views of Baptists than the original warrants. The preposition is not *ek* (out of), but *apo* (from). The act was immersion (see proof in the note on 28: 19), and the next act after the immersion might be, in the conception of one writer, a going *up out* of the water, and in the conception of another, a going *away from* the water. In Acts 8: 39 the writer fastened upon the act which immediately followed the baptism, and therefore used the other Greek preposition, *ek* (out of): And when they [Philip and the eunuch] were come *up out* of the water. Jesus, however, was not less certainly immersed than the eunuch, but Matthew conceives of the next act as a going *from* the water. Ellicott, an Episcopalian, says in his Life of Christ, "The Forerunner *descends* with his Redeemer into the rapid waters of the now sacred river." Alford, also an Episcopalian, and a scholar of great distinction, says, "The moment that Jesus was gone *up out of* the water, behold," etc. ; showing that he does not regard the use of the Greek preposition *apo* (from) in this verse as adapted to awaken any doubt concerning the question whether Jesus went down into the water and was immersed. Alexander's remark here is singular, "that even if John did submerge, in this and other cases, this was no more essential to the rite than nudity." *Were opened unto him*—Unto Jesus; not, perhaps, to the others, John excepted. John 1: 32. *Like a dove*—In the form of a dove. See Luke 3: 22; *In bodily shape*. Concerning the characteristics of the dove, see note on 10: 16.

17. *My beloved Son*—It is impossible to reproduce, neatly, in our language, the peculiarly expressive words of the original. Two articles are used, the one before Son, the other before beloved, thus: The Son of me, the beloved; or, The Son, the beloved, of me. God has many sons; but concerning the sense in which Jesus was the Son of God, see note on 16: 16. The material heavens seemed to open. Heaven itself opened, after his resurrection, to receive him, and therefore heaven has been opened to receive all God's adopted sons. The emblem of the Spirit may be on the head, but the Spirit himself may not be in the heart. The church-edifice may be ornamented with the dove, but the Spirit of God may long ago have fled from the church.

2 And when he had fasted forty days and forty nights, he was afterward a hungered.

CHAPTER IV.

JESUS TEMPTED; BEGINS HIS MINISTRY.

780 U.C. Jan., A.D. 27.

1. *Then*—Immediately after his baptism; or, as Trench suggests, it may "rather denote the divine order in which the events of the Saviour's life followed one another, and is intended to call our attention to this." First came "baptism with" [in] "water and the Holy Ghost, then baptism with," [in] "the fire of temptation." *Led up*—From the valley of the Jordan. *Of the Spirit*—Luke (4:1) represents Jesus as being full of the Holy Ghost when he returned from the Jordan. The Spirit, then, was no other than the third in the Trinity. "He was led by the good Spirit to be tempted of the evil." *Into the wilderness*—Barnes directs us back to 3:1; but it was "a wilder region than that;" for (Mark 1:13) he was with the wild beasts. The precise locality is unknown, though tradition assigns it to a mountain a little west of Jericho called Quarantana, in allusion to our Lord's forty days of fasting. "The aspect of the whole region," says Dr. Olin, "is peculiarly savage and dreary." Dr. Robinson computes the mountain as twelve hundred or fifteen hundred feet in height. Thomson says: "The side facing the plain is as perpendicular, and apparently as high, as the rock of Gibraltar." There is no special reason to doubt that in this case tradition is correct.

To be tempted—Not merely to be put to the test as Abraham, when required to put his only son to death, but to be solicited to evil. But how could Jesus be solicited to evil? If he had the least movement of desire toward the objects which Satan presented, was not that sinful? If he had no movement of desire toward them, how can it be said that he was tempted? how, that he gained a victory? A perfectly satisfactory explanation by beings who are seldom tempted without at least in some measure sinning, is difficult, and, perhaps, impossible. The objects which Satan presented were of course objects of thought. But merely *thinking* of them was not sin. If Jesus positively *desired* them, the desiring them was sin; much more was it sin if he delighted to think of them; and still more if he chose them. But he neither chose them, nor delighted to think of them, nor positively desired them. Somewhere, perhaps, between thinking of them and actually desiring them, there may have arisen in the Saviour's mind a state which he himself knew was a state of temptation. This is probably as near to the solution of the difficulty as the most prolonged speculation would be likely to bring us. As to the object of the temptation, it should be considered, first, that all the sufferings which Jesus bore in passing through it, were a part of his sufferings endured for man; secondly, that they conduced "to perfectness of *official* qualification." In proof of the latter, see Heb. 2:10, with Prof. Ripley's note in his excellent Commentary on that Epistle. Thirdly, should be considered the moral effect of the temptation and victory upon disciples in every age.

Of the devil—Barnes says, "The name is sometimes given to men and women." With the article it is never applied to a human being. *The* devil is used to designate the prince of evil spirits. The attempt to show that by "the devil" is not meant a real person is as fruitless

3 And when the tempter came to him, he said, If thou be the Son of God, command

that these stones be made bread.

4 But he answered and said, It is written, Man shall not

---

as would be the attempt to show that Jesus Christ is not a real person. In the earlier Bible times, when the personification of evil would be most probable, much less is said of the devil; but in the later times, when the personification of evil would be less probable, the existence of the devil is brought out with great clearness. Jesus says in the *explanation* of the parable of the tares, *The enemy that sowed them is the devil*. See also John 8 : 44; 14 : 30. One may profess to have no belief in the devil's existence, yet may be very much in the habit of using the name. The devil is not found in cities only. He that denies the existence of the devil gives reason to fear that the devil has not left him untouched. The holiest being may be tempted. Extraordinary illumination may be followed by extraordinary temptations. Temptations may be greater in solitude than in a crowd, yet solitude should be often sought. He that goes into solitude in disgust with society may be sure that he was not led into it by the Holy Spirit.

2. *Fasted.*—Luke (4 : 2) says, And in those days he did eat nothing. Jesus afterward said of John, He came neither eating nor drinking, but this is not so strong a statement. We seem to do no violence to the record, if we consider it as teaching that the abstinence was total. That he was afterward hungry, implies that during the fast he was in a preternatural state. Moses (Ex. 34 : 28) and Elijah (1 Kings 19 : 8) each fasted forty days.

3. *The tempter came*—How? In a bodily, visible form? or, in suggestions made to the mind? or, thirdly, is this a mere personification of the Saviour's own thoughts? The last is utterly inadmissible; for it locates evil in the heart of Christ himself. It is impossible, without doing violence to the language of the entire narrative, to regard the evil, and the presentation of the evil, as otherwise than external. As to the first and the second questions, does not such phraseology as Matthew has employed, prove that *he* believed it to be a bodily appearance? But Matthew's method of representation must have been derived originally from Jesus. In relating the facts to his disciples, would Jesus, the only witness of what occurred, have used language so adapted to make upon their minds the impression that the tempter came in a bodily form, if he came only in the other way?

In this first temptation, Satan appeals to the appetite for food. If Jesus is the Son of God (see 3 : 17, *This is my beloved Son*), it is not to be supposed necessary that he should remain in want. He may work a miracle; but a miracle wrought only to supply himself with food, will imply distrust of him who has sent him to save men, and that would prove that he was *not* sent. *If*—Satan would goad him by this word to the selfish, distrustful act of turning stones into bread. Bread made of stones would have given, under the circumstances, no nourishment to the Holy Son of God.

4. *It is written*—In Deut. 8 : 3. Jesus repels the tempter by argument, but not by argument drawn from reason. The appeal is made to the written word, which is a method not less reasonable than an appeal made directly to reason itself. Reason was used, used reasonably, but not exclusively, not authoritatively. As the Israelites had learned, by having manna instead of common food, that God is not limited in his resources, so Satan should know that it is not necessary that Jesus, for the support of his life, should have *bread*. God can sustain him in some other way,

live by bread alone, but by every word that proceedeth out of the mouth of God.

5 Then the devil taketh him up into the holy city, and setteth him on a pinnacle of the temple,

6 And saith unto him, If thou be the Son of God, cast thyself down: for it is written, He shall give his angels charge concerning thee; and in *their* hands they shall bear thee up, lest at any time thou dash thy foot against a stone.

7 Jesus said unto him, It is

---

either by another kind of food supplied in the ordinary manner, or miraculously; or, as he had been sustained during the forty days, without material food. *Man*—Jesus here implies that he is human. *By every word;* "every arrangement of the divine will." See John 4: 32.

5. In this second temptation, the appeal is made to the spirit of presumption. *Taketh him*—bodily, but not, as Dr. Whedon says, "by transporting his person so with the quickness of a thought, that he is not to be conceived as on his way at any intermediate point." Neither these words nor any others in the narrative imply that he was carried through the air at all. Matthew (17: 1) says, And after six days Jesus *taketh* Peter, James, and John his brother, and bringeth them up into an high mountain, apart. No one supposes that Jesus transported the men through the air; but the Greek word for *taketh* is the same in both cases.

The holy city—Holy because the centre of the Old Testament theocracy. *A pinnacle of the temple*—Concerning the temple see note on 21: 12. It is impossible to determine what part of the temple is meant by the pinnacle (the definite article ought to have been used). Some say that Herod's royal porch is meant, which rose six hundred feet over the ravine of Kedron. It is the pinnacle from which, according to an unsupported tradition, James was thrown. The idea that it was a point so inaccessible that it could not have been reached unless both Satan and Jesus had gone through the air, is without foundation.

Many persons, in looking down a precipice from a great height, as at Niagara Falls, are conscious of a bewilderment and a daring, in which they are tempted to throw themselves down the precipice. If this is a constitutional peculiarity of men, we see in the form of the second temptation the peculiar subtlety of "the serpent." What place is too sacred for Satan to enter? If the devil led Jesus to so holy a place as the house of God, is it surprising that he leads some professors of religion into the ball-room and the theatre?

6. *It is written*—In Ps. 91: 11, 12. A wonderful stroke of policy! As our Lord had repelled the first attack with Scripture, Satan imitates him by turning to Scripture himself. Familiarity with the Bible is no proof of saintship. Some men, without belief in the supernatural character of any of the facts narrated in the Scriptures, have made the Bible a life-study. Satan has been accused of unfairness in applying to Jesus words which the Psalmist applies to the servants of God in general. There was no unfairness on that ground, for the promise made to God's servants in general was as good for Jesus as for others. Satan has also been very unjustly accused of unfairness in omitting the words, *To keep thee in all thy ways;* but there is no proof that the omission was designed. It has been suggested that the words were quoted from

CHAPTER IV.

written again, Thou shalt not tempt the Lord thy God.

8 Again, the devil taketh him up into an exceeding high mountain, and sheweth him all the kingdoms of the world, and the glory of them;

9 And saith unto him, All these things will I give thee, if thou wilt fall down and worship me.

10 Then saith Jesus unto him, Get thee hence, Satan: for it is written, Thou shalt worship the Lord thy God, and him only shalt thou serve.

---

the Septuagint. This is a translation of the Hebrew of the Old Testament in Greek, made in Alexandria, Egypt. The five books of Moses were translated nearly three hundred years before Christ; and, as is probable, the remaining books gradually, so that not far from the first of the Christian Era, all the Old Testament books existed in Greek. The Septuagint and the Hebrew are here so alike, that Satan may as well be supposed to have quoted from the latter as from the former. Had Jesus complied with Satan's suggestion, it would not have been trust in God, but vanity. The "fraud" consisted in applying the passage to an act neither necessary nor required. Misapplication of Scripture may work infinite mischief.

7. *Written again*—In Deut. 6: 16. Our Lord does not deny the justness of the sentiment, but his method of dealing with the tempter implies approval of the maxim, "Scripture must be interpreted by Scripture." Satan tempted Jesus to tempt God. One may tempt God by unnecessarily exposing one's self to evil, and at the same time expecting to be kept from harm. Contact with evil must be the contact of opposition, not of embrace. We may tempt God by fearing lest our wants may not be supplied.

8. The third temptation is an attempt to excite worldly ambition. *Taketh*—Not forcibly, not against his will. Which of the mountains of Palestine is meant we have no means of knowing, and therefore supposition is useless. *All the king-doms*, etc.—The way in which they were shown is not intimated. That they were presented in a vision, or that Satan merely pointed out the direction of the several kingdoms, or that Jesus saw them in imagination, or that only portions of Palestine are intended, are all assumptions. Luke (4: 5) says that the kingdoms were shown *in a moment of time*. In whatever way it was done, the result was that all the kingdoms of the world,—especially of the heathen world over which Satan had long held sway,—with their riches and splendor, their art and their military power, were presented to the mind of Jesus for the purpose of inflaming desire.

9, 10. A truth and a lie may be found in very close proximity. Satan was indeed "the prince of this world." John 12: 31; 14: 30; 16: 11. With few exceptions, the kings and nobles and people of all lands constituted one vast kingdom of evil, with Satan as the sovereign. This was a truth. Affirming that he had power to transfer this kingdom to another was a lie. No such power had been given; and, besides, from the nature of the case, such transfer was impossible. The kingdom of evil originated with Satan, and had grown up to its enormous dimensions by his influence. Jesus could not have become the sovereign of Satan's kingdom without becoming just what Satan himself was. But it may not have been the intention of Satan to tempt Jesus by offering to transfer his kingdom as a kingdom of evil, but only as a kingdom, flattering him that in a splendid, vis-

11 Then the devil leaveth him, and, behold, angels came and ministered unto him.

12 ¶ Now when Jesus had heard that John was cast into prison, he departed into Galilee;

13 And leaving Nazareth,

ible form his Messianic power might be at once established, but knowing that if he yielded, the establishment of that power would be prevented. If this view is correct, it was a temptation to reject the slow, painful, purely spiritual, unpopular method which it was the will of God should be adopted. *Written*—In Deut. 6: 13, quoted from the Septuagint.

11. *Leaveth him*—Not implying that he may not return. See Luke 4: 13; 22: 53; John 14: 30; Matt. 27: 46. James (4: 7) says, *Resist the devil*, and he will flee from you. *Angels came and ministered*—Not spiritual strength, for this he had shown in resisting the temptations, but peace, comfort, and perhaps food. Elijah, when hungry, was visited by an angel. 1 Kings 19: 4–8. Jesus is now prepared for his great work. He has gained the victory over the greatest temptations offered to men, but gained it not by striking the tempter dead by the breath of his will, which would have been a victory of no spirituality and no sublimity, but by refusing to yield to the tempter. He has conquered not for himself only, but for all his people. In many a man's life there is a *turning point* at which the soul leaps madly into the embrace of the Evil One, or becomes so confirmed in love and faith that disloyalty to God is made well-nigh impossible. Judas is an example of the former; Peter of the latter. Temptation, however, cannot be expected to cease in the present life; and, as in the case of the Israelites on their journey from Egypt to Canaan, *the real giants may come last*. God's word is security, not against attacks from the devil, but against defeat. When devils go, angels come. Notice the many interesting points of resemblance and of unlikeness between the temptation of Jesus and that of Adam.

781 U.C. April, A.D. 28.

12, 13. The events recorded in these verses did not occur till more than a year after those narrated in the preceding verse. Where Jesus was, and what he did during the interval, will be seen when we come to the study of John. So far as Matthew's report shows, we are now to examine the beginning of our Lord's ministry, but it must not be inferred that Matthew was ignorant of the fact that a year of his ministry had already passed away. The Holy Spirit did not see fit to lead our evangelist to record the labors of the first year.

John . . . into prison—This event occurred probably in March, A.D. 28, in the year of Rome 781. Herod's wickedness brings the gospel to the publicans and sinners of Galilee all the sooner. *Capernaum*—"The contest between the rival claims of the two most probable spots is one of the hottest, and at the same time the most hopeless, in sacred topography." It is certain that it was "upon the sea-coast," that is, by the Sea of Galilee, and it was doubtless on the western side of the sea. Khan Minyeh, Tell Hûm three miles further north, 'Ain Mudawarah, or the Round Fountain, and a spot very near Bethsaida, near the Upper Jordan, have their respective advocates. As recently as 1866 was reported "the discovery" [at Tell Hûm] "of a synagogue in a state of fine preservation, remarkable for its elegant architecture, and belonging in all probability to an age earlier than that of Christ. It may have

CHAPTER IV.   53

he came and dwelt in Capernaum, which is upon the sea coast, in the borders of Zabulon and Nephthalim:

14 That it might be fulfilled which was spoken by Esaias the prophet, saying,

15 The land of Zabulon, and the land of Nephthalim, *by* the way of the sea, beyond Jordan, Galilee of the Gentiles;

16 The people which sat in darkness saw great light; and to them which sat in the region and shadow of death light is sprung up.

17 ¶ From that time Jesus began to preach, and to say, Repent: for the kingdom of heaven is at hand.

18 ¶ And Jesus, walking by the sea of Galilee, saw two brethren, Simon called Peter, and Andrew his brother, casting a net into the sea: for they were fishers.

---

been one of the Galilean synagogues in which the Saviour himself taught and performed some of his mighty works." As Dr. Hackett remarks, however, this of itself would not settle the question of the name of the town. *Sea-coast*—See note on vs. 18. *Zabulon and Nephthalim*—Territories which, named after two of the sons of Jacob, were in the northern part of Palestine and extended on the east to the Sea of Galilee. Zabulon lay on the southern side of Nephthalim.

14–16. *By Esaias*—In 9: 1, 2. The quotation is made *freely* from the Hebrew itself. The substance of the thought is fairly expressed, though the words are not exactly similar to those of the prophet. The prophecy is generally regarded as having distinct reference to the times of the Messiah. The northern portions of Palestine were more exposed to the deteriorating influence of the Gentiles than the central portions. The people were far from the centre of national worship. They were not so much given to reflection upon religion, nor so much to religious observances, as those who lived nearer Jerusalem. The people having less social refinement, their depravity took on coarser forms. Hence they are represented as sitting in darkness and in the region of the shadow of death. The darkness was wide-spread, reaching *beyond Jordan;* not, perhaps, in this case, east of the river, but toward its sources, and even to Galilee of the Gentiles, by which is meant Upper Galilee, where Gentiles were more numerous. Now that Jesus has begun to dwell in one of their principal cities, the words of Isaiah are fulfilled. A great light shines upon them.

17. *From that time*—From the time he went from Nazareth and made Capernaum his home. *Began to preach*—He had already labored several months in Judea, and had preached more or less; but he now begins his work in Galilee. It may have reference, also, to the fact that John, being in prison, has ceased to preach. The Baptist having closed his labors as the forerunner, the Messiah himself enters more actively upon his distinctive work. *To preach*—"to publish orally." *Repent*—See note on 3: 2. The message is substantially the same as John's; but it should be borne in mind that genuine repentance, as evinced by those who have knowledge of Christ, always implies faith in Christ as the Saviour from the sin committed. Mark (1: 15) gives the message in the fuller form: Repent ye and believe the gospel.

18. *Sea of Galilee*—So called, because the province of Galilee

5 *

19 And he saith unto them, Follow me, and I will make you fishers of men.

20 And they straightway left *their* nets and followed him.

21 And going on from thence, he saw other two brethren, James *the son* of Zebedee, and John his brother, in a ship with Zebedee their father, mending their nets; and he called them.

22 And they immediately left the ship and their father, and followed him.

23 ¶ And Jesus went about all Galilee, teaching in their synagogues, and preaching the gospel of the kingdom, and

---

bordered its western side. It was also called Lake of Gennesaret (Luke 5: 1), from the plain which lay "at its north-western angle," and Sea of Tiberias (John 6: 1), from the city of that name, which stood on its western side. It is mentioned in Josh. 11: 2, by the name of Cinneroth. It is "of an oval shape, about thirteen geographical miles long, and six broad. Its most remarkable feature is its deep depression, being no less than seven hundred feet below the level of the ocean. The great depression makes the climate of the shores almost tropical. Snow very rarely falls, and though it often whitens the neighboring mountains, it never lies here. As the beach is everywhere pebbly, it has a beautiful sparkling look. The lake abounds in fish now, as in ancient times. In the time of Christ no less than *nine* cities stood on the very shores of the lake; while numerous large villages dotted the plains and hillsides around. This region was then the most densely peopled in all Palestine."—*Smith's Dict. of the Bible.* On the borders of this sea, our Lord spent most of his public life. Concerning the *Plain* of Gennesaret, see note on 14: 34. *Peter and Andrew*—See note on 10: 2. *Net*—There were two kinds, the *casting* net, which is the kind here meant, and the *drag* net mentioned in *Matt.* 13: 47. The latter was used with a boat. The former was *cast*, or thrown, by the fisherman from the shore. Though fish are now, as formerly, very abundant in the Sea of Galilee, yet, as Porter says, "The fishery, like the soil of the surrounding country, is sadly neglected. One little crazy boat is the sole representative of the fleets that cov-

FISHING NET.

ered the lake in N. T. times, and even with it there is no deep-water fishing."—Two men to one net,—an instructive fact.

21, 22. *James and John*—See note on 10: 2. *He called them*—These four men are now, for the first time, distinctly called to be constant followers of Jesus, though (John 1: 37-42) Andrew, Simon, John, and perhaps James, had known him before, in Judea, and in a general sense had been called to be his disciples. The call is instantly and cheerfully obeyed. All is left, even the father, and the father himself makes no opposition. That he was aged, and needed his sons' support, is without proof. Fishing is still to be the business of the disciples, but fishing of a very different kind.

Here is the beginning of organized effort to save the world. A mustard-seed, but it will grow to be

healing all manner of sickness, and all manner of disease, among the people.

24 And his fame went throughout all Syria: and they brought unto him all sick peo-

---

a great tree! A leaven that will eventually leaven the whole lump! As to the composition of the apostolic body, see the paragraph preceding the note on 10: 5.

23. Our Lord's labors in Galilee have been very conveniently arranged by Andrews, in his "Life of our Lord," into alternate sojourns in Capernaum and Circuits. Before his final departure from Capernaum and Galilee, he made *nine circuits*. Thus there were *nine sojourns*. These are not all recorded, however, in the Gospel of Matthew. One of the circuits is reported, summarily, in this 23d vs. How many of the four hundred and four towns and villages which Galilee is said to have contained, Jesus visited, we have no means of knowing. *Teaching in their synagogues*—These buildings were erected for prayer, and the reading of the Old Testament. Our Lord often taught in them, and performed in them many of his miracles. Unlike the temple, synagogues were not used for sacrifices. There is no proof that they came into use till many centuries after the completion of Solomon's Temple. Nearly every town had one, and some had more. They were so located that when entering them, persons would be looking toward Jerusalem. Every synagogue had an ark, or chest, containing a copy of the Law. It had "chief seats" (23: 6), or seats of honor, " to which the wealthy and honored worshipper was invited," and a reading-desk on a platform, from which the Scriptures were read. Connected with the synagogue were "elders," to which reference is made in Luke 7: 3, over whom was a "ruler," as, for example, Jairus (Luke 8: 41); the "minister" (Luke 4: 20), whose duty it was "to open the doors, to get the building ready for service." "The officers of the synagogue exercised in certain cases a judicial power." Matthew 10: 17 proves that even punishment was sometimes inflicted in the building itself:—*And they will scourge you in their synagogues.*

Preaching the gospel of the kingdom—The good news of the kingdom. See, in Luke 4: 16-22, a very beautiful illustration of our Lord's method of preaching the good news in synagogues.

24. *Syria*—The large territory on the north of Palestine, in which, among other towns, were Antioch on the west, and Damascus on the east, and the interesting mountain range of Lebanon. Through all this wide and distant region did the fame of Jesus spread, even in the earlier part of his Galilean ministry. Not only were the sick healed to whom the Saviour went, but sick ones were brought to him from different and distant points. *All sick people*— The general statement. Then follows the specification. *Torments*—Possibly, according to one writer, " acutely painful paralysis, complicated with neuralgia;" according to another, "cramp, twisting the limb round as if in torture." Precisely what is meant, no one can certainly tell. *Possessed with devils*—Devils, or demons, are recognized throughout the gospels as actual beings. James (2: 19) says, The devils also *believe and tremble*. See also Rev. 16: 14. The more correct view of demoniacal possession makes the person both diseased and possessed; but possession, not disease, was the characteristic. It is probable that possession was generally the result of vice in the grossest forms. Repeated and earnest attempts have been made to show that "posses-

ple that were taken with divers diseases and torments, and those which were possessed with devils, and those which

sion" is only symbolic of evil; or, that in seeming to recognize demons in human beings, Christ only *accommodated* himself to the prevalent Jewish belief. But, 1. Jesus used language which implied his own perfect recognition of the personality and indwelling of demons. Examine with care Luke 11: 14-26. Jesus was truthful, and opposed to superstition. He could not therefore have uttered these words if he knew that such a phenomenon as demoniacal possession had no existence. We need not hesitate to say that, uttering such words with such knowledge, Jesus could have no claim on our confidence. The language which he employed was not, then, an "accommodation" of himself to popular opinion. 2. The evangelists themselves use language which proves that they sincerely believed in the reality of demoniacal possession. This would be generally admitted. Though like all the Jews, except the Sadducees, they had doubtless believed in it before they became disciples of Christ, yet, *as evangelists*, they could not have used language so unequivocally showing continued belief in possession, had they not been strengthened in their opinion by the evident belief of Jesus himself. They speak of demons as *coming out* of men and *entering into* swine; to demons they attribute given physical phenomena; they represent the demoniacs themselves as confessing that they were possessed with demons; and they make a distinction between diseased persons and demoniacs.

What was demoniacal possession? "The demoniac was one whose being was strangely interpenetrated ('*possessed*' is the most exact word that could be found) by one or more of those fallen spirits, who are constantly asserted in Scripture ... to be the enemies and tempters of the souls of men. He stood in a totally different position from the abandoned wicked man, who morally is given over to the devil. This latter would be a subject for punishment; but the demoniac for deepest compassion. There appears to have been in him a *double will* and *double consciousness*,—sometimes the cruel spirit thinking and speaking in him, sometimes his poor crushed self crying out to the Saviour of men for mercy; a terrible advantage taken and a struggle between sense and conscience in the man of morally divided life. Hence it has been not improbably supposed, that some of these demoniacs may have arrived at their dreadful state through various progressive degrees of guilt and sensual abandonment. 'Lavish sin, and especially indulgence in sensual lusts, superinducing, as it would often, a weakness in the nervous system, which is the especial bond between body and soul, may have laid open these unhappy ones to the fearful incursions of the powers of darkness.'" To refer the phenomena of modern "spiritualism" to demons, is, in the present state of knowledge, hasty. If they should be referred, however, to any sort of spiritual beings, they should be ascribed to demons.

Lunatic—Derived from the Latin word *luna*, and originally applied to the subject, because the disease was believed to be influenced by changes in the moon. Lunacy was probably epilepsy, "a disease of the brain which causes persons affected with it to fall down suddenly, and is attended by convulsive stupor." See the graphic account of a case in Mark 9: 14-29. Sometimes the lunatic was possessed.

The palsy—"A loss of the power of voluntary motion and feeling, one or both coming on, sometimes grad-

were lunatic, and those that had the palsy; and he healed them.

25 And there followed him great multitudes of people from Galilee, and *from* Decapolis, and *from* Jerusalem, and *from* Judea, and *from* beyond Jordan.

CHAPTER V.

AND seeing the multitudes, he went up into a moun-

---

ually, but more often suddenly, and extending at one time to a part, at another time to the whole body. It is a kind of station-house on the way to apoplexy, where passengers stop, not merely to stay over night, but to rest many days, or even years. A great injury inflicted on the brain, either by pressure or other cause, will induce a complete loss of motion and feeling, and this extending to the whole structure, brings likewise a loss of consciousness, which is apoplexy. A smaller degree of pressure, or a less injury upon the same brain, would occasion a loss of motion only, or, if a loss of feeling were experienced also, it would only extend to a part of the body, and consciousness would remain. This would be palsy. The disease is like apoplexy in kind, but stops short of it in degree."—*Dr. Ira Warren.*

25. *Decapolis* was a district lying chiefly on the east side of the Jordan. It contained ten cities. Hence its name. "This region, once so populous and prosperous, from which multitudes flocked to hear the Saviour, and through which multitudes followed his footsteps, is now almost without an inhabitant. Six out of the ten cities are completely ruined and deserted." *From beyond Jordan*—The territory lying on the east side of the Jordan south of Decapolis, and called Perea, from the Greek word *peran*, which means *beyond*. Though Jerusalem was a part of Judea, and Decapolis was itself beyond Jordan, this apparent mixing or confusing of the localities specified need create no difficulty.

It is a general and not uncommon style of representation.

CHAPTER V.

THE SERMON ON THE MOUNT.

781 U.C. Midsummer, A.D. 28.

It must constantly be borne in mind that Matthew does not profess to give the details of the Saviour's life in the order of time. The delivery of the discourse, for example, which we are now to examine, was preceded by much that Matthew was not led by the Spirit of God to report; and there is considerable reason to suppose that the discourse is introduced earlier than it might have been in relation to some of the events which are given further on. Let the student keep in mind the object for which Matthew wrote, and he will see why the evangelist thought the order of time, as to the details, of little importance. The question whether this discourse and that given by Luke are the same will be considered in the notes on Luke 6: 20-49.

The object of the Sermon on the Mount should be attentively considered. It is possible to explain the discourse so that it will seem to be in opposition to those parts of the Bible which teach the necessity of Christ's sufferings as the ground of justification. The sermon is a favorite with those who have no belief in the substitutional character of Christ's death. But as we ought not to overlook those passages which teach the necessity of good works,

tain: and when he was set, his disciples came unto him:

2 And he opened his mouth, and taught them, saying,

so we ought not to forget those which inculcate the necessity of the atonement. Neither the one class of passages nor the other comprises all that the Holy Spirit has spoken to men concerning the way of salvation. The Sermon on the Mount was intended to bring out not both the great features of the Christian system, believing and doing, but only, or chiefly, one—doing. The other, believing, is as clearly to be seen elsewhere as doing is to be seen here. Christ's teaching was progressive. Compare the Sermon on the Mount with the discourse in John 14-17. Even the most discerning and spiritual of the Lord's disciples needed such instruction as they received on the mount to prepare them for the richer instruction given them at the Supper. Jesus, in short, did not intend that the former should be regarded as his final, complete word, as he did not intend that his personal teachings all combined should be so regarded. He intended to speak, as he did speak, after his return to heaven, through the apostles, and thus the epistles are as truly his instructions to men as the words he spoke at the Supper and on the Mount.

The necessity of such preparatory instruction as is given in the Sermon is evident from the following considerations: In the time of Christ, outward righteousness, "ritualism," was mistaken by the Jews for inward righteousness. The mistake pervaded almost the entire nation. They must be made to see it. They must be taught the worthlessness of the most conscientious adherence to mere rites. They must be made to see what that righteousness is which God long ago required through Moses, and which some of their ancestors had signally illustrated. Intimations of Christ's willingness to aid them in attaining such righteousness are made in the numerous promises which the Sermon contains. Thus the Old Covenant and the New Covenant are put, not in opposition, as they sometimes are, but in harmony. "I am bound to confess," says Tholuck, "that the farther my studies have extended, the more clearly have I seen that the religion of the Old Testament and the Gospel constitute one revelation, and the higher has been my consequent estimate of the loftiness and depth of the Jewish economy." In this connection Rom. 3: 31 is important. It is impossible to conceive of a more effective method of breaking up whatever erroneous views of the Old Covenant the disciples were still cherishing.

PLAN OF THE SERMON.

CHAP. 5: 3-16. *Introduction.*—A. The blessedness of the righteous. *a.* Of the poor in spirit. *b.* Of the sorrowing. *c.* Of the meek. *d.* Of those that long for righteousness. *e.* Of the merciful. *f.* Of the pure in heart. *g.* Of the peacemakers. *h.* Of the persecuted for righteousness' sake. *i.* Of the persecuted for Christ's sake. B. The influence of the righteous. *a.* A preserving power. *b.* An enlightening power.
17-20. *Subject.*—THE SUPERIOR CHARACTER OF THE RIGHTEOUSNESS REQUIRED.
21-48. Illustrations of the subject—Part I. Murder; Adultery; Divorce; Perjury; Revenge; Limited Love.
CHAP. 6: 1-7: 12. Part II. Almsgiving; Prayer; Fasting; Trusting God for the supply of our physical wants; Charitableness in judging; Care in communicating truth; Certainty of receiving the Father's benevolent interposition; Loving others as ourselves.
13-27. *Conclusion.*—*a.* Enter the way pointed out. *b.* Beware of false guides. *c.* The consequence of giving heed to his words. *d.* The consequence of not giving heed.

1. *The multitudes*—Rev. Dr. W. M. Thomson, who was a missionary in Syria for twenty-five years, says in his "Land and the Book": "Should a prophet now arise with a tithe of

CHAPTER V.   59

3 Blessed *are* the poor in spirit: for theirs is the kingdom of heaven.

4 Blessed *are* they that mourn: for they snall be comforted.

---

the celebrity of Jesus of Nazareth, there would quickly be immense assemblies about him from Galilee, and from Decapolis, and from Jerusalem, and from Judea, and from beyond Jordan. Bad, and stupid, and ignorant, and worldly as the people are, their attention would be instantly arrested by the name of a prophet, and they would flock from all parts to see, hear, and be healed. There is an irresistible bias in Orientals of all religions to run after the mere shadow of a prophet, or a miracle-worker." How highly favored are the multitudes who are now permitted to hear such a teacher as the Lord Jesus Christ! *Seeing . . . . he went*—Not to avoid them, but to secure a more convenient place from which to address them. *His disciples*—Not merely the twelve, but all who, as pupils, desired instruction. The people generally who were in attendance heard the discourse, for 7:28 says that the people were astonished at his doctrine. *A mountain—The* mountain; either some definite mountain, or the mountainous region in distinction from the lower lands. Robinson contends that either of the several mountains on the western side of the Sea of Tiberias might answer the conditions. There is, however, a mountain which has been designated as the Mount of the Beatitudes, though Robinson attaches little value to the tradition, and Hackett cannot say that he has "any great confidence in it." The name of the traditional mountain is Kurun Hattin, the Horns of Hattin, Hattin being the name of a village near the foot of the mountain, and Horns having been suggested by the shape. "The tradition," says Stanley, "cannot lay claim to any early date; it was in all probability suggested first to the Crusaders by its remarkable situation. But that situation so strikingly coincides with the intimations of the Gospel narrative, as almost to force the inference that in this instance the eye of those who selected the spot was for once rightly guided. It is the only height seen in this direction from the shores of the Lake of Gennesaret. The plain on which it stands is easily accessible from the lake, and from that plain to the summit is but a few minutes' walk. The platform at the top is evidently suitable for the collection of a multitude, and corresponds precisely to the 'level place' [Luke 6:17. mistranslated 'plain'] to which he would 'come down' as from one of its higher horns to address the people. Its situation is central, both to the peasants of the Galilean hills and the fishermen of the Galilean lake, between which it stands, and would therefore be a natural resort both to 'Jesus and his disciples' when they retired for solitude from the shores of the sea, and also to the crowds who assembled 'from Galilee, from Decapolis, from Jerusalem, from Judea, and from beyond Jordan.'"

2. *Opened his mouth*—In Gen. 29:1 are the words (the translation given by Dr. Conant in his revised version of Genesis), And Jacob *lifted up his feet, and went* to the land of the sons of the East; "a mode of expression," says a note, "by which the Hebrew indicates anything of formal and grave import, as in this case the undertaking of a long and difficult journey. Compare the similar purport of the phrase, 'He opened his mouth and taught them,' Matt. 5:2."

3. *Blessed*—Happy is regarded by some as a more exact expression of

5 Blessed *are* the meek: for they shall inherit the earth.

6 Blessed *are* they which do hunger and thirst after right-

the meaning. Though the only question should be, Which word best represents the original? the writer cannot forbear to say that the old Saxon word, *blessed*, seems to have something divine about it. *Happy* has indeed, like *blessed*, been consecrated by Christianity to an exalted use; but it was cradled in the doctrine of chance. *Hap* was chance, luck; and happiness, therefore, was a state of pleasure resulting from good luck. Though the word has sprung out of its old pagan sense, and has put on a truly Christian meaning, yet even now it gets tossed about much more freely among the rough things of the earth than the word *blessed*. Happiness is applied to almost all sorts of pleasure; blessedness only to that which is exalted and refined.[1]

The poor in spirit—In these words is struck the first blow against the prevailing righteousness of the times, yet Jesus calls the hearers back only to what had already been taught by their own prophets. One who has no material possessions may be wanting in the kind of poverty here meant; one who abounds in them may abound in this also. That voluntary poverty to which Romanism attaches such merit is the worst possible illustration of poverty of spirit. Nor can the Lord mean poor in respect to mental culture. A mean, craven spirit is equally remote from the quality described. Jesus rebuked the church in Laodicea for saying, I am rich, and increased with goods, and have need of nothing, and for not knowing that it was wretched, and miserable, and poor, and blind, and naked. Rev. 3: 17. Poverty of *spirit;* therefore an internal state, which, however, is more likely to characterize those who have little property than those who have much. It must mean consciousness of spiritual want; that is, of sinfulness and ignorance, which always leads to deep self-abasement. That men do not need a supernatural revelation, a Saviour of supernatural origin, substitutional righteousness as the ground of all personal righteousness, is an assumption that does not spring from poverty of spirit. Modern spiritualism and poverty of spirit are essentially contrary the one to the other. Rationalism is the offspring of pride. *The kingdom of heaven*—See note on 3: 2, second paragraph. *Theirs*—They are members of it; or, since the kingdom is essentially internal, it is a possession lodged in the spirit. The deeper the poverty, the ampler the riches. "In the view of those Jews whose senses were dazzled with brilliant pictures of the Messiah's kingdom, this commencement of his discourse contrasted strongly with the whole circle of their ideas; but to those in whom the law had fulfilled its office, and who were brokenhearted, such language was a balm."

4. *They that mourn*—Poverty of spirit leads to mourning, not merely at the introduction of the soul into the kingdom of God, but throughout this life. The mourning must be viewed "as a continuous condition of the soul," caused

---

[1] Some may be interested in considering the application of the word *Blessed*, as a title, to the Virgin Mary, by the Church of Rome. From henceforth all nations shall call me *Blessed*. Luke 1: 48. A note in the Roman Catholic version says: "These words are a prediction of that honor which the Church in all ages should pay to the blessed Virgin. Let Protestants examine whether they are in any way concerned in this prophecy." They *here* examined, and their decision is, in the words of Rev. Frederick Meyrick, that "the notion that there is conveyed in the word any anticipation of her bearing the title of ' Blessed' arises solely from ignorance." In the judgment of the critic, the original (one word) merely means "count happy."

CHAPTER V.

eousness: for they shall be filled.

7 Blessed *are* the merciful: for they shall obtain mercy.

---

by continuous consciousness of poverty of spirit. *Shall be comforted*—Immediately and ever after, but in the highest degree in heaven. This is a continuous state as well as the other. According to Paul, it is possible to be *sorrowful yet always rejoicing*. Christ himself is the Comforter. The effects of his coming had been described by the prophets under precisely this conception. Says Isaiah (40: 1), *Comfort ye, comfort ye, my people. To comfort all that mourn*, etc. Isa. 61: 1, 2, 3. See the whole of the beautiful description. In Luke 2: 25, Simeon is represented as waiting for the Consolation of Israel; and when the aged saint saw the child Jesus, he exclaimed, Lord, now lettest thou thy servant depart in peace according to thy word. Mourning without being comforted is not the true conception of a member of Messiah's kingdom. Joy which is not born of mourning under conscious poverty of spirit is spurious.

5. Another shaft aimed at the false righteousness of the times. *The meek*—Those who bear evil with patience and humility. The doctrine of the world at that time, and even to this day, is contrary to that which is here taught. It was held by the ancient Britons that patience avails nothing except to bring upon us yet heavier evils. This had not been the teaching even of the Old Testament, for Ps. 37: 11 says, *The meek shall inherit the earth*. But Jesus must be understood as giving to this Old Testament doctrine a richer meaning than even the most spiritual men of his day were able to perceive. The truly meek of our Lord's time expected to inherit the earth in the sense that the Messiah's kingdom, of which they were to be members, was about to be set up in the Holy Land. This, so far, was not an incorrect understanding of the Old Testament. But Jesus uses the words to express the ever growing and at last universal supremacy which the patiently suffering members of his kingdom shall attain. The proud monarchs of the world must give place. The mighty change has been in progress ever since Christ spoke on the Mount. Sensitiveness relative to our personal rights is not enjoined by Jesus as a virtue. Too little meekness is still a fault even in many disciples of Christ.

6. Those who are poor in spirit, who mourn, and are meek, cannot but hunger and thirst after *righteousness*. This word has been explained by some as the imputed righteousness of Christ, by some as personal righteousness, and by others as both. The context requires it to be understood as personal righteousness, but other parts of the Scriptures teach us that Christ's righteousness, imputed through faith, lies at the basis of personal righteousness. Righteousness "is that state of mind which corresponds to the moral requirements of God's righteousness." This is what men find impossible of attainment by their own exertions; but it is attainable through Christ. Examine with care Rom. 8: 2-4. This righteousness in its perfect realization is indispensable to perfect blessedness, but in heaven it will be the possession of every believer. *Hunger and thirst*—Figures expressing intense desire. They are suggestive of pain. When, in heaven, the soul is *filled* with righteousness, the element of pain will be wanting, but not the desire.

7. The Pharisees scarcely had a conception of the quality which Jesus here commends. See, in evidence, 9: 13, But go ye *and learn what that meaneth*, I will have mercy and not sacrifice; 12: 7, But

8 Blessed *are* the pure in heart: for they shall see God.

9 Blessed *are* the peace-makers: for they shall be called the children of God.

10 Blessed *are* they which

---

if ye had known what this meaneth, I will have mercy and not sacrifice, ye would not have condemned the guiltless; 23: 23, in which the Pharisees are denounced for omitting the weightier matters of the law, judgment, *mercy,* and faith. The mercy which Jesus commends is a *Christian* virtue. To him who manifests it God will show mercy, while, strictly speaking, it is the mercy of God first manifested that inspires the soul with the spirit of mercy. Thus we must ever pray, *And forgive us our debts, as we forgive our debtors.* The methods of mercy are various. "This beatitude comprises every degree of sympathy and mutual love and help."

8. *The pure in heart—*The Pharisees aimed to make clean the outside of the platter. They appeared righteous unto men, but within were full of hypocrisy. They failed, therefore, in this respect, also, to manifest the righteousness of the law. But even sincerity and inward integrity are not all that is embraced in the Saviour's words. Purity of heart expresses essentially the same as righteousness in vs. 6. That, however, is represented as desired; this as obtained. It is a freedom from all moral pollution, embracing great delicacy of conscience, superiority to all debasing associations of thought, the use of the appetites, propensities, affections, and will in accordance with the will of God,—the result of a divinely exerted power. *Shall see God—*Not the essence of God. Seeing God in that sense is the exclusive prerogative of Christ. Not that any man hath seen the Father, *save he which is of God,* he hath seen the Father. John 6: 46. *Seeing—*Not an act of the understanding only, not "intuitions of reason," not an act of the resurrection-body, but "the most intimate fellowship with God." It is through the faith that works by love that such fellowship is attained. Hence the faintest breathings of love prove that the soul has entered into fellowship with God. The vision of God thus begun here will become clearer forever. Christ will be seen in heaven by the eye of the resurrection-body, and doubtless by the redeemed spirit before the body is raised,—how, we have no means of knowing; but the chief thing intended, both before the resurrection and after, is fellowship with God.

9. *Peace-makers—*Not the peaceable, but those who make peaceful them that are at enmity. They are the opposite of strife-makers. The virtue was taught under the Old Covenant, but it was not generally understood in the wide and spiritual sense in which it is intended by Christ. Being himself the great Peace-Maker (see the beautiful passage, Eph. 3: 13-19), Jesus raises peace-making to a higher position than it is possible for men to attain till they have come into peace with God by him. Peace-making, in the widest sense, is bringing men into harmony with God. *The children of God—*Implying that persons of this description, (1.) Have their origin with God; (2.) Are like God. God, then, is a Peace-Maker, which is distinctly taught in Col. 1: 20, 21. *Shall be called—*Not merely shall be, but shall be recognized as such. Peace-making is the legitimate business of all the subjects of Christ's kingdom. "On the spot where Jesus had described the kingdom of heaven and pronounced the meek and the peace-makers blessed, the most bloody battles have been fought! On the 5th of July, 1187,

are persecuted for righteousness' sake: for theirs is the kingdom of heaven.

11 Blessed are ye, when *men* shall revile you, and persecute *you*, and shall say all manner of evil against you falsely, for my sake.

12 Rejoice, and be exceeding glad: for great *is* your reward in heaven: for so persecuted they the prophets which were before you.

13 ¶ Ye are the salt of the earth: but if the salt have lost his savour, wherewith shall it

---

the celebrated battle of Hattin took place, in which the last remnant of the Crusaders was destroyed on the height of Tell Hattin, after the army had been beaten by Sultan Saladin in the valley. Again, on the plain of Jezreel, Bonaparte defeated, in 1799, with three thousand men, an army of twenty-five thousand Turks."

10. *Persecuted*—Not merely by the operation of unjust law, but also in other ways. *For righteousness' sake*—On account of your own righteousness. Thus plainly does Jesus apprise his followers that even righteousness will secure the world's active hatred. The forces of evil were marshalled against Jesus himself when an infant, and the greater the contrast became between his righteousness and the false righteousness of the times, the more intensely was he persecuted. Persecution is the most terrible chapter in human history. Persecution has often been waged in the name of Christianity, but never by Christianity herself. The sufferings must be borne for righteousness' sake, or there is no blessedness in the suffering.

11. The *ninth* beatitude, though not so reckoned by many eminent interpreters. It is generally regarded as only an expansion of the thought expressed in vs. 10; but there is an important advance in the thought. Here it is persecution for *Christ's* sake to which Jesus prefixes a distinct blessing. That a promise is not expressed in this verse is no objection to the view. The promise is in vs. 12. Slandering Christians, of which Jesus here speaks, has always been very common. History is full of illustrations of this kind of persecution. *Falsely*—Christians must so live that what is alleged against them shall have no foundation in fact.

12. *Be exceeding glad*—Exult. It is stronger than rejoice. *Your reward*—A reward may, or may not, be a reward of merit. In this case, the idea of meritoriousness is to be excluded. "It is inconceivable," says Tholuck, "that man can render by his virtues any service to God, any more than in taking a draught of the fountain the thirsty traveller renders that fountain a service." See Rom. 4:4; Luke 17:10. The teaching of infidelity that men have "a natural, inalienable right to the providence of God" (*Theodore Parker*), is not the doctrine of Christ. *The prophets*—Jeremiah was scourged and put in the stocks (Jer. 20:2); Zechariah was stoned (2 Chron. 24:21); and Jewish writers affirm that Isaiah was sawn asunder.

Nine blessings; nine characteristics of the righteous; nine promises. He that desires the blessings must have the characteristics. He that desires the fulfilment of the promises must have faith. How exalted the righteousness described! How earnestly should it be sought!

13. Jesus now speaks of the *influence* of such righteousness as he has described. In this verse he represents his disciples as a *preserving* power. *Salt*—Nothing is more

be salted? it is thenceforth good for nothing, but to be cast out, and to be trodden under foot of men.

14 Ye are the light of the world. A city that is set on a hill cannot be hid.

15 Neither do men light a

---

useful than sun and salt, says an old Roman proverb. Homer calls salt divine, and another ancient Greek writer speaks of it as an emblem of righteousness. "Attic salt" is a phrase used for wit. Salt is universally used for seasoning and preserving. So the disciples of Christ, not the apostles only, are a seasoning and preserving power in a world which is unsavory and full of tendencies to corruption. They are such *by the active effort which they make to save men. Have lost his savor*—"I have often," says Thomson, "seen just such salt, and the identical disposition of it that our Lord has mentioned. A merchant of Sidon, having farmed of the government the revenue from the importation of salt, brought over an immense quantity from the marshes of Cyprus,—enough, in fact to supply the whole province for at least twenty years. This he had transferred to the mountains, to cheat the government out of some small percentage. Sixty-five houses in Jûne—Lady Stanhope's village—were rented and filled with salt. These houses have merely earthen floors, and the salt next the ground, in a few years, entirely spoiled. I saw large quantities of it literally thrown into the street, to be trodden under foot of men and beasts. It was 'good for nothing.' Similar magazines are common in this country, and have been from remote ages, as we learn from history, both sacred and profane; and the sweeping out of the spoiled salt and casting it into the street are actions familiar to all men."

"Maundrell, who visited the lake at Jebbûl, tells us that he found salt there which had entirely 'lost its savor.' Indeed, it is a well-known fact that the salt of this country, when in contact with the ground, or exposed to rain and sun, does become insipid and useless. So troublesome is this corrupted salt, that it is carefully swept up, carried forth, and thrown into the street. No man will allow it to be thrown on to his field, and the only place for it is the street, and there it is cast to be trodden under foot of men." It is not necessary, however, to suppose that Jesus meant "that every trace of the peculiar taste of salt were wanting," but only that it has from some cause been so far injured as to be unfit either for seasoning or preserving. Here is no such doctrine as that a renewed soul will finally perish. If a disciple has lost the disposition to work as an instrument in saving men, there is no *human* power by which it can be restored to him. What God's grace may do for him is to be learned from other parts of the Bible. Or, like all similar ones in the epistles (Heb. 6: 6), this *if* may be understood as a warning note to keep us from final ruin. Means to keep all the children of God from apostasy must be used. *My sheep shall never perish*. In the light of *these* words, all such hypothetical expressions should be interpreted. The salt of *the earth*—Of the people of the earth. Christians are, not may be, or ought to be, or will become, but are, the means, etc.

14. *Ye are the light*—Not only a different figure, but a different sentiment. This teaches that Christians both as individuals and as organized churches, are (their *present* characteristic) an enlightening power; that is, a power for communicating *knowledge* to men; not only by their righteousness, but by the effort

candle, and put it under a bushel, but on a candlestick; and it giveth light unto all that are in the house.

16 Let your light so shine before men, that they may see your good works, and glorify your Father which is in heaven.

17 ¶ Think not that I am come to destroy the law, or the prophets: I am not come to destroy, but to fulfil.

---

which that righteousness leads them to put forth in disseminating truth,—truth, not so much a system of Christian principles as an efficacious life from Christ. Jesus declares himself to be the light of the world. John 8: 12. His followers are children of light. 1 Thess. 5: 5. Mark as very important, For ye were sometime darkness, *but now are ye light in the Lord.* Eph. 5: 8. That was the true light which lighteth every man that cometh into the world. John 1: 9. Jesus, then, is the source of all the light that shines from his disciples. *Of the world*—Compare Mark 16: 15. *A city on a hill*—As a city so located could not but be seen, so a true disciple cannot but be seen. "One of the most striking objects," says Stanley, "in the prospect from any of these hills, especially from the traditional Mount of the Beatitudes, is the city of Safed, placed high on a bold spur of the Galilean Anti-Lebanon. Dr. Robinson has done much to prove that Safed itself is a city of modern date. But, if any city or fortress existed on that site at the time of the Christian era, it is difficult to doubt the allusion to it, in 'the city lying on the mountain top.'" As Jesus is known to have drawn some of his illustrations from objects toward which his eye was directed, there is danger lest we attempt to account for all his illustrations in the same way.

15, 16. The obligation of Christ's disciples to let their light shine before men is illustrated by the use which is made of a family *lamp*,—the correct rendering of the Greek. Men act appropriately, consistently, putting the lighted lamp not under a bushel,—*the* bushel, the family measure—but on a *candlestick*,—the lamp-stand. The lamp, that is, is put *where it will do that for which it was lighted.* Good *works*—Not meritorious. The idea of merit is not embraced in the words. The glory of our Father must be the end. *The bushel*—Of indolence, of spurious modesty, of unauthorized customs, of excessive interest in the forms of religion (ritualism), of worldly care. The churches of Christ are the great preserving power and the great enlightening power; but the churches can be such only as the individual members are such. The evidence of discipleship is twofold: 1. The righteousness which is described in vs. 3–12; 2. That active effort to purify and enlighten the world which is described in vs. 13–16. Many strangely overlook the latter. Christ gives no preference to the one over the other. He can have little righteousness who makes no effort to make others righteous. Let all the light that now shines upon the world from Christ be extinguished, and how dense would be the darkness! How intense would be the light were every Christian what he ought to be!

17–20. *The subject of the sermon stated,* vs. 17–19 being preliminary to the conciser form in vs. 20.

17. *Think not*—Why this special caution? Did the Jews suppose that the Messiah, whenever he might come, would destroy the law? There is reason to believe that they held the opposite opinion. But not many of the hearers of this sermon had attained to the conviction that the Messiah had appeared. Yet they

18 For verily I say unto you, Till heaven and earth pass, one jot or one tittle shall in no wise pass from the law, till all be fulfilled.

19 Whosoever therefore

knew enough of the preacher to be convinced that he was greatly unlike the teachers whom they had been accustomed to hear. They were therefore in danger of thinking that *this Jesus* purposed to destroy the ancient law. Such an opinion would itself be an obstacle to their acceptance of him as the Messiah. This is one way of accounting for the use of the words, *Think not*. But they may have been used merely as an impressive way of *calling attention* to the fact that, in founding the new kingdom, he would not destroy that law which constituted the life of the old. See the same phrase, 10 : 34. *The law or the prophets*—The entire ancient economy as represented in the written law, both moral and ceremonial, and in the writings of the prophets, which two leading portions of the Old Testament stand for the whole. *To fulfil*—To give it "a deeper and holier sense,"—not deeper than it really had before he came, but deeper than those who lived before he came perceived, or could perceive. We are told that a Greek writer of a former age likens the ancient law to a sketch, which the painter does not destroy, but *fills up*. Says Tholuck : "Christ has come to perfect, to fill up with religious knowledge and life, all that in the Old Testament revelation existed in outline." Says Luther in Tholuck : "To show the real kernel and true significance of the law, that men might learn what it is, and what it requires." The rites of the Mosaic law, as mere rites, are abolished, but as an idea they were expressed by Jesus Christ with wonderful clearness and power. His vicarious sufferings *filled up* the sketch drawn in the ritual law. But he also fulfilled the law by putting his followers upon a course which, with his gracious help, issues in the attainment of the righteousness which the law requires. See Rom. 8 : 4, *That the righteousness of the law might be fulfilled in us,* etc. ; Rom. 3 : 31, Do we then make void the law through faith? God forbid. Yea, *we establish the law;* Rom. 10 : 4, *Christ is the end of the law* for righteousness to every one that believeth. The believer in Christ does not render *conscious* obedience to the law, but he renders conscious obedience to Christ, and as Christ requires all that the law requires, obedience to Christ is all the same as obedience to the law; only as rendered to Christ obedience involves the great, crowning act of abjuring all reliance on that obedience as the ground of justification. Thus Christ fulfils the law, and yet the law is abolished.

18. *Verily I say*—A solemn, authoritative form, "fixing, as it were, the stamp of truth upon the assertion which it accompanied." These things saith the *Amen* [the Verily], the faithful and true Witness. Rev. 3 : 14. Sometimes the affirmation is made still more solemn by repetition, as in John 3 : 3, *Verily, verily,* I say unto thee, Except a man be born again. *One jot*—The smallest letter in the Hebrew alphabet ('). *Tittle*—The little horns or points such as may be seen in the following Hebrew letters, ר, ך.¹ *Till heaven and earth*—Not while time shall last, shall the least require-

¹ It has been remarked already, that in the time of Christ, not the Hebrew, but the Septuagint translation of the Hebrew (into Greek) was in common use. Is it possible that this reference to the jot and the tittle of the *Hebrew* alphabet rather than to any part of the *Greek*, indicates that our Lord, even if he did use the Septuagint, regarded not the Greek but the Hebrew Scriptures as the authoritative word of God?

shall break one of these least commandments, and shall teach men so, he shall be called the least in the kingdom of heaven: but whosoever shall do and teach *them*, the same shall be called great in the kingdom of heaven.

20 For I say unto you, That except your righteousness shall exceed *the righteousness* of the scribes and Pharisees, ye shall

---

ment of the law pass away without receiving that fulfilment by Christ which constitutes the very end for which it was given. In being fulfilled in Christ, the form of the law as mere law passes away, though even then the substance remains. In Deut. 6 : 4 are the words, *The Lord our God is one Lord.* By dropping the mere point or horn in the last letter of the word translated *one*, the word would mean *another;* and so the Rabbins were accustomed to say that if ד (daleth) were changed into ר (resh), the foundations of the world would be shaken,—so immutable even in their judgment is the law.

19. The best interpreters are not quite agreed what is the meaning of these words. The general sentiment which our Lord intended to convey seems to be this: In that new kingdom which I am to found, will be required an estimate of the law very different from that which prevails among the scribes and Pharisees. The entire law, even the least things in it, must be regarded as of importance. Character must be estimated according to the estimate in which God's commands are held. He that shall break, undervalue, through some more or less needless mistake of his judgment, one jot or one tittle of the law, and shall teach men so, shall be regarded as so deficient in Christian character that he must be considered as the least of my subjects; but he that shall do and teach even the one jot or the one tittle, shall be regarded as the highest among my subjects. Both classes, the least as well as the greatest, are in Messiah's kingdom. Both are attached to God's commandments, and therefore the righteousness of both is vastly superior to that of the Pharisees, but the two are not equal in righteousness.

20. The subject more concisely expressed: *The superior character of the righteousness required. Your righteousness*—Not the righteousness which is imputed by faith, though that is the foundation of this, but personal righteousness. See note on vs. 6. *The scribes*—This class of persons will come before us so often in our study of the Gospels that some knowledge of it is indispensable. The scribes were the most influential persons in Palestine in religious affairs. It was chiefly by them that the doctrinal opinions of most of the Jews were shaped. They were the custodians and interpreters of the law, and of the Jewish religious writings generally. Most of the scribes of earlier times were good men; as, for example, Ezra. See the book of Ezra, 7 : 10. The one aim of those early scribes was to promote reverence for the law, to make it the ground-work of the people's life. They would write nothing of their own, through fear that less worthy words should be raised to a level with those of the oracles of God. They carefully studied the Old Testament, and laid down rules for transcribing it with the most scrupulous precision. At last they fell into idolatry of the letter, and reverence for the word was destroyed. The words of the scribes were honored above the law. It was a greater offence to offend against them than against the law. They were as wine while the precepts of the law were as water. Thus the

in no case enter into the kingdom of heaven.

21 ¶ Ye have heard that it was said by them of old time, Thou shalt not kill ; and whosoever shall kill shall be in danger of the judgment :

22 But I say unto you, That whosoever is angry with his brother without a cause shall be in danger of the judgment: and whosoever shall say to his brother, Raca, shall be in danger of the council : but whoso-

---

first step was taken toward annulling the commandments for the sake of their own traditions. Ceremonial laws became far more important than moral laws, and some of the plainest moral duties were evaded. In our Lord's time had accumulated a vast amount of *scribe-learning*, which consisted of interpretations of the law handed down from several of the previous ages,—*traditions*. These were made a study by Jewish youth. The scribes belonged to the party of the Pharisees. They sympathized with them, not with the Sadducees. Hence they are often mentioned together. One of the most distinguished of the scribes was Hillel, born about 112 B.C., of whom it was said, if the heavens were parchment, and all the trees of the earth pens, and all the sea ink, it would not be enough to write down his wisdom. Hypocrisy was the great characteristic of the scribes in the times of our Lord.—*Condensed from Smith's Dictionary of the Bible. Shall exceed*—1. In quantity ; 2. In quality. *In no case*—Not by any means. It is implied that if they shall have the righteousness taught by Moses, that is, in the fulfilled form in which it is taught by Christ, they will be members of the kingdom.

Jesus now proceeds to illustrate the righteousness required. His purpose is, not to disparage the law, but to exalt it. Observe especially that it is his purpose to show not only how much more comprehensive and spiritual it is than the scribes and Pharisees teach, but how much more so than even ancient and sincere expounders of the law taught. May the Spirit of God impress upon our hearts these rich interpretations of our Lord, that, hungering and thirsting for righteousness, we may be filled.

ILLUSTRATIONS. — CLASS I.

21. *First illustration. Ye have heard*—From the scribes in the synagogues and the temple. *By them* —*To* them. This is held by eminent scholars as demanded by usage in Matthew and other books of the New Testament. Even the English reader must be struck with the contrast thus brought out : Said *to them* of old time, but I say *unto you*. *Them of old time*—The people of the time in which traditional interpretations of the law began to be taught. *Thou shalt not kill*—This was the command as given by Jehovah to the people through Moses. *Whosoever shall kill*, etc.—This was the traditionary, superficial interpretation of the law which the scribes of our Lord's day affirmed had been taught to the people in former times, and which they themselves were accustomed to urge as the right one. The interpretation made disobedience to the law consist in doing the mere outward act. It was making the law a merely civil law. He that actually *took life* should be held accountable. He is in danger of *the judgment*—A court founded by Moses (Deut. 16: 18) in every city, consisting of seven judges, with power to condemn to death.

22. Jesus affirms that this commandment has a deeper meaning. It is more than a civil law. It em-

CHAPTER V. 69

ever shall say, *Thou* fool, shall be in danger of hell-fire.

23 Therefore if thou bring thy gift to the altar, and there

---

braces more than the outward act. It forbids even anger, that state of feeling of which there may be no proof except the person's own consciousness; of which, even if it should burst out in hot words, the courts would take no cognizance. *Raca*—Worthless, brainless. *Fool*—Impious, godless. It refers to moral characteristics rather than to intellectual. Many suppose that three degrees of guilt are intended: 1. The lowest, that which arises from concealed anger; 2. That which arises from anger bursting out in the opprobrious word, *Raca;* 3. That which arises from a still more passionate state, and showing itself in the yet more severe and contemptuous term, *fool*. This gradation in guilt is connected by such interpreters with gradation in punishment: 1. That which could be inflicted by the judgment, the lowest court; 2. By the council, the Sanhedrim, the highest court; 3. The punishment of hell-fire. From this view Dr. Alexander strongly dissents, affirming that it is difficult to see how the angry utterance of *fool* indicates greater guilt than that of *Raca*. We see no difficulty, however, in the usual explanation. "Malignant" anger, as Alexander calls it, is not affirmed, but causeless anger. This, however slight, exposes to punishment; and whether it is greater guilt to call a man fool than Raca is not the question. The *anger* which leads one to call his brother fool *may* be greater than that which makes him say Raca, and that is sufficient to save the common interpretation at this point from inconsistency.

Hell fire—The original is in this form,—*the gehenna of fire*. On the west and the south sides of Jerusalem, not on the south only, as Barnes and many others affirm, is a deep ravine called Valley of Hinnom, in Hebrew, Ge-Hinnom, from which *gehenna* is derived. "On the southern brow, overlooking the valley at its eastern extremity, Solomon erected high places for Molech (1 Kings 11: 7), whose horrid rites were revived from time to time in the same vicinity by the later idolatrous kings. Ahaz and Manasseh made their children 'pass through the fire' in this valley (2 Kings 16: 3; 2 Chron. 28: 3; 33: 6), and the fiendish custom of infant sacrifice to the fire-gods seems to have been kept up in Tophet, at its south-eastern extremity, for a considerable period. To put an end to these abominations the place was polluted by Josiah, who rendered it ceremonially unclean by spreading over it human bones and other corruptions, from which time it appears to have become the common cesspool of the city, into which its sewage was conducted, to be carried off by the waters of the Kidron, as well as a laystall" [dunghill] "where all its solid filth was collected."—*Smith's Dictionary.* Barnes, in his note upon this verse, says that "it was necessary to keep fires continually burning there." This statement, made by many others also, rests upon very slender authority. Dr. Samuel C. Bartlett says, in his "Life and Death Eternal," "Still more destitute of foundation is the assertion by Mr. Barnes and others, that 'this valley was called *the gehenna of fire.*'" According to Dr. Bartlett, *gehenna* did not have in the time of Christ *two meanings*, a primary and usual meaning as the name of a valley south of Jerusalem, and an unusual and secondary or figurative meaning, denoting the place of punishment. It had but one meaning, *punishment in the future world, hell.* The Jews used it repeatedly

rememberest that thy brother hath aught against thee;

24 Leave there thy gift before the altar, and go thy way;

---

in that sense. Even Dr. Alger (Unitarian), in his "Doctrine of a Future Life," says that "this is a fact about which there can be no question." Dr. Bartlett's view is supported by Prof. E. P. Barrows, formerly of the Theological Seminary, Andover, who writes to the former, that it appears to him certain that in our Lord's day the word *gehenna* "had come in well-established theological usage—probably long before the beginning of the Christian era—to signify hell, that is, the *place of torment for the wicked;* and that this was the only sense of the word."

This word, hell-fire, *gehenna*, being used by Christ in this verse to express punishment in the future world, the other words, *judgment* and *council*, must be used to express the same, but in less degree. That these refer to future punishment is also evident from the fact that of *such* violations of the sixth commandment no Jewish court would take cognizance. The courts tried for actual murder, not for anger. *Without a cause*—It is possible, then, to be angry without sinning. Anger is ascribed to Jesus (Mark 3:5); and Paul (Eph. 4:26) says, Be ye angry and sin not. Even the term *fool* may be used without sin; for Jesus (23:17, 19) addresses the scribes and Pharisees as *fools*. Luke 24:25 is not to the point, for in the Greek, *fools*, addressed to his disciples, is not the same word, but one that was often used in a milder sense, and there it means, *dull in understanding.* We may interpret the words of Jesus too literally. The right spirit *may* exist even when the word *fool* is used. The wrong spirit may exist when other words are used, or none at all. Yet it must be confessed that if a disciple of Christ can address, without sin, one of his fellow-men in the terms in which Jesus addressed the Pharisees, he must have attained to a remarkable degree of that righteousness which the Saviour enjoins in the Sermon on the Mount.

23, 24. *Therefore*—The practical application. They are addressed as Jews, and therefore the phraseology used is drawn from the peculiar forms of Jewish worship. *Thy gift* —Some say, "any kind of gift,— sacrificial or eucharistic." Others restrict it to the sacrificial. The man is suposed to have arrived at the altar, but just as he is about to deliver his offering to the priest, he remembers, not that he has some ground of complaint against his brother, but that his brother has some complaint, not necessarily some ground for it, against himself. Instantly he must suspend this act of worship, and perform a duty, which, for the time, is paramount. The offering of the gift will not be acceptable to God till he has become reconciled to his brother. The reconciliation is not supposed to be mutual. The offerer is under obligation to "remove the offence and make friendly overtures to his brother." This is Alford's view. Tholuck considers the person addressed to be the offender, and the other as having a just ground of complaint. So long as the offerer neglects the duty here enjoined, he is guilty of breaking the sixth commandment. The latter is the view more commonly held. We think that both may be correct. The offerer should cease to make his offering in case either fact is remembered. What was intended for his hearers as Jews has been appropriated, as Christ meant it should be, by Christians; "and so arose that beautiful custom of the early Church, of the mutual act of forgiveness among members of

first be reconciled to thy brother, and then come and offer thy gift.

25 Agree with thine adversary quickly, while thou art in the way with him; lest at any time the adversary deliver thee to the judge, and the judge deliver thee to the officer, and thou be cast into prison.

26 Verily I say unto thee, Thou shalt by no means come

Christian families before the celebration of the Holy Communion."

ALTAR.

The altar—God commanded Moses to make two altars: 1. The altar of burnt offering, on which a fire was required to be kept constantly burning, which is supposed to be "the symbol and token of the perpetual worship of Jehovah." This stood outside the temple. 2. The altar of incense. This was also called the golden altar, whereas the other was the brazen. It stood in the Holy Place. The former is the altar to which the Saviour refers. The word *altar* is very improperly applied in some Christian churches to the communion-table or to any other part of a *Christian* house of worship. Not one instance of such a use is to be found in the New Testament. In Heb. 13 : 10 it is said, indeed, *We have an altar*, whereof they have no right to eat which serve the tabernacle, but, as Dr. Ripley remarks in his excellent Notes on Hebrews, "The altar which believers in Jesus are here represented as having is *the cross* on which our Lord endured his sacrificial and propitiatory death, or offered up himself as our sacrifice. It is here employed as the visible emblem of the Christian religion. . . . It is indeed only by a figure of speech, though a very easy and appropriate figure, that it is called an altar." For Protestants to speak of the communion-table, or of that part of the building where it is located, as the *altar*, is simply an imitation of the language of Romanism, borrowed from that dispensation which was only a shadow of good things to come.

25, 26. Jesus here teaches, in language drawn from *the law*, that reconciliation with one whom we have offended, should be immediate. Literally, the language is tantamount to this: If you are prosecuted for debt, effect a settlement with the plaintiff, your creditor, your adversary, while you are on the way with him to the magistrate, lest coming before the magistrate you shall be thrown by his decision into prison to suffer the penalty of the law. Among the Jews, imprisonment for debt could not be prolonged beyond "the seventh year, or at farthest

out thence, till thou hast paid the uttermost farthing.

27 ¶ Ye have heard that it was said by them of old time, Thou shalt not commit adultery:

28 But I say unto you, That whosoever looketh on a woman to lust after her, hath committed adultery with her already in his heart.

29 And if thy right eye of-

---

the year of jubilee." It has been affirmed that "in later times the sabbatical or jubilee release was superseded by a law, probably introduced by the Romans, by which the debtor was liable to be detained in prison until the full discharge of the debt." This is not considered by all as certain. This 26th verse has been quoted in proof, but it does not quite prove it. Jesus is not here referring specially and exclusively to the duty of obeying the sixth commandment by being willing to satisfy the plaintiff in a case of prosecution for debt. He *may* intend to include even such a case, but he speaks more comprehensively. He means to enforce the duty of effecting, immediately, a settlement with any man between whom and yourself is a difficulty, of whatever kind it may be. Life is brief, and punishment for cherished sin is certain. The injured party should not be allowed, by your delay, to confront you in the next world. You should agree with him while you are in the way with him,—while both are on their journey together toward the judgment-seat of Christ. *Till thou hast paid*, etc.—"In the case of any book but the Bible, criticism would have taken the meaning of this passage to be simply that the judicial proceedings were to be executed against the offender according to the utmost rigor of the law."—*Tholuck.* But from these words in part the Church of Rome forces the doctrine of purgatory, and a certain class of Universalists the doctrine of restoration. The impossibility of paying the debt is the meaning which Matt. 25 : 46 and many other passages require. *Farthing*—"A small brass coin equal to two mites," or about two-fifths of one cent.

27, 28. *Second illustration.* They had also heard from the scribes that it was formerly said, Thou shalt not commit adultery. Such was the prohibition of the law itself. The superficial interpretation of it by the scribes is to be supposed, though it is not expressed; for, in these illustrations generally, Jesus is not criticising the law, but the meaning which the scribes told the people had been given it from the earliest times. We must suppose, therefore, that, in *this* illustration, the Saviour is aiming his words against the notion that infraction of the seventh commandment consists only of the overt act. Jesus affirms that even the use of the eye *for the purpose* of inflaming lust is a violation of the command. This ampler breadth of meaning must be regarded as forbidding all impure associations of thought, and contact with all literature, with all paintings, with all sculpture, with all theatrical exhibitions, that are adapted to produce them. The success of the theatre, for any considerable period, depends upon its resting on a basis of licentiousness. A moral theatre would soon get smitten with paralysis and die. Jesus here affirms that a single, momentary act of impurity, *in the heart*, is a violation of the law. This form of inward unrighteousness has doubtless always been a very prevalent sin, and actual infraction of the seventh commandment has also been fearfully prevalent, both in the higher and the lower classes of society. The churches of Christ should give no quarter to the sin.

CHAPTER V.

fend thee, pluck it out, and cast *it* from thee: for it is profitable for thee that one of thy members should perish, and not *that* thy whole body should be cast into hell.

30 And if thy right hand offend thee, cut it off, and cast *it* from thee: for it is profitable for thee that one of thy members should perish, and not *that* thy whole body should be cast into hell.

31 It hath been said, Whosoever shall put away his wife, let him give her a writing of divorcement:

32 But I say unto you, That whosoever shall put away his wife, saving for the cause of

---

29, 30. Such unrighteousness must be subdued, however difficult, or the punishment of the future life must be suffered. This is taught in figurative language. It must be figurative, for mutilation of an eye or a hand would not necessarily result in greater purity of heart. It might make *a bad matter worse*, by giving birth to intenser self-righteousness. *Right eye . . . right hand*—Selected because they are almost universally prized above the left. *Offend*—Not in the modern sense of displease, but, to cause thee to sin. *Pluck out . . . cut off . . . cast it from thee*—1. Resolutely deny yourself the object desired; 2. Cease desiring it. To aid you in subduing desire for a wrong object, cut the last and the least tie of connection between yourself and it. But it is not possible, in this world, to dissolve connection between every tempting object and one's self. The point of our Saviour's command, therefore, lies in the extinction of the desire for it. *Profitable*—For your advantage. Jesus had no hesitancy in sometimes presenting this lower view. It is by no means, however, that selfish view which has been called the "utilitarian"; namely, that the virtue of an act consists in its being *useful* to the doer. It will be profitable to lose an object which may be so strongly desired that parting from it may seem like parting with a right eye, rather than to lose one's entire self by being cast into hell. *Hell*—Gehenna, concerning the meaning of which see note on vs. 22, second and third paragraphs.

31, 32. *Third illustration. It hath been said*, must be understood as in the previous cases. The law of Moses concerning divorce (Deut. 24:1, 2) is as follows: When a man hath taken a wife, and married her, and it come to pass that she find no favor in his eyes, because he hath found *some uncleanness in her:* then *let him write her a bill of divorcement*, and give it in her hand, and send her out of his house. And when she is departed out of his house, she may go and be another man's wife. *But I say unto you*, must not be understood as implying that Jesus here sets himself in opposition to Moses. What he still opposes is the loose interpretation given the law by scribes and Pharisees, that interpretation being implied, not expressed. Concerning the opinions of the Jews upon divorce and concerning the nature of the Mosaic requirement more will be said in considering 19:3–9. Prof. Hovey says upon the verses before us, in his treatise on "The Scriptural Law of Divorce": "For a husband to put away his wife, by giving her a bill of divorce according to the Jewish law, for any other reason, is to authorize and tempt her to commit adultery by marrying another. And of this sin he is guilty, whether the wife is ever married the second time or not. But while the passage before us teaches by implication that a Jew

fornication, causeth her to commit adultery: and whosoever shall marry her that is divorced committeth adultery.

33 ¶ Again, ye have heard that it hath been said by them of old time, Thou shalt not forswear thyself, but shalt perform unto the Lord thine oaths:

34 But I say unto you, Swear

might put away his wife without sin, provided she was an adulteress, and marry another woman, it does not teach that a wife, thus divorced for good cause, had a right to marry again. According to the law of Moses she was to be put to death, and also her paramour. And, though this law was not rigidly enforced at the time of Christ, it may be presumed that an adulteress was generally unable to take position again as a lawful wife by marriage to a second husband. It appears, therefore, that the process of divorce, in order to be valid before God, must be a criminal process, and that only crime can justify it. When it rests on any other ground, it is without effect; the parties remain husband and wife as before."

*Causeth her to commit adultery—*Dr. Conant's view of these words differs from Dr. Hovey's. He says: "I understand this as equivalent to *makes her an adulteress,* in the same sense in which it is said (1 John 5: 10), *he that believeth not God hath made him a liar;* not that God thereby becomes a liar, or that she becomes an adulteress, but simply is treated as such. By repudiating her, for which the only just cause was adultery, he makes her appear as one guilty of that crime." Dr. Hovey's explanation is the common one.

33–37. *Fourth illustration.* In Lev. 19: 12 are the words, *And ye shall not swear by my name falsely;* and in Num. 30: 2, If a man vow a vow unto the Lord, or *swear an oath to bind his soul* with a bond, *he shall not break his word,* he shall do according to all that proceedeth out of his mouth. These, probably, are the verses, condensed, which Jesus represents the scribes as quoting. Some say that *thou shalt perform unto the Lord thine oaths* is the "weakening" interpretation of the scribes. Thus understood, the meaning is, Oaths in which the name of *God* occurs ought to be performed; but oaths by heaven, by earth, by Jerusalem, by the head, need not be kept. It is better, however, to regard these words, equally with the others, as quoted, though freely, from the law, and the superficial explanation of the scribes as understood. The result is the same. That which, in the scribes and Pharisees, wore the appearance of special reverence for God, indicated the existence of more than common irreverence. "Aben Ezra [1170 A. D.] speaks of the practice of swearing as universal in his day, so that he says, men swear daily countless times, and swear that they have not sworn." Thomson says: "This people are fearfully profane. Everybody curses and swears when in a passion. No people that I have ever known can compare with these Orientals for profaneness in the use of the names and attributes of God. The evil habit seems inveterate and universal.... The people now use the very same sort of oaths that are mentioned and condemned by our Lord. They swear by the head, by their life, by heaven, and by the temple, or, what is in its place, the church. The forms of cursing and swearing, however, are almost infinite, and fall on the pained ear all day long." Swearing among the Jews in the time of our Lord was also very common. It is not, then, merely against false swearing, perjury, that our Lord protests, but against "evasions of conscience."

CHAPTER V.

not at all; neither by heaven; for it is God's throne:

35 Nor by the earth; for it is his footstool: neither by Jerusalem; for it is the city of the great King.

36 Neither shalt thou swear by thy head, because thou canst not make one hair white or black.

37 But let your communication be, Yea, yea; Nay, nay:

34, 35. *Swear not at all*—Is Christ here condemning all oaths whatever, or is he condemning oaths of a certain class? In no case is the rule, Compare Scripture with Scripture, more important. Without such comparison, the conclusion of the Quakers is inevitable. Neglect of the rule leads them to believe as strongly that Christ does *not require* baptism in water and the commemoration of the Lord's death by the use of bread and wine, as it leads them to believe that he *does require* total abstinence from oaths. What answer should be given to the question may be apparent from the following considerations: *a.* There were oaths in ancient times which the Author of the Bible commanded. See Ex. 22: 11; Deut. 6: 13; 10: 20; Isa. 65: 16. *b.* The New Testament represents God himself as swearing by himself. Heb. 6: 13. *c.* Jesus allowed himself to be put under oath by the high priest. 26: 63, 64. *d.* Paul used the oath. Gal. 1: 20; 1 Cor. 15: 31 (the latter not so evident in the English as in the Greek). *e.* It is difficult to see anything in the *nature* of the oath which is sinful. *f.* After appearing to forbid all oath-taking whatever, Jesus *specifies;* and what does he specify? Swearing by heaven, by the earth, by Jerusalem, by the head. Swearing by God is *not* specified, which is very remarkable if he intended to include it, universally, in the general prohibition, Swear not at all. From these considerations it may be inferred that the words *not at all* must be taken with limitation. *For it is God's throne*—You are as truly culpable, therefore, as if you should swear by God himself. *His footstool*

—Equally to be blamed therefore. *The city of the great King*—Beautiful for situation, the joy of the whole earth, is Mount Zion, on the sides of the north, *the city of the great King.* Psalm 48: 2. As they themselves held that Jerusalem was, figuratively, the dwelling-place of Jehovah, the irreverence of daily swearing by Jerusalem was not essentially less than that of swearing by Jehovah.

36. According to Alexander, after a few earlier expositors, the reason given against swearing *by the head* is equivalent to this: "Thou canst not make (or bring into existence even) one hair (whether) white or black. It is then a denial of man's power, not to change the color of his hair, which is continually done by artificial means, but to produce one of any color, which, however trivial the effect may be, is a creative act." As has been remarked, "our Lord did not refer to artificial but to natural changes: this is seen from the fact that he mentions also the *white* hair, that of *age.* How miserable, then, is the observation of Ottius, that Christ is alluding to Herod, who, according to the account of Josephus, had *the vanity to dye his hair.*"—*Tholuck.* The meaning is simply this, thou art entirely dependent on God, as even thine inability to control the color of a hair of thy head shows. It is essentially the same, therefore, to swear by your head as to swear by God. Using such an oath, then, on every trivial occasion, is as truly a sin as to use on trivial occasions the name of God.

37. *Your communication*—This must be explained in harmony with

for whatsoever is more than these cometh of evil.

38 ¶ Ye have heard that it hath been said, An eye for an eye, and a tooth for a tooth:

39 But I say unto you, That ye resist not evil, but whosoever shall smite thee on thy right cheek, turn to him the other also.

---

the explanation, already given, of the words, Swear not at all. This, therefore, must mean, Your communication in ordinary, daily life. Abstain wholly from profane swearing. It is a rule for the regulation of private life. "The true oath consists in the simple asseveration, uttered in perfect consciousness and under a sense of the presence of God, before him and in him."—*Lange*. *Cometh of evil*—Either of evil in the abstract, or of him who is the source of all evil, the devil,—probably the former.

Though the judicial oath is not here condemned, yet even that has been used with such frequency as to give it oftentimes substantially the character of a profane oath. It is desirable that judicial oaths be greatly diminished in number.

38. *Fifth illustration*—It should still be kept in mind that Jesus is illustrating the righteousness which he, as the fulfiller of the law, requires. *An eye for an eye*, etc.—This was the requirement of the law. See Ex. 21 : 24; Lev. 24 : 20; Deut. 19 : 21. The *form* of the law is derived from what has been called the *lex talionis*; that is, that law which prevailed in the ruder form of society, by which the injured person retaliated upon the injurer by inflicting upon him *the same kind* of suffering as he had himself received. But while the form of the law was in imitation of the *lex talionis*, there is no evidence that the execution of the law was generally in accordance with the form. The intention was considered as met if the punishment was in proportion to the offence. The interpretation to which the superficial righteousness of the scribes led, was such as to encourage the spirit of revenge both in necessary resort to law and in private life. But was not that the very spirit of the Mosaic legislation? Nothing is more contrary to the fact. The *lex talionis*, private revenge, had long been the only principle by which men had been governed. The law of Moses took away the right of private revenge. It gave the right of punishment to the civil magistrate. It was, therefore, a rebuke to the *spirit of revenge*. See Lev. 19 : 18; Prov. 24 : 29; Lam. 3 : 27-30. The Old Testament itself confutes, therefore, the slander uttered by Theodore Parker against the character of the Mosaic legislation. The law, *Eye for eye*, was a public enactment intended to repress crime, and is the basis of all human government. The Jews, however, as we have reason to believe, seldom resorted to the law in the right spirit. The law was just. While as a general thing it required its penalties to be used, it did not forbid occasional forgiveness for a personal wrong, and it never justified the use of its penalties in a spirit of revenge.

39. *But I say*—As before, placing himself in opposition to the scribes, not in opposition to the law. He applies his higher view of the law to four cases. *Resist not evil*—We are required to resist the devil and all moral evil. The meaning is, resist not "a common, unprovoked insult." *Smite thee on thy right cheek*, etc., must not be pressed with slavish literalness. It is conceivable that even the spirit of revenge might prompt a man to turn the other cheek. Jesus was struck by one of the officers with the palm of the hand, and turned

CHAPTER V.

40 And if any man will sue thee at the law, and take away thy coat, let him have *thy* cloak also.

41 And whosoever shall compel thee to go a mile, go with him twain.

42 Give to him that asketh

the other cheek, not literally, but by the gentleness with which he bore it. John 18: 22-23. Paul was smitten on the mouth at the command of the high priest, and, "in the grace with which he recovered his self-possession, the frankness with which he acknowledged his error," he shews that he himself felt that in the quick outburst of the words, *God shall smite thee, thou whited wall,* he had *not* turned the other cheek. " A blow on the cheek was the utmost mark of contempt, such as few would dare to inflict on any one but a slave." The Saviour's direction, then, amounts to this: Do not avenge an insult; bear it with gentleness; suffer *double* rather than retaliate. Going to law for the attainment of our rights is not always wrong, though there are many cases in which the disciples of Christ better suffer even from men of the world than to do so. That Christians, members of the same church, should go to law with one another, either in pagan countries or Christian, is contrary to the law of Jesus Christ, revealed through the apostle Paul: 1 Cor. 6: 1-7.

40. Second case. Rather than indulge in that spirit of retaliation which the false interpretation of the scribes was continually fostering, they should be willing to give up the *cloak* (the outside garment which the poor used as a covering by night, Ex. 22: 26, 27), to him who would wrong them of the *coat*, — the under garment worn next the skin. Do not indulge in bitterness toward him who would invade that right concerning which men are so sensitive, — the right of property. This is a case which too frequently occurs.

41. Third case. *Compel thee to go*—Impress thee. Simon was, *perhaps*, compelled, impressed, by legal authority, to aid in bearing the cross. 27: 32. The original word was derived from the Persian. "Cyrus, or, according to Herodotus, Xerxes, was the first to establish relays of horses and couriers at certain distances on all the great roads, in order that the royal letters and messages might be transmitted with the greatest possible speed. These" [public couriers] " had authority to *press* into their service men, horses, ships, or anything that came in their way, which might serve to hasten their journey." A similar system had been introduced by the Roman government into Palestine, but it was very obnoxious to the Jews. Some think that Jesus refers not to legal requisitions, but to "acts of constraint in private life," taking his phraseology, however, from the well-known practice of the Roman government. The duty enjoined is, be ready to yield to the exaction, governmental or private, which one may make upon you, even to doubling your service, rather than to manifest revenge.

42. Fourth case. A literal interpretation of these words would be a false one, and acting accordingly would multiply beggars, vagabonds, and knaves. Sympathy should be neither hoarded nor wasted. An enlightened judgment and a loving heart will save us from turning away the asker and the borrower, even if their demands are a little extravagant, rather than indulge toward them impatience and fretfulness.

These four cases of the application of the true spirit of the law,

thee, and from him that would borrow of thee turn not thou away.

43 ¶ Ye have heard that it hath been said, Thou shalt love thy neighbour, and hate thine enemy.

44 But I say unto you, Love your enemies, bless them that curse you, do good to them that

---

An eye for an eye, show how delicate and far-reaching is the righteousness to which Jesus would bring the world. Notice the gradation from gross personal insult to mere asking and borrowing.

43. 44. *Sixth illustration.* Love thy neighbor—Lev. 19: 18. This was the law. The "outrageous" addition by the scribes was, Hate thine enemy. Christ brings out the long-obscured meaning of the law by teaching them, in opposition to the scribes, that they must *love* their enemies, etc. But did not the law mean by neighbor, primarily, the Jews, and only the Jews? Notice in the verse from which the law is quoted the evident allusion to Jews: Thou shalt not avenge, nor bear any grudge against, *the children of thy people*, but thou shalt love thy neighbor as thyself. Did the law, then, command Jews to love only Jews? Such is the representation of those who take pleasure in berating the entire Jewish economy. Of course, and with perfect propriety, the primary reference is to the duty of loving their own people, but this requisition was intended to discipline them into love for others also. It contains no intimation that their love was to be *restricted* to Jews. *Hate thine enemy*—Not foreigners only, but any one, even a Jew. But Christ teaches that they are not only not to retaliate, but are to cherish the spirit of love toward the wrong-doer. But their love must not be the mere disposition; the disposition must be *acted out* in praying for him. This does not imply that we are to be indifferent to the sin of the wrong-doer. Our enemies are to be loved in the same sense in which God loves them.

Loving an enemy had been enjoined under the old covenant. Prov. 24: 17, 18. It had been very beautifully illustrated, too, by Joseph, David, Elisha, and Job. But as the Jews generally had never attained to so high a state, and were now, under continued false teaching, farther from it than ever, Jesus reinforces with his own divine authority the true meaning of the law. Thus, again, he fulfils righteousness.

Infidels have aimed to take credit from the Old Testament and from Jesus, by affirming that love to enemies was enjoined by pagan moralists. The fact is admitted, but both the Old Testament and Jesus gain greatly by the comparison; for, though Socrates, Plato, and other pagan moralists taught the duty, they put it upon a selfish basis:—"Hatred of enemies will injure yourself; or, self-respect forbids it." It is related that Socrates, having been struck in the face by a drunken man, the wise man was content to set over the wound the words, "N. did this."—"'Help your friends, damage your enemies,' was the maxim even of the wise men of the people."

It may have been noticed that in some versions, *Bless them that curse you, do good to them that hate you, . . . which despitefully use you*, and, are wanting. This is because there is very little evidence from ancient manuscripts that they ought to be in the text,—a point concerning which biblical scholars are agreed.

No English reader should be surprised to learn that, like all other books that have descended from antiquity, copies, or manuscripts of the Bible, as they were made by

CHAPTER V.

hate you, and pray for them which despitefully use you, and persecute you;

45 That ye may be the children of your Father which is in heaven: for he maketh his sun to rise on the evil and on the good, and sendeth rain on the just and on the unjust.

46 For if ye love them which

---

hand, before printing was invented, contain *variations of reading*, so called. That is to say, one copy *varies* from another in the spelling of a word, in the omission of a word, or in the location of a word. So far as concerns the doctrines and the facts of Christianity, these variations are of no importance whatever. That the variations are so slight is to be attributed to that universal, particular providence which is ever superintending the kingdom of Christ. The first edition of "Hamlet," only a very small part of Shakespeare's writings, was published in 1603. The variations in the several editions of that one play are far greater than those of the entire New Testament, written more than fifteen hundred years before. The second edition, 1604, appeared with the statement on the title-page, "Enlarged to almost as much againe as it was, according to the true and perfect coppie." In the edition of 1623 are wanting entire passages which appeared in 1604. In editions of the present century these passages have been restored. It is of course desirable that the comparatively unimportant variations in the ancient manuscripts of the Sacred Scriptures should be examined and compared, that the true reading in every case may be adopted, and a copy of the Hebrew and the Greek Scriptures be produced, that shall be as nearly correct as possible, even in the minutest particular. This is precisely the work which distinguished and devout men have been doing. The recent discovery of a very excellent and very old (4th century) manuscript, in a convent at the foot of Mount Sinai, has added greatly to the importance of this kind of labor. We cannot be too grateful for the many favoring providences by which the scholarship of modern times has the means of accomplishing so much in the department to which reference is made. Believing that the English reader should be able to share in the benefits, the writer will not hesitate to apprise him of so many of the changes in question as are of sufficient importance to call for it.

45. The *motive* that distinguishes the teaching of Jesus from that of pagan moralists is *likeness to God*, expressed in the words, That ye may be *the children* of your Father which is in heaven. But is not the desirableness of likeness to God taught by heathen? It is taught in similar words but with dissimilar meaning. Plato, who lived many years before Christ, means by likeness to God only the avoidance of sensuality, and devoting one's self to philosophy.

For he maketh his sun, etc.—"A beautiful illustration of the all-embracing love of God." Seneca, who was born A. D. 2 or 3, has in his writings a similar saying: Nam et sceleratis sol oritur et piratis patent maria,—*For even upon the wicked the sun arises, and seas lie open to the use of pirates. His sun*—God, then, is distinct from nature, and therefore pantheism, the doctrine that God and nature are one, is a lie. God is seen by devout Christians as working in all physical phenomena. A pantheist, looking out of his window in the sunshine, or in a rain-storm, may consistently enough say, *I shine! I rain!* for, according to his own teaching, he, as a part of nature, is God.

love you, what reward have ye? do not even the publicans the same?

47 And if ye salute your brethren only, what do ye more than others? do not even the publicans so?

48 Be ye therefore perfect, even as your Father which is in heaven is perfect.

46, 47. Jesus here enforces the duty of loving even those who do not love them, by the consideration that otherwise their love is as narrow in principle as that of the publicans. The Roman government was supported largely by taxes, which were either direct or indirect. The latter were the customs. These were farmed out, let out, to Roman knights, who, being men of wealth and social position, became responsible for their collection. As that which came to the government was called *publicum*, that is, for the public, the state, these officers were called *publicans*. But these are not the class here mentioned by that name. The New Testament publicans were a lower set of men, employed to do the *work* of collecting. With some exceptions, they were a hard, exacting set of men. They were held by the Jews to be as bad as the heathen. 18: 17. In the public estimation, publicans were yoked with "sinners." 9: 11. They embezzled to enrich themselves. The more they exacted, the more they could embezzle. "Among the Greeks they were called *cheats, plunderers, prostitute-keepers, adulterers*." "Theocritus considered the bear and the lion the most cruel among the beasts of the wilderness; and among the beasts of the city the publican and the parasite." "Left to themselves, men of decent lives holding aloof from them, their only friends or companions were found among those who, like themselves, were outcasts from the world's law."

Salute—Common forms of salutation among the Jews were, Peace be with thee! Art thou in health? The Lord be with you! The Lord bless you! Go in peace! Hail! "Arabians have similar forms, but the followers of Muhammed never address the salutation, Peace be on you, to one whom he knows to be of another religion; and if he find that he has by mistake thus saluted a person not of the same faith, he generally revokes his salutation."

Brethren — Any one between whom and themselves exist special ties, whether national, religious, or natural. How cutting to the scribes and Pharisees this calm lowering of them to the level of the two most hated classes! Bigotry is a sin that should be driven from the world. Had all men had the righteousness which Christ enjoins, it never would have entered it. Bigots are fewer than formerly, but there are many yet. If one should love one's enemies, it ought not to be difficult to love Christ's disciples of whatever name. Oneness of denominational name, however, or oneness in organization, is not a necessary condition of the most enlarged catholicity. *What do ye more*—What do ye that excels in *quantity* and *quality?*

48. *Therefore*—In view of what has been said in the last five verses; or, as some think, of all that has been said. *Perfect*—Much difference of opinion exists relative to the meaning of this word; some say: Be complete; be not wanting in any element of righteousness; have them all. Had Jesus preceded the direction by *a complete list* of Christian traits, this interpretation would have been less doubtful, though the fact that he did not do so is not decisive against it. *As your Father in heaven*—The perfection, then, whatever is meant by it,

CHAPTER VI.

TAKE heed that ye do not your alms before men, to be seen of them: otherwise ye is to be in imitation of perfection in God. But in vs. 45, God is represented as loving all men irrespective of character and condition. That, so far, is perfect love, and if we love in like manner, our love, so far, is perfect. We do not affirm that this exhausts the meaning of the word *perfect*, but if we keep before us the exact point which our Lord had in view, this seems to be the conclusion to which we must come. That the idea of the attainability in this life of sinlessness is involved in the word cannot be proved.

CHAPTER VI.

ILLUSTRATIONS: CLASS II.

The superior character of the righteousness required is still the subject. The illustrations in Part I. are drawn chiefly from current doctrines; of Part II. from current practices, the aspect being that of motives.

1. A general proposition embracing alms-giving, prayer, and fasting. *Take heed*—There is great danger, then, of doing what is forbidden. Watchfulness against the danger must be maintained. *Alms* —A Greek word meaning *righteousness*, instead of the word here rendered *alms*, is the true reading. See note on 5: 44, last paragraph. *Do not your righteousness*—See vs. 20. *To be seen*—For the purpose of being seen, implying desire for the praise of men. But had they not already been commanded to let their light shine before men? Not that they might be seen, but that God might be seen in the good works which he would enable them have no reward of your Father which is in heaven.

2 Therefore when thou doest *thine* alms, do not sound a trumpet before thee, as the hyp-

to do. *Reward*—See note on 5: 12.

2. *First Illustration. Therefore* —A specification under the general precept in vs. 1. *Alms*—The term was derived from the Greek word for which it here stands. It was formerly written *almosine, almosie, almous, almose, almesse, almoyn,* and *almes*. In the Greek it was more comprehensive, meaning *compassion*, so that true alms-giving was the bestowal of gifts upon the poor in the spirit of compassion. The English word is applied almost exclusively to gifts bestowed upon beggars. The Pharisees attached great value to alms-giving. "Alms are the salt of the kingdom," was a proverb. "It is related of the Rabbi Abba, who is represented to have been a model of benevolence, that in order not to hurt the feelings of the poor, he used to go about with an open bag on his back, full of alms, to which the poor might help themselves." "In every city there were three collectors. The collections were of two kinds: (1.) Of money for the poor of the city only, made by two collectors, received in a chest or box in the synagogue on the Sabbath, and distributed by the three in the evening; (2.) For the poor in general, of food and money, collected every day from house to house, received in a dish, and distributed by the three collectors. The two collections obtained the names respectively of 'alms of the chest,' and 'alms of the dish.' Special collections and distributions were also made on fast days."

A trumpet—Doubtless a figurative expression to denote the ostentatious method in which the alms

ocrites do in the synagogues and in the streets, that they may have glory of men. Verily I say unto you, They have their reward.

3 But when thou doest alms, let not thy left hand know what thy right hand doeth:

4 That thine alms may be in secret: and thy Father which seeth in secret himself shall reward thee openly.

5 ¶ And when thou prayest, thou shalt not be as the hypocrites *are:* for they love to pray standing in the synagogues and in the corners of the streets, that they may be seen of men. Verily I say unto you, They have their reward.

6 But thou, when thou prayest, enter into thy closet, and when thou hast shut thy door, pray to thy Father which is in

---

of the Pharisees, both in the synagogues and in the streets, were conferred. Doing God's will by showing compassion to the poor was not the end, but intense love of the praise of men. Had no one been present, it would have been much less, if anything at all, that beggars would have got from a Pharisee. *The hypocrites*—This word was derived from one which meant *to act upon the stage.* A hypocrite was an actor. As stage-playing implied that the actor did not feel but only pretended to feel, so the Pharisees only pretended to feel for the poor, and were therefore called hypocrites. Here was none of the righteousness which God required even through the institutions of Moses. *Have their reward*—Have it fully, all they bargain for. The Greek is stronger than our version makes it.

3, 4. *Right hand . . . left hand.* The Greeks and the Romans called the hands *brothers. Not . . . know* —Our benefactions may be known as having come from us; it is often impossible that it should be otherwise; but we are to make no attempt to let others know it. We are to be so indifferent to human praise as not to care whether men know that we have given or not. So easily excited is the love of human applause, that we ought, so far as possible, to conceal from men what we do for objects of benevolence. This form of righteousness is too uncommon in Christian churches. Many of the modern ways of raising money for the kingdom of Christ are adapted to strengthen the kingdom of Satan. The more spiritual members of a church should no longer allow the world or worldly members to control them in this respect. *Seeth in secret*—He maintains his existence and carries on his operations in secret. *Himself* is emphatic. *He* will reward thee, though what thou doest may be unknown to all others. *Openly*—No stress should be laid upon this word, as the original is now rejected from the critical editions of the Greek Testament. See note on 5:44, last paragraph.

5, 6. *Second Illustration.* Many of those who lived under the Old Covenant had the true conception of prayer, and were themselves remarkable for the sincerity and spirituality of this form of worship; but in our Lord's time the false righteousness of the Pharisees was manifest in nothing more clearly than in the hollowness of their prayers. As among Roman Catholics, the form was scrupulously observed, but the spirit of prayer as evinced in Moses, Hannah, David, and Jeremiah, was wanting. "Daily prayer was repeated three times, at 9 o. c., at 12, and at 3; people assembled in the synagogues for prayer on Sabbath,

secret; and thy Father which *do:* for they think that they seeth in secret shall reward thee openly.

7 But when ye pray, use not vain repetitions, as the heathen do, for they think that they shall be heard for their much speaking.

8 Be not ye therefore like unto them: for your Father

Monday, and Thursday. He who prayed properly was to spend nine hours a day in prayer." The Rabbis taught "that the pious people of old time waited an hour, and prayed an hour, and then waited another hour. . . . Eighteen prayers were to be used daily. . . . Prayer was offered up in the street, above all, at the hour of prayer; at that hour, whoever was riding on an ass was obliged to dismount. Prayer was to be so earnest, that even if one were saluted by the king when engaged in prayer, one ought not to acknowledge it: if a serpent wound itself around one's foot, still one might not remove it."

In the synagogue—Why should this have been condemned? He speaks not against praying *in that place*, but only against praying there to be seen of men; that is, to get credit with men for being very righteous. *The corners of the streets*—Points where two streets met, and where, therefore, a larger number of people would be likely to be. Had a Pharisee happened to be at such a place when either of the appointed hours of prayer had arrived, he would be very glad that it had so happened, and, perhaps, though there is no proof that it was ever done, he would time his walk so as to bring him to a street corner at the hour. *Thy closet*—An upper room, or "any place of privacy." That he might *not* be seen of men, Peter went upon the house-top to pray. Acts 10: 9. The roof of the Jewish house was nearly flat, and was "surrounded by a breastwork or wall to prevent one from falling, which is as high as the breast." It should not be inferred that Jesus intended to disapprove offering prayer in the hearing of others. He prayed in the presence of others himself, and in the use of the plural in the Lord's Prayer taught his disciples to do so. *Enter thy closet . . . shut thy door*—Figurative expressions by which he would warn us against the sin of the Pharisees. They prayed to men; they ought to have prayed to God, whether they were praying in the synagogue or in an upper room. They were as guilty of hypocrisy in prayer as in almsgiving.

"Read on this book;
That show of such an exercise may color
Your loneliness. We are oft to blame in this—
'Tis too much proved, that with devotion's visage,
And pious action, we do sugar o'er
The devil himself."—*Shakespeare.*

7, 8. *Use . . . vain repetitions* —The original is one word,—*battologesete,*—a verb. It is believed to have originated in imitation of the sounds made by stammerers, and its meaning in this place is probably the same as *much speaking* with which the verse ends. Jesus once prayed all night, and in the garden he prayed three times and used the same words. Several successive hours have been spent in prayer by many of the most consistent Christians. What the Saviour condemns, then, is the notion that the efficacy of prayer depends on the frequency with which it is offered, and on the repetition of brief, disconnected appeals to Jehovah, such as is known to have prevailed among the heathen in their prayers to false gods. The priests of Baal spent half a day in crying, *O Baal! hear us.* 1 Kings 18:26. The worshippers of Diana, all, with one voice, about the space of two hours, cried out, Great is

knoweth what things ye have need of, before ye ask him.

Diana of the Ephesians! As the Greeks had about thirty thousand gods, some of them with a variety of names, it was simply impossible for a Greek to avoid senseless repetitions. In an ancient Latin author, one is represented as begging his wife to cease belaboring the gods with thanks, and as accusing her of judging of them by herself, since she could believe nothing unless it should be said a hundred times. Wearisome repetitions of words distinguish the Muhammedans and many of the heathen of our own day. The following, taken, abbreviated, from a Manual of Prayers prepared for Roman Catholics, is a specimen of vain repetitions in the Church of Rome.

God the Father of heaven, have mercy on us.
God the Son, Redeemer of the world, have mercy on us.
God the Holy Ghost, have mercy on us.
Holy Mary,
Holy Mother of God,
Holy Virgin of virgins,
Mother of Christ,
Mother most pure,
Mother most chaste,
Mother undefiled,
Mother inviolate,   } Pray for us.
Virgin most prudent,
Virgin most venerable,
Mirror of Justice,
Seat of Wisdom,
Queen of Angels,
Queen of Patriarchs,

For your Father knoweth—But Jesus knew that this is no reason why we should not pray.

The Lord's Prayer.

It has been affirmed, chiefly by men of little reverence for our Lord, that this prayer was borrowed. Some have said that it was borrowed with almost verbal exactness from the Zend Avesta, the sacred books of the fire-worshippers in Persia and the Parsees in India,

9 After this manner therefore pray ye : Our Father which

the latter having been driven from Persia by the Muhammedans. The assertion has been proved to be utterly without foundation. "There is," says Tholuck, "only one single passage in the Zend Avesta which bears a resemblance, and that only an apparent one, to the fifth petition." Others have affirmed that it was borrowed in part from Jewish Rabbis. From the writings of Jewish Rabbis can be culled expressions which are *somewhat like* the first, the second, the fourth, and the sixth petitions, but there is no proof that they are the source whence these were taken. "For the fifth, *And forgive us our debts,* we cannot adduce even one apparent parallel."—*Tholuck.*

The connection of the prayer with what precedes is manifest. Jesus had just warned them against the notion that prayer is acceptable in proportion to the amount of word-praying. That was speaking negatively. He now speaks affirmatively. He gives them a specimen of the kind of prayers which they should offer. We should ever bear in mind, however, that it is the right spirit, rather than this particular form of words, which he enjoins. It is possible to offer the Lord's Prayer, and doubtless it often is offered, in a prayerless spirit. The twofold question has been much discussed, whether this form of prayer was intended to be obligatory, and whether it is evidence that written prayers should be used instead of extemporary. The latter part of the question could not have been seriously proposed till after the "church," in consequence of having lost the spirit of prayer, had begun to use written prayers. Then a defence of the new method was natural. One of the most eminent scholars in the Church of England (Alford) says : "It is very improbable that the prayer was

CHAPTER VI.

art in heaven, Hallowed be thy name.

10 Thy kingdom come. Thy will be done in earth, as *it is* in heaven.

11 Give us this day our daily bread.

12 And forgive us our debts, as we forgive our debtors.

13 And lead us not into

---

regarded in the very earliest times as a set form delivered for liturgical use by our Lord." The offering of the Lord's Prayer by the pastor, in all non-Episcopal churches, as an invocation, would, in the judgment of the writer, be well. It is difficult to see how this *divine* form can be evidence that the churches of Christ should use prayers written by *men uninspired*.

PLAN OF THE PRAYER.

Introduction.	Petitions.		Conclusion.
	A.	B.	
1. Father.	1. Hallowed *thy* name.	1. Give *us*.	1. *Thine* is the kingdom.
2. Our.	2. *Thy* kingdom.	2. Forgive *us*.	2. *Thine* the power.
3. In heaven.	3. *Thy* will.	3. Lead *us* not.	3. *Thine* the glory.

It will be observed that the first set of petitions directs the mind to God—*thy;* the second, to ourselves —*us*. The conclusion calls it back to God, there to rest forever. "The Lord's Prayer, apprehended by a Christian and spiritual understanding, implies such a depth of religious feeling, such an intense sense of our relation to God, and such a strength of faith, that it has been regarded by the large majority of praying Christians as not so much an expression of their actual state of mind, as the type of that condition which they were striving to attain."—*Tholuck.*

9. *After this manner*—Briefly, comprehensively, spiritually. Let the state of your hearts be such that, without any fixed, definite purpose to do so, you will be impelled to pray in this manner, or *in any other that shall be substantially like it*. *Father*—Then we are not orphans. God is the Father of all men,—a truth seen by many of the heathen, though dimly, for Jupiter was called father of gods and men. The word here put upon our lips shows that Jesus Christ knew God to be a true person, distinct from inanimate nature and from the human mind. Plato, a celebrated Greek philosopher, born more than four hundred years before Christ, recommended that atheists (one kind) be put into the house of correction (literally, *place for making people sober*) for five years, and that if not *sobered* by that time, they be put to death. Denial of the personality of God *is insanity*, though Plato's method of cure would make more hypocrites than believers. The spirit of sonship, lost by sin, is restored by Christ, and is thence called the spirit of adoption. This has ever been unknown to the best heathen minds. *Our* Father. Then men are brothers. . There are times when the soul cannot but lay its wants before the Father exclusively of the wants of all others, but the true, normal state of every Christian man, in prayer, is that of oneness with all who, even in the lower sense, are God's children,—how much more with those who are children in the higher sense, whatever their denominational connection! He who is not habitually in this state should be alarmed at the narrowness of his spirit. There is nothing contradictory between the spirit of universal Christian fellowship and conscien-

temptation, but deliver us from evil: For thine is the kingdom,

tious adherence to that form of church government, and to those rites, which one believes to be based upon divine authority. *Who art in heaven*—In the visible heavens and beyond, a conception figuratively expressed, and naturally suggested by the conviction that God is superior to earthly things. The Jews, however, had just views of God's omnipresence. *Behold, the heaven and the heaven of heavens cannot contain thee.* 1 Kings 8: 27. *Whither shall I go from thy Spirit? or whither shall I flee from thy presence?* Ps. 139: 7. There is a locality where Jesus now is, and the holy angels are, and the resurrection-bodies of the redeemed are to be. That is heaven. *Hallowed be thy name*—God's *name* is not a mere appellation, as Jehovah, Lord, etc., nor is it merely the essential nature of God, but it is that nature *as manifested to us*. These words, as used in prayer, imply that the soul recognizes God as holy, and *feels* him to be such. Explaining them as expressing the desire that God's name may not be taken in vain would not exhaust the meaning; yet profane swearing is a fearfully abounding proof that God is still but little recognized on earth as holy. Anxiety concerning our own names is both foolish and sinful. He that hallows the name of God will be as much honored by God's providences as will be for his good.

10. *Thy kingdom come*—See note on 3: 2, second paragraph. The kingdom had already been introduced. It is here conceived as extending both in space and time, till, in the latest ages, it shall comprise the people of all lands, and as completed at last in heaven itself. God in Christ is the king; believers are the subjects. "We pray that it may come in us; we pray that we may be found in it." Earthly kingdoms are only the scaffolding of God's kingdom. *Thy will be done*—This is not a mere repetition of the second petition. That contemplates the reign of God rather in its wholeness; this rather in its extension over individuals; yet neither view excludes the other. One may be truly a subject of the kingdom without being an exemplification of the complete fulfilment of God's will. That the will, however, may be brought into entire subjection to God's will, not absorbed in it, so as almost to lose its personality, as Madame Guyon seems to teach, should be our constant prayer. This should be the prayer of each one, not for himself only, but for all mankind, and that with the conviction that Christ contemplates a state, even on earth, in which a very high degree of personal righteousness shall mark the individual members of his kingdom, to be perfected at last in heaven. *As it is in heaven*—Considered as the abode of angels. *As* refers chiefly to completeness.

11. The form is now changed from *Thy* to *Us*. Jesus permits us to begin on the lower part of the scale of wants. *Bread*—Whatever is needful for the nourishment of our physical natures. *Daily*—Bread sufficient for the day. The original is a difficult word; for in the twelve hundred Greek books which have come down to us, it is not to be found. This is the only place in the entire Greek language in which it occurs, Luke 11: 3 being only a parallel verse. The attempt has been made to show that it means, *belonging to the morrow*, as if we are taught to pray, *Give us to-day the bread for to-morrow;* or, *Give us our future bread day by day.* There is no satisfactory evidence that our own version, *daily*, is not correct. *This day*—We are not to pray for to-morrow's bread. We may not need any, and if we do, it will be time enough to pray for it when to-

CHAPTER VI.

and the power, and the glory, for ever. Amen.

14 For if ye forgive men their trespasses, your heavenly Father will also forgive you:

15 But if ye forgive not men

---

morrow has become to-day. The duty of praying for bread does not release one from the duty of working for it. *For even when we were with you, this we commanded you, that if any would not work, neither should he eat.* 2 Thess. 3: 10. Indolence, however, is not much given to praying. Why offer prayer for daily bread, if one has laid in his barrel of flour? One's dependence on God, even after that has been done, is a sufficient answer.

12. A higher want. *Debts*—Sins. *As*—Not expressive of condition, much less of measure, but of similarity. Do for us what *in kind* shall be like that which we do for others. *Debtors*—Possibly in a commercial sense, but more probably referring to some offence committed. Men are bankrupts. They have nothing to pay. He who withholds the latter part of this petition will get nothing if he offers the former part.

13. A still higher want. Having prayed that sin may be forgiven, the soul next prays that it may not be be brought into temptation, but may be delivered from evil. But James (1: 2) tells us to *count it all joy when we fall into divers temptations.* He also forbids us to say when we are tempted that we are tempted of God; *for God,* he says, *cannot be tempted with evil, neither tempteth he any man;* but every man is tempted, when he is drawn away of his own lust and enticed. Distinguish between the circumstances, the outward condition, that may become the occasion of temptation, and the inward yielding to sin, and the contradiction disappears. The subject of temptation may be viewed thus: 1. Temptations, tests, trials, are not pleasant. Conscious of weakness, the believer naturally shrinks from them. Jesus did so in the garden. Our Lord permits us, therefore, to pray that we may not be led *into such circumstances* as will put our characters strongly to the test. 2. But as a matter of fact we are sometimes led into circumstances precisely of that sort. The test which is then applied may be a means of good. 3. Therefore, we should count it all joy to have been led into them, and thus, not otherwise, we shall be improved. 4. But through its depravity, the soul, resisting the beneficial tendency of the test, may "be drawn away and enticed." *But deliver us from evil*—Some regard this as a distinct petition, the seventh, but the connection with the previous clause is so close that the two may be regarded as one petition. *Evil*—Evil in general, "evil in every form."

Thine is the kingdom, etc.— Whether this doxology is a genuine part of the Lord's Prayer has been much discussed. It is not a question between believers and infidels. Scholars of the greatest reverence for the word of God are not in agreement concerning it. We present a brief outline of the facts on both sides of the question: 1. This part of the Lord's Prayer is found in not one of the six most ancient manuscripts, nor in five others of later date, known to the learned as written in a *small, running* hand, instead of being written like the first-named in *large capitals,* nor in the ancient Latin versions, nor "in the writings of most of the early fathers, some of whom wrote commentaries on the Lord's Prayer." 2. It *is* found in a Syriac translation which has generally been regarded as made in the second century, called the Peschito version. Though this is a version of great value, its value as an

their trespasses, neither will your Father forgive your trespasses.

16 ¶ Moreover when ye fast, be not, as the hypocrites, of a sad countenance: for they disfigure their faces, that they may appear unto men to fast.

Verily I say unto you, They have their reward.

17 But thou, when thou fastest, anoint thine head, and wash thy face;

18 That thou appear not unto men to fast, but unto thy Father which is in secret: and

---

evidence of the genuineness of the last sentence of the Prayer has been considerably weakened by the discovery in 1842 of another Syrian version of the Gospels; for the newly discovered manuscript is considered as proving that the Peschito was *much changed* long after it was made. The doxology is also found in two other Syriac versions, the one made in A. D. 508, the other possibly in the fifth or sixth century; in an Egyptian version, fourth century, perhaps; in an Ethiopic version, fourth; in an Armenian, fifth; in a Gothic, fourth; in a Gregorian version, sixth; in "nearly all the five hundred or more cursive" [the small, running letter] "manuscripts in which the sixth chapter of Matthew is preserved." Most of *these* manuscripts are assigned to the tenth and sixteenth centuries, inclusive. It may be added that this part of the Lord's Prayer is now excluded from *all* critical editions of the Greek Testament but one, and that the scholars, however devout, who would defend it as a genuine part of the Prayer, are very few in number. Dr. Schaff says: "It was probably inserted in the beginning of the fourth century from the liturgies and the *primitive habit* of the Christians in praying the Lord's Prayer." Yet he also says, strangely: "No one can doubt the eminent propriety of this solemn conclusion which we are accustomed to regard from infancy as an integral part of the prayer of prayers, and which we would now never think of sacrificing to critical considerations in our popular Bibles and public and private devotions. Probably it was the prevailing custom of the Christians in the East from the beginning to pray the Lord's Prayer with the doxology. Compare 2 Tim. 4: 18."

It has been very beautifully said that "when the whole number of the sons of God shall have reached their goal, a pure doxology will arise in heaven: Hallowed be the name of God. His kingdom is come. His will is done. He has forgiven our sins. He has brought temptation to an end. He has delivered us from the evil one. His is the kingdom, and the power, and the glory, for ever. Amen."

14, 15. *For* connects these verses with the fifth petition. We must not conclude that forgiving a fellow-man is the only or the chief condition of forgiveness by our Maker. Penitence, faith, etc., are also conditions. Should we forgive before the wrong is confessed? Yes, in the sense of cherishing no revenge and using active measures to do the injurious person good. See 5: 44. Though God does not forgive till the sin is acknowledged, yet he took the first step in bringing men to repentance. *We love him, because he first loved us.* 1 John 4: 19.

16-18. *Third Illustration.* The only public fast which Moses required was that of the Great Day of Atonement, Lev. 23: 27, where the Hebrew translated *shall afflict your souls* is understood to mean that abstinence from food which is the result of true humiliation of spirit. No private fasts were required, though

CHAPTER VI.

thy Father which seeth in secret shall reward thee openly.

19 ¶ Lay not up for yourselves treasures upon earth,

in the Old Testament many such fasts are recorded. Hannah, who afterward gave birth to Samuel, David when lamenting the death of Abner, Nehemiah weeping over the desolate state of Jerusalem, fasted in the sense of abstaining from food. During their captivity in Babylon, the Jews kept four public fasts a year. "Public fasts expressly on account of unseasonable weather and of famine, may perhaps be traced in the first and second chapters of Joel." Fasting, when it proceeds from a right spirit, is not condemned by our Lord; for (17:21) he says, *Howbeit this kind goeth not out but by prayer and fasting.* But as in many other cases, so also in this, the righteousness of the Pharisees was false. Fasts had been greatly multiplied, and had been connected with various "other signs of humiliation, such as abstinence from the use of water, of anointing oil, of razors, with the besprinkling of ashes, the putting on of mourning." The Pharisees fasted not under conscious poverty of spirit, but to make a show of piety for the purpose of gaining the praise of men. They gave their faces a look of sadness by disfiguring them, and they disfigured them by going with uncombed, unanointed heads and unwashed faces. It was their aim to catch the eyes of others. Such fasting was as bad as continual feasting. Jesus tells his hearers to anoint the head and wash the face; that is, to "appear as usual" when they fast. Obedience to this direction presupposes true humiliation, and this presupposes a return to the simpler requirement of Moses. "The number of annual fasts in the present Jewish calendar has been multiplied to twenty-eight." The numerous fasts of the Roman Catholic Church and of the Episcopal Church—Lent, for example, continu-

ing forty days in commemoration of our Lord's fasting in the wilderness—are unauthorized, and are unquestionably detrimental to spirituality. An Episcopal journal, 1867, says: "We never met with a family which made any real difference in regard to the quantity or quality of food consumed in Lent."

19-34. *Fourth Illustration.* The duty of resisting worldliness and of making God the sole object of trust is the thought running through the remaining part of the chapter. It has been thought difficult to see the connection with what precedes; and it is indeed true that the direct reference which has hitherto been made to the scribes and the Pharisees is suspended. But it is plain that our Lord still shapes his discourse by their well-known characteristics. They were covetous, grasping. *Which devour widows' houses.* Mark 12:40. Against such worldliness, especially as cherished under the garb of piety, Jesus proceeds to warn his hearers.

19-21. Some very excellent men, as George Müller, founder of the well-known Orphan Asylum of Bristol, England, regard such precepts as forbidding them to accumulate material possessions. Such a literal interpretation overlooks other passages. Neither Abraham, nor Job, nor Joseph of Arimathea, nor Joanna the wife of Chuza, was reproved for owning property. Our condition may be such that we shall commit no sin in giving away all that we have, and thenceforth accumulating nothing, but there is nothing in these precepts that requires it. See 2 Cor. 12:14, where the writer speaks of the duty of parents to *lay up* for their children.

The 21st verse is the key to the meaning. Our *hearts* are not to be set upon earthly treasures. We are not to *trust* in riches. Mark 10:24.

where moth and rust doth corrupt, and where thieves break through and steal:

20 But lay up for yourselves treasures in heaven; where neither moth nor rust doth corrupt, and where thieves do not break through and steal:

21 For where your treasure is, there will your heart be also.

22 The light of the body is the eye: if therefore thine eye be single, thy whole body shall be full of light.

23 But if thine eye be evil, thy whole body shall be full of darkness. If therefore the light that is in thee be darkness, how great *is* that darkness!

24 ¶ No man can serve two masters: for either he will hate

In buying we are to be as though we possessed not. 1 Cor. 7:30. We are not to lay up treasure for *ourselves*, but are to be rich toward God. Luke 12:21. We must lay it up for the purpose of using it in glorifying our Creator; and whether we are successful in this respect or not, must make as the chief end of life the attainment of righteousness. Our earthly goods must not be our *treasures*. *Moth*—An insect often mentioned in the Old Testament as well as in the New. It is also mentioned by ancient uninspired writers. The evidence from these sources is abundant that its habits four thousand years ago were similar to those which the moth of modern times has. It was very fond of clothes, old or new. *Rust*—Not merely rust in the present sense of the word, but whatever may tend to destroy— "the wear and tear" of things. The opinion that it means a species of worm that destroyed corn is not well supported. *Break through*—Dig through, for thieves in Palestine could obtain access to houses with but little difficulty by digging through the mud walls. *In the dark they dig through houses.* Job 24:16. *Where your treasure is*, etc.—More surely than the well-aimed arrow will hit the mark, for it is the heart that begins to lay the treasure up. The spirit of these precepts is equally binding upon the rich and the poor. It is equally applicable to one who makes his *reputation* in study, or in public affairs, the end of life. "What a man loves, that is his God. For he carries it in his heart, he goes about with it night and day, he sleeps and wakes with it; be it what it may, wealth or pelf, pleasure or renown."

22, 23. Jesus here illustrates by means of the eye the danger of continuing in our natural darkness. The last sentence is the application. What precedes is the figure. All parts of the body have ownership in the light of the eye, and of course will have plenty of light if the eye has light. *Single*—Not in the sense of sound, healthy, but as opposed to *double*. He whose eye is directed toward only one object is supposed to have all the light necessary to see that object with distinctness. *If thine eye be evil*—Evil in the sense of not being single,—seeing two objects or more at the same time, and therefore not seeing either clearly. So if the light within, which some say is the reason, others the conscience, others the *faculty* by which spiritual things may be discerned, —the last seems to be the more probable,—fails to do its office, the darkness of the whole inner man is fearfully great. Thus Jesus enforces the thought of the three preceding verses,—that we must seek one thing, and that the highest good.

24. *Two masters*—The idea of master implies *absolute control;* that is, one is not *master* unless he has control exclusive of all others. One who should attempt to serve *two*

the one, and love the other; or else he will hold to the one, and despise the other. Ye cannot serve God and mammon.

masters would find it, from the nature of the case, impossible. The one or the other must be subordinate; and so complete is the surrender of the will implied in serving a master, that it is impossible not to hate any other who might be seeking to gain the control. Some suppose that *holding to the one and despising the other* is a mere repetition of *hating the one and loving the other*; but it is better to understand a double alternation thus: He will either hate A and love B, or he will cleave to A and despise B. The application is made in the last sentence. *Ye cannot serve God and mammon*—Ye, in contrast with him who cannot serve two human masters. *Mammon*—Not, as Barnes and some others say, the name of a Syrian idol. There is no evidence that the Syrians ever worshipped an idol of that name. The word means *riches*, and here riches is personified as the other master. It is as impossible for one to serve both God and Riches as for a servant to be controlled by two masters. Service rendered to God as the rightful sovereign implies that no service is rendered or can be rendered to Riches, and service rendered to Riches implies that none is paid or can be paid to God. The idea that the service rendered to God is in its very nature opposed to the service rendered to Riches is of course implied; but the point is this: that having either as *master* implies that it is impossible for the other to be master. The amount of riches that may come in competition with God is not stated. It may be very small. The object served in preference to God may be books, as well as gold. It may be a friend, a wardrobe, the theatre, the opera, reputation.

25 Therefore I say unto you, Take no thought for your life, what ye shall eat, or what ye shall drink; nor yet for your

25. *Take no thought*—The common explanation is, Be not *anxious*, as if it were a given *degree* of concern that is forbidden. Dr. Conant thinks the idea of degree is not that which Jesus intended to express. He considers it "a prohibition, rather, of concern *for the future*," calling attention to vs. 34, Sufficient unto the day is the evil thereof. Admitting that the idea of anxiety, that is, of a *high degree* of concern, is not intended, yet the concern, whether more or less, which is prohibited, seems to refer to the *current* day as well as to the future. Jesus has already taught us to pray, Give us this day our daily bread. Any concern respecting our temporal wants which contradicts the spirit of this petition is to be repressed. *Is not the life?* —Not the *soul*, in the popular sense, though the original is sometimes so used, for Christ teaches us to be very anxious relative to the soul, but the principle of animal life. *Meat*—Food. The argument is, As God gave you your life, he will of course give you the means of preserving it. But we are not to be indifferent to our bodily wants. 1 Tim. 5:8; 1 Cor. 9:11; 1 Cor. 16: 1-13; 2 Cor. 9:5. In these passages is enjoined the duty of providing for the wants of others. It cannot, therefore, be sin to make some provision for our own wants. But if concern relative to our physical wants indicates distrust of God, and therefore want of righteousness, how little must be the righteousness of him, who, though having abundant daily supplies, is corroded with desire to accumulate riches!

"The clergyman," says Tholuck, "will indeed find the comforting assurance of the text not by the sceptical complaint, Has it then never

body, what ye shall put on. Is not the life more than meat, and the body than raiment?

26 Behold the fowls of the air: for they sow not, neither do they reap, nor gather into barns; yet your heavenly Father feedeth them. Are ye not much better than they?

27 Which of you by taking thought can add one cubit unto his stature?

---

happened that a man who has sought first the kingdom of God and his righteousness has died of starvation? . . . Assuredly, in the ordinary course of life, he who strives after the righteousness of God, which righteousness of course includes diligence in his calling in life, will experience the truth of the consolation of the text: for *extraordinary* cases there are other extraordinary texts of consolation."

26. The duty of making God our trust to the exclusion of all concern relative to our temporal wants is enforced by reference to the birds. God feeds them. But whence the propriety of reminding us that they neither sow, nor reap, nor gather into barns? How could they be expected to do so? and if we understand our Lord as saying that they do nothing toward supplying themselves with food, that is not correct. Birds build their own nests and seek their own food. God so constituted them (instinct), and so constituted nature, that through their active habits their wants are supplied. But not even their instinct leads them to attempt to raise the material of food, yet God supplies them. *Much better* —Superior in rank, capacity, and possible destiny. Jesus here distinctly recognizes the duty of men to work,—to sow, to reap, etc. 2 Thess. 3: 10, 11: For even when we were with you, this we commanded you, that *if any would not work, neither should he eat.* For we hear that there are some which *walk among you disorderly, working not at all,* but are busy bodies. But men must have such confidence in their heavenly Father that they shall follow their several occupations with no special anxiety relative to the result, —a very high type of righteousness, but a type demanded by our Saviour. In the fourth century was a sect of Christians called Euchites, an order of monks, who, believing themselves to have reached "the summit of perfection, discarded all the occupations of common life,—all manual labor, by which the monks were used to provide for their own support and for the relief of others, but which *they* regarded as a degradation of the higher life of the spirit. They were for living by alms alone, and were the first *mendicant friars.*" To such men the birds would have set examples worth following.

27. *By taking thought*—Not by an effort of your thinking power, but by indulging in anxiety respecting your present and future physical wants. *One cubit*—A variable measure, but eighteen inches is the length commonly assigned. *Stature* —Scholars differ concerning the meaning, in this place, of the Greek word. It often means *age.* The only question is whether it here means age or stature. Dr. Conant prefers the latter, but, "in deference to the opinion of many eminent scholars," gives the other rendering in the margin. On the whole, we prefer *age.* In Luke 12: 26 is the additional thought: If ye then be not able to do that thing *which is least,* why take ye thought for the rest? But eighteen inches would be *a great addition to a man's stature.* It has been objected to the meaning, *age,* that the cubit is a measure of space, not of time, but the objection is of little weight. David says, 'Thou hast made *my days as a hand-breadth.* Here a measure of space is applied

CHAPTER VI.

28 And why take ye thought for raiment? Consider the lilies of the field, how they grow; they toil not, neither do they spin:

29 And yet I say unto you, That even Solomon in all his glory was not arrayed like one of these.

30 Wherefore, if God so

---

to time. The reasoning is this: If you cannot add so little as a cubit to your life, why should you show such concern relative to your temporal affairs as shall imply distrust of God?

28, 29. "With reference to clothing," says Tholuck, "the Saviour might a second time have taken an illustration from the animal kingdom; for instance, he might have alluded to the peacock, as Solon did to Crœsus when he sought to humble him; but the figure he selects is more tender, and at the same time better suits his purpose. For he points out the glorious adornment in which one of the most unassuming of the products of creation is invested." If the lily, as described by Dr. Bowring, is the kind to which Jesus referred, it could scarcely be called "one of the most unassuming of the products of creation." The popular mind conceives of the lily of this verse as white, but it is affirmed that the white lily does not grow wild in Palestine. Dr. Bowring saw in Galilee, in April and May, a lily, the color of which was "a brilliant red; its size about half that of the common tiger lily." Dr. Thomson believes "the beautiful Hûleh lily" to be the flower referred to. "This Hûleh lily is very large, and the three inner petals meet above, and form a gorgeous canopy, such as art never approached, and king never sat under, even in his utmost glory. And when I met this incomparable flower, in all its loveliness, among the oak woods around the northern base of Tabor and on the hills of Nazareth, where our Lord spent his youth, I felt assured that it was this to which he referred. . . . Nothing can be in higher contrast than the luxuriant, velvety softness of this lily, and the crabbed, tangled hedge of thorns about it." This illustration is more forcible than that taken from the birds, for the lilies do less than the birds toward prolonging their existence. *Solomon in all his glory*—Wealth gives lustre to a monarch, and this king's reputation among his contemporaries for wealth was great. See 2 Chron. 9, where is graphically depicted the visit of a queen, and where are many other details which illustrate the magnificence of his reign, as his "great throne of ivory," the number of his horses and chariots, etc. The extent to which Solomon engaged in commerce has led to the just remark that "the overwhelming riches of this eminent merchant-sovereign are perhaps not surprising." The temple which he built is among the evidences of his "glory." Yet even Solomon was not arrayed like one of the lilies of Galilee. If the arrangements of Providence are such in respect to lilies, God's children should have no distrust of his willingness to clothe them, they still being supposed to use their free powers in sowing, reaping, etc.

How different from man's standard of judging is God's! An ivory throne, chariots, servants, gold, peacocks, and apes are man's ideal of glory! 2 Chr. 9: 21. God chooses the lily. Jesus was tenderly interested in the birds and plants; so his disciples ought to be. Not with the sentimentalism of a mere artist did Jesus love to talk of nature, but he loved nature as the work of the Infinite Mind.

30. *The grass*—The herbage. *Wherefore* seems to make it neces-

clothe the grass of the field, which to-day is, and to-morrow is cast into the oven, *shall he not much more clothe* you, O ye of little faith?

31 Therefore take no thought, saying, What shall we eat? or, What shall we drink? or, Wherewithal shall we be clothed?

32 (For after all these things do the Gentiles seek:) for your heavenly Father knoweth that ye have need of all these things.

33 But seek ye first the kingdom of God, and his righteousness; and all these things shall be added unto you.

34 Take therefore no thought for the morrow: for the morrow shall take thought for the things of itself. Sufficient unto the day *is* the evil thereof.

---

sary to include the lilies, but it should be *and* instead of wherefore. Lilies would of course be cut down with the herbage generally; but there is an advance in the thought here. "The scarcity of wood in Palestine is very great, especially in the southern part; so that the people are obliged to resort to the use of almost everything that is capable of being burnt, in order to procure the means of warming their houses in winter, and of preparing their daily food. They not only cut down, for this purpose, the shrubs and larger kinds of grass, but gather the common withered grass itself, and the wild flowers, of which the fields display so rich a profusion."— *Hackett*. To-day ... to-morrow— Even the best grasses are comparatively short-lived, and as to the lily, "one south wind sweeping across the plain will in four and twenty hours leave all its beauty faded, parched, and dead." *Oven*—"It consists of a large jar made of clay, about three feet high, and widening toward the bottom, with a hole for the extraction of the ashes. Occasionally, however, it is not an actual jar, but an erection of clay in the form of a jar, built on the floor of a house. ... It was heated with dry twigs and grass, and the loaves were placed both inside and outside of it." *Of little faith*—This part of the discourse, then, was addressed specially to his disciples, for others have *no* faith.

32. *The Gentiles*—Making the supply of their temporal wants the end of life was and still is the characteristic of the heathen; and therefore it would be heathenish in Christ's disciples to do the same thing. The Pharisees despised the heathen, and yet in worldliness the Pharisees and the heathen were alike. *Your heavenly Father knoweth*—A truth of infinite value.

33, 34. The conclusion of the train of thought beginning at vs. 19. *The kingdom of God* is explained in the note on 3: 2. *First* refers not to time, but to importance. *His righteousness*—The personal righteousness which is the subject of this sermon. It should be the object of every day's aim. *All these things*— All the temporal supplies of which Christ has spoken. See Rom. 8:32: *He that spared not his own Son*, etc. Reader, are you doing what Jesus Christ here commands you to do? *No thought for the morrow*—The conclusion is repeated, and that for the purpose of enforcing it anew. *Morrow*—Not, strictly, the entire future of your life on earth, but the coming day. The morrow will be anxious for itself; that is, to-morrow will bring its own cares. If you are anxious under the wants of to-day and anxious concerning the wants of to-morrow, your anxiety will be doubled. Of course the sin will be doubled. *The evil thereof*—Its cares. If the course from which

CHAPTER VII.

JUDGE not, that ye be not judged.

2 For with what judgment ye judge, ye shall be judged: and with what measure ye mete, it shall be measured to you again.

3 And why beholdest thou the mote that is in thy brother's eye, but considerest not the beam that is in thine own eye?

4 Or how wilt thou say to thy brother, Let me pull out the mote out of thine eye; and, behold, a beam is in thine own eye?

5 Thou hypocrite, first cast out the beam out of thine own eye; and then shalt thou see clearly to cast out the mote out of thy brother's eye.

---

we are dissuaded will double the load, what a load do those poor creatures carry who indulge in anxiety relative to *all* their future days on earth, assuming, as such persons generally do, that they shall live to old age! "Life is no series of chances with a few providences sprinkled between to keep up a justly failing belief, but one providence of God."—*Unspoken Sermons by George McDonald.*

CHAPTER VII.

The connection between this part of the sermon and what precedes is more obvious than some have thought. The superiority of the righteousness required by the law, and fulfilled by Christ, continues to be the subject. The scribes and Pharisees were still in our Lord's eye; for they were uncharitable in judging (1-5); they did not treat others as they wished to be treated themselves (12); they were false teachers and bore bad fruit (15-20); they said, but did not (21-27).

1. *Fifth Illustration. Judge not*—Do not assume to sit in judgment upon men. The spirit of censoriousness is the thing prohibited. *That ye be not judged*—By God, in whatever way, whether through men as instruments of providence, or through Jesus Christ at the Day of Judgment. That censoriousness, rather than judgment universally, is the sin condemned, is evident from 18: 15-17; 1 Cor. 5: 11 and 6: 5, in all which the duty of church discipline is enjoined. See, also, John 7: 24: *Judge not according to the appearance, but judge righteous judgment.* Indifference to error or to sin is not taught. The Sermon on the Mount is itself the best reproof of false liberality, for it is throughout a judgment of sin and error. Assumption of authority by the civil power concerning matters of religion is forbidden. History tells sad tales of trial and death for opinions' sake. There is a medium course between intolerance and indifferentism.

2. *With what judgment*, etc.—Your judgment of others shall be made the standard by which you shall be judged. "No indulgence shall be shown to those who have shown no indulgence to others." Innumerable illustrations of this truth may be drawn from the history of persecution. *Again*—No importance should be attached to this word. It should disappear from the translation.

3-5. The point is this: that we must not be guilty of hypocrisy by proposing, as if in love, to cure a brother of a fault when indulging one of our own still greater. Possibly Jesus means to refer to a greater fault of *the same kind;* for mote (splinter) and beam, it will be noticed, are the same in kind. We

5 ¶ Give not that which is holy unto the dogs, neither cast ye your pearls before swine, lest they trample them under their feet, and turn again and rend you.

7 ¶ Ask, and it shall be given you; seek, and ye shall find; knock, and it shall be opened unto you:

8 For every one that asketh receiveth; and he that seeketh findeth; and to him that knocketh it shall be opened.

9 Or what man is there of you, whom if his son ask bread, will he give him a stone?

10 Or if he ask a fish, will he give him a serpent?

11 If ye then, being evil, know how to give good gifts unto your children, how much

say possibly, for the point should not be pressed. *Pull*—*Cast out* is better. Notice the gradation; beholding, casting out. One might not attempt the latter who would do the former, though the former would be very likely to lead to the latter. *First cast out*—It is duty to aid your brother to get rid of the splinter, but you must first get rid of the beam which is in your own eye. This direction must not be perverted by neglecting all effort for another's good under the plea that we are not perfect. *Shalt see clearly* —Personal righteousness is a divine qualification for making others righteous. The smallest fault, like a splinter in the eye, is painful till removed; the sooner out the better.

6. The connection with the preceding verse is not clear, but it may be this: Though you ought to attempt to make your brother better, yet discriminate. Some are like dogs and swine. All effort to make *them* better will be a waste. *That which is holy*—Meat consecrated as sacrifice. *Dogs and swine* were unclean by the law of Moses. *Pearls* —Then, as now, held in high estimation. *Under*—With. *Again* is superfluous. Sacrificial meat and pearls are truths respecting spiritual things. This precept may be greatly perverted by withholding truth from those who give little promise of receiving it, yet are not such that they should be regarded as swine or dogs. God had a purpose of mercy relative to Matthew the publican, the woman who was a sinner, and one of the thieves on the cross.

7-11. The righteousness described must be sought with prayer. *Ask; seek; knock*—The second expressing more earnestness than the first, and the third more than the second. *Every one*, etc., *receiveth*—This is true even in the ordinary relations of life. How much more is it to be expected that in the higher relations which we sustain to God, we shall obtain what we ask! In vv. 9-11, Jesus illustrates from the more specific relation existing between parents and their children. It is an argument from the less to the greater. No father would mock his starving child by giving him a stone instead of bread, or a serpent instead of a fish: it would be doing violence to his nature. He has the capacity to see what his children need. He is indeed *evil*, depraved, yet he has lost neither capacity nor parental affection. The *nature of God* is such as to insure good things in answer to your prayers. It is *more* certain that your heavenly Father will hear you, for it is more thoroughly accordant with his nature. *Good things*—In Luke 11: 13, the Holy Spirit. So far, then, as the gift of the Holy Spirit is embraced in these verses, the promise need not be limited by the condition in 1 John 5: 14, inasmuch as prayer for the Holy Spirit is *known* to be in accordance with the will of God; but there are

more shall your Father which is in heaven give good things to them that ask him?

12 Therefore all things whatsoever ye would that men should do to you, do ye even so to them: for this is the law and the prophets.

13 ¶ Enter ye in at the strait gate: for wide *is* the gate, and broad *is* the way, that leadeth to destruction, and many there be which go in thereat:

14 Because strait *is* the gate, and narrow *is* the way, which leadeth unto life, and few there be that find it.

15 ¶ Beware of false proph-

---

many things for which we pray concerning which the will of God may be positively unknown. It is better for us and for our friends that some of our prayers should not be answered. "Monica, dreading the persecutions which were then threatening the metropolis, prayed to God that he would not suffer her son to go to Rome: he went notwithstanding, and it was in Italy that he found Christ." This son was Augustine, the celebrated church father, born in the middle of the fourth century, whose conversion was a most remarkable illustration of the grace of God. We should be careful to pray for bread, not for a stone. It is better that the prayer be lost if offered for that which will not nourish.

12. The Golden Rule. *Therefore*—The connection is thought by some to be obscure, but this seems to be a conclusion from the statement of the preceding verse. As God bestows his love upon you in the "good gifts" of his providence and grace, so should you bestow yours upon your fellow. But in what measure? In the same measure in which you, in similar circumstances, would desire him to bestow his love upon you. Is the rule original with Jesus? Jesus himself makes no such claim. He affirms it to be a requisition of the Law and the Prophets; that is, so far as concerns our relations to one another, it is the great principle underlying the teachings of the Law and the Prophets, though as pre-existent he was himself the source of all the truth of the Old Testament. Gibbon, in his "Decline and Fall of the Roman Empire," shows his antipathy to Christianity by saying that he read the Golden Rule in a moral treatise of Isocrates, written four hundred years before the publication of the Gospel. But it appears that "in *all* the parallel sayings from the classics and the rabbinical writings, there is to be found" [only] "the *negative* expression." Jesus states the duty in the *positive* form. In the writings referred to is announced little more than the duty of refraining from doing to others the wrong which they do to us. That is a *silver* rule. Jesus enjoins active beneficence: only his is worthy the name of Golden Rule.

CONCLUSION OF THE SERMON.

13, 14. These verses contain an exhortation to lead the life of righteousness which has been described. The duty is enforced in figurative terms. The life is represented as a narrow way at the beginning of which stands a *strait*, that is, narrow, gate. It is so represented, 1. Because it is a life in which the requirements of Christ put severe curbs on the sinful powers of men; 2. Because it is a life of trials arising from the opposition of men to truth and holiness. *Few that find it*—Not merely, as some think, in that early age of the Christian cause, but even now. Nominal Christians are many, but real disciples are still a minority. *Wide is the gate and broad the way*—Not wholly on account of the number which go in,

ets, which come to you in sheep's clothing, but inwardly they are ravening wolves.

16 Ye shall know them by their fruits. Do men gather grapes of thorns, or figs of thistles?

17 Even so every good tree bringeth forth good fruit; but a corrupt tree bringeth forth evil fruit.

18 A good tree cannot bring forth evil fruit, neither *can* a corrupt tree bring forth good fruit.

19 Every tree that bringeth not forth good fruit is hewn down, and cast into the fire.

20 Wherefore by their fruits ye shall know them.

21 ¶ Not every one that saith unto me, Lord, Lord,

---

but because of the large scope which men give to the sinful actings of their hearts. Let there be but one such man, and there is a wide gate and a broad way. The ends of the two ways are different. The broad way does not at last empty all its travellers into the narrow way. The narrow way leads to life. Lev. 18:5; 1 Tim. 6:19. *Life*—See remarks concerning the meaning of this word in the note on 25:46. *Destruction*—This is one of the words on which reliance has been placed for proof that the wicked will be *annihilated*. It has been confidently asserted that the Greek word means annihilation. Though this position has not been taken by men distinguished for breadth and accuracy of scholarship, many of the people have been greatly deceived by the *appearance* of scholarship in some of the books written in its defence. A very thorough refutation of the error has been made by Dr. Bartlett ("Life and Death Eternal"). The word does *not* mean annihilation, but *ruin*, the destruction not of being, but of well-being. "'I am lost, *destroyed*, or perished,' was a common Attic phrase, meaning, I am in the last degree miserable or unfortunate." If the word means *annihilation*, the words in Hosea 13:9, O Israel, *thou hast destroyed thyself*, mean, O Israel, thou hast *annihilated* thyself. It is difficult to see how Israel could have been annihilated and yet continue in existence, as the nation did, many hundred years after. It is difficult to see how the ointment which a woman poured on the Saviour's head could have been annihilated, though it must have been if the Greek word here translated *destruction* means annihilation; for in the question, To what purpose is this *waste?* the original of the word waste is the same as is here rendered destruction. Substitute the word annihilation in any passage in the Bible for the word destruction, and the absurdity is manifest. *Enter*—Go. Men are free, then, though in vv. 7-11 they are commanded to pray for God's help. *At* the strait gate—Through it. There must be no stopping on the threshold.

15-20. The narrow way may be missed through bad guidance. *False prophets*—Teachers who profess to give you truth, but give you falsehood. It need not be restricted to Pharisees and scribes, nor to those who were soon to arise, deceiving if possible the very elect, but may be applied also to false teachers in all ages. *Sheep . . . wolves*—The antipathy between them is great, but not greater than the contradiction between the reality and the appearance in false teachers. *Fruits*—Not their teaching, but the effects of their teaching, both on themselves and on others; the effects viewed in the light not of morality merely, but of the inward righteousness taught by Jesus. However correct

CHAPTER VII.

shall enter into the kingdom of heaven; but he that doeth the will of my Father which is in heaven.

22 Many will say to me in that day, Lord, Lord, have we not prophesied in thy name? and in thy name have cast out devils? and in thy name done many wonderful works?

23 And then will I profess unto them, I never knew you: depart from me, ye that work iniquity.

24 ¶ Therefore whosoever heareth these sayings of mine,

---

may be the moral habits of the teacher and of his inner circle of admirers, the question is, Does his teaching give men more impressive views of the evil of sin and more loving reverence for the holiness of God? Apply the question to the propagators of modern "spiritualism," to the entire body of infidel and semi-infidel teachers, and to the teachers of Romanism. An illustration is drawn from nature. As the nature, good or bad, of a tree is seen in its fruit, so the nature of the teacher is seen in the effects of his doctrine. *Grapes*—The fruit of the vine. They were sometimes of very large size. Grapes of Eschol were borne on a stick resting upon men's shoulders. Clusters have been seen in Syria ten or twelve pounds in weight. There is a vine "at Hampton Court which covers a space of twenty-two hundred square feet." "A bunch of Syrian grapes was produced at Wellbeck, which weighed nineteen pounds, and measured in length twenty-three inches, and nineteen and a half inches in its greatest diameter. It was sent as a present from the Duke of Portland to the Marquess of Rockingham, and conveyed a distance of twenty miles, on a staff, by four laborers; two of them bore it in rotation, thus affording a striking illustration of the proceeding of the spies." *Thorns*—See note on 13:7, 22.

21-23. Notice the related words, *prophets*, in vs. 15, and *prophesied*, in vs. 22. Jesus, then, is still referring to the false teachers, while, as is evident from the first two words in vs. 24, *Therefore, whosoever*, he would have all, teachers and taught, consider themselves as intended. Professing at the Day of Judgment to have taught the truths of the kingdom, and even to have cast out demons, will not be accepted by Christ the Judge as evidence of qualification for the kingdom of heaven. One must have *done the will of God* (12:50; John 7:17); that is, have attained to the righteousness enjoined in the Sermon. *In that day*—The Day of Judgment, which is not in this world, but in the next. *Lord, Lord*, is not the repetition of the formalist, but of the zealot. Whether the term should ever be applied to Jesus was not long ago gravely debated in a National Convention of Unitarians. Jesus himself says (John 13:13), *Ye call me Master, and Lord: and ye say well; for so I am.* Cast out devils—Not that they had actually done so; for (Mark 9:39) no man who shall do a miracle in the name of Jesus can lightly speak evil of him. See the graphic account of the *failure* to cast out an evil spirit in Jesus' name, Acts 19:13-16. Notice in vs. 13 the words *took upon them*, that is, attempted. See, also, the account of Simon Magus in Acts 8:9-24. *Will profess*—Will openly declare, in contrast with their own hypocrisy. *I never knew you*—Never had any loving recognition of you as mine, as you had none of me as yours. *Depart from me*—This shows that the destruction spoken of in vs. 13 is not annihilation. *From me*—Therefore from all who are like me; therefore from heaven. Separation from Christ is the essence of hell. *Work iniquity*

and doeth them, I will liken him unto a wise man, which built his house upon a rock:

25 And the rain descended, and the floods came, and the winds blew, and beat upon that house; and it fell not: for it was founded upon a rock.

26 And every one that heareth these sayings of mine, and doeth them not, shall be likened unto a foolish man, which built his house upon the sand:

27 And the rain descended, and the floods came, and the winds blew, and beat upon that house; and it fell: and great was the fall of it.

28 ¶ And it came to pass, when Jesus had ended these sayings, the people were astonished at his doctrine:

29 For he taught them as *one* having authority, and not as the scribes.

The disposition to do so is still in them, and, therefore, they are unfit for the presence of those whose highest delight is to do the will of God.

24-27. The duty of doing as well as hearing, and the awful consequences of not doing what we have heard, are here graphically set forth. It is not meritorious working, however, which is inculcated in this word *do*. The Sermon proceeds upon the assumption that men have no natural righteousness, and that they need strength from heaven to attain what is here taught. *A wise man*— One who adopts means which are adapted to secure an end, especially a good end. *Rock*—This is simply one element of the figurative description, and yet it cannot but suggest Christ, who is elsewhere distinctly represented as a *Rock*. *Floods*— Streams. *Rain, rivers, winds*—Nature roused to exert itself in three different modes, as if bent on destroying. *A foolish man*—One that uses bad means to secure an end. Both the wisdom and the folly involve a large moral element. The folly is not so much a difficulty of brain as of heart. *Great was the fall of it* —Greater than the fall of an empire. The idea of doing the will of Christ while rejecting or essentially modifying his teachings, is absurd. The plea of amiability or of kindness to the poor is worthless against the rejection of the Bible as a supernatural revelation.

28, 29. *Ended these sayings*—The reference is to all the Sermon. It would appear, therefore, that it was all delivered at one time, and not, as some say, at different times. *Doctrine*—The word is used not in the current theological sense, but in the sense of instruction. *Astonished* —The righteousness which Jesus had enjoined was unlike what they had been accustomed to hear. *Not as the scribes*—*They* taught so superficial a righteousness that their teaching wanted "life and spirit."

Reader! having completed the examination of this wonderful discourse,—wonderful, as has been said, for "that living spirit which inspires it; that creative power which energizes in every sentence, and in the whole structure and march of the discourse; that vast oratorical sweep which in a few brief words or phrases now rises to the loftiest heights, and now in calm dignity again descends; that sublime force of thought which reaches even the most distant truths, and grows resistless with every step of its onward march,"—such questions as these press upon the attention: 1. Have I a distinct conception of the righteousness required of the disciples of Christ? 2. Have

CHAPTER VIII.

WHEN he was come down from the mountain, great multitudes followed him.

I earnestly sought such righteousness? 3. Have I committed the mistake of seeking it as means of securing merit with the Father? 4. Or, have I accepted as the foundation of it the righteousness of Christ? 5. Have I perverted Christ's righteousness by professing to rely upon it for salvation, while remiss in seeking the personal righteousness which Christ teaches in the Sermon on the Mount?

CHAPTER VIII.

A SERIES OF MIRACLES.

781 U.C. Midsummer and Autumn, A.D. 28.

Having presented Jesus to his readers as the fulfiller of the ancient law, Matthew in this chapter and the following sets forth his claims as evinced in his miracles: he is doer as well as teacher. The miracles here recorded were not wrought in the order in which they are reported. This we learn with the help of the other evangelists. They were selected and grouped by Matthew, and the selection was happily made. The cases are various. Leprosy, palsy, fever, a tempest, demoniacal possession, an issue of blood, blindness, death itself, are all shown to have been under the complete control of Christ's will. Two cases of possession are reported, but they are not alike. The two cases of palsy are different, since one is connected with forgiveness of sin, while the other is not. The scenes of the miracles were sea and land, house and hill-side. Some were wrought on Jews and some on Gentiles. They were wrought on persons of different ages and of both sexes.

9*

2 And, behold, there came a leper and worshipped him, saying, Lord, if thou wilt, thou canst make me clean.

3 And Jesus put forth *his*

One was performed at such a distance that the subject was not even visible to the Saviour's natural eye. In no case was there a process of healing: the cure was instantaneous. These miracles—and the same is true of all that are reported in the Bible—were *not violations of nature*. Violations of nature, that is, of "laws" under which he himself placed nature, can with no propriety be affirmed of the Creator. Miracles were merely *interferences with the usual course of nature* without disturbing it. The regularity of natural events is precisely that which made miracles possible.

There is no evidence that evil spirits ever worked miracles, and therefore the miracles of Jesus prove the truth of the revelation which he professed to make. But his miracles had other though subordinate ends, as the physical and the spiritual good of the subject. The theory that the disciples *honestly mistook* natural events for miracles requires such a method of explaining the details of the narratives, that it makes them more incredible than miracles themselves. This is called the *Naturalistic* theory. The *Mythic* hypothesis is that by which the narratives of miracles are supposed to be myths, or legends, not histories. How the human mind could have been so imposed on as to be willing to accept fables, instead of the facts which were so fresh in their memories, has never been shown. Such narratives as these and real myths have so little resemblance that it is impossible to put them in the same class of writings. Read the myths in any of the Classical Dictionaries, and the difference will be immediately seen.

hand, and touched him, saying, I will; be thou clean. And immediately his leprosy was cleansed.

1. *Followed him*—Many of them only with the feet, not with the heart.

2. *A leper*—Leprosy, from a Greek word meaning scale, was a disease of the skin. It was well known among the Jews in early times, and in Lev. 13: 14 are sundry directions concerning the treatment of the disease. It was not always easy to determine whether a person was affected by this or by some other and milder disease. If suspicion of leprosy was awakened, an examination was made by the priest, and if, after fourteen days as the extreme limit, the usual proofs of leprosy were wanting, the person was pronounced clean. Uncleanness was pronounced upon him who was known to have taken the disease. Lepers were required to dress in mourning. Lev. 13: 45. They were not to come in contact with other persons, but were allowed to go about towns and even into synagogues. In Lev. 14 is prescribed what must be done for their recovery, the most important thing being the duty of appearing before the priest and offering a sacrifice. "The disease, as it is known at the present day, commences by an eruption of small reddish spots slightly raised above the level of the skin, and grouped in a circle. These spots are soon covered by a very thin, semi-transparent scale or epidermis, of a whitish color, and very smooth, which in a little time falls off, and leaves the skin beneath red and uneven. As the circles increase in diameter the skin recovers its healthy appearance toward the centre; fresh scales are formed, which are now thicker, and superimposed one above the other, especially at the edges, so that the centre of the scale appears to be depressed. The scales are of a grayish-white color, and have something of a micaceous or pearly lustre. The circles are generally of the size of a shilling or half crown, but they have been known to attain half a foot in diameter. The disease generally affects the knees and elbows, but sometimes it extends over the whole body; in which case the circles become confluent" [flow together]. "It does not at all affect the general health." It was not contagious, but it could be transmitted from parent to child. It was regarded as incurable. In the middle ages a terrible disease prevailed in Europe which was called leprosy, but the true name of which is *elephantiasis*. "Leper or lazar-houses abounded everywhere: as many as two thousand are said to have existed in France alone."

The directions which Moses gave for the treatment of lepers were not merely for sanitary ends. Ceremonial uncleanness was attributed to the leper, and this doubtless symbolized the great and painful fact of moral uncleanness. "The leper was the type of one dead in sin: the same emblems are used in his misery as those of mourning for the dead." *Worshipped*—Bowed down to him, after the oriental style. Gen. 44: 14. Moses cried unto the Lord for Miriam; this man cries unto Jesus for himself. *If thou wilt*—Not a sign of unbelief, but a form of begging him to be willing to do what he believes he has power to do.

3. *Put forth his hand*—A "prophecy" of the coming good. How unlike mesmerism! The cure was effected by the same sort of power that raised the dead, and no dead man has been raised by mesmeric power. *Touched him*—This was forbidden by the law of Moses. Lev. 5: 3. Why forbidden? That the ceremonial uncleanness might not be communicated. But as Jesus made the leper clean by touching

CHAPTER VIII. 103

4 And Jesus saith unto him, See thou tell no man; but go thy way, shew thyself to the priest, and offer the gift that Moses commanded, for a testimony unto them.

5 ¶ And when Jesus was entered into Capernaum, there

him, it was impossible that the act should make *him unclean*. Thus the act was a violation of the Mosaic precept only in appearance. Such is the freedom even of the law when not slavishly understood. Putting forth the hand was simply an outward sign of the inward act of the will. *Was cleansed*—1. Cured of the disease; 2. Restored to ceremonial purity. The distinction which the Mosaic economy made between things clean and things unclean was intended to teach the people the holiness of God and their own sinfulness. The method, as related to a people with their degree of knowledge, shows divine wisdom; 3. Possibly, also, renewed in heart.

4. *See*—It gives importance to the command. Such a prohibition was not laid upon every one whom he healed (Mark 5: 19); but generally Jesus required that persons should refrain from saying much concerning their cure. Why? 1. His nature forbade him from appearing to press his claims in a noisy, demonstrative manner. Matt. 12: 16-20. This may have been the principal reason. 2. Had not Jesus thus restrained the excitable, wonder-seeking nature of the people, their attention would have been completely turned from the truth he preached to the miracles he wrought. 3. In some cases the injunction of silence may have sprung from the desire to promote the spiritual good of the healed by saving him from the spirit of boasting. In addition to these reasons there existed in the case of the leper one of a more specific kind. Having been cleansed, his first duty was to secure from the priest in Jerusalem a statement of his freedom from the disease, and to make the required offering. Lev. 14. *For a testimony unto them*—To the people, that the priest regarded him as healed. Thus even the prejudiced priest shall be made to give, unwittingly, testimony to the miraculous power of Jesus. Had this been the only miracle which Jesus wrought, it would have been sufficient evidence of his Messiahship. "I will!" What authority! and independence! and consciousness of power to do it in his own strength! The apostles healed in the name of Jesus; Jesus in his own name.

5. The miracle which we have just examined is considered by some as having taken place several weeks earlier than the miracle wrought upon the centurion's servant. See Mark 1: 40; Luke 5: 12. Others think it was performed just before; that is, after Jesus had descended from the mountain, but before he had entered Capernaum. *Was entered*—This is one of several similar instances of bad grammar in our common English version. Strictly speaking it implies that some other person or persons entered Jesus into the city as a father enters his son at college, or as a vessel is entered at the custom house; but this is not the meaning which Matthew intended. *Had entered* is the proper rendering of the Greek, and is correct English. *Capernaum*—See note on 4: 13. It was probably a military station. *Centurion*—a Roman officer commanding a century, which was originally a hundred men, but afterwards from fifty to a hundred. Sixty centuries made a Roman legion. The number of legions in a Roman army varied. The number of centurions mentioned in the New Testament is at least four: 1. The one mentioned in the verse before

came unto him a centurion, beseeching him,

6 And saying, Lord, my servant lieth at home sick of the palsy, grievously tormented.

7 And Jesus saith unto him, I will come and heal him.

8 The centurion answered and said, Lord, I am not worthy that thou shouldest come under my roof: but speak the word only, and my servant shall be healed.

9 For I am a man under authority, having soldiers under me: and I say to this *man*, Go, and he goeth; and to another, Come, and he cometh; and to my servant, Do this, and he doeth *it*.

10 When Jesus heard *it*, he marvelled, and said to them

---

us; 2. The one who is named in connection with the scenes at the crucifixion; 3. Cornelius, of Acts 10; 4. Julius, to whom Paul was entrusted when sent to Rome as a prisoner. As Dr. Hackett remarks, in Smith's Dictionary, these all appear in a favorable light. The centurion before us, though a Gentile, had no faith in the gods which were worshipped in the larger part of the Roman Empire. He may have adopted the Jewish religion, and so have been a proselyte. He was at any rate favorably disposed toward it; for he had built the Jews of Capernaum a synagogue. Luke 7: 5. *Came unto him*—Not himself, but by messengers, elders of the Jews. Luke 7: 3. Jesus can be found in the city as well as in the desert and on the mountain. Soldiers not less than others may go to Christ. Havelock was a man of much prayer; so have been many others of military renown.

6. *Servant*—Not one of the soldiers, but a common servant, perhaps a slave. *Palsy*—See note on 4: 24, last paragraph. *Grievously tormented*—Not with devils, but suffering excruciatingly with the disease. He was threatened with immediate death. Luke 7: 2. There are some features in this man's case which are not generally found in palsy; a disease in which men do not suffer much.

7. *I will*—That settled the question. The preliminary act of going to the centurion's house was not done. Christ is not bound to one set of acts preliminary to great results.

8-10. Here are the two great qualities, humility and faith, each wonderfully developed. *Humility:* "He knew and felt himself, as a heathen, to be out of the fold of God, a stranger to the commonwealth of Israel; and therefore unworthy to receive under his roof the Redeemer of Israel." *Faith:* Jesus is now near the house. Luke 7: 6. The fact of his proximity would have been seized by some as a staff for their weak faith to lean upon. The centurion needs no such support. *Speak the word*—The true reading —see this explained in the note on 5: 44, last paragraph—requires the rendering, *only say in a word*. The centurion felt that it was not indispensable that Jesus should come to his house. The argument in vs. 9 is this: *My relations are such* that I am able to believe that whatever command you shall give, even at this distance from my servant, will be obeyed. But what were the relations? 1. He was *under* authority. He was therefore accustomed to obey. 2. He was *in* authority, and was therefore accustomed to receive obedience. He had no doubt, therefore, that a word from such a being as Jesus would secure the healing of his servant. *So great faith*—Faith consists of two elements: the assent of the intellect

CHAPTER VIII.

that followed, Verily I say unto you, I have not found so great faith, no, not in Israel.

11 And I say unto you, That many shall come from the east and west, and shall sit down with Abraham, and Isaac, and Jacob, in the kingdom of heaven:

12 But the children of the kingdom shall be cast out into outer darkness: there shall be weeping and gnashing of teeth.

13 And Jesus said unto the centurion, Go thy way; and as thou hast believed *so* be it done unto thee. And his servant was healed in the self-same hour.

14 ¶ And when Jesus was

---

and the trust of the heart. The intellect assents to just so much of the truth of religion as God makes known, and the heart trusts him with respect to it. The definition, then, is equally applicable to Abel, Abraham, the centurion, and Paul. God had communicated certain truths respecting Jesus Christ to the intellect of the centurion. To these his intellect gave assent, and to Christ himself his heart yielded trust. The mere assent of the intellect to the truth is not the faith which the Old Testament and the New extol. *He marvelled*—Not that he had hitherto been ignorant of the centurion's faith. He wept at the grave of Lazarus, but he knew some days before he began to weep that Lazarus was dead. Jesus had the characteristics of man though he was God. *Not in Israel*—Israel, that is, the descendants of Jacob, ought to have had great faith; for to Israel God had made known more truth pertaining to himself than to all others of the race, but the centurion, a Roman, one of a people to whom no supernatural revelation had been given, had greater faith than Israel.

11, 12. *The kingdom of heaven*—The kingdom of heaven perfected; that is, heaven itself. *From the east and west*—Gentiles of all nations. Isa. 45: 6; 49: 5, 6. Thus from China on the east to California on the west is the prophecy in the constant process of fulfilment. *Sit down*—Recline. It should have been so rendered. See the posture explained in the note on 9: 10. *With Abraham*—This is a figure by which the Jewish mind was accustomed to think of the happiness of heaven. *The children of the kingdom*—Of the Jewish theocracy, which was a type of the kingdom of the Messiah. Not all of them shall be cast out; for a remnant shall be saved. See Rom. 11. *Outer darkness*—The figure of a feast is still preserved, the guests being supposed to be in a brilliantly lighted room, and so the unbelieving Jews are conceived as being in the darkness outside. *Weeping and gnashing* imply both misery and rage. This Gentile was a true descendant of Abraham, for he had Abraham's faith. Great opportunities and little improvement. The last first.

13. *Said unto the centurion*—Unto the messengers whom he had sent. Luke 7: 10. *The self-same hour*—No importance should be given to the peculiar strength of the expression. It is stronger than the original requires. *In that hour* is more correct. The short prayer of this Gentile soldier brings a quicker answer than the long prayers of the scribes and Pharisees.

14. *Peter's house*—Peter afterward said, We have left *all*. If he was the owner of the house, and the owner when he said this, yet there is no misrepresentation in saying that he had left all. Every man, the wealthiest, is required to hold all things at God's disposal. This is

come into Peter's house, he saw his wife's mother laid, and sick of a fever.

15 And he touched her hand, and the fever left her: and she arose, and ministered unto them.

16 ¶ When the even was come, they brought unto him many that were possessed with devils: and he cast out the spirits with *his* word, and healed all that were sick:

17 That it might be fulfilled

---

the essential thing, without which no man can be a disciple. As the house was in Capernaum, Peter must have moved from Bethsaida, which is called (John 1: 44) the city of Andrew and Peter. *His wife's mother*—His mother-in-law. The apostle, who is claimed as the founder of a church whose popes, bishops, and priests are not allowed to marry, was himself married, and he took his wife with him on his missionary tours. See 1 Cor. 9: 5. The fact that the mother-in-law, after her miraculous cure, ministered, served at the table, is no evidence that the daughter was dead. The mother would naturally have desired to do this in gratitude. *Laid*—Lying, that is, in bed.

15. *Touched her hand*—This is another instance of an outward sign of the inward act of the will. *She arose*, etc.—She was not only cured of the fever, but was saved from the weakness which invariably follows recovery from fever when effected by physicians. Men healed of the malady of sin should minister to those around them. The church is doing this more freely than ever, but tens of thousands of her members care only to be ministered unto.

16. *When the even* (evening) *was come*—Mark (1: 32) gives the time more definitely: And at even *when the sun did set*. We must infer from Mark (1: 21) that it was the evening immediately following the Jewish Sabbath, which began at sunset and ended at sunset. People brought their sick friends, then, to Jesus immediately after the Sabbath. The explanation is to be found in the self-righteous scrupulosity with which, under the false teaching of the scribes, they regarded the day. The stricter Pharisees undertook to determine the *instant* when the Sabbath began. "They therefore called the time between the actual sunset and the appearance of three stars, and the Talmudists decided that 'if on the evening of the Sabbath a man did any work after *one* star had appeared, he was forgiven; if after the appearance of *two*, he must offer a sacrifice for a doubtful transgression; if after *three* stars were visible, he must offer a sin offering:' the order being *reversed* for works done on the evening *after* the actual Sabbath." According to Thomson, this form of intense self-righteousness still exists among many of the Jews of Palestine. "A profane and most quarrelsome fellow once handed me his watch to wind just after sunset on Friday evening. It was now his Sabbath, and he could not work." The Rabbis teach that a Jew " must not carry so much as a pocket-handkerchief, except within the walls of his city. If there are no walls, it follows, according to their perverse logic, that he must not carry it at all. To avoid this difficulty here in Safed" [a city near the Sea of Galilee], "they resort to what they call Erŭv. Poles are set up at the ends of the streets, and *strings* stretched from one to the other. This string *represents a wall*, and a conscientious Jew may carry his handkerchief anywhere within these strings." *Possessed*—See on 4: 24. *Cast out the spirits*—"Spiritual-

CHAPTER VIII.

which was spoken by Esaias the prophet, saying, Himself took our infirmities, and bare *our* sicknesses.

18 ¶ Now when Jesus saw great multitudes about him, he gave commandment to depart unto the other side.

19 And a certain scribe came, and said unto him, Master, I will follow thee whithersoever thou goest.

20 And Jesus saith unto him, The foxes have holes, and the birds of the air *have* nests; but the Son of man hath not where to lay *his* head.

21 And another of his dis-

---

ism," with its shameful accompaniments, will in like manner be cast out of men when God has tolerated it as long as he sees to be best.

17. *Esaias*—Isaiah 53: 4: *He hath borne our griefs and carried our sorrows.* It will be impossible to give even the briefest outline of what has been written relative both to the passage in Isaiah and to Matthew's use of it. The question has been, In what sense did Jesus *take* our infirmities, our diseases, and *bear* our sicknesses or sorrows. The answer should be allowed to depend not on our preconceived theological opinions, but upon a careful and extended consideration of the manner in which the original words are used. We have no doubt that those are correct who have affirmed, after the most thorough and critical investigation, that it is not a *removal away from us* of our infirmities and sicknesses that the words express, but a removal by bearing them *as a burden first upon himself.* "These sicknesses and discords of man's inner being, every one of which as a real consequence of sin, and as being at every moment contemplated by him as such, did press with a living pang into the holy soul of the Lord."—*Trench.*

Notice how our Lord spent this Sabbath,—not in rest, not in exclusive private communion with God, but in labor for the good of others. Mark 1: 21-31. Spiritual activity on the Sabbath in his followers, therefore, must be acceptable to Christ. Let us bear with cheerfulness the fatigue which such activity may produce.

18. Jesus could not consent to be always surrounded by a crowd. It was neither for his own good nor for theirs. *The other side*—Of the Sea of Galilee. See note on 4: 18. The number of cities then, as now, was much smaller on the eastern side.

19. Before entering the ship he is accosted by a *scribe*. See concerning the scribes the note on 5: 20. *Master*—Teacher. *I will follow thee*—Very few of the scribes would have been willing to make such an avowal. Most of them were hostile to Jesus. There is an air of self-confidence even in this man that does not promise well. It has been suggested that it may have been Judas Iscariot; but where nothing is known silence is a virtue.

20. The reply of our Lord tends to confirm the suspicion that the man's spirit was not that of a true disciple. He seems not to have counted the cost. *Foxes have holes*—Foxes were accustomed, as they still are, to burrow in the ground and to resort to old ruins. *Nests*—Haunts, or dwelling-places, one of which was the mustard-plant When it is grown, it is the greatest among herbs, and becometh a tree: so that *the birds of the air come and lodge in the branches thereof.* 13: 32. *The Son of man*—See note on 12: 8, second paragraph. *Not where to lay his head*—We should be careful not to put into

ciples said unto him, Lord, suffer me first to go and bury my father.

22 But Jesus said unto him, Follow me; and let the dead bury their dead.

23 ¶ And when he was entered into a ship, his disciples followed him.

24 And, behold, there arose a great tempest in the sea, insomuch that the ship was

---

these words, as has sometimes been done, more than they were intended to express, as the idea of suffering from abject poverty. There is reason to believe that Jesus generally had both food and shelter. But he had no home of his own. After he left his parents, he was entirely dependent on others for the supply of his temporal wants. He that made all surrenders all, that those who have nothing may have all.

21, 22. *Disciples*—In the wider sense, not implying the faith which works by love. Many who followed Jesus were disciples only *in the feet*. *Bury my father*—Now lying dead. To suppose the father still living, though aged, and the request to be this, Suffer me to take care of my father till he shall have died and been buried, does little toward softening the apparent severity of the Saviour's requisition; for even upon that supposition one might say, as the infidel Celsus, of the second century, did say, that Jesus "demanded what was inconsistent with duty to parents." *Let the dead bury their dead*—This is to be explained by a well-known figure of rhetoric, employed also by uninspired writers, by which a word used in one sense is repeated in a different sense. The meaning may be expressed thus: Let those who are dead in sin bury those who are dead physically. As to the alleged severity of the requisition, he who enters into the spirit of our Lord's teachings will have no difficulty in seeing that Jesus is here dealing with a man who had made no thorough consecration of himself to his service. To such a man it was proper that the severest possible test should be applied. The requirement is similar to that in which one was commanded to sell all his property and give to the poor in order to become a disciple. Had Jesus not seen that the rich man's state of mind was such as to require the test, he would have allowed him to keep his property; and had he not seen that this man's state was such as to require the test applied to him, he would have allowed him to bury his father. The test, therefore, is not essentially severer than is applied to all who profess a willingness to become followers of Christ. Jesus must have all, and have all immediately. To do something else *first* is what *love* cannot ask.

23. *A ship*—See note on 14: 13, under the same word. *Disciples*—In the narrowest sense, that is, the twelve apostles, as they were afterward called. We shall find these fishermen less at home on the sea than the carpenter's son.

24. *A great tempest*—"Small as the lake is," says Thomson, "and placid, in general, as a molten mirror, I have repeatedly seen it quiver, and leap, and boil like a caldron, when driven by fierce winds from the eastern mountains, and the waves ran high,—high enough to fill or 'cover' the ships, as Matthew has it. In the midst of such a gale 'calmly slept the Son of God,' in the hinder part of the ship, until awakened by the terrified disciples." "Those winds are not only violent, but they come down suddenly, and often when the sky is perfectly clear." "To understand the causes of these sudden and violent tempests, we must remember that the lake lies low,—six hundred feet

CHAPTER VIII.

covered with the waves: but he was asleep.

25 And his disciples came to *him*, and awoke him, saying, Lord, save us: we perish.

26 And he saith unto them, Why are ye fearful, O ye of little faith? Then he arose and rebuked the winds and the sea; and there was a great calm.

27 But the men marvelled, saying, What manner of man is this, that even the winds and the sea obey him!

28 ¶ And when he was

---

lower than the ocean; that the vast and naked plateaus of the Jaulan rise to a great height, spreading backward to the wilds of the Hauran, and upward to snowy Hermon; that the water-courses have cut out profound ravines and wild gorges, converging to the head of the lake, and that these act like gigantic *funnels* to draw down the cold winds from the mountain."

Was covered with the waves—*Was becoming covered*, say some, so as to "obviate all necessity for qualifying these words." But what necessity for qualifying them? An officer of a brig has just informed the writer that on his passage from Cuba to Boston, the waves, in a storm of not very uncommon power, *covered the deck*, and completely immersed himself and men. This little ship may have been similarly swept by the waves of the Sea of Galilee. *But he was asleep*—How great the contrast between the Lord's state and that of the sea! But the sleep was not less natural than the tempest. He who could wake the dead could have passed from Bethlehem to Calvary without sleep, but he was God *manifest in the flesh*. The well-known wakefulness which the commander and officers of a ship have in a storm is in wonderful contrast with this sleeping of Jesus. Christ felt safe in the wildest rockings of nature, but not, like a child, through ignorance of physical forces. He knew what terrific power dwells in one drop of water. Jesus and Jonah, each in a storm at sea. Let the Sabbath-school teacher speak of the differences.

25, 26. *Lord, save us: we perish*—Here are, 1. Consciousness of danger; 2. Faith in Jesus. Yet their faith was not perfect. Their little faith, however, was better than none; for it leads them to cry, Lord, save! Had it been perfect, they would not have cried at all. They all cried. United prayer is duty. *Then he arose*—The sublimity of the act is surpassed only by that which created light. *Rebuked* implies personification of the winds and the sea. Nature can take different postures of reverence before her great Creator. The idea of Lange that "the ultimate ground of this rebuke lay in the fact that the disturbances of nature were caused by unclean spirits," is without sufficient foundation. How much more obedient to their Lord are winds and waves than the human will unrenewed! Yet when Jesus Christ speaks, what a change comes over the boisterous passions of a Saul, an Augustine, a Luther, a John Bunyan!

27. *The men*—The disciples, and, if there were sailors on board, them also. *What manner of man* refers to nature and character. This miracle must have greatly confirmed the disciples' faith in Jesus, if not as the Messiah, yet as a being endowed with some special divine authority. The ship in the storm suggestive of the Christian and of a Christian church in peril. The result full of comfort to every believer.

28. *Into the country of the Gergesenes*—Two different cities have been claimed as the locality where this remarkable miracle was wrought:

come to the other side into the country of the Gergesenes, there met him two possessed with devils, coming out of the tombs, exceeding fierce, so that no man might pass by that way.

29 And, behold, they cried out, saying, What have we to do with thee, Jesus, thou Son

---

Gadara and Gergesa. Barnes says that "Gadara was a city not far from the Lake of Gennesareth," and that "Gergesa was a city about twelve miles to the south-east of Gadara, and about twenty miles to the east of the Jordan." On the contrary, Gadara is ten miles from the lake, a great distance, as we shall see, considering what occurred. Gergesa is now regarded as much more probably to be recognized in the ruins found by Thomson, seen by a few later travellers, on the eastern side of the lake, and called by the natives Kersa or Gersa. These ruins are a little west of north from Gadara, and near the lake. Thomson forcibly states the difficulties in the way of Gadara. The swine "must have run down the mountain for an hour and a half, forded the deep Jarmuk, quite as formidable as the Jordan itself, ascended its northern bank, and raced across a level plain several miles before they could reach the nearest margin of the lake,—a feat which no herd of swine would be likely to achieve, even though they were possessed." In his "Illustrations of Scripture," Dr. Hackett considers that the conditions of the narrative could have been naturally fulfilled in the region of Gadara, but in the American edition of Smith's Dictionary, 1867, he evidently regards the vicinity of the ruins of Gersa as the more probable scene of the miracle. He quotes from Mr. Tristram's "Land of Israel": "The bluff behind is so steep and the shore so narrow, that a herd of swine rushing frantically down must certainly have been overwhelmed in the sea before they could recover themselves. While the tombs of Gadara are peculiarly interesting and remarkable, yet the whole region is so perforated everywhere by these rock-chambers of the dead, that we may be quite certain that a home for the demoniac will not be wanting, whatever locality be assigned for the events recorded by the evangelists." According to Thomson, "the walls" [of Gersa] "can be traced all round." "It is within a few rods of the shore, and an immense mountain rises directly above it, in which are ancient tombs. . . . The lake is so near the base of the mountain, that the swine rushing madly down it could not stop, but would be hurried on into the water and drowned." "This discovery of the site of Gergesa," says Andrews, "removes all topographical difficulties from the sacred narrative."

Possessed—See note on 4: 24. *Coming out of the tombs*—Concerning the Jewish tombs see note on 27: 60. "I have often met," says Tristram, "in the outskirts of Caiffa" [Haifa, at the foot of Mount Carmel] "a maniac who dwells in similar tombs." Quoted by *Dr. Hackett in Smith's Bible Dictionary. Exceeding fierce*—They were desperate cases. *No man might*—No man *could* pass that way. There is no road which sin does not make dangerous. These demoniacs are a painfully exact likeness of men in the worst stage of sin, and to that stage all sin tends. There met him *two*. Sinners of the worst stage like to be together.

29. The devils are quicker to recognize the divine nature of Jesus than are some human beings. *What have we to do with thee?*—This form of words occurs several times in the New Testament. Jesus

CHAPTER VIII.

of God? art thou come hither to torment us before the time?

30 And there was a good way off from them a herd of many swine feeding.

31 So the devils besought him, saying, If thou cast us out, suffer us to go away into the herd of swine.

32 And he said unto them, Go. And when they were come out, they went into the herd of swine: and, behold, the whole herd of swine ran violently down a steep place into the sea, and perished in the waters.

33 And they that kept them fled, and went their ways into the city, and told everything, and what was befallen to the possessed of the devils.

34 And, behold, the whole city came out to meet Jesus: and when they saw him, they besought *him* that he would depart out of their coasts.

---

used it in addressing his mother at the marriage festival in Cana. It means substantially this: "What have we in common? Our relations are wholly different. . . . It always implies reproof, although sometimes a friendly one."—*Tholuck*. *Before the time*—The devils speak through the men. So strong is their aversion to the worse torment which they are conscious of deserving, that Jesus seems to them to have come before the time appointed for their final doom. They dread the loss of the satisfaction which they take in tormenting others. When they can torment neither men nor swine, their own misery will be terribly increased. *Son of God*—On the meaning of these very important words, see the note on 16: 15-17.

30, 31. *Many swine*—Mark (5: 13) says there were about two thousand. *A good way off*—Not several miles, as would have been the case had Gadara been the locality, but some distance up the hill. The distance may be judged in part by the supposed capacity of the animals to run. *Suffer us to go*—Some writers, as Barnes and Dr. Whedon, would defend our Lord against the cavils of objectors by the consideration that he did not command the evil spirits to go into the swine, but only *permitted* them to do so. No defence is needed. Jesus Christ, as the Son of God, had the *right* to send the devils anywhere, and no man has the right to call that right in question. Possibly the swine were kept by Jews, and in that case they deserved to lose them, for God had long before forbidden swine's flesh to the Jews; but as no man knows that the owners were Jews, the defence is good for nothing. The truth is, after all, that according to the oldest manuscripts the true reading in the Greek requires the rendering *Send us away*, instead of, *Suffer* us to go. The devils prefer swine to hell.

32. *Go*—Not only *out* of the men, but *into* the swine. The mercy of the former is not in the least tarnished by severity in the latter. According to Paige, an American Universalist commentator, the demoniacs were merely crazy men, and their insanity was transferred by Jesus to these two thousand pigs! *Perished*—The swine. The devils, alas! are still alive.

33. *Fled*—"The devils could not overtake them," says Bengel. It is not doing justice to their sagacity to suppose that they tried to do so: Jesus was still not far off.

34. *The whole city*—So many of the people went out that it is rhe-

CHAPTER IX.

AND he entered into a ship and passed over, and came into his own city.

2 And, behold, they brought to him a man sick of the palsy, lying on a bed: and Jesus seeing their faith said unto the sick of the palsy: Son, be of good cheer; thy sins be forgiven thee.

3 And, behold, certain of the scribes said within themselves, This *man* blasphemeth.

4 And Jesus knowing their thoughts said, Wherefore think ye evil in your hearts?

5 For whether is easier, to say, *Thy* sins be forgiven thee; or to say, Arise, and walk?

6 But that ye may know that the Son of man hath power on earth to forgive sins, (then saith he to the sick of the palsy,) Arise, take up

---

torically correct to say that the whole city went out. *Besought him*— What a fearful prayer! They make no examination of his claims. They attempt no compromise. They must be altogether rid of him. Many in our times would rather lose Christ than swine.

With the exception of the raising of the dead, this miracle, in its twofold character, is one of the most remarkable that Jesus wrought.

CHAPTER IX.

THE SERIES OF MIRACLES CONTINUED.

1. Jesus now returns to the western side of the sea. *His own city*— Capernaum, called his own city because it was his place of residence.

2, 3. *Palsy*—See note on 4:24, last paragraph. *Their faith*—Both of the sick man and of his friends. See Mark 2:4 for evidence that it was very great. *Son*—A form of address which, like *daughter* in vs. 22, is a beautiful illustration of the tenderness of the Saviour's sympathy with the afflicted. *Thy sins*— This is not decisive that his disease was caused by his sins, but it makes it probable. He was evidently oppressed by the consciousness of sin. *Be forgiven*—Are forgiven. The original is in the indicative mode. It is not, however, a mere announcement of forgiveness, but an **affirmation** that *he now* forgives. *Said within themselves*—Thought. *Blasphemy* —See note on 12:31, 32. They considered him as speaking blasphemy because he seemed to them to assume the prerogative of God. Such language *was* blasphemy if Christ was not God. But such direct forgiveness of this man's sin is proof of the Lord's deity. He forgives sin, however, as God in human flesh, as the Son of man on earth.

4. *Knowing their thoughts*—See John 2:24, 25. He knew them, not by shrewdly guessing them, but by a power which no created being has.

5, 6. *Whether*—An old form of pronoun, equivalent to the more modern *which*. *Easier to say* the one, or *to say* the other. We can see no greater case in *doing* the one than the other. "It would be easier for a man, equally ignorant of French and Chinese, to claim to know the last than the first; not that the language of itself is easier; but that, in the one case, multitudes could disprove his claim; and, in the other, hardly a scholar or two in the land." —*Trench*. So the scribes might object, It is easy enough *to say*, Thy sins are forgiven, but what is the proof that it has been done? Jesus

CHAPTER IX.

thy bed, and go unto thine house.

7 And he arose, and departed to his house.

8 But when the multitudes saw *it*, they marvelled, and glorified God, which had given such power unto men.

9 ¶ And as Jesus passed forth from thence, he saw a man named Matthew, sitting at the receipt of custom: and he saith unto him, Follow me. And he arose, and followed him.

10 ¶ And it came to pass, as Jesus sat at meat in the house, behold, many publicans and sinners came and sat down with him and his disciples.

11 And when the Pharisees saw *it*, they said unto his disciples, Why eateth your master with publicans and sinners?

---

takes them at their thought, and proceeds to do what is harder, namely, *to say*, that is, to claim the power to say, Rise up and walk. If at his word the man shall be cured of his malady, it will prove that the claim *to forgive sins* is founded on truth. *Thy bed*—Bedsteads seem not to have been wholly unused in Palestine; but the poorer people used mats, or their outside garment, for a bed. *That ye may know*—Miracles, then, are proofs of Christ's authority to found a religion which shall be characterized for true forgiveness of sin. Jesus forgives sin now that he is in heaven. *Son of man*—See on 12: 6, 8, second paragraph. *Arise*—But he was completely disabled. True. But it is reasonable to make the attempt to do what to the world may seem to be absurd, on condition that Christ commands us to do it. One may have formed such habits of sin that repentance may seem to be impossible, but if God commands one to repent, repentance is a perfectly reasonable act.

8. *Such power unto men*—The multitude, though not yet recognizing the deity of Jesus, are struck with the fact that uncommon power has been manifested.

9. *From thence*—The point of departure is not definitely stated. The event is probably related out of its chronological order. *Matthew*—See note on 10: 3. *At the receipt of custom*—Probably near Capernaum, on the great road from Damascus, which crossed the Jordan north of the Sea of Galilee and ran down the western side through the city. The customs or toll which Matthew was here accustomed to collect was for the Roman government, of which, as should be borne in mind, the Jews were subjects. Concerning the class of persons, publicans, to which Matthew belonged, see note on 5: 46. *Follow me*—A call to active discipleship. The call to apostleship seems to have been made later. He may have been a disciple in heart before.

10, 11. There is great difference of opinion concerning the question whether Matthew's feast and the events recorded in connection with it are in the chronological order. We shall assume as on the whole probable that they are. *Sat at meat* —Reclined at table. Sitting was the earlier posture. Reclining on couches came with a higher civilization. "Generally speaking, only three persons reclined on each couch, but occasionally four or even five. The couches were provided with cushions on which the left elbow rested in support of the upper part of the body, while the right arm remained free: a room provided with these was described as 'spread,'

12 But when Jesus heard *that*, he said unto them, They

Mark 14: 15, A. V." [Authorized version], "'furnished.' As several guests reclined on the same couch, each overlapped his neighbor, as it were, and rested his head on or near the breast of the one who lay behind him. The ordinary arrangement of the couches was in three sides of a square, the fourth being left open for the servants to bring up the dishes. The couches were denominated respectively the highest, the middle, and the lowest,—the terms being suggested by the circumstance of the guest who reclined on another's bosom always appearing to be *below* him. The protoklisia ['uppermost rooms'] (Matt. 23: 6), which the Pharisees so much coveted, was not, as the authorized version represents it, 'the uppermost *room*,' but the highest seat in the highest couch,—the seat numbered 1 in the annexed diagram."—*Smith's Bible Dictionary.*

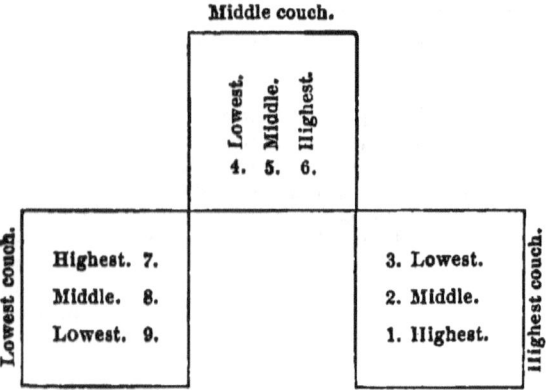

Publicans and sinners—The feast was made for Jesus by Matthew in his own house. The company was great (Luke 5: 29), and, in addition to the Saviour and his disciples, consisted of persons with whom he had been classed, and with whom, doubtless, he had been more or less accustomed to associate. By sinners is meant persons of dissolute life. *When the Pharisees saw it*—If by the Pharisees seeing Jesus with such persons, is meant seeing him with the natural eye rather than learning the fact a little time after, it follows that they either had been invited to the entertainment, or had happened in, or had been looking in upon the party from the door. The first is quite improbable. That sort of intercourse with that sort of persons would have spoiled all their righteousness. Either of the other acts would not have been incongruous with oriental freedom. *Said unto his disciples*—"The Pharisees," says Bengel, "acted in an underhand manner, cunningly, or at least with cowardice. To the disciples they said, Why does your Master do so? to the Master, Why do your disciples do so?" This is correct; but sometimes the Pharisees addressed their captious criticisms of Jesus to Jesus himself. A large dinner or tea party is either right or wrong, according to the end for which it is called and the conduct of those assembled. The style of conversation at Matthew's feast, had Jesus not been there, would probably have been very worldly, and it

CHAPTER IX.

that be whole need not a physician, but they that are sick.

13 But go ye and learn what *that* meaneth, I will have mercy, and not sacrifice: for I am not come to call the righteous, but sinners to repentance.

14 ¶ Then came to him the disciples of John, saying, Why do we and the Pharisees fast oft, but thy disciples fast not?

---

would not be strange if it had been very gross. Jesus being present, conversation upon worldly things must have been felt to be out of place, and vulgarity would have blushed to open its mouth. Christians need not fear either disgrace or contamination in associating for a good purpose with bad men. An important crisis in our Lord's ministry: he turns from Pharisees to publicans.

12, 13. Here are both a defence of himself and a rebuke of the Pharisees, expressed first in a figure and then without a figure. *To call the righteous*—It has been common (see Barnes) to explain these words as meaning *righteous by pretence*—as the Pharisees indeed were; in other words, it has been held that Jesus argues with them from their opinion of themselves. "You think you are righteous. Very well, I did not, then, come to call you." The explanation will be seen to be unnecessary if we consider that in the Greek there is no article. I am not come to call *righteous men* is the true rendering. This removes all appearance of seeming to admit that there is, by natural birth, such a class of persons as the righteous. *Go ye and learn*—You have *come in ignorance*, though you have come supposing that you know. *Go*—*Go away*, and learn; give yourselves up to an examination of your own Scriptures. He quotes Hosea 6: 6. *I will have*—I desire. Jesus is not here putting mercy and sacrifice (the latter meaning their entire ceremonial system) in opposition, but he teaches that mercy stands first in importance. A similar form of expression may be seen in John 6: 27. *Labor not for the meat which perisheth*, but for that meat which endureth unto everlasting life. The original of the words, *to repentance*, is wanting in several of the best manuscripts. It is genuine, however, in Luke 5: 32. The services of public worship must not be neglected under pretence that religion consists merely of mercy to our fellow-men. Mercy to our fellow-men must not be wanting under the plea that religion consists in worshipping God.

14. *Then came*—Perhaps immediately after the conversation with the Pharisees. Scribes (Luke 5: 30, 33) and Pharisees (Mark 2: 18) united with the disciples of John in this criticism of our Lord. How singular the union! These may have been some of John's more legal disciples, they not having recognized the Messiahship of Jesus. There is no proof that their fasting, as some have affirmed, was in consequence of John's imprisonment. *Fast oft*—See note on 6: 16, to which may be added that the fasting of which they speak was without any divine authority. The stricter Pharisees fasted twice a week: Luke 18: 12. "The number of annual fasts in the present Jewish Calendar has been multiplied to twenty-eight." *Why?*—The question refers not to their own fasting, but to the neglect of it by Christ's disciples. The Saviour's laxity in contrast with their own strictness is the point. With all their fasting they were less spiritual than the disciples of Jesus. Ritualism may give birth to laxity, and utter bold reproofs against those who do not accept its teachings.

15 And Jesus said unto them, Can the children of the bride-chamber mourn, as long as the bridegroom is with them? but the days will come, when the bridegroom shall be taken from them, and then shall they fast.

16 No man putteth a piece of new cloth unto an old garment; for that which is put in to fill it up taketh from the garment, and the rent is made worse.

17 Neither do men put new wine into old bottles: else the

---

15. Clothing the thought in imagery drawn from customs attending oriental marriages, Jesus replies that there is no reason why his disciples should fast. He is still with them. By and by, when he is taken from them, they will be so sorrowful that there will be more fitness in fasting. *Children of the bride-chamber* — Special friends who attended the bridegroom when he set forth from his house to go for his betrothed. See note on 25: 1-11 concerning marriage customs among the Jews. Jesus must not be understood as teaching that, after his return to heaven, his followers in all future ages of the church are to live in sorrow. It gives no authority to the teachings of the Romanists that the church should have many fasts, Lent, etc., etc. Jesus merely states the fact that his present disciples will be thrown into sorrow, for the time being, by his death. He elsewhere teaches that the children of the New Covenant should be characterized for joy. Christ is the bridegroom; the church is the bride. How calmly though not as yet very clearly does Jesus foretell his death!

16, 17. By two additional figures, Jesus still teaches, in the case of his disciples, the unfitness of fasting. It would be an attempt to combine the spiritual religion of the new dispensation with the antiquated forms of the old, and would certainly result in disaster. The metaphors in which the thought is expressed are "as simple and intelligible as they are wonderfully profound and full of fine meaning." *New cloth*—Unfulled, and therefore whenever it shall "full" it will tear away the old and make a worse rent. The new cloth represents the teachings of Jesus Christ which lead to joyousness of spirit. *Old garment*—The unauthorized legal fasting to which these disciples of John and the Pharisees were attached; and this may be considered as standing for the entire system of self-righteous working which had long been growing up in the nation. To place the chief dependence upon that which implied, at least in their system of fasts, a sorrowful state, and to regard the doctrines of the new teacher, which were adapted to awaken joy, as subordinate, was like *patching* an old garment with unfulled cloth. It was unfitting, incongruous. *The rent made worse*—This has been lamentably fulfilled in the history of all State Churches; e. g., the Church of England (Episcopal), and the Church of Scotland (Presbyterian), and the Lutheran Church in Germany. The persistent effort which has been made in the Church of England and in the Episcopal Church of the United States to *patch* the evangelical system into the legal in the form of Puseyism, is cause of sincere grief to every lover of pure Christianity. The rent is made worse, in a multitude of individual cases, when the soul attempts to mend its long-worn robe of self-righteousness with some little patch

CHAPTER IX.

bottles break, and the wine runneth out, and the bottles perish: but they put new wine into new bottles, and both are preserved.

18 ¶ While he spake these things unto them, behold, there came a certain ruler, and worshipped him, saying, My daughter is even now dead: but come and lay thy hand upon her, and she shall live.

19 And Jesus arose, and followed him, and *so did* his disciples.

---

taken out of the gospel. The old garment must be thrown away, and a wholly new garment procured.

By the next metaphor, the thought is advanced a little. *New wine*—Unfermented. Concerning the wines of Palestine, see note on John 2: 10. See also the latter part of the note on 26: 27. *Old bottles*—" Vessels of metal, earthen, or glass ware for liquids were in use among the Greeks, Egyptians, Etruscans, and Assyrians, and also no doubt among the Jews, especially

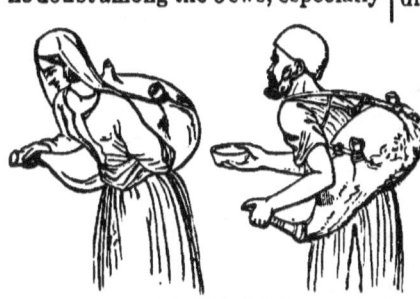

WATER-SKINS.

in later times." But the bottles here referred to were *skins* of animals, and were doubtless made as leathern " bottles " are now made in Western Asia. " When the animal is killed, they " [Arabs] " cut off its feet and its head, and they draw it in this manner out of the skin, without opening its belly.... They afterwards sew up the places where the legs were cut off and the tail, and when it is filled they tie it about the neck." Dr. Hackett saw many such skin bottles in his travels in Egypt and Syria. He says: " That bottles of this shape... were common in the days of the patriarchs and the Pharaohs, I had interesting proof in one of the tombs near the Ghizeh pyramids. Among the figures on the walls I saw a goat-shaped bottle, as exactly like those now seen in Cairo, as if it had been painted from one of them by a modern artist." *The bottles break*—Becoming old, they will not expand as the wine ferments. New wine, therefore, must be put into new skins. The point is still this, that the reason why his disciples do not fast is, that there would be no *fitness* in doing so. He is with them, and therefore they should rejoice rather than fast. If this explanation exhausts the meaning which Jesus intended, as perhaps it does, yet it is in keeping with the spirit of the words to say that the gospel cannot be restrained by the stiff ceremonies of Phariseeism. Not the forms of even the old, divinely appointed, economy, though once required, will answer. The few, simple, elastic forms which Jesus authorized are those which suit the free, living spirit of the gospel. Christ must be received exclusive of all destructive combination with the dried forms of legalism. It would be contrary to our Lord's teaching in his Sermon on the Mount to suppose that he is here setting Christianity in opposition to the spirit of the Old Covenant.

18, 19. *While he spake*—While he *was speaking* these things to John's disciples. *There came a certain ruler*—According to the latest critical edition of the Greek Testament, we should here read, There came *in a*

20 ¶ And, behold, a woman, which was diseased with an issue of blood twelve years, came behind *him*, and touched the hem of his garment:

21 For she said within herself, If I may but touch his garment, I shall be whole.

22 But Jesus turned him about, and when he saw her, he said, Daughter, be of good comfort; thy faith hath made thee whole. And the woman was made whole from that hour.

23 And when Jesus came

---

ruler, that is, into Matthew's house. *Ruler*—That officer of the synagogue that presided over the elders of the synagogue. *Worshipped*—Bowed down. *Even now dead*—Has just now died. Mark says, *Lieth at the point of death;* Luke, *She lay a dying*. She was not then dead, but was dying; and as Jesus very soon received a message (Mark 5:35) that she was actually dead, Matthew, making no report of the coming of the messenger, seems to be under a kind of necessity to report the fact of the death just at this point. Such was the freedom which the Holy Spirit granted him under the power of inspiration. *But come*—Though his faith is great, it is not so great as that of the centurion, for the latter believes that Jesus can cure his servant without coming; yet the centurion is a Gentile, and this man is a son of Abraham. *Followed him*—Was following. He had not yet reached the house.

20, 21. *Behold*—It was a new case, arresting the Lord's steps on his way to the house of death. To the ruler every moment of the delay must have seemed an hour, but should the child die, Jesus is conscious—and how calm in the consciousness!—of power to grapple with death itself. Twelve years of malady, and that malady making her by the law unclean, poverty induced by protracted medical treatment (Mark 5:26), and despair of help from human sources, cannot but touch the Saviour's heart. *Behind him*—Timidity, caused partly by her reverence, and partly, perhaps, by her disease. *The hem*—The fringe. Num. 15:38, 39.

"It was in the first instance the ordinary mode of finishing the robe, the ends of the threads composing the woof being left in order to prevent the cloth from unravelling." This woman, like the Jews generally (see note on 23:5, last paragraph), seems to have attached great sanctity to the fringe. There may have been mixed with her faith some erroneous views of the Saviour's miraculous power. *Said within herself*—There is something affecting in the silence of her effort. *Touched*—According to the Mosaic law, she was unclean. Her uncleanness was communicable. In touching Jesus, therefore, she was guilty of violating the letter of the law.

22. *Of good comfort*—Of good cheer: take courage. *Her faith* made her whole, not as an element of character, not because it had essential merit, but as the act by which she looked away from herself to Christ. No pilot steers by the light on his own vessel. The brazen monument which Eusebius, about 300 A.D., says was standing in his time, and which was then believed to have been erected by this woman in honor of her deliverer, is regarded by Dr. Robinson as more probably erected in honor of some emperor.

23. This work of mercy being done, Jesus proceeds at once to the case which called him from the house of feasting to the house of mourning. *Minstrels*—Flute-players, hired for the occasion. The practice is still continued in some oriental countries, though its expensiveness confines it chiefly to the more wealthy. "It

CHAPTER IX. 119

into the ruler's house, and saw the minstrels and the people making a noise,

24 He said unto them, Give place: for the maid is not dead, but sleepeth. And they laughed him to scorn.

25 But when the people were put forth, he went in, and took her by the hand, and the maid arose.

26 And the fame hereof went abroad into all that land.

27 ¶ And when Jesus departed thence, two blind men followed him, crying, and saying, *Thou* Son of David, have mercy on us.

---

was incumbent on even the poorest Israelite, at the death of his wife to provide at least two pipers and one woman to make lamentation." Speaking of the deaths which occurred when Joppa was taken by the Romans, Josephus says, "And a great many hired mourners with their pipes." *Making a noise*—Lane, speaking of the modern Egyptians, says: "After death the women of the family raise cries of lamentation called welweleh or wilwáe, uttering the most piercing shrieks, and calling upon the name of the deceased, O my master! O my resource! O my misfortune! O my glory! The females of the neighborhood come to join with them in this conclamation: generally, also, the family send for two or more *neddábehs*, or public wailing women."

24. *Give place*—He requests the flute-players and the people to withdraw. *Not dead, but sleepeth*—This he affirms in consciousness both of his power and his purpose to restore her to life. Her death was *transient*, and therefore she was not dead in the sense in which almost all mankind die. For that reason he affirms that she sleeps. As Dr. Bartlett well expresses it, "Physical death includes not only the departure, but the *returnless* departure, of the spirit: in this sense she was not dead." Jesus represents Lazarus as *sleeping*, though he afterward tells the disciples that he is dead. It was in that case, also, the *transient* nature of the death that suggests the peculiar appropriateness of the term *sleep*. *Laughed him to scorn*—Not only laughed, but laughed in *derision* at what he had just said. As Dr. Wayland once remarked, they have not laughed much since. Modern infidelity laughs at much that Jesus said and did, yet claims to be eminently Christian. These mourners are not disposed to think that all their piping and clamor have been premature. Perhaps, also, they have an eye to their pay.

25, 26. *The people*—The crowd (so also in vs. 23), put out, not by force, but by command. It included all but the parents and the three disciples, Peter, James, and John. Mark 5: 37, 40.

27. *Thence*—From the house of Jairus. "Blindness is extremely common in the East from many causes; e. g., the quantities of dust and sand pulverized by the sun's intense heat; the perpetual glare of light; the contrast of the heat with the cold sea-air on the coast, where blindness is specially prevalent; the dews at night while they sleep on the roofs; small-pox, old age, etc.; and perhaps, more than all, the Muhammedan fatalism, which leads to a neglect of the proper remedies in time. . . . *Ludd*, the ancient Lydda, and Ramleh, enjoy a fearful notoriety for the number of blind persons they contain. The common saying is that in Ludd every man is either blind or has but one eye. Jaffa is said to contain five hundred blind out of a population of five thousand at most. *Two*—They were partners in sorrow. *Son of David* —These words were equivalent to *Messiah*. See the latter part of the

28 And when he was come into the house, the blind men came to him: and Jesus saith unto them, Believe ye that I am able to do this? They said unto him, Yea, Lord.

29 Then touched he their eyes, saying, According to your faith be it unto you.

30 And their eyes were opened; and Jesus straitly charged them, saying, See *that* no man know *it*.

31 But they, when they were departed, spread abroad his fame in all that country.

32 ¶ As they went out, behold, they brought to him a dumb man possessed with a devil.

---

note on 1: 1. See, also, 22: 42–45. The application of them to Jesus by these men is not proof, however, that they had arrived at the conception of his Messiahship. It proves at least this, that they knew Jesus as a descendant of David.

28, 29. *Into the house*—Perhaps the house in which he lived when he was in Capernaum. Though not healed on the way, they persist in following him till he hears their prayer. *Yea, Lord*—Faith's answer is prompt and brief. *Touched*—As in the case of the leper, an outward sign of the inward act of the will. It was not at all necessary as a means of cure. *According to your faith*—Each believed that Jesus was able to cure his blindness, to cure it wholly; not both eyes partially, not one eye only; and therefore each was cured. Had Jesus seen that either of the men believed that he was able or willing to open only one eye, the spiritual disqualification would have been so great that he would doubtless not have opened even one.

30, 31. *Straitly charged*—Sternly charged. It implies threatened displeasure. They had addressed him as the Messiah, and would be likely after their cure to proclaim him as such through all the region. Jesus knew what evil results might arise from their doing so: 1. Awakening such enthusiasm among the people as to draw too largely upon his time in working miracles; 2. Stirring up the malice of the Pharisees so as to hasten his death before the time. *Spread abroad his fame*—The disregard of their benefactor's request is to be disapproved, not, as it is said to have been done by Romish expositors, applauded. This miracle is a beautiful illustration of the truth that Christ is the light of the world. Reader! are you yet spiritually blind? Cry for light. Give the quick response of faith, *Yea, Lord!* No restriction is now put upon the cured. Go, preach!

32. *As they went out*—The men that had been cured of blindness. *A dumb man possessed*—The dumbness was in consequence of the possession, for (vs. 33) when the devil departed he was able to speak. On the general subject of demoniacal possession see note on 4: 24. *Dumb*—Devils are not straitened in their efforts. They make some persons clamorous (8: 28, 29) and others dumb. Nor was Christ straitened. He cast out both noisy devils and still devils. A Universalist commentator says that this man was "probably an insane man, who fancied he could not speak, or he would not;" which illustrates the rationalistic character of Universalism. The fact is, that the Jews themselves made a distinction between merely diseased persons and persons who were both diseased and possessed. Mark (7: 32–35) reports the cure of a deaf mute who was not possessed.

CHAPTER IX.

33 And when the devil was cast out, the dumb spake: and the multitudes marvelled, saying, It was never so seen in Israel.

34 But the Pharisees said, He casteth out devils through the prince of the devils.

35 And Jesus went about all the cities and villages, teaching in their synagogues, and preaching the gospel of the kingdom, and healing every sickness and every disease among the people.

36 ¶ But when he saw the multitudes, he was moved with compassion on them, because they fainted, and were scattered abroad, as sheep having no shepherd.

37 Then saith he unto his disciples, The harvest truly *is* plenteous, but the laborers *are* few:

38 Pray ye therefore the

---

33. *Never so seen in Israel*—Israel was the most remarkable nation, and this, in the judgment of the people, was the most remarkable thing yet done in Israel. The feelings which they express may, however, be the culmination of the feelings which have been awakened by all the miracles of the day. They will yet see greater things. The regeneration of men is a fuller manifestation of Christ than opening blind eyes or casting out a dumb devil.

34. Criticism (vs. 11) means hostility, though it is not necessary to suppose the Pharisees of vs. 11 to be the same as are mentioned here. It is probable, however, that they are the same. The rationalists of our times deny the fact: the Pharisees admitted the fact, but attributed the act to the prince of devils working through the active co-operation of Jesus himself. This absurd charge will be often repeated. It will be considered at greater length in the notes on 12: 22-28.

35. *All the cities and villages*—By a comparison with Mark 6: 1-6, it seems probable that the cities and villages referred to were in that part of Lower Galilee in which Nazareth was situated. *Preaching and healing*—This twofold work has been done with great success by some modern missionaries. Christianity aims to bless both body and soul.

36. *When he saw*—Not in one place only, but wherever. *Fainted* —Harassed. Fainted is not strong enough for the true reading of the original. The allusion is not chiefly, if at all to their physical state. They had no good guides in things spiritual. The scribes were very poor shepherds. The condition of the people had long been deplorable. In the picture which Matthew here gives of our Lord, is a wonderful blending of the human and divine. Respecting Christ as a shepherd, see notes on John 10.

37, 38. *Harvest*—Of Jews, primarily, but in the large sense in which Jesus used it, of the Gentiles in all times. *Plenteous*—Great. *Laborers few*—He was the only laborer, it has been said, which is true in the strict sense; yet it is not to be supposed that the apostles, whom he is about to send forth into active service, had hitherto done nothing. Laborers is a comprehensive term, not to be restricted to ministers. "Idleness in the Lord's work is a sin." *Pray*, etc.—Taken in connection with the fact that he will immediately exercise his authority in sending forth the twelve, and very soon seventy more, the direction *to pray* for more laborers should foreclose all objections drawn from the supposed incompatibility of the human will and the divine will. We learn

Lord of the harvest, that he will send forth laborers into his harvest.

CHAPTER X.

AND when he had called unto *him* his twelve disciples, he gave them power *against* unclean spirits, to cast them out, and to heal all manner of sickness and all manner of disease.

2 Now the names of the twelve apostles are these: The

---

from this direction that we are not to confine ourselves to the Lord's Prayer. The life of Christians, whether ministers or otherwise, ought not to be a life of ease.

CHAPTER X.

JESUS COMMISSIONS AND SENDS THE TWELVE.

782 U.C. Winter, A.D. 29.

1. Where the important event here recorded took place it is impossible to tell, but it is most probable that it occurred at some point in the circuit referred to in vs. 35 of the last chapter. The public labors of Jesus have now been prosecuted about two years. About one year and three months remain before his death. It will be observed that most of the twelve disciples were kept under the Saviour's instruction nearly twenty-four months before they were considered as qualified to be sent forth as apostles. "*Twelve* (3×4) appears in twelve tribes, twelve stones, and twelve gates (Rev. 21: 19-21); twelve thousand furlongs of the heavenly city (Rev. 21: 16); one hundred and forty-four thousand sealed (Rev. 7: 4)." Nothing mysterious, however, should be considered as expressed in this number of the apostles. Some definite number must be chosen, and this would be naturally suggested by the number of the Jewish tribes. *Power against*—Power *over*. *Unclean spirits*—Wicked demons, of whom Satan is the prince. Unclean because wicked. Acts 19: 12.

2. *Apostles*—Persons *sent out*. All the Gospels except John's, and the Acts, have catalogues of the apostles. In the following table the names are arranged in the order in which they are given. The book of Acts, it should be borne in mind, was written by Luke.

	Matt. 10: 2-4.	Mark 3: 16-19.	Luke 6: 14-16.	Acts 1: 13.
1.	Simon Peter,	Simon Peter,	Simon Peter,	Peter,
2.	Andrew, his brother,	James,	Andrew,	James,
3.	James, son of Zebedee,	John,	James,	John,
4.	John, his brother,	Andrew,	John,	Andrew,
5.	Philip,	Philip,	Philip,	Philip,
6.	Bartholomew,	Bartholomew,	Bartholomew,	Thomas,
7.	Thomas,	Matthew,	Matthew,	Bartholomew,
8.	Matthew,	Thomas,	Thomas,	Matthew,
9.	James, son of Alpheus,	James,	James,	James,
10.	Lebbeus, Thaddeus,	Thaddeus,	Simon Zelotes,	Simon Zelotes,
11.	Simon the Canaanite,	Simon,	Judas, brother of James,	Judas, brother of James.
12.	Judas Iscariot.	Judas Iscariot.	Judas Iscariot.	

It will be observed that Peter holds the first place in all the catalogues, Philip the fifth, James the ninth; and that the other nine are arranged by all the writers in groups of three each, under these three names, Judas being invariably put last. In this sense, the apostles' names are given in classes. In the fourth catalogue, the name of Judas Iscariot

CHAPTER X.

first, Simon, who is called Peter, and Andrew his brother; James *the son* of Zebedee, and John his brother;
3 Philip, and Bartholomew; Thomas, and Matthew the publican; James *the son* of Alpheus, and Lebbeus, whose surname was Thaddeus;
4 Simon the Canaanite, and

---

is of course wanting. *Simon, who is called Peter*—*Cephas* is the name by which Jesus is reported in John 1: 42 as addressing this apostle. It is a Chaldee word, and as Jesus and the apostles spoke Chaldee, not Greek, it is the name by which Jesus must have always addressed him. It comes from the old Hebrew word *Ceph*, which means rock. *The first*—He is named first in all the catalogues, and was prominent above all the others in energy and zeal. He often spoke and acted as the representative of the others, but, contrary to the teachings of the Romanists, he was never accorded any superiority of rank, and he never claimed any. See more in respect to this in the note on 16: 18, 19. *Andrew*—We have no means of determining whether he was younger or older than his brother Peter. Bethsaida was their original home (John 1: 44), but from Mark 1: 29 it must be inferred that they had removed to Capernaum. Concerning the labors and death of Andrew nothing is certainly known, though tradition affirms that he suffered death on a cross in the shape of the Greek letter X, which is therefore called St. Andrew's cross. *James*—Jacob is the real name in the original. James is the English form, the time of its introduction into our language being uncertain. His father's name was Zebedee, and his mother's Salome. Except Judas, he is the only one of the twelve of whose death we have definite knowledge. He was put to death by Herod. Acts 12: 2. Like Peter and Andrew, he had been bred a fisherman. Very little is reported of his labors. *John*—James' brother. This is the man who is to write the richest of all the narratives of his Master's life, the most spiritual of all the epistles, and the only prophetical work of the New Testament.
3. *Philip* was of Bethsaida. A few interesting things are related concerning him which will be examined in their order, but not much is known of his apostolic life. *Bartholomew*—That is, son of Talmai. There is some reason to suppose that he is the same as Nathanael. He is reported as having preached in India, by which may be meant Arabia Felix. *Thomas* means *twin*. See John 11: 16: Thomas which is called *Didymus*, that is, *twin*. John is the only evangelist who speaks of any of his traits of character. John 11: 16; 20: 24-29. The tradition that Thomas founded the church in Malabar has little to support it. *Matthew*—Concerning the class to which he belonged,—the publicans, —see note on 5: 46. In Luke 5: 27, he is called Levi. It is worthy of especial notice that Matthew had humility enough to designate himself the publican, and the other evangelists magnanimity enough to omit the designation. This is another instance of the freedom which was granted to the evangelists by the Holy Spirit. *James the son of Alpheus*—Much investigation and reasoning have been expended upon the question whether this James and James the brother of the Lord are the same. Some take the affirmative and others the negative. There are insuperable difficulties in the way of a decisive answer. *Lebbeus*—In Mark this apostle is called *Thaddeus*, and he is believed to be the same as is called by Luke in his Gospel and

Judas Iscariot, who also betrayed him.

5 These twelve Jesus sent forth, and commanded them,

the Acts *Judas*, brother of James. By this theory, he had three names. He was the author, as some think, of the Epistle of Jude, but others hold that that epistle was written by Jude the Lord's brother.

4. *Simon the Canaanite*—Neither, as Barnes, a native of Cana, nor a descendant of Canaan, which this method of writing the word leads many to think. The word should be spelled *Cananite*. A still better spelling would be *Kananite*. The word means zealot, from which we are probably to infer that Simon had been exceedingly zealous for the Mosaic law. It is an error to suppose that he was so called in consequence of belonging to a political sect called Zealots, for that party did not arise till several years later. *Judas Iscariot* — Iscariot need not be considered as a surname. Several of the theories respecting its origin are fanciful. The most common opinion has been, though it has little to support it, that Judas was a native of Kerioth, a town in the southern part of Judea. "The position of his name, uniformly the last in the lists of the apostles in the Synoptic Gospels" [Matthew, Mark, and Luke], "is due, it may be imagined, to the infamy which afterwards rested on his name; but, prior to that guilt, it would seem that he took his place in the group of four which always stand last in order, as if possessing neither the love, nor the faith, nor the devotion which marked the sons of Zebedee and Jonah." *Prof. E. H. Plumtre, in Smith's Dictionary*, says:— "There are more signs in the Gospels that Judas had a strong and sturdy intellect than that some of the other disciples had, . . . but he had no largeness of mind nor loftiness of aim which fitted him for great exploits; . . . he was mean,

sordid, miserly, but still not insensible to the attractions of the opposite character; . . . he had enough of moral sentiment to know the right and put on the semblance of it. . . . The sins of Judas were those of deliberate intent; the sins of Peter were those of sudden lapse. . . . There is no other *kind* of objection to the fact that the Most High in his providence allowed Judas to be one of the *first* preachers of the gospel, than to the fact that he has in his providence allowed other unfit men to be *eminent* preachers of it, or that he has allowed unworthy men to sit on the bench of justice, or to reign on the throne which, even although they were 'ordained of God,' they have tarnished. The mystery here is the old mystery of moral evil." *Who also betrayed him*—How calmly stated! How free from personal feeling!

THE COMPOSITION OF THE APOSTOLIC BODY.

As the selection of men to make the first general promulgation of Christianity and to found Christian churches, was the most important act of our Lord's life, save that of actually surrendering himself to a sacrificial death, we pause for the purpose of briefly considering the composition of the apostolic body. Its bearings upon questions pertaining to the ministry of modern times, and to the spirit which should govern the churches in the choice of pastors, make the subject one of much practical importance. As Judas soon dropped wholly out of the apostolic ranks, we shall not include him in what we purpose to say. Matthias, however, who was chosen to fill his place, and Paul, who, though there was "a divine irregularity about his call." was as

saying, Go not into the way of the Gentiles, and into *any* city of the Samaritans enter ye not:

---

truly an apostle as any other, will both be included.

The two grand characteristics of the apostolic body were *Unity and Diversity*.

1. *Unity*—The apostles were all men; not one of them an angel, not one of them a woman. They were all Jews; all believers in the unity and holiness of God; all believers in Jesus Christ; were of the same official rank; were one in doctrine and practice and general aim. They were one, not organically, but through the possession of a common life,—that derived from Christ.

2. *Diversity*—They were not all Palestinian Jews. Only one had been born into the rights of Roman citizenship. Some of them were married; at least one lived and died unmarried. Some had followed one kind of worldly calling, and some another. Paul was summoned from the highest social position; Matthew from the lowest. While probably all were endowed with an ardent temperament, the temperaments of those best known differed, and only one, Paul, had the temperament to which belong the highest qualities. Some were men of ordinary intellectual ability; others of the highest. One was constitutionally sceptical; another practical; another intuitive; another logical. James was conservative; Paul was progressive; John held the balance pretty evenly between the two. One, in addition to some youthful Greek culture, was learned and trained to think even if judged by the highest Rabbinic standard. The labors, the successes, the trials, of some are narrated, while those of others are kept secret with God. Some are known as writers; some as preachers; others as both preachers and writers. Some spent life chiefly in large cities; others elsewhere.

Some were more useful in converting men and organizing them into churches; some in instructing them; others equally useful in doing both. Some were mere narrators of the facts of Christianity; others bold defenders of the truth against the errorists of their times. Some have a world-wide reputation, while of others nothing is known but their names. Such were the diversities of the apostles, yet they awoke among themselves no jealousies, no contempt, no coldness. The men were one in sentiment, in doctrine, in purpose, and in joy over each other's success.

These diversities are repeated, by divine intention, in ministers of modern times. Not all the diversities of modern ministers, however, are the result of divine intention, as, for example, those which are born of perversion of Scripture and of self-neglect.

The composition of the apostolic body illustrates the wisdom of Christ, and teaches many impressive lessons both to ministers and to churches.

THE LORD'S ADDRESS TO THE TWELVE.

5. *Go not into the way of the Gentiles*—Direct not your way to Gentiles. Samaria was the region located in the central part of Palestine, having Judea on the south and Galilee on the north. The city of Samaria stood on a hill "rising abruptly from the bosom of a beautiful valley to a height of some four hundred feet, and surrounded by a circle of hills still higher, except partially on the west." Its central position "made it admirably adapted for a place of *observation*, and a fortress to awe the neighboring country. And the singular beauty of the spot, upon which, to this

6 But go rather to the lost sheep of the house of Israel.

7 And as ye go, preach, saying, The kingdom of heaven is at hand.

8 Heal the sick, cleanse the lepers, raise the dead, cast out devils: freely ye have received, freely give.

9 Provide neither gold, nor silver, nor brass in your purses;

10 Nor scrip for *your* jour-

---

hour, travellers dwell with admiration, may have struck Omri, as it afterward struck the tasteful Idumean." The city was built by Omri, King of Israel, who named it Samaria after the name of the owner, *Shemer,* of whom Omri bought the hill for two talents of silver. 1 Kings 16: 23, 24. On a tablet which Mr. Layard rescued from the ruins of Nineveh was found the name Beth Omri, which means House of Omri, a method of designating this very city.

Samaritans—Whether the Samaritans in the time of Christ were wholly of heathen origin, or whether they were a mixed race, partly Jewish and partly heathen, it would appear to be certain that at first they were all heathen; for in the year 721 B.C. the inhabitants of Samaria and the adjacent cities were carried away captive into Assyria, and their places were filled with "men from Babylon, and from Cuthah, and from Ava, and from Hamath, and from Sepharvaim." Concerning the character of the Samaritans and the relation existing between them and the Jews, see note on John 4: 9, 20. Neither of the prohibitions contained in this verse arose from the national prejudices against Samaritans and Gentiles so common among the Jews; for Jesus ever showed perfect freedom from national prejudices; but it arose, doubtless, from knowledge that his kingdom would spread more rapidly both among Jews and others by beginning with Jews. The prohibition was soon removed, and the largest liberty was granted in preaching the gospel of the kingdom. Ye shall be witnesses unto me, both in Jerusalem, and in all Judea, *and in Samaria, unto the uttermost part of the earth.* Acts 1: 8.

6. *Lost sheep* (9: 36)—Sinners of the nation of Israel. "All sinners," says a volume of Notes intended for the people, "are like lost sheep, as being cared for and sought after by appointment of Christ. But such of them as have been baptized and have come into this outward covenant relation are more especially like the lost sheep of the house of Israel." The notion that my child is any the less sought as a lost sheep by the good Shepherd, because he was not baptized in infancy, is without scriptural sanction. Infant baptism brings no one into nearer relation to God.

7. *Preach, The kingdom . . . is at hand*—How much ampler and richer the message which they were afterward authorized to deliver! This message was preparatory to that. The time had not quite come for preaching distinctly that Jesus is the Messiah. *Kingdom of heaven*—See note on 3: 2.

8. They were to prove the truth of their message by miracles, but they were *to sell* neither miraculous power nor truth. The mercenary spirit of Simon Magus and the noble obedience of Peter to this item of his Lord's instructions are recorded in Acts 8: 18, 20.

9, 10. He now speaks of their equipment. *Purses*—Girdles. See note on 3: 4. "They were used as pockets, as among the Arabs still, and as purses, one end of the girdle being folded back for the purpose." *Gold, silver, brass*—The different

RUINS OF SAMARIA.

ney, neither two coats, neither shoes, nor yet staves: for the workman is worthy of his meat.

---

kinds of current money. By brass was meant, not as with us a compound of copper and zinc, with which the ancients were not probably acquainted, but copper and tin. *Scrip*—A bag carried by shepherds and travellers, and slung over the back. The English word implies the *scraping* together of things. *Two coats,* etc.—The spirit of these directions has been better expressed, we think, by Dr. Thomson, than by any other writer. "The entire 'outfit' of these first missionaries shows that they were plain fishermen, farmers, or shepherds; and to such men there was no extraordinary self-denial in the matter or the mode of their mission. We may expound the 'instructions' given to these primitive evangelists somewhat after the following manner: Provide neither silver, nor gold, nor brass in your purses. You are going to your brethren in the neighboring villages, and the best way to get to their hearts and their confidence is to throw yourselves upon their hospitality. Nor was there any departure from the simple manners of the country in this. At this day the farmer sets out on excursions quite as extensive, without a para in his purse; and the modern Moslem prophet of Tarshīha thus sends forth his apostles over this identical region. Neither do they encumber themselves with two coats. They are accustomed to sleep in the garments they have on during the day, and in this climate such plain people experience no inconvenience from it. They wear a coarse shoe, answering to the sandal of the ancients, but never take two pair of them; and although the staff is an invariable companion of all wayfarers, they are content with *one.* Of course such 'instructions' can have only a general application to those who go forth, not to neighbors of the same faith and nation, but to distant climes and to heathen tribes, and under conditions wholly diverse from those of the fishermen of Galilee; but there are general principles involved or implied which should always be kept in mind by those who seek to carry the gospel to the masses of mankind either at home or abroad."

Neither shoes, nor yet staves—Mark (6:8) says, Take nothing *save a staff* only, and *be shod with sandals. Staff* is the translation of the true reading in Matthew, and the singular was actually employed in English Bibles before the commonly received version was made. It was a mistake in King James' translators to use the plural. But the substitution of *staff* for *staves* makes the contradiction between Matthew and Mark appear all the greater. The former says, Provide not a staff, and the latter says, Take nothing save a staff. The contradiction is only apparent. The spirit of the entire direction relative to their equipment is this: Make no extra preparation. If you have a staff let that one staff suffice (Mark). If you have none, be not particular to provide even one (Matt.); or, perhaps even Matthew means, Provide no staff in addition to the one you have. Such candor as we show in interpreting uninspired books will save us from regarding such little variations as evidence against the veracity of the evangelists. As to the shoes or sandals, they were not to be so wanting in faith as to provide themselves with an extra pair. For proof, however, that these directions were not intended to be of permanent obligation, see Luke 22: 35, 36. *Worthy of his meat*—Of his living, whatever is necessary to support life. They were to go with entire conviction that the general principle which prevails under the divine government, that he who works shall not want

11 And into whatsoever city or town ye shall enter, inquire who in it is worthy; and there abide till ye go thence.

12 And when ye come into a house, salute it.

13 And if the house be worthy, let your peace come upon it: but if it be not worthy, let your peace return to you.

14 And whosoever shall not receive you, nor hear your words, when ye depart out of that house or city, shake off the dust of your feet.

15 Verily I say unto you, It shall be more tolerable for the land of Sodom and Gomorrah in the day of judgment, than for that city.

---

bread, will hold good in their own case.

11. *Who in it is worthy*—Here is reference not to personal merit, but to readiness to receive them as teachers of religion. Devout, spiritual Jews, who were waiting for the kingdom of God, were to be sought as promising more success in their mission, and as likely to afford them a better temporary home as a centre of operations. Spiritual ministers seek spiritual people. Families where Christ would not be welcome are not likely to be fond of entertaining Christ's servants. *There abide*—Luke says, Go not from house to house. "The reason is very obvious to one acquainted with oriental customs. When a stranger arrives in a village or an encampment, the neighbors, one after another, must invite him to eat with them. . . . It also consumes much time, causes unusual distraction of mind, leads to levity, and every way counteracts the success of a spiritual mission." —*Thomson*.

12, 13. *Salute it*—See note on 5: 47, second paragraph. Religion does not forbid the common courtesies of life. Christians should have such kindness of spirit as shall make them observant of all the reasonable forms of society, and ministers pre-eminently so. The salutation is not to depend on the worthiness of the house. That largeness of heart which characterizes intelligent piety is superior to the little petty conventionalities of life. If the family show no sympathy with their heavenly mission, and so would find their presence positively unpleasant, they are to withdraw their salutation, that is, themselves.

14. *Shake off the dust*—See Acts 13: 51. It was an expressive symbolic act, equivalent to saying, You are so utterly polluted that we cannot allow a particle of your dust to cleave to us. We can have no association with you. By the same kind of act, the stricter Jews expressed their non-fellowship with Gentiles whenever they passed from a heathen territory into Palestine. For an instance of shaking dust from the "raiment," see Acts 18: 6.

15. The punishment which rejecters of the gospel shall receive is here very forcibly expressed by reference to the fate of Sodom and Gomorrah. It was formerly held that the Dead Sea was formed at the time of the overthrow of these cities. But it is now seen that there is nothing in the Bible that justifies the opinion, and much in the results of an examination of the entire valley of the Dead Sea and of the River Jordan to make its continued acceptance impossible. Dr. Robinson holds that "a lake must have existed where the Dead Sea now lies, into which the Jordan poured its waters long before the catastrophe of Sodom." It has recently been argued that the Old Testament

16 ¶ Behold, I send you forth as sheep in the midst of wolves: be ye therefore wise as serpents, and harmless as doves.
17 But beware of men: for

"seems" to require us to locate Sodom on the north of the Dead Sea, though the same writer admits that "the long-continued tradition and the names of existing spots seem to pronounce with almost equal positiveness that it was at its *southern* end." That the southern end, below the peninsula, is the true locality, seems, in the present state of our knowledge, much the more probable. "In what precise manner 'the Lord overthrew the cities' is not clearly indicated in the records either of Scripture or of natural remains. The great difference of level between the bottoms of the northern and the southern ends of the lake, the former being a depth of thirteen hundred, the latter only of thirteen, feet below the surface, confirms the theory that the southern end is of recent formation, and, if so, was submerged at the time of the fall of the cities."—*Stanley.* The cities were not overwhelmed with water but with fire. Their destruction is often referred to in the Scriptures as a very signal illustration of the displeasure of God; but Jesus Christ affirms that the punishment which awaits those who will not receive the message of eternal life, will be a yet more signal manifestation of God's displeasure.

In the day of judgment—For evidence that Jesus refers to punishment after the death of the body, see 25: 31-46; John 5: 28, 29. It is appointed unto men once to die, but *after this the judgment.* Heb. 9: 27. See also 1 Cor. 5: 10. As remarked by Dr. Bartlett, after quoting these and many other passages: "If these do not show that at the last day, the day of final judgment, the day of Christ's coming in glory, all the wicked as well as the good will stand before him in conscious activity to receive public sentence, nothing can show it." The application of the passage before us to the destruction of Jerusalem is in violation of all just principles of interpretation. Jesus preached a day of judgment: the world still needs to hear it preached.

16. The Lord proceeds to apprise them of the persecutions which they will suffer through their entire term of service, and to exhort them to bear all with fortitude. *I send*— When Christ sends, fear may well be dismissed. *In the midst*—Not *into*, for they are already among wolves. Christ never apologized for the spirit of persecution. With him, a persecutor is a wolf. The bodies which have persecuted for religious opinion's sake are churches only in name. The church of Christ is to be sought elsewhere. Their exposure to persecution is a reason why they should be *wise as serpents.* The serpent does not seem to *us* to be distinguished for sagacity, but that the ancients and many in all past ages have taken this view of the reptile is certain. The apostles must show wisdom in not needlessly exposing the infant cause to persecution, and in doing the best thing possible for it when persecution shall arise. *Harmless as doves*—Simple as doves, that is, free "from all taint of evil." The writer has heard the objection that when these birds fight, they fight with terrible fury. Very likely, for what is done rarely may be done all the more vigorously. Yet the dove is constitutionally gentle, meek, pure, or it could not have been regarded by the ancients as the symbol of these qualities in others. In Syria it was "so venerated as to be regarded as holy, and

they will deliver you up to the councils, and they will scourge you in their synagogues;

18 And ye shall be brought before governors and kings for my sake, for a testimony against them and the Gentiles.

19 But when they deliver you up, take no thought how or what ye shall speak: for it shall be given you in that same hour what ye shall speak.

20 For it is not ye that speak, but the Spirit of your Father which speaketh in you.

21 And the brother shall

---

forbidden as an article of food." The two qualities here enjoined upon the apostles, and by inference to be regarded as required of all ministers of the word, are not necessarily contrary, yet are very difficult of realization in the same person. They have been seen in perfect combination only in Christ. They were largely developed in Fenelon. The wisdom of the serpent without the simplicity of the dove makes one crafty, as the "old" serpent was; the simplicity of the dove without the wisdom of the serpent makes one weak, as Eve at last was. God *gave* both qualities to Eve, but she lost her simplicity. But I fear, lest by any means, *as the serpent beguiled Eve through his subtlety*, so your minds should be corrupted *from the simplicity that is in Christ*. 2 Cor. 11: 3. The unity of character resulting from the combination of both qualities may be considered as partly constitutional, but it is chiefly the result of a divine operation upon the heart. It is not so much intellectual as moral.

17, 18. *Beware of men*—A strange, yet most needful warning. Children of your Father, yet beware of them. *Councils*—"The lesser courts, of which there were two at Jerusalem, and one in each town of Palestine." *Synagogues*—See on 4: 23. The officers of the synagogue had judicial power, not so great as that of the higher courts, but sufficient to allow them to order scourging,—a strange act for such a place, and a punishment, which, for religious opinions, was not required by the law. It is less strange that Jews, eighteen centuries ago, were intolerant, than that some nominal Christians of the nineteenth century are. *Governors*—Roman officers serving in Palestine, called Proconsuls, Pro-prætors, Procurators; or, rulers in general, wherever their administration might be. *Testimony against*—Testimony *to*, that is, to them on behalf of the truth. The meaning is not, against their unbelief, though that would be an indirect result of their testifying. As they had already been told not to go to the Gentiles, Jesus here refers to the future enlargement of their mission, not to this first brief service. Persecution gives power to an infant cause, but no thanks for it are due to the persecutors. Persecuted ministers and missionaries of more recent times are in honorable company. *Blessed* are ye when men shall persecute you.

19, 20. *No thought how or what*—This is a prohibition, not of all previous reflection, but of all anxiety. Anxiety would prove that they are distrusting God. Help will be given them from above. This is a promise that when they are in such circumstances as are here named, they shall receive special inspiration to speak aright. It is no proof that even the apostles were to attempt to preach with no preparation. How much less does it prove that

CHAPTER X.

deliver up the brother to death, and the father the child: and the children shall rise up against *their* parents, and cause them to be put to death.

22 And ye shall be hated of all *men* for my name's sake: but he that endureth to the end shall be saved.

23 But when they persecute you in this city, flee ye into another: for verily I say unto you, Ye shall not have gone over the cities of Israel, till the Son of man be come.

24 The disciple is not above *his* master, nor the servant above his lord.

25 It is enough for the dis-

---

others may do so! In 1 Tim. 4: 13, 14, Paul says, Till I come, *give attendance to reading*, to exhortation, to doctrine. *Neglect not the gift which is in thee. . . . Meditate upon these things; give thyself wholly to them; that thy profiting may appear to all.*

21, 22. Drop the articles in vs. 21, as the Greek permits, and the description will be more forcible: Brother will deliver up brother, and father child, and children will rise up against parents. It is a twofold truth that love to Christ and hatred of Christ are stronger than the strongest earthly ties. The history of the Christian religion yields many illustrations of it. *Hated of all men* —Men either love Christ or hate him. Those that hate *him* hate those that love him. *All* who hate Christ will hate them. Not all who do not love Christ are *conscious* of hating him, and not all who hate him hate him in the same degree. But all who do not love him are, in a very criminal sense, *against* him, and may, therefore, come at any time into a state of *conscious* hatred. *Endureth to the end*—Holds out in his discipleship till his trials are over. It is a comprehensive expression, and may, therefore, refer to trials that might come upon them in the siege of Jerusalem, or to any other trials even to the close of life. Observe that he who shall endure to the end will thereby prove that Christ had given him the true (the eternal) life, and that he that shall not endure to the end will thereby prove that he had not been made alive.

23. *Flee*—Not under the motive of self-interest. That is not the kind of virtue which Jesus teaches. The direction has reference not to mere personal safety, but to the more rapid success of his cause; and he solemnly assures them that they shall have room enough to work in, and will scarcely have accomplished all when the Son of man shall have come. *Till the Son of man be come*— Some (Barnes) say, in the destruction of Jerusalem; others (Dr. Whedon), at Christ's resurrection; others, in the scenes of the Pentecost; others, at the end of the world. We incline to the first, but feel by no means certain that that expresses the Lord's meaning. *Son of man*— See note on 12: 6-8, second paragraph.

Courting martyrdom, as was done by some in the early part of the fourth century, is here virtually condemned. "It behooves us," said Origen, born 185 A.D., "neither at all times to avoid danger, nor at all times to meet it. But it needs the wisdom of the Christian philosopher to examine and decide what times require that one should withdraw himself, and what that he should stand fast, ready for the conflict, without withdrawing himself, and still more without fleeing."

24, 25. The first of these verses is a proverb, used by Jewish Rabbis. *Beelzebub*—A god worshipped by the Philistines. A king of Israel, who

ciple that he be as his master, and the servant as his lord. If they have called the master of the house Beelzebub, how much more *shall they call* them of his household?

26 Fear them not therefore: for there is nothing covered. that shall not be revealed; and hid, that shall not be known.

27 What I tell you in darkness, *that* speak ye in light: and what ye hear in the ear, *that* preach ye upon the housetops.

28 And fear not them which kill the body, but are not able to kill the soul: but rather fear him which is able to destroy both soul and body in hell.

---

met with an accident, sent to this god to inquire whether he should recover. 2 Kings 1: 2. The deity is supposed to have been so named as protector of the people against flies. Baal means *lord*, the whole name, *lord of flies*, or *fly-god*. But the true reading is *Beelzebul*. Some have suggested that *b* was changed into *l* to make the sound more agreeable to the ear. It is *possible* that the change was accidental. But it seems probable that the Jews changed the spelling so as to express more fully their dislike of idolatry, Beelzebul meaning, as is probable, *lord of the dunghill*. *Master of the house*—Head of the family, —a beautiful appellation as applied by Christ to himself. All who accept him as their Saviour are members of his family. How bitter and contemptuous the spirit that could have surnamed such a being as Jesus Christ, *Lord of the Dunghill!* But Theodore Parker shows quite as contemptuous a spirit toward Christ in the manner in which he speaks of the Lord's Supper. "The Lord's Supper," he says, "I don't like, as it is now administered. It is a heathenish rite, and means very little, I think." He recommends coming together in a parlor and eating, if one likes, curds and cream and baked apples.

26, 27. He encourages them still further. *Nothing covered*, etc., *may* refer, as the words elsewhere do, to the exposure of hypocrisy, but the two verses may alike refer to the fact that the truths which the Lord has spoken to them privately must be preached by them openly. They must not be deterred by fear of persecution. What he tells them they must preach as publicly as if they should·stand upon the tops of the houses. "Our Lord spent most of his life in villages, and accordingly the reference here is to a custom observed only in such places, never in cities. At the present day local governors in country districts cause their commands thus to be published. Their proclamations are generally made in the evening, after the people have returned from their labors in the field. The public crier ascends the highest roof at hand, and lifts up his voice in a long-drawn call upon all faithful subjects to give ear and obey."—*Thomson*. Our Lord's teachings are light, though given in darkness. Since darkness sometimes speaks boldly, with what courage should light speak always! Timidity in the preacher of truth, especially in an atmosphere infected with rationalism, is a sin and a shame.

28. This verse is one of vast importance, and one in the attempt to expound which Universalism shows special weakness. *And fear not*— Rendering this, as it may be, And be not afraid of, brings out more clearly the contrast between fearing persecutors and fearing God. *Be not afraid of your persecutors . . . but fear God*. A singular but unsupported interpretation of the last

CHAPTER X.

29 Are not two sparrows sold for a farthing? and one of them shall not fall on the ground without your Father.

30 But the very hairs of your head are all numbered.

31 Fear ye not therefore, ye are of more value than many sparrows.

---

member of this verse is that which teaches that the being whom we are exhorted to fear is the devil. But, 1. We are nowhere else exhorted to fear the devil; 2. The devil has no *power* th punish in hell, but equally with all who serve him is in God's power; 3. James (4 : 12) says, There is *one lawgiver, who is able to save, and to destroy.* This teaches that God is the only dispenser of life and death. *To destroy*—Not, *to annihilate.* See remarks upon the word *destruction* in the notes on 7 : 13, 14. Observe that it is both *body and soul* that God is able to destroy. Representing God as raising up the body after it has been dead for untold ages only for the purpose of immediately annihilating it, is making God too much like boys that build only for the sake of overturning. The soul is destroyed, not by losing its existence, but by being punished, and punishment in non-existence is impossible. Therefore annihilation is a lie. It may be added that *Apollyon*, in Rev. 9 : 11 ("the angel of the bottomless pit"), is derived from the Greek word meaning *to destroy.* It would be singular if Destruction himself has nobody to reign over in the bottomless pit! *The soul*—This is expressly distinguished by our Lord from *the body.* The body may be killed, while the soul may remain untouched. Therefore materialism is a lie. *In hell*—See the second and third paragraphs in the notes on 5 : 22.

29–31. He still further strengthens their faith by reminding them of God's universal and therefore particular providence, selecting the sparrow as an illustration. *Sparrows* are still very abundant in Palestine, one hundred species having already been observed. The English Tree Sparrow is often seen in and about Jerusalem. "At the present day the markets of Jerusalem and Jaffa are attended by many 'fowlers' who offer for sale long strings of little birds of various species, chiefly sparrows, wagtails, and larks. . . . It may well excite surprise how such vast numbers can be taken, and how they can be vended at a price too small to have purchased the powder required for shooting them. But the gun is never used in their pursuit. The ancient methods of fowling to which we find so many allusions in the Scriptures are still pursued, and, though simple, are none the less effective." *A farthing*—About one cent and a half. Not one of *these* birds, so insignificant, falls on the ground, that is, to perish, without *your Father.* To explain the last two words as *your Father's notice,* is cold; and besides, the argument in that case would minister little comfort to the disciples. If they are here apprised that they may perish by the hand of persecution, they certainly can find very little support in the mere fact that they shall not perish without being seen by their Father. God's oversight is not withdrawn when the sparrow perishes. It perishes in accordance with God's will. God is as truly the superintendent of the sparrow in its dying as he was in its living. But *they* are worth so much more than many sparrows that even the hairs of their head are all numbered; that is, God's government extends over them in all the *minutest particulars* of life. They should go forth to their work, therefore, without fear.   5 : 31.

32 Whosoever therefore shall confess me before men, him will I confess also before my Father which is in heaven.

33 But whosoever shall deny me before men, him will I also deny before my Father which is in heaven.

34 Think not that I am come to send peace on earth: I came not to send peace, but a sword.

35 For I am come to set a man at variance against his father, and the daughter against her mother, and the daughter-in-law against her mother-in-law.

36 And a man's foes *shall be* they of his own household.

37 He that loveth father or mother more than me is not worthy of me: and he that loveth son or daughter more than me is not worthy of me.

38 And he that taketh not his cross, and followeth after me, is not worthy of me.

The spirit of these beautiful directions should be appropriated by pastors of the present times, in the more formal relations which they sustain to churches and incorporated societies.

32, 33. Another reason why they should be courageous in their work. *Whosoever*—Not the apostles only. "'He will not confess the confessing Judas, nor deny the denying Peter,' because the confession of the former was hypocritical, the denial of the latter a transient weakness, followed immediately by the deepest repentance." *Shall confess*—Not a mere oral act, though that is included, but a life of continual faith and service.

34-36. Jesus guards them against that timidity and against that compromise of the truth which might spring from seeing division arise from their labors. They must go forth to their work with the distinct understanding that their Master came into the world for the very purpose of breaking up the wretched union of men in sin— even of parents and children. Compare these verses with vs. 21. That puts forward the active hostility of unbelievers against believers; this the necessary opposition of believers to unbelievers. The hostility of unbelievers will be the *result* of the truth preached. The necessary opposition of believers was purposed. *I am come to set a man against.* Had the apostles not set men at variance with men, one of two things would be certain: either that all men immediately received Christ, or, that the message which had been preached was not the truth. *The daughter-in-law*—A bride. There is a kind of preaching that keeps men peaceful in sin. A church should not be alarmed at the mere fact that the preaching of its pastor stirs up hatred.

37. *Loveth...mother more than me* —What audacity of presumption if Christ was not more than human! How could the holiest angelic spirit have dared to bring himself into such rivalry of love with one who, as nature teaches, should be loved more than all other created beings? One of such purity and modesty never could have made such a demand unless conscious of *uncreated* excellence.

38. *His cross*—A plain allusion to the manner of his own death, which, however, the disciples themselves could not then have perceived, though not ignorant of crucifixion as a method of punishment, or of the fact that many of those condemned to suffer it were compelled to carry their own cross. The only Christ that we are to follow is one who first bore the cross, and was then borne by it. Following such a one is being crucified with him.

CHAPTER X.

39 He that findeth his life shall lose it: and he that loseth his life for my sake shall find it.

40 ¶ He that receiveth you receiveth me: and he that receiveth me receiveth him that sent me.

41 He that receiveth a prophet in the name of a prophet shall receive a prophet's reward: and he that receiveth a righteous man in the name of a righteous man shall receive a righteous man's reward.

42 And whosoever shall give to drink unto one of these little ones a cup of cold *water* only

---

39. *Findeth . . . shall lose: loseth . . . shall find*—It is clear that this is one of the cases in which the same word is used, in the same sentence, in different senses. Let the *dead* bury their *dead* is another instance. So also in John 3: 8. The *wind* bloweth where it listeth: . . . so is every one that is born of the *Spirit*. Here the same Greek word is used where our common version very properly uses the two words *wind* and *spirit*. So in the verse before us, *life*, and *it* which stands for life, cannot both refer to life in the same sense; for it is not true that he who loses natural life for Christ will find natural life. Natural life ends with the death of the body. The meaning may be expressed thus: He that finds his physical life shall lose spiritual life; and he that loses his physical life shall find spiritual life. It may be more fully expressed thus: He that attempts to preserve his natural life, avoiding all possible exposure in my cause for the sake of the worldly good that he imagines to be embraced in the continuance of his physical life, shall lose true spiritual life in the world to come. On the other hand, he who, willingly exposing his natural life in my cause, loses it, will find true spiritual life in the next world. Dr. Bartlett well expresses it thus: He who will lose his life in a lower sense for Christ shall save it in the highest sense conceivable.

40. *Receiveth you*—Not into his house merely, not, necessarily, into it at all. That might be done and nothing more. He must receive them as messengers of Christ, not merely as neighbors or as men. If he receives them as Christ's messengers, he will receive the message, all the message. If he receives the message, he will yield himself to its influence. In receiving Christ it is impossible not to receive the Father also. He who thinks he trusts in God, while not receiving Christ and not receiving Christ's messengers, is lying under a fearful and fatal mistake.

41. This verse is an extension of the general principle expressed in the preceding verse. To receive a prophet (a religious teacher) in the name of a prophet is to receive him because he is a prophet; that is, from regard to his work. That must be the motive. *A prophet's reward*—Will prove himself to be so united in spirit with the prophet that he shall obtain bliss similar to that of the prophet himself. The same explanation must be made of the latter part of the verse, only it must be borne in mind that by righteous man is meant any Christian man in more private life.

42. *These*—Probably pointing to them. *Little ones*—Disciples. Whoever does the smallest favor, represented by a cup of cold water, to a disciple of Christ, and does it because he is Christ's disciple, implying of course that the doer is himself a disciple, shall not lose his reward. *His reward*—That which, in accordance with God's gracious

in the name of a disciple, verily I say unto you, he shall in no wise lose his reward.

CHAPTER XI.

AND it came to pass, when Jesus had made an end of commanding his twelve disciples, he departed thence to teach and to preach in their cities.

2 Now when John had heard in the prison the works of Christ, he sent two of his disciples,

3 And said unto him, Art thou he that should come, or do we look for another?

4 Jesus answered and said

---

and sovereign purpose, will be appropriately his. It would be a mistake to regard the act as meritorious ground of justification.

CHAPTER XI.

A MESSAGE FROM JOHN; THE LORD'S OPINION OF JOHN.

781 U. C. Midsummer, A.D. 28.

1. *And it came to pass when*—It has been already stated that Matthew does not report all the events of our Lord's life in the order of time. It should be noticed accordingly that the date placed at the head of this chapter is earlier than the date of the chapter preceding. *He departed thence*—It is impossible to determine the point of departure. *Their cities*—Cities in the southeastern part of Galilee. "The Lord gives himself no rest, but enters immediately upon new labors."

2. John's imprisonment is judged by Andrews to have occurred in March, the year of Rome 781, A.D. 28, and this message to have been sent to Jesus in the following midsummer. According to Josephus, the place of John's confinement was the castle of Machaerus, which was on the eastern side of the Dead Sea, a long distance from the region in which Jesus was then laboring, but the evangelists are silent respecting the question of location. *Had heard in prison*—How? *And all the disciples of John showed him* of all these things. Luke 7: 18. Reports of Christ's miracles and discourses reached the ears of the Baptist in spite of the lustful tyrant.

3. *He that should come*—The Coming One,—a phrase by which Old Testament writers designated the expected Messiah. See Ps. 40: 7; 118: 26. The sense is, Art thou The Coming One, that is, the Messiah, of whom the prophets wrote? or, are we to look for another? This is no evidence of doubt that Jesus was a being of wonderful excellence, that he had wrought miracles, or even that he was a real messenger from God. Is it evidence of doubt that Jesus was the Messiah? is a question concerning which even the most distinguished interpreters are not agreed. It seems to the writer of these notes that John should by no means be regarded as in a state of painful doubt, but *as desirous to receive some strengthening word from Christ*. What he had already heard from the lips of his own disciples must have brought him fresh life in the prison of Machaerus, and this very report of what they had seen must have created a desire to hear from Jesus himself. This explanation runs clear of two extremes: the one, that the message was sent only with reference to John's disciples; the other, that John was "in danger of being offended at him," that "it was prompted by doubt and disappointment about Christ's conduct."

4, 5. *Shew again*—Report. *Again*

CHAPTER XI.

unto them, Go and shew John again those things which ye do hear and see:

5 The blind receive their sight, and the lame walk, the lepers are cleansed, and the deaf hear, the dead are raised up, and the poor have the gospel preached to them.

6 And blessed is *he*, whosoever shall not be offended in me.

7 ¶ And as they departed, Jesus began to say unto the multitudes concerning John, What went ye out into the wilderness to see? A reed shaken with the wind?

8 But what went ye out for to see? A man clothed in soft

---

conveys a wrong impression. The original makes no allusion to a *second* time. According to Luke (7: 21), Jesus, before the very eyes of John's disciples, cured many of their infirmities and plagues, of evil spirits and blindness. *The dead are raised*—He had raised the daughter of Jairus, and (Luke 7: 11-15) the son of the widow of Nain. Jesus does not say even now that he is the Messiah, but the messengers are to tell John what they have seen and heard. As John is familiar with the prophecy of Isaiah (61: 1) in which these things are mentioned as characteristic of the Messiah, he will have received from Christ the strengthening word which he sought.

6. *Shall not be offended in*—Shall not take offence at, in consequence of finding that I am different from the ideal Messiah whom he has been expecting. Why should this be considered, as it is by so many, a reproof of John? Is the supposition consistent with the character given him in vv. 7-11? It may have been intended chiefly for the disciples who were listening,—both John's and his own. He that stumbles at Christ loses Christ's blessing. Stumbling at Christ's supernatural origin and atoning death is stumbling at Christ himself.

7. Not to save John's personal reputation with the people, but to exalt John's mission, our Lord proceeds to speak of John's character and relation to himself. *A reed*— One kind of reed, not now growing in Egypt, but found in Syria, is the papyrus, which, before parchment came into use, was used for writing paper. "Dr. Hooker saw it on the banks of Lake Tiberias, a few miles north of the town. . . . The papyrus plant has an angular stem from three to six feet high, though occasionally it grows to the height of fourteen feet; it has no leaves; the flowers are in very small spikelets, which grow on the thread-like flowering branchlets which form a bushy crown to each stem; it is found in stagnant pools as well as in running streams, in which latter case, according to Bruce, one of its angles is always opposed to the current of the stream." It is not certain that this is the reed which grew in the region where John had baptized, as it is well known that there were several species. *Shaken with (by) the wind*—Either a man of no account, like the reeds that grew on the banks of the Jordan, or a man of vacillating will.

8. The Lord ascends a step higher. Supposing them to have gone to see, not a reed, but a man, did they go to see one of luxurious style of living? *Soft raiment*—Garments of the finer, more expensive material. It stands for what would be likely to characterize persons of wealth or elevated position. He means to say that the man whom they went to see was not one of the sort that is commonly found in kings' courts. Luxury leads to levity; simplicity to sobriety. Christian

raiment? behold, they that wear soft *clothing* are in kings' houses.

9 But what went ye out for to see? A prophet? yea, I say unto you, and more than a prophet.

10 For this is *he*, of whom it is written, Behold, I send my messenger before thy face, which shall prepare thy way before thee.

11 Verily I say unto you, Among them that are born of women there hath not risen a greater than John the Baptist: notwithstanding, he that is least in the kingdom of heaven is greater than he.

12 And from the days of John the Baptist until now the kingdom of heaven suffereth violence, and the violent take it by force.

---

self-denial, however, has had in many ages of the Christian era some remarkable illustrations in court-life.

9, 10. The third illustration is another step in advance. Did they go to see a prophet? *More than a prophet*—More than "the evangelical prophet" Isaiah, because acting in the character of a forerunner of the Messiah. Jesus does not say that *they* considered John as more than a prophet, but that he whom they went out to see *is* more than a prophet. In fact they had failed to understand John's true position. Our Lord quotes from Mal. 3: 1. He must have had more than human or even angelic familiarity of acquaintance with the Father to have presumed to appropriate those words to himself.

11. *Verily* shows, as elsewhere, his conviction of the certainty of what he affirms. *Hath not risen a greater*—Jesus here takes the *fourth* step in his method of bringing out John's official relation to himself. He is equal to the greatest of mankind, for he is my forerunner; which cannot be said of any other man. Though he is in the old dispensation, he is the last, and stands, therefore, next to me. But to be in the old dispensation is not equal to being in the new. Why not? Because the new is that to which by divine ordination the old looks. The new is the completion of the old.

He that is in the new is, *in his relations* to me, greater than John. John came to herald the coming of the kingdom of which, when come, my disciples are actual members. It is, then, a comparison *of states in this world*, not of character, or of destiny. When Herod had taken off this bold reprover's head, John was himself in the kingdom of heaven in its (to him) completed form, and therefore became greater than the greatest of Christ's disciples in the kingdom of heaven in its incompleted form in the world.

We cannot hold with some that Jesus intends to institute a comparison between John as born of a woman and others who are born of God. John was as truly born of God as Matthew. The remark of Dr. Whedon, in his Commentary, that one who is truly *in* the kingdom of God is "*above making such a mistake as poor John . . . committed*," is hardly justified by the Lord's representation of his character.

12, 13. These verses seem intended still to exalt John by comparing his work with that of the prophets. The prophets and the law, that is, the writers of the law, did little more than to announce beforehand in one way or another what had recently been taking place. *From the days*—Including the time in which John preached. *Until now*—Not excluding the time to come, even to the end of the new dispen-

CHAPTER XI.

13 For all the prophets and the law prophesied until John.
14 And if ye will receive *it*, this is Elias, which was for to come.
15 He that hath ears to hear, let him hear.
16 ¶ But whereunto shall I liken this generation? It is like unto children sitting in the markets, and calling unto their fellows,
17 And saying, We have piped unto you, and ye have not danced; we have mourned unto you, and ye have not lamented.
18 For John came neither

---

sation. All the time in which John preached was characterized for the intensity of interest with which men rushed to hear the word and toward the open door of the kingdom of God. It is not implied that all who rushed toward the door succeeded in entering it. The view which makes our Lord represent men as committing the "mistake" of trying "to hurry, violently, the kingdom into a premature existence" (Dr. Whedon), is based upon the view, untenable, we think, that John had been guilty of a similar "mistake" in sending the messengers to Jesus. It is not the generally received explanation.

14, 15. *If ye will receive it*, implies that the hearers had not yet come to a cordial recognition of the truth that John was the personage whose coming was foretold by Malachi (4:5) under the name of Elias (Elijah): Behold, *I will send you Elijah the prophet* before the coming of the great and dreadful day of the Lord. *Elijah* "has well been entitled 'the grandest and the most romantic character that Israel ever produced.' Certainly there is no personage in the Old Testament whose career is more vividly portrayed, or who exercises on us a more remarkable fascination. His rare, sudden and brief appearances; his undaunted courage and fiery zeal; the brilliancy of his triumphs; the pathos of his despondency; the glory of his departure, and the calm beauty of his reappearance on the Mount of Transfiguration,—throw such a halo of brightness around him as is equalled by none of his compeers in the sacred story." It was believed by many of the Jews that Elijah would reappear for the relief of the nation, and indeed "he is recorded as having often appeared to the wise and good Rabbis,—at prayer in the wilderness, or on their journeys,—generally in the form of an Arabian merchant. At the circumcision of a child, a seat was always placed for him, that, as the zealous champion and messenger of the 'covenant' of circumcision, he might watch over the due performance of the rite. During certain prayers the door of the house was set open that Elijah might enter and announce the Messiah.... So firm was the conviction of his speedy arrival, that when goods were found and no owner appeared to claim them, the common saying was, 'Put them by till Elijah comes.'" At the feast of unleavened bread, as observed by the modern Jews, "A cup of wine is poured out for him, and stands all night upon the table. Just before the filling of the cups of the guests the fourth time, there is an interval of dead silence, and the door of the room is opened for some minutes to admit the prophet." See Matt. 16:14; 17: 3, 4; 27:47; John 1:21. The resemblance between John and Elijah is very striking. *Ears to hear*—One of our Lord's solemn methods of calling attention.

16-19. The general meaning is plain; that the generation of that

eating nor drinking, and they say, He hath a devil.

19 The Son of man came eating and drinking, and they say, Behold a man gluttonous, and a wine-bibber, a friend of publicans and sinners. But wisdom is justified of her children.

20 ¶ Then began he to upbraid the cities wherein most of his mighty works were done, because they repented not:

21 Woe unto thee Chorazin!

---

day was indisposed to accept wisdom (vs. 19) as preached by either of the great teachers whom God had sent. It was pleased with neither John nor Jesus, though in some respects so unlike. John could not be accused of going to marriage festivals or to dinner-parties: he was abstemious, taught his disciples to fast, was plain in his apparel, was strict in his method. But they said he was possessed. Jesus was gentle and compassionate (vv. 28, 29). He conformed, so far as they were innocent, to the usages of social life. But they said he was a glutton and a wine-bibber, and took persons of the lowest moral character as his associates. Thus far all is plain, but the details of the similitude which Jesus employs have given to many considerable difficulty.

To illustrate the fault-finding spirit of that generation, Jesus uses the fact that the children of those days *played wedding and funeral*. They divided themselves into two parties. Some *piped*, played the flute, and the others were expected to dance, but would not. They did not like to play wedding. So the players proposed to play funeral, and fell to *mourning;* singing dirges. That pleased the other children no better. They would not *lament*—Beat the breast,—the common sign of sorrow. It was attempted to carry on these plays in the *market*—public places where the people were accustomed to gather for talking, or for buying and selling. The playing or speaking children represent John and Jesus; the complaining children, that generation. There is an apparent contradiction between these verses and vs. 12, for that says that people are rushing toward the kingdom; this, that people have resisted the teachings both of John and Jesus. That, however, refers to the people, this rather to the scribes and Pharisees; for it was these, chiefly, who were severe in their style of talking concerning the two teachers. It has never been easy for the Lord's disciples to satisfy the world, provided they live so as to satisfy Christ. "Radical" criticism is uncandid. Had the doctrine of Jesus flattered men more, Jesus himself would have been persecuted less.

Wisdom justified, etc.—Wisdom is here personified, as it is in Proverbs. *Her children*—The wise. The wise justifying their mother is equivalent to this: The wise prove by their conduct that what comes from heaven professing to be wisdom is wisdom.

20. *To upbraid*—To reprove with mingled grief and anger at their continued impenitence. *Mighty works*—Miracles. *The cities*—The people of the cities. He speaks of the rejection of his claims by *individuals*. Some who would be unwilling to be considered rationalists are accustomed to speak of miracles, however genuine, as of little value as an evidence of the Saviour's authority to teach. Jesus, as is here seen, regarded them in a different light. He upbraided the cities, because they did not repent under the evidence coming from his miracles. The miracles are a strong evidence even for those who know them only by report.

CHAPTER XI.

woe unto thee Bethsaida! for if the mighty works, which were done in you, had been done in Tyre and Sidon, they would have repented long ago in sackcloth and ashes.

22 But I say unto you, It shall be more tolerable for Tyre and Sidon at the day of judgment, than for you.

23 And thou, Capernaum, which art exalted unto heaven,

21-24. There is no reason to doubt that these towns were situated on or near the shore of the Lake of Gennesareth, but the exact location has been much in dispute. *Chorazin*—"And here" [two miles from the ruins of Tell Hum, which are on the north side of the lake] "we are among the shapeless heaps of Chorazin, which attest most impressively the fulfilment of that prophetic curse of the Son of God. I have scarcely a doubt about the correctness of the identification, although Dr. Robinson rejects it, almost with contempt. But the name, Khorazy, is nearly the Arabic for Chorazin; the situation—two miles north of Tell Hum—is just where we might expect to find it; the ruins are quite adequate to answer the demands of history; and *there is no rival site.*"—*Thomson.* "Discoveries more recently made have strengthened this presumption from the name and position of *Chorazy.* Mr. Grove, speaking of the excavations by Messrs. Wilson and Anderson, says: 'The ruins of Chorazin at Kerazeh' (so he writes the word) 'turn out to be far more important than was previously suspected; they cover a much larger extent of ground than *Tell Hum*, and many of the private houses are almost perfect, with the exception of the roofs; the openings for doors and windows remaining in some cases. All the buildings, including a synagogue or church [?], are of basalt, and it is not till one is right in among them that one sees clearly what they are; fifty or one hundred yards off they look nothing more than the rough heaps of basaltic stones so common in this country.'"— *Hackett.*

Bethsaida—"Until the discovery by Reland of the fact that there were two places of the name, one on the west and one on the east side, the elucidation of the various occurrences of the two was one of the hardest knots of sacred geography." The Bethsaida in which some of the apostles were born has been located by Dr. Robinson at a spot on the north-western side of the lake, and, as the word means *house of fish*, it is not unlikely that the town lay on the shore. There was another Bethsaida on the eastern side of the river, at the north-eastern extremity of the lake, which was "rebuilt and adorned by Philip the Tetrarch, and raised to the dignity of a town under the name of Julias, after the daughter of the emperor." Dr. Thomson, however, rejects the "*invention* of a second Bethsaida as wholly unnecessary," and says that Reland, "who first started the idea, confesses that he has no authority for it, but merely resorts to it . . . to solve" a difficulty. Dr. Thomson believes the town to have been built on both sides of the Jordan; and Dr. Hackett thinks this supposition might aid in understanding certain statements in the Gospels which have hitherto been attended with much difficulty. *Capernaum*—See note on 4: 13.

Tyre and Sidon—Celebrated ancient cities of Phœnicia Proper, which was "a narrow undulating plain" on the eastern coast of the Mediterranean, "only twenty-eight miles in length, and in average breadth about a mile." Though so small, it long held commanding influence in the world. Its latitude was about the same as that of South Carolina. The two cities were about twenty

shalt be brought down to hell: for if the mighty works, which have been done in thee, had been done in Sodom, it would have remained until this day.

24 But I say unto you, That

---

miles from each other. Tyre was about one hundred and two English miles from Jerusalem. Its government was a monarchy. It was celebrated for its commerce, its wealth, its mechanical arts. Its merchants were "merchant princes." It imported gold from Arabia, silver, iron, lead, and tin from Spain, and copper from districts on the south of the Black Sea. It drew wheat, oil, honey, and balm from Palestine, wine from Damascus, lambs from Arabia, linen from Egypt, ivory and ebony from an island in the Persian Gulf. The religion of Tyre and Sidon was idolatrous. The people were not Jews, but heathen. It was a very wicked city. *Sidon* or *Zidon* means *fishery*. It was celebrated for the skill of its mechanics, and, like Tyre, was long distinguished for its prosperity. Like its southern neighbor, it was given to idolatry. It still exists under the name of Saida. *Sodom*—See note on 10: 15.

Jesus contrasts Capernaum with Sodom, and Chorazin and Bethsaida with Tyre and Sidon. The ancient cities had no such manifestation of the power and the goodness of God as the modern Galilean cities had had in the miracles of Jesus. *Would have repented*—They ought to have repented as it was. Rom. 1: 20. With what sublime independence of all dogmas, whether of theology or philosophy, does Jesus assume the freedom of the human will! *Would have repented! Sackcloth*—" A coarse texture of a dark color, made of goats' hair. It was used, 1. For making sacks; and, 2. For making the rough garments used by mourners, which were in extreme cases worn next the skin." *Ashes* were sprinkled by many of the ancients upon their persons as a sign of mourning. Esther 4: 1; Job 2: 12.

Hell—In 5: 22 is the word *hell* in connection with *fire*. But not the same Greek word is used. There, as we have seen, the word is Gehenna, meaning the place of punishment after death, and is properly translated hell. Here the word is Hades. What does *this* word mean? It is very generally held that it means, not the place of future punishment, but *the world of disembodied human spirits irrespective of character*. If this is its true import, the English word *hell* leads the reader astray. Of those who consider this as its true meaning, some (Dr. Conant and the Revised New Testament of the Bible Union) would render it *underworld;* and others, objecting to that as also tending to lead astray, would not translate it at all, but use the word itself (Hades). The etymological meaning of the term is *invisible*. The original, general notion of the word, therefore, has reference to *the future world as invisible*.

Some are unable to accept, fully, the above view of the word. Prof. N. H. Griffin (Williams College) says:[1] "We do not find, in the Scriptures, a passage which requires the term Hades to be referred to any indiscriminate abode of the dead, other than the grave: there is not a passage which speaks of a righteous man as going to it, or being connected with it. . . . In fact, we know of *no term, of any kind, in the Scriptures, denoting any place, beyond this world, that is common to the righteous and wicked.* They are all distinctive, denoting either a place of happiness or misery." According to Prof. Griffin, the only difference between Gehenna and Hades is, that Gehenna always refers to the future punishment of the wicked, while Hades is also

[1] Bibliotheca Sacra, January, 1856.

CHAPTER XI.

it shall be more tolerable for the land of Sodom, in the day of judgment, than for thee.

25 ¶ At that time Jesus answered and said, I thank thee, O Father, Lord of heaven and earth, because thou hast hid these things from the wise and prudent, and hast revealed them unto babes.

26 Even so, Father; for so it seemed good in thy sight.

---

often used of the grave. Prof. Bartlett takes substantially the same view. Both writers hold that "a sort of heathen mythology has been forced upon the sacred writers," admitting that in heathen classics the idea of an indiscriminate abode of the righteous and wicked as disembodied spirits is found in the term Hades, but denying that Hades is ever so used in the New Testament. "Throughout the New Testament," says Prof. Bartlett, "Hades seems invariably viewed as the enemy of man, and from its alliance with sin and its doom, as hostile to Christ and his church. In many instances, it is with strict propriety translated 'hell.'" In support of the view which they present, both professors quote Luke 16: 23: And in *hell* [Hades, not Gehenna] he lifted up his eyes, being *in torments.* In the passage before us, hell is used as the opposite of heaven.

The day of judgment—Future with respect to Sodom, for *temporal* ruin had fallen upon it long before. *Shall be more tolerable*—Future, then, with respect to Tyre and Sidon. *Would have remained*—Many of the "liberal" thinkers of our times virtually bind all natural laws in the bonds of necessity. The people of Capernaum had more light than the people of Sodom. But we have more light than the people of Capernaum. Our criminality is greater, therefore, than even theirs, if we believe not. The punishment, then, must be greater.

25, 26. *I thank thee*—Not mere thanks, but a thankful confession of the Father's justice and grace. *Because*—That. *Hast hid*—How? "Those," says a Methodist commentator, "who understand by this text that God has from all eternity made salvation impossible to be attained by a fixed part of mankind, wrong divine justice, and abuse our Lord's words." The same writer assumes that "Calvinists and other predestinarians" believe that God's plan predestinates and fixes all the wicked acts of wicked men, and then fixes their damnation for committing those decreed acts. If there is *one* of the thirteen thousand Baptist churches in the United States that has adopted Articles of Faith that teach such a view of God's government, we have yet to learn the fact. Nor are such doctrines taught or held by the Congregational, or the Presbyterian, or the Episcopal churches. *How hid?* Not in any manner that conflicts with the teachings of our Lord, *Ye will not* come to me that ye might have life. *The wise and prudent*—Those who, like the scribes and Pharisees, profess to have great spiritual discernment, but have none. It is also applicable to those who profess to know so much by means of nature, or reason, or "intuition," or "the inner light," or communion with spirits through a "medium," that they need no written revelation. *These things*—The spiritual lessons which are to be derived from the Saviour's words and works. Revealed to whom? To *babes*—That is, the humble, teachable, those who acknowledge their want of wisdom. It would not be just, however, to infer from the Saviour's words that any of our race are naturally, that is, without divine assistance, disposed to receive Christ as their spiritual king. The point of harmony between God's

27 All things are delivered unto me of my Father: and no man knoweth the Son, but the Father; neither knoweth any man the Father, save the Son, and *he* to whomsoever the Son will reveal *him*.

28 ¶ Come unto me, all *ye* that labor and are heavy laden, and I will give you rest.

29 Take my yoke upon you, and learn of me; for I am meek and lowly in heart: and ye shall find rest unto your souls.

---

action upon men in giving them spiritual life and their own free acts always escapes us. God never acts upon men for the purpose of making them sin, but it is matter of fact that God does not reveal the Son by his Spirit to all. Millions of our race have died without knowing Christ even by name. *Seemed good*—Therefore not arbitrary. Whether we can see it or not, God sees good reason for hiding,—they are wise in their own eyes.

27. *All things*—Everything pertaining to the mediatorial kingdom. *Are delivered to me*—It must not be inferred that Christ was not equal with the Father. In *these* words he says nothing whatever concerning his original, essential nature; but speaks only of his relations to the Father in the work of mediation. *That* work belongs peculiarly to the Son, and being so understood by the Father, all the things embraced in that work may be said to have been *delivered by the Father to the Son*. *Knoweth the Son*—His person and work in the deeper sense. *No man* —A peculiarly unfortunate rendering, as if the Father himself were a man. *No one* is correct. *No one* knows the Son *but the Father*. A similar change should be made in the next clause: Neither knoweth *any man* (any one) the Father. The Father knows the Son and the Son the Father in a sense which can never be revealed to any created being whatever; but that knowledge of the Father and of the Son which is possible to men through the Holy Spirit is indefinite in measure and richness. That we cannot know the Father, except through Christ, is a sentiment than which none is more obnoxious to the modern rationalistic philosophy. "The moment," said one of its disciples,[1] "we call ourselves by the name of Christ, we lose, if not the spirit, the true expression, of truth." "Religion," said another, "is the affirmation of the spirit made in the soul of man, —the report which the spirit makes of itself. So we can say, 'I know.'" *The Son will reveal*—The Son *is pleased* to reveal.

28. How sweetly do these words fall upon the ear! *Shall be brought down to hell*, and *hid from the wise and prudent*, sounded like the knell of the hopes of many, but now he shows the deep tenderness of his spirit and the all-embracing character of his love; *Come, all*. *That labor*, etc.—The Jewish people were bending under the weight of traditions, and some of them were conscious of the load. The invitation, however, is not restricted to those who are conscious of their burdens. Jesus would awaken in all the consciousness of the load they are carrying, that they may be induced to come. *Rest*—Not bodily or intellectual ease, which would be no relief, but "*rest in the soul*, which shall make all yokes easy and all burdens light." *Me . . . I*—The full preciousness of the meaning will not be seen unless these pronouns are regarded as emphatic, distinguishing Jesus Christ from the heartless, heavily loading scribes, and from all others who profess ability to give men rest.

29. *Yoke*—As the ox is brought

[1] In Horticultural Hall, Boston, May 31, 1867.

30 For my yoke *is* easy, and my burden is light.

CHAPTER XII.

AT that time Jesus went on the sabbath day through the corn; and his disciples were a hungered, and began to pluck the ears of corn, and to eat.

2 But when the Pharisees saw *it*, they said unto him, Behold, thy disciples do that

---

under control by means of the yoke, so a human being may be said to be under the yoke if he is under control. An old Greek classic speaks of the "*yoke of bondage*," and Paul (1 Tim. 6: 1) says, Let as many servants as are *under the yoke*, etc. Peter says (Acts 15 : 10), Now therefore why tempt ye God, *to put* [by putting] *a yoke* upon the neck of the disciples, which neither our fathers nor we *were able to bear?* In his letter to the Galatians (5 : 1) Paul says, Be not entangled again with the *yoke of bondage*. The yoke which Jesus here commands us to take cannot be that against which his own apostles inveighed. *His* yoke is the precepts which he enjoins. But, as we saw in our study of the Sermon on the Mount, his precepts are even more exacting than those of Moses; that is, they are the precepts of Moses *fulfilled*,—developed into their true, original meaning. *Take*—The soul must choose it and be cheerful in its choice. *Meek and lowly*—Qualities which are generally deemed desirable in the learner are here professed by this divine teacher. Jesus looks with love upon that which is low, though he is above all. Rationalism is unfit by its intense pride to teach the world.

30. *My yoke is easy*—Notice here, also, the emphatic *my*, by which his yoke is contrasted with that of the scribes and Pharisees. But if his precepts are even more rigorous than those of Moses (see above), how can he say that his yoke is easy, when his apostles seem to speak of the law of Moses as a yoke of bondage? The apostles never spoke of the law of Moses as a *heavy* yoke, except so far as it was used as a means of justification. Moses spoke of Christ. The entire system of Moses had no significancy except as the shadow of Christianity. He, therefore, who used the Mosaic precepts, not in *their true import*, but as the ground of justification, took upon himself a heavy, galling yoke. Christ's yoke is easy, because obedience to his precepts is *not* required as a ground of justification. *My burden light*—The explanation must be essentially the same as that of the easy yoke.

CHAPTER XII.

THE DISCIPLES PLUCKING EARS OF GRAIN; JESUS HEALING A WITHERED HAND, AND FALSELY ACCUSED BY THE PHARISEES, ETC.

781 U.C. Summer, A.D. 28.

1. *At that time*—Indefinite. The incident, after the manner of Matthew, seems not to be related in chronological order. The date placed at the head of the chapter is taken, like all such dates, from "Andrews' Life of Christ," yet the reader should be apprised that there is great uncertainty relative to the matter. *The sabbath-day*—The Jewish Sabbath, answering to our Saturday. The field lay, probably, near Capernaum, within a sabbath-day's walk of the city. *Through the corn*—The grain-fields. In the United States the word *corn* is commonly used for maize, Indian corn, though it is also a general word for different kinds of grain. Indian

which is not lawful to do upon the sabbath day,

3 But he said unto them, Have ye not read what David did, when he was a hungered, and they that were with him;

4 How he entered into the house of God, and did eat the shewbread, which was not lawful for him to eat, neither for them which were with him, but only for the priests?

5 Or have ye not read in the law, how that on the sabbath

---

corn was unknown in Palestine. The field here referred to was probably either barley or wheat.

2. *When the Pharisees saw it*— The suggestion has been made, and it is not unreasonable, that they had followed him out of Capernaum to see if his walk was more than their scrupulous notions regarded as lawful on the Sabbath. *Not lawful*— Not taking the grain, but taking it on the Sabbath. The law said (Deut. 23: 25), *When thou comest into the standing corn of thy neighbor, then thou mayest pluck the ears with thy hand;* but thou shalt not move a sickle unto thy neighbor's standing corn. "When travelling in harvest-time," says Thomson, "my muleteers have very often thus prepared parched corn in the evenings after the tent has been pitched. Nor is the gathering of these green ears ever regarded as stealing. After it has been roasted, it is rubbed out in the hand, and eaten as there is occasion. . . . So also I have often seen my muleteers, as we passed along the wheat-fields, pluck off ears, rub them in their hands, and eat the grains, unroasted, just as the apostles are said to have done." The Pharisees (those here mentioned were probably of Capernaum) were stricter than the law. It was held that "he who reapeth grain on the Sabbath, to the quantity of a fig, is guilty. And plucking corn is as reaping." Sowing the poisonous seeds of traditionalism was no sin! Plucking a few heads of grain on the Sabbath to appease hunger was a crime! Such is the spirit of ritualism in all times.

3. *What David did*—See the account in 1 Sam. 21: 1-6. *Have ye not read?*—Their criticism was, therefore, the more inexcusable.

4. The city in which the incident occurred was Nob, where, in the time of Saul, the tabernacle was kept. According to Dr. Robinson, "it must have been situated somewhere upon the ridge of the Mount of Olives, north-east of the city." *Shew-bread*—Twelve loaves of bread kept on a table in the Holy Place, first, of the tabernacle, and afterward of the temple, one week, and on the Sabbath eaten by the priests, new loaves supplying the place of those eaten. The original word means "*bread of the face or faces.*" In translating into German, Luther used *Schaubrode*, "from which our subsequent English versions have adopted the title *shew-bread*." By bread of the face is meant *bread of the presence;* that is, the presence of God. It was probably a symbol of spiritual bread. It was to be eaten by none but priests,—that was the *letter* of the law. But David ate it when hungry in his flight from Saul, and the Pharisees are not known to have blamed him. They of course justified the act on the ground that in a case of that sort it was no violation of the law, for the law was more merciful than to let men starve, if eating some of the shew-bread would prevent it. But the disciples were not violating even the letter of the law. To say that their act was equivalent to harvesting on the Sabbath was a species of violence in interpretation to which none but the Pharisees were equal.

5. But Jesus and his disciples were in no danger of starving. An-

CHAPTER XII.

days the priests in the temple profane the sabbath, and are blameless?

6 But I say unto you, That in this place is *one* greater than the temple.

7 But if ye had known what *this* meaneth, I will have mercy, and not sacrifice, ye would not have condemned the guiltless.

8 For the Son of man is Lord even of the sabbath day.

9 And when he was departed thence, he went into their synagogue:

---

other line of defence is therefore taken. The priests were required to do even more work on the Sabbath than on any other day; for they were to bake the shew-bread and to offer four lambs instead of two. There is no evidence that the Pharisees regarded these as profane acts, though upon their own principles they ought to have so regarded them. But if they could find no fault with the priests for working on the Sabbath, and twice as much as usual, and in the temple itself, why should they blame him and his disciples for plucking, rubbing, and eating corn to appease hunger?

6-8. Jesus concludes his defence with wonderful force. David was a king, the men who offered the sacrifices were priests, the temple was greater than both priests and king, but Jesus is *greater than the temple* ("the True Temple of God on earth"),—another of those remarkable sayings which prove Jesus to have been the most arrogant of men if he was not one in nature with the Father. It is not surprising, considering their blindness, that the Pharisees soon became exasperated. Jesus accuses them of not understanding their own Scriptures. Hosea 6: 6. See note on 9: 13, where the same quotation is found. *The guiltless*—The disciples who had plucked the ears of grain. He means to say that they are blameless in respect to the act in question. In how much higher sense was Christ blameless! *Who did no sin!*

Son of man—The evangelists never call Christ the Son of man, but Christ often called himself so. 1. The appellation presents Christ in his humanity. He was truly man as well as truly God, and, remembering that in a few years after his ascension a sect arose under the name of Docetæ (*Seemists*), which affirmed that he did not have a body of flesh, but only *seemed* to have; that he was not a real man, we shall see the importance of the designation. 2. It expresses the *humiliation* of his state. "It was as the Son of man that he humbled himself; it is as the Son of man that he is exalted; it was as Son of man, born of a woman, that he was made under the law, and as Son of man that he was Lord of the Sabbath day; as Son of man he suffered for sins. . . . It was as Son of man that he had not where to lay his head. . . . Only the pure in heart will *see God*, but the evil as well as the good shall see their Judge: 'Every eye shall see him.'"

Lord of the Sabbath—He had, therefore, the right to abolish it, but neither here nor elsewhere does he intimate a purpose to do so. He had the right to interpret the Sabbatic law both by words and practice according to what he knew was its true import. See more on this important subject in the note on Mark 2: 27, 28. Whether Jesus Christ should be called Lord, as was once gravely debated in a Christian Convention, so called, admits of a ready answer; for if he is Lord of the Sabbath, of what, or of whom, may he not be Lord?

9. The incident about to be related occurred, it would seem, in

MATTHEW.

10 ¶ And, behold, there was a man which had *his* hand withered. And they asked him, saying, Is it lawful to heal on the sabbath days? that they might accuse him.

11 And he said unto them, What man shall there be among you, that shall have one sheep and if it fall into a pit on the sabbath day, will he not lay hold on it, and lift *it* out?

12 How much then is a man better than a sheep? Wherefore it is lawful to do well on the sabbath days.

---

the synagogue of Capernaum (Luke 6: 6), and on another Sabbath, probably the next one. *Was departed*, like *was entered*, is not good English. It should be *had departed*, or, *departing*.

10. This miracle, wrought upon the Sabbath, may be regarded as *proof* that Jesus was indeed Lord of the Sabbath. "The withered hand of Jeroboam (1 Kings 13 : 4-6), and of the man (Matt. 12 : 10-13), is such an effect as is known to follow from the obliteration of the main artery of any member, or from paralysis of the principal nerve, either through disease or through injury. A case, with a symptom exactly parallel to that of Jeroboam, is mentioned in the life of Gabriel, an Arab physician. It was that of a woman whose hand had become rigid in the act of swinging, and remained in the extended posture. The most remarkable feature in the case, as related, is the remedy, which consisted in alarm acting on the nerves, inducing a sudden and spontaneous effort to use the limb,—an effort which, like that of the dumb son of Crœsus, was paradoxically successful."—*Smith's Dictionary*. This illustration fails to meet the case in the text. The withered hand of the Gospel is more than a *rigid* hand. "The disease, which probably extended throughout the whole arm, was one occasioned by a deficient absorption of nutriment in the limb; it was in fact a partial atrophy, showing itself in a general wasting of the limb, with a loss of its powers of motion, and ending with its total death. When once thoroughly established, it is incurable by any art of man."—*Trench*. It may be added that Christ never attempted to cure by alarm. *They*—The scribes and Pharisees. *Accuse*—Enter a complaint before the court of seven in Capernaum. Bent on taking his life, they are now trying to get what they can make serve as sufficient evidence against him. Life given to this man's hand will be one means of bringing Christ to death, and so unnumbered millions to life.

11, 12. Jesus replies to the catechising Pharisees by arguing from the less to the greater, taking his illustration of the less from their own course of procedure; and the less is a thing of so little value, that it can be said of it, How much better is a man! Afterward the Jews became stricter respecting even raising a sheep from a pit on the Sabbath. It was taught that it would be right, however, to lay down a plank that it might walk out itself! But would the man have died had the cure been postponed, as a sheep might have died if not rescued? Reply: 1. The physician was there; 2. No divine law made it a sin to cure him on the Sabbath; 3. Health and happiness one day sooner were desirable; 4. It was well that the enmity of the Pharisees should be brought out. *Lawful to do well*—A good deed must not be postponed. Physicians ought not to postpone visiting a patient till the Sabbath, provided his case will permit the visit to be made on Saturday. Many persons postpone *sending* for a physician till the Sabbath, for the sake

CHAPTER XII.

13 Then saith he to the man, Stretch forth thine hand. And he stretched *it* forth; and it was restored whole, like as the other.

14 ¶ Then the Pharisees went out, and held a council against him, how they might destroy him.

15 But when Jesus knew *it*, he withdrew himself from thence: and great multitudes followed him, and he healed them all;

16 And charged them that they should not make him known:

17 That it might be fulfilled which was spoken by Esaias the prophet, saying,

18 Behold my servant, whom I have chosen; my beloved, in

"*saving time.*" Conscientious physicians will make every possible effort to attend the public worship of God. Had Jesus met this man the day before, he would not have postponed the cure till the Sabbath, for the sake of saving time.

13. Christ really did no work; he cured the man by the mere act of his will; telling the man to stretch forth his hand, was not *work*. This is one of our Lord's most wonderful miracles, as not the least thread of connection is to be seen between the act of his will and the cure. It is also a very instructive case. Our Lord commanded the man to do what to him was impossible. Had any other, not endowed with power to work miracles, commanded him to do it, the effort to do it would have been unreasonable. It is reasonable to attempt to do whatever Christ commands. Christ commands men to repent, and therefore the effort to repent is a perfectly reasonable act. Men need, however, the aid of the Holy Spirit to do this very thing. To say that men have the power "to will to obey if they will use it" (a Methodist writer), is much like saying that men may will, if they will to will to will, and so on without end. Stretching forth the hand was the man's own act, and only his; ministering strength to him to do it was Christ's act, and only his. Repentance is the sinner's act, and his only; the strength by which he repents is Christ's, and only Christ's.

14. *Held a council*—Not, called together the great national Sanhedrim, or any other council, but held an informal consultation. Enmity to our Lord was now becoming strong, and was attempting organization. The Pharisees everywhere were almost a unit in their opposition. There was doubtless some concert between those at Jerusalem and those at Capernaum. The difference between the ritualism of that day and the rationalism of this: That admitted the reality of the miracles, but rejected him that wrought them; this denies the miracles, but claims the name of Christian.

15. *Withdrew*—Not through fear. He had shown his superiority to fear by healing the man on the Sabbath before their eyes, their former criticism (vs. 2) notwithstanding. He withdrew that his work might not be cut short before all had been done that was necessary for laying the foundation of his kingdom. Had he permitted himself to be taken and put to death then, many a bruised reed would have been broken, and much smoking flax would have been quenched.

16. See note on 8: 4.

17. Not, so that it *was* fulfilled. The correctness, in all cases, of the form, that it *might be* fulfilled, implying purpose, "may now be regarded as a settled point."

whom my soul is well pleased: I will put my Spirit upon him, and he shall shew judgment to the Gentiles.

19 He shall not strive, nor cry; neither shall any man hear his voice in the streets.

20 A bruised reed shall he not break, and smoking flax shall he not quench, till he send forth judgment unto victory.

21 And in his name shall the Gentiles trust.

22 ¶ Then was brought unto him one possessed with a devil, blind and dumb: and he healed him, insomuch that the blind and dumb both spake and saw.

23 And all the people were amazed, and said, Is not this the Son of David?

24 But when the Pharisees

18-21. The words are quoted from Isa. 42: 1-4. The Holy Spirit, speaking through Matthew, applies them to Jesus Christ, though uttered by the prophet more than seven hundred years before. Those who deny all prophecy will of course deny that Isaiah spoke these words concerning the coming Messiah, but the application here made settles the question. Some have referred them to the Jewish people; some to Cyrus; some to Isaiah himself. *Shall show judgment to the Gentiles*—Shall make known "the religion of Jehovah, as revealed in the gospel." As the Gospel according to Matthew was intended primarily for Jews, this reference to the conversion of Gentiles shows that Matthew wrote in no exclusiveness of spirit. *Shall not strive*, etc.—Unlike false leaders in religion, Jesus was distinguished for gentleness of manner and spirit. *Bruised*, etc.—A partly-broken reed will he not break in two. *Flax*—Made into a wick. *Smoking*—Dimly burning. A dimly burning taper he will not extinguish. Souls oppressed by the consciousness of sin he will not destroy. Souls in whom there is a spark of desire for spiritual life, he will not reject. Though expressed negatively, it is a strong affirmation that Christ will cherish the least measure of spiritual sensibility. This he will continue to do till he send forth *judgment unto victory*; till, by his righteous decision, he shall crown the conflict in victory. A *bruised reed* will secure Christ's attention. He who insists that his own spirit is the source of light will get little light from Christ. *Gentiles trust*—Hope. Thus, again, does Matthew show the largeness of his vision. In what untold millions of cases has this prophecy been fulfilled! Here is authority for foreign missions. The victory of Christ is victory without the sword.

781 U.C. Autumn, A.D. 28.

22. *Blind and dumb*—In consequence of the possession. See note on 4: 24, third paragraph. *Insomuch*—So that.

23. *Is not this the son of David?* —*Is this the son of David?* was the form of the question in the original edition (1611) of King James' translation, but in some later editions, including that of the American Bible Society (1867), it appears with a negative. Do *not* men gather grapes of thistles? is at once seen to convey a false impression. The negative in the verse before us is equally out of place. Observe the difference. Is *not* this, expresses positive conviction that Jesus is the son of David. *Is* this the son, etc., expresses doubt whether he is or not, which implies the disposition to inquire. It is hardly correct, therefore, to say that "these fresh displays of love surprised and melted

CHAPTER XII.

heard *it*, they said, This *fellow* doth not cast out devils, but by Beelzebub the prince of the devils.

25 And Jesus knew their thoughts, and said unto them, Every kingdom divided against itself is brought to desolation; and every city or house divided against itself shall not stand:

26 And if Satan cast out Satan, he is divided against himself; how shall then his kingdom stand?

27 And if I by Beelzebub cast out devils, by whom do your children cast *them* out? therefore they shall be your judges.

28 But if I cast out devils

---

their hearts." As to the meaning of the words, *son of David*, see note on 9: 27, last few lines.

24. Evidently there is a conspiracy between the Pharisees of Capernaum and those of Jerusalem; for scribes, most of whom, as we have already seen, were Pharisees, had come from the capital. Mark 3: 22. *This fellow*—This man. No contempt was expressed, whatever degree of it may have been felt. *Beelzebub*—Beelzebul. See note on 10: 25. They virtually admit that Jesus has wrought miracles.

25, 26. *Knew their thoughts*—Not necessarily because they had spoken them. It is more probable that they had spoken only to the bystanders in an undertone. He shows the absurdity of their charge in a manner which at first sight seems to credit the kingdom of Satan with more harmony than it is generally supposed to have. But the kingdom of evil, while in itself it is distinguished for chaos, is a unit against the kingdom of Christ. It is only the union of the powers of darkness against Christ that keeps it from disorganization and ruin. Let that union cease and Satan fall to casting out himself, and his kingdom will be ruined. But it is Satan's object to preserve his kingdom, and therefore he will not be guilty of the suicidal act of casting out himself. As Christ has begun the work of driving Satan from the world, it is absurd to suppose him to be doing it with Satan's help, which their charge implies. *Every kingdom*—Any kingdom.

Jesus here assumes the existence of Satan as a distinct person. What Universalism denies (see Paige's Commentary and the writings of Universalists generally), Theodore Parker admitted, but Parker held that Jesus was mistaken! Mr. Parker's admission is at once an illustration of the candor which it is possible for full-grown rationalism to show, and of contempt for the intelligence and honesty of Jesus.

27. *By whom . . . your children*—Your disciples, who are like you in spirit and aims. It has been held that they worked real miracles. But, (*a.*) There is nothing in the Bible which proves that God ever helped wicked men to work miracles; (*b.*) A thorough examination of Exodus 7 and 8 will show that the magicians of Egypt wrought only imitations of miracles, and that at last they were unsuccessful even in these. See Bush's Notes on Exodus; (*c.*) Acts 19: 13 speaks of certain Jews, *exorcists*, who attempted to call over them which had evil spirits the name of the Lord Jesus. By other sources of information, it is well known that exorcism was much practised by the Jews. "In the schools of the Pharisees a so-called higher magic was taught, by which demons were to be expelled and drawn out of the noses of persons possessed, by means of certain roots, by exorcism, and by magical formulas supposed to have been derived

by the Spirit of God, then the kingdom of God is come unto you.

29 Or else, how can one enter into a strong man's house, and spoil his goods, except he first bind the strong man? and then he will spoil his house.

30 He that is not with me is against me; and he that gathereth not with me scattereth abroad.

31 ¶ Wherefore I say unto you, All manner of sin and blasphemy shall be forgiven unto men: but the blasphemy against the *Holy* Ghost shall not be forgiven unto men.

32 And whosoever speaketh a word against the Son of man,

---

from King Solomon.'" It was of course pretended by these disciples of the Pharisees that their alleged expulsion of evil spirits was effected by divine help. It was legitimate for Jesus to use their pretensions as the basis of his self-defence. If he casts out devils by Beelzebub, they have no possible means of proving that it is not by the same sort of help that their disciples cast them out. Jesus makes no admission of the validity of their pretensions. *Therefore . . . your judges*—Therefore your own judges shall convict you of inconsistency and partiality. The logic of unbelief limps, and the spirit of unbelief is uncandid.

29. Jesus affirms in figurative language that he is *stronger* than Satan. *The strong man*—Satan. *The house*—This world. *His goods*—Men and all their instruments of evil. *Spoil* his goods—Seize them. Christ is stronger. He has come into this world, which is Satan's house, and taken from him, already, a great multitude. In this, Christ has shown his power over Satan. Seizures will continue to be made, and at last Satan will be completely bound and cast into the bottomless pit. Rev. 20: 1–3. Who will then pretend to doubt that Jesus cast out devils by the Spirit of God?

30. *Not with me . . against me*—A general maxim, teaching that neutrality is impossible. *Gathereth . . . scattereth*, is regarded by many expositors as a mere repetition of the former; but perhaps it indicates a more active state. It may be an allusion to the work of harvesting. There are different degrees of guilt, but all are on the side of Satan who are not on the side of Christ. Pharisees and Sadducees, self-righteous moralists and sceptics, are alike in this,—that they are not with Christ. Acceptance of Christianity as a system is possible while one is rejecting Christ himself. With *me*—Christ must be received and loved as a person.

31, 32. The leading thought is, that blasphemy against the Holy Spirit can never be forgiven. To enforce it the more strongly, the sin is contrasted with all other sin, and even with all other blasphemy. It is even contrasted with words spoken against Jesus Christ regarded as the Son of man; that is, against Christ in his humiliation. What, then, is the nature of the sin? The Pharisees had charged him with casting out devils by Satan. He had affirmed that he cast them out by the Spirit of God. The circumstances, therefore, seem to require us to say that the sin consisted in ascribing to Satan what was done by the Holy Spirit in Christ. If we turn to Mark 3: 30, we find the evangelist himself affirming, *Because they said, He hath an unclean spirit.* Some say that the sin was not so much a single act as a state; but it was both a state and an act. The act was the utterance of the words, This man does not cast out devils but by Beelzebub the prince of devils, and the

CHAPTER XII. 155

it shall be forgiven him: but whosoever speaketh against the Holy Ghost, it shall not be forgiven him, neither in this world, neither in the *world* to come.

33 Either make the tree

---

utterance of the words presupposes a blasphemous state of heart.

This sin cannot be forgiven. Why not? It is a great dilution of the meaning to answer, Because those who commit it will not repent. This is very true, but in the consequences with which this sin is visited we see *retribution*. The retribution, however, is not arbitrary. It has relation to character. God does not grant repentance to him who commits it, and he does not grant it because the sin is the highest possible insult, since the Holy Spirit, against whom the calumny is uttered, is the only agent by whom God's love in the atonement can be made efficient in conversion and final salvation. Jesus teaches, in vs. 32, that it is a great sin to speak a word against the Son of man, but that is a sin for the forgiveness of which God's grace has made provision. Blasphemy, in its most general meaning, is evil speaking, then evil speaking of things sacred. *Holy Ghost*—The third in the Trinity. He is not to be regarded as merely the spirit of the Father. This was the view of Sabellius in the third century, and is held, substantially, by some small but well-known sects of the present day. He is not indeed so separate from the Father as to be another and entirely independent God, but he is so separate as to have his own distinct personality. He is mentioned in the Old Testament, but, in accordance with the progressive nature of revelation, less clearly than in the New. The Holy Spirit is God, for the attributes of God are ascribed to him. He is represented in the Scriptures as knowing, loving, choosing, interceding, which shows that he is not a mere *influence* of the Father.

This world . . . the world to come—These phrases were used by the primitive Christian writers to designate this world and the world that comes after death. The mere statement, It shall not be forgiven him, would have been sufficient to show that the future life was included; but Jesus gives strength to the declaration by the additional words. Mark reports our Lord as saying, *Hath never forgiveness, but is in danger of eternal damnation*. Universalist commentators deny that there is reference to the future world; but the denial avails nothing against such unequivocal language, and against the fact that the Jewish schools taught that the sin of blaspheming the name of God *could be washed away by death*. It was doubtless against this tradition that our Lord uttered the words, *neither in the world to come*. These words are used by Romanists in support of their doctrine of purgatory, but they give no support to the opinion that *any* sin will be forgiven in the next world. If they do not express the eternity of future punishment, the Greek language was incapable of expressing it, and of course equally incapable of expressing the eternity of future bliss. Whether these men had committed the sin in question or not, they were clearly on the very margin, to say the least, of that terrible state against which Jesus warned them.

The distress of *tender consciences* lest the sin against the Holy Spirit has been committed is quite useless. Committal of the sin and fear lest the sin has been committed are never found together. He that has committed it is insensible and calumnious. Grieving the Spirit and resisting the Spirit are heinous sins; but God has made provision by which they can be forgiven. Blaspheming the Holy Spirit is a different sin.

good, and his fruit good; or else make the tree corrupt, and his fruit corrupt: for the tree is known by *his* fruit.

34 O generation of vipers, how can ye, being evil, speak good things? for out of the abundance of the heart the mouth speaketh.

35 A good man out of the good treasure of the heart bringeth forth good things: and an evil man out of the evil treasure bringeth forth evil things.

36 But I say unto you, That every idle word that men shall speak, they shall give account thereof in the day of judgment.

37 For by thy words thou

---

33. The meaning of this verse is thus expressed by Dr. John J. Owen: "If I do good, consider me as good, and act consistently.... The character of a man is determined by his actions. The Pharisees could be at no loss in respect to our Lord's true character, inasmuch as his life and the tendency of his doctrines were good. They had no excuse, therefore, for their malicious charge of his collusion with Satan." Christ's life, outward and inward, was good; therefore his nature was good. Man's life is bad; therefore his nature is bad.

34, 35. *Generation of vipers*— Brood of serpents. See note on Matt. 3: 7, last paragraph. What intensity of wickedness Jesus must have seen in their hearts! for, observe that, though infinite in tenderness, he calls them what the austere John had called those Pharisees that came to be baptized. *How can ye*— Not physically, but morally impossible—as impossible for them to speak good things, as for a serpent to send forth healing instead of poison. "The term *generation of vipers* indicates that depravity is born. As the viper's nature is derived by propagation from its original parents, so man's moral nature is derived from his progenitors."—*Dr. Whedon.* Yet Jesus would not have called Nicodemus, though a Pharisee, and ignorant of the nature of the new birth, nor the impenitent young man of whom Mark (10: 21) speaks, one of a brood of vipers. The phrase, therefore, indicates not mere depravity, but an intense degree of it. *Abundance of the heart* — Overflowing of the heart. It is a general proposition, as applicable to a good man as to a bad man, but here applied to the Pharisees. Their hearts overflowed with evil; of course they spoke evil. A good man's heart overflows with good; therefore he speaks good things. The thought is expressed in vs. 35, under the simple figure of a treasure. *A good man ... bringeth forth*—The good man *sends* forth. The good man's heart being a treasure which grace has filled with pure thoughts, devout affections, holy desires, sends forth good words. Such a man cannot speak such words as you Pharisees have just applied to me, nor be guilty of such deeds as you are doing in plotting my death. The evil man's heart being a treasure of unsound reasonings relative to sacred things, and of corrupt desires, base motives, it sends forth evil things.

36, 37. *Idle word* — A word, which, like an idle man, does no good. There is no necessity for saying, as many do, that the context requires us to understand the word in a stronger sense. The Saviour takes the occasion to affirm that even for a *useless* word, we must give account at the day of judgment. *Account thereof*— Of it in all its wide-spread rela-

CHAPTER XII.

shalt be justified, and by thy words shalt thou be condemned.

38 ¶ Then certain of the scribes and of the Pharisees answered, saying, Master, we would see a sign from thee.

39 But he answered and said unto them, An evil and adulterous generation seeketh after

---

tions. A useless word is wrong in itself, but the measure of its sinfulness cannot be estimated exclusively in that way. A useless word is a sign of a useless thought, and many useless words are signs of many useless thoughts; that is, of a heart which needs cleansing. The effect of a useless word upon other persons will be taken into account. Useless words, then, cannot be otherwise than hurtful, and though the wrongfulness of them is so much less than that of blasphemy, yet, since they are indications of the state of the heart, we shall by them be justified or condemned. It would be a perversion of these general sayings of our Lord, to affirm that our words are to be the only standard by which we are to be either condemned or justified. Matt. 25: 35-46 teaches us that *deeds* will be taken into the estimate; and Romans 2: 16 shows that the *thoughts* will also be weighed.

Justified—Be declared just. The New Testament reveals *four* methods of justification: (*a.*) By grace (Rom. 3: 24); (*b.*) By the death of Christ (Rom. 5: 9); (*c.*) By faith (Rom. 5: 1); (*d.*) By works (James 2: 24.) But these methods are not equally efficient. They are not co-ordinate. They do not hold precisely the same relation to the person justified. In other words, works must not be exalted to the level of faith; faith must not be exalted to a level with Christ's sufferings or God's grace. Without grace, the atonement, and faith, we strike upon the hidden sands of Arminianism; without works, against the rocks of Antinomianism. Oh! what efficiency, harmony and glory in God's method of saving men! Grace—forfeited love — provides the atonement, awakens faith, constrains to good works. If we are justified by our works (which includes our words), it is not in consequence of any merit in ourselves.

38. *Master*—Teacher; spoken, perhaps, in derision of his pretensions. *A sign from thee*—As Luke (11: 16) says, A sign from *heaven*. We have, by combining the two, A sign which *you* may bring *from heaven*, in distinction from these miracles which you bring rather from the earth. Christ himself was the great sign from heaven. They could not see him as such; how, then, could they see him as a sign from "the deep realm of death"? vs. 40.

39. *Adulterous*—Some say, both literally and spiritually, and in proof of the former refer to 5: 31, 32. The old prophets often represented the relation which Israel sustained to God under the figure of marriage, God the husband and Israel the wife. Relapse into idolatry or other gross sins was, therefore, called adultery. The present state of the nation was one of great departure from the true ideal of fidelity to God, which is enough of itself to account for our Lord's use of the term adulterous. *Seeketh after a sign*—Not denying that Jesus wrought miracles, but rejecting them as evidence of the divinity of his mission. He affirms, not that no sign shall be given, but no such sign as they demand. A sign shall be given, which he calls the sign of the prophet Jonas (Jonah), "that is, the sign which had typi-

a sign; and there shall no sign be given to it, but the sign of the prophet Jonas:

40 For as Jonas was three days and three nights in the whale's belly; so shall the Son of man be three days and three nights in the heart of the earth.

---

cally appeared in the history of Jonah, 2: 1." Jonah was one of the prophets of Israel; some say, the first. His father's name was Amittai. His own name means *dove.* "Jonah was probably born about 850 B.C. . . . He was a child when Homer was an old blind bard, singing his rhapsodies on the eastern shores of the Mediterranean."

40. The story of Jonah is here so unequivocally sanctioned by our Lord as historical, that the wit which has been expended upon it has been most justly called "profane." The theory that "the 'fish' was no animal at all, but a ship with the figure of a fish painted on the stern, into which Jonah was received after he had been cast out of his own vessel!"—"that just as the prophet was thrown into the water, the dead carcass of some large fish floated by, into the belly of which he contrived to get, and that thus he was drifted to the shore," would not be made much more absurd by supposing further that Jonah was no man at all, but only the offal which the sailors threw over about the time the **storm** subsided. The event was either historical, or it was not. If it was, Christ spoke precisely as we should expect him to speak. If it was not, he spoke in a manner which no honest teacher would have employed. Therefore, if we reject the account as historical, the gravest doubts are thrown over the moral character of Jesus, which is the result to which all rationalism tends.

In the whale's belly—If the above view is correct, it matters very little whether the animal was a whale, or a shark, or some other large fish. Excessive attempt to explain the details in the record of a miracle may lead to scepticism; yet within the limits which sincere reverence for the word of God will observe, some attempt is allowable. Dr. Thomson insists that we should believe the fish to have been a whale, regarding the absence of whales in the Mediterranean at the present day as creating no difficulty, since "the multiplication of ships in this sea, after the time of Jonah, frightened them out of it, as other causes have driven all lions out of Palestine, where they were once numerous. . . . Our Lord calls it a whale, and I am contented with his translation; and whale it was, not a shark." Our Lord does *not* call it a whale: King James' translators do. The Greek word may mean *any large fish.* "The Mediterranean formerly abounded in a species of carcharias, or dogfish, specimens of which are still found there, though in less numbers. . . . Its throat and maw are sufficiently capacious to lodge, without crowding, a man of the largest size." Dr. Baird, of the British Museum, says that in the River Hooghly, below Calcutta, he had seen a white shark swallow a bullock's head and horns entire. "Certainly the preservation of Jonah in a fish's belly is not more remarkable than that of the three children in the midst of Nebuchadnezzar's 'burning, fiery furnace.'"

So shall the Son of man, etc.—The burial and resurrection of our Lord is the sign which was to be given to that generation and to all the following generations. The fact of the resurrection of Jesus was wielded by the apostles with great power. It was their chief reliance as an argument in support of the Messiahship of Jesus. *In the heart of the earth*—Not, as some have

CHAPTER XII.

41 The men of Nineveh shall rise in judgment with this generation, and shall condemn it: because they repented at the preaching of Jonas; and, behold, a greater than Jonas *is* here.

42 The queen of the south shall rise up in the judgment with this generation, and shall

---

said, in Hades, but in the earth, that is, buried. To deny this as the meaning because the body of Jesus was put into a rock instead of the ground, or because it was not put very deep in the earth, is the merest trifling. *Three days and three nights*—Jesus was entombed on Friday afternoon, and, as he rose on Sabbath morning, he lay in the tomb, according to our manner of reckoning, much less than three days and three nights; but the Jewish method of expressing such a fact was different. They reckoned a part of a day, if only an hour, as a whole day, and a part of a night as a whole night. Jesus rose on *the third day*. How clear to us, though obscure to them, this reference to his death! Ministers of the present times and Sabbath-school teachers should give more prominence to the fact of the resurrection of Jesus. It is still an argument of wonderful power.

41. He contrasts their conduct, that is, chiefly, that of the scribes and Pharisees, under his preaching, with that of the people of Nineveh under the preaching of Jonah. *Nineveh*—"It is now," says Mr. Barnes, in the "revised and corrected" edition of his Notes on the Gospels, 1842, "so completely destroyed that geographers are unable to ascertain whether it was on the eastern or western bank.... The very situation is unknown. If it seem strange that ancient cities are so completely destroyed that no remains of brick or stone are to be found, it should be remembered that they were built of *clay*, dried only in the sun, and not burned." Since these words were penned, Nineveh has been laid open to the eyes of men. The enormous and shapeless mounds that lie along the banks of the Tigris, and extend eastward several miles, have opened their rich treasures of knowledge; "and some of them must mark the ruins of the Assyrian capital." Through the eyes of Layard and others, the world has been permitted to look upon palaces, gateways, chambers, and halls, drinking-vessels, vases, parts of a throne, colossal representations of kings, slabs inscribed with biblical names, as Jehu, Hezekiah, and Sennacherib, all traceable to a period many hundred years before Christ.

The time of Jonah's visit to Nineveh is put by Layard at 750 B.C., but some place it B.C. 840. The destruction of the city is believed to have occurred B.C. 606, possibly twenty years earlier. It would have been destroyed before had not the king and people reformed in some degree their life at the preaching of the Jewish prophet. Jesus contrasts with their repentance the unbelief of the Jews, and affirms that the men of Nineveh will condemn (by their example) this generation for their impenitence under the preaching of one who is greater than Jonah. Jesus, dear reader, is still preaching,—preaching to you, and more fully and solemnly than he preached to the Pharisees.

42. Our Lord draws another illustration from the heathen world, for the purpose of rebuking the impenitent Pharisees. *The queen*—A queen, referring not so much to her as an individual as to her character. She was of the *heathen* world. *The south*—Sheba, a kingdom in the southern part of Arabia; not Seba, a kingdom of Ethiopia. Arabian writers refer to her under the name of Bilkees, but no reliance

condemn it: for she came from the uttermost parts of the earth to hear the wisdom of Solomon; and, behold, a greater than Solomon *is* here.

43 When the unclean spirit

---

can be put upon their statements. Nor can any reliance be placed upon the traditions of the Abyssinians, who give her the name of Maqueda. *Rise up in the judgment*—"Not rise from the dead at the day of judgment, but stand at the bar to be tried."—*Alexander.*

Solomon—Concerning the "*glory*" of this monarch see note on G:

NINEVEH.

29. Excepting perhaps the first few years of his life, Solomon was one of those men in whom the moral is less amply developed than the intellectual, and the intellectual much marred by the sensual. Whether his apostasy was sincerely confessed, we could more certainly tell if he had left any expression of penitence approaching that which his own father made in the fifty-first Psalm. Whether he "fell from grace" is not at all the question. Did he have any grace? is the point. On the whole the question may as well, perhaps, be left unanswered. *The wisdom,* etc.—Respecting this there can be but one opinion; and it is because a heathen queen went from her *very distant country,* here called the uttermost parts of the earth, to hear it, that she, too, at the day of judgment, will condemn by her example those of the Jews who rejected Christ. *A greater than Solomon*—Greater in origin, authority, *wisdom,* and *goodness.* "On the lowest view which serious thinkers

CHAPTER XII.

is gone out of a man, he walketh through dry places, seeking rest, and findeth none.

44 Then he saith, I will return into my house from whence I came out; and when he is come, he findeth *it* empty, swept, and garnished.

45 Then goeth he, and taketh with himself seven other spirits more wicked than himself, and they enter in and dwell there: and the last *state* of that man is worse than the first. Even so shall it be also unto this wicked generation.

46 ¶ While he yet talked to the people, behold, *his* mother and his brethren stood without, desiring to speak with him.

47 Then one said unto him, Behold, thy mother and thy

---

have ever taken of the life of Jesus of Nazareth, they have owned that there was in him 'one greater than Solomon.'"

43-45. Jesus here exposes the fearful moral state to which the people of Israel are coming. Not all the details are easy to be understood; the outline is plain. The clue is in the closing sentence: Even so shall it be with this generation. What shall be? This generation shall be worse at last than it is now. This is expressed in the form of a similitude. He makes use of a fact which, judging from the similitude itself, must have sometimes occurred; namely, the return of a devil to him out of whom it had been cast. *Walketh through dry places*—Goes through deserts, which, in consequence of their desolateness, it was natural to regard as the resort of evil spirits. *Seeking rest*—The words indicate merely the restlessness of an evil spirit that has been cast out of a man. *Will return into my house*—He resolves to repossess the man. *Garnished*—Set in order. *Empty, swept, and garnished*—It is a mistake to suppose that each of these three words has a distinct meaning. They should be grouped together, and be held as meaning merely, *all ready for him. Seven other spirits*—A definite for an indefinite number. *More wicked*—Then there are degrees of depravity in devils as well as in men. *Worse than the first*—He is more thoroughly possessed, and, by implication, beyond recovery. Such are the facts by which our Lord expressed the fearfulness of the moral state into which the Pharisees in particular, and the Jews generally, soon came. The demon of idolatry—so some explain it—had been cast out by the sufferings through which the Jews had passed centuries before in the Babylonian captivity. That left the house empty. Real righteousness, however, did not enter. See the Sermon on the Mount for proof. The people had only the appearance of devotion to the service of God. Their state was therefore "inviting to the unclean spirit." They rejected, and continued to reject, God's remedy for sin. Under the intensified spirit of evil they grew worse and worse, till their state was more deplorable than ever, even crucifying the Son of God himself.

46. *His brethren*—Brothers, which is the more proper term for the expression of natural relationship. Whether they were real brothers, or cousins, will be considered in the note on 13: 55. *Stood* — Were standing, not for a moment merely, for Luke (8: 19) says, They could not come at him for the press. They were waiting outside the crowd. He was in the house, and probably in Capernaum. *Desiring* — Seeking. The former is too weak.

47. *One said unto him*—They sent in a messenger; or perhaps the fact of their attempting to speak

brethren stand without, desiring to speak with thee.

48 But he answered and said unto him that told him, Who is my mother? and who are my brethren?

49 And he stretched forth his hand toward his disciples, and said, Behold my mother and my brethren!

50 For whosoever shall do the will of my Father which is in heaven, the same is my brother, and sister, and mother.

CHAPTER XIII.

THE same day went Jesus out of the house, and sat by the sea side.

2 And great multitudes were gathered together unto him, so

---

with him was passed along through the crowd, till those who were nearest him (Mark 3: 32) told him. Why did they desire to speak with him? Mark says (3: 21), And when his friends heard of it, they went out to lay hold on him, *for they said, He is beside himself*. The multitude pressed upon him for so long a period that he had no time to eat. His mother and brothers were either fearful lest his abstinence and labors should be injurious to his health, or lest the animosity of the Pharisees should result in his arrest.

48. *Who is my mother?* etc.— These questions were doubtless intended as a reproof. Jesus knew better than they how long to speak to the people. It is not the only time that he reproved his mother, though he always did so with great gentleness and respect. See Luke 2: 48, 49; John 2: 4. What becomes of the Roman Catholic doctrine of "Immaculate Conception"? and what shall be said of the idolatry that prevails among Romanists veiled by the thin disguise of "veneration and invocation"? The following is taken from a Roman Catholic "Manual of Devotion": "O holy and glorious Virgin Mary, I commit my soul and body to thy blessed trust this night, and forever, especially in the hour of my death;" and the following also: "I confess to Almighty God, to blessed Mary, . . . that I have sinned exceedingly, in thought, word, and deed."

· 49, 50. Spiritual relationship superior to natural is the sentiment here expressed. The affection which Jesus bore to Mary as his *mother* was sincere and deep (John 19: 26, 27), but the love which he had because she did the will of his Father was greater. Natural ties are characteristic of only this life. They are from necessity limited. They may exist without the hallowing influence of the spiritual. "Spiritualism," in the present perverted sense of that word, has shown itself in many of its chief adherents as disgustingly indifferent to the most sacred of earthly ties. Jesus taught just views of the relation of the earthly to the spiritual. How sweet the ties between Jesus Christ and those who do the will of God! How great, therefore, should be the love of these toward one another! The silence of Jesus relative to a father harmonizes with the report of the evangelists that he had none. When the demands of earthly friends come in comparison with God's claims, they should be disregarded.

CHAPTER XIII.

JESUS ILLUSTRATES THE FOUNDING AND THE DEVELOPMENT OF HIS KINGDOM IN SEVEN PARABLES.

781 U.C. Autumn, A.D. 28.

1, 2. *The same day*—Probably

CHAPTER XIII.

that he went into a ship, and sat; and the whole multitude stood on the shore.

3 And he spake many things unto them in parables, saying, Behold, a sower went forth to sow;

4 And when he sowed, some

---

the same day on which the closing incident of the last chapter occurred. *The shore* — The beach. "Along the edge of this secluded basin" (the sea Galilee), says Stanley, "runs the whole way round from north to south a level beach. . . . On this *beach*, which can be discerned running like a white line all round the lake," etc.

3. *Spake . . . in parables* — A *fable* is a species of composition which represents a brute creature as talking and acting like a man, and that not in things moral, but in things pertaining to common prudence. A *myth* is a composition representing the actions of the deities of heathen. A *proverb* is thought condensed in a very brief form, and expressing, either in simple or figurative language, some moral or prudential sentiment. An *allegory* is a representation of one person or thing, by another person or thing, so complete that the two seem to be alike, yet one is literal, and the other moral or spiritual, the latter being the real meaning of the former. "Pilgrim's Progress," by John Bunyan, is an allegory. For an example of proverbs, see those written by Solomon. Myths may be found in Classical Dictionaries, having been collected from ancient Greek and Latin profane authors. For specimens of fables, see those of Æsop. The *parable* is different from them all. It expresses spiritual truth without that violation of the laws of nature which is a characteristic of the fable, and it expresses it in such a way as to compel comparison of one thing with another; as, for example, of the preacher with the sower, or the truth with the seed. It is an interesting fact that our Lord never employed the fable for conveying instruction. That form would not have been in harmony with the dignity of his character.

It has been inquired whether these seven parables were uttered on different occasions, and were grouped in their existing order by Matthew. It is more probable that they were spoken on the same occasion. It has also been questioned whether he had employed this method of teaching before. It is certain that he had employed it very little, if at all. His method had been more like that of the Sermon on the Mount. He never wholly dispensed with it, but from the time at which the present chapter opens, the *parabolic* method was that which he chiefly employed. Why, will soon appear. The parables which are now to be examined are intended to teach the development of his kingdom from its beginning to its completion at the Day of Judgment.

THE SOWER.

A sower—The beach on which the crowds stood is the eastern boundary of the beautiful plain of Gennesareth. Mr. Stanley, when visiting the spot, felt that he saw disclosed every feature of the great parable. "There was the undulating cornfield descending to the water's edge. There was the trodden pathway running through the midst of it, with no fence or hedge to prevent the seed from falling here and there on either side of it, or upon it; itself hard with the constant tramp of horse, and mule, and human feet. There was the 'good,' rich soil, which distinguishes the whole of that plain and its neighbor-

seeds fell by the way side, and the fowls came and devoured them up:

5 Some fell upon stony places, where they had not much earth: and forthwith they sprung up, because they had no deepness of earth:

6 And when the sun was up, they were scorched; and because they had no root, they withered away.

7 And some fell among thorns; and the thorns sprung up, and choked them:

8 But other fell into good ground, and brought forth fruit, some a hundredfold, some sixtyfold, some thirtyfold.

9 Who hath ears to hear, let him hear.

10 And the disciples came, and said unto him, Why speakest thou unto them in parables?

---

hood from the bare hills elsewhere descending into the lake, and which, where there is no interruption, produces one vast mass of corn. There was the rocky ground of the hillside protruding here and there through the cornfields, as elsewhere through the grassy slopes. There were the large bushes of thorn,—the 'Nabk,' that kind of which tradition says that the crown of thorns was woven,—springing up, like the fruit-trees of the more inland parts, in the very midst of the waving wheat." *Went forth*—From his house, from the village.

4. *Fell by the way-side*—The roads in Palestine are not fenced or walled. They ran through cultivated fields, or along the border. In sowing, therefore, some of the seed would be likely to fall upon the path or road. *Fowls devoured*—Stanley saw larks and sparrows busy picking up seeds which had fallen upon the road over which he was travelling.

5, 6. *Stony places*—The rocky places. *Stony* places, especially on land recently cleared, may be very productive; for the roots will work with remarkable persistence between the stones to the needed depth. Large rocks with a very thin layer of soil is meant. Seed sown there would spring up quickly. The sun that helps a deeply rooted plant kills one that grows out of a thin soil.

7. *Fell among thorns*—"Every one who has been in Palestine must have been struck with the number of thorny shrubs and plants that abound there. The traveller finds them in his path, go where he may. Many of them are small, but some grow as high as a man's head. The Rabbinical writers say that there are no less than twenty-two words in the Hebrew Bible denoting thorny and prickly plants. The prevalence of such shrubs, say agriculturists, shows a luxuriant soil. If proper care be not taken they soon get the upper hand and spread in every direction."—*Hackett*. Rev. Dr. Smith, missionary at Beirut, assured Dr. Hackett that he had seen thistles which "rose above his head, even when mounted on horseback." There is "another thorny plant and troublesome weed, the rest-harrow, which covers entire fields and plains, both in Egypt and Palestine."

8. *Some an hundred fold*—This would be a large increase from the soil of Palestine in its present state under Turkish indolence, but it can be shown that in many parts of the land the soil must have been capable of it. "In the time of Christ the country was densely peopled, and the fields were protected from the depredations of birds, mice, and insects, and also from cattle and other animals which now trample under foot so much of the grain." Then Isaac sowed in that land, *and*

CHAPTER XIII.

11 He answered and said unto them, Because it is given unto you to know the mysteries of the kingdom of heaven, but to them it is not given.

12 For whosoever hath, to him shall be given, and he shall have more abundance: but whosoever hath not, from him shall be taken away even that he hath.

13 Therefore speak I to them in parables: because they seeing see not; and hearing they hear not, neither do they understand.

14 And in them is fulfilled the prophecy of Esaias, which saith, By hearing ye shall hear, and shall not understand; and seeing ye shall see, and shall not perceive:

15 For this people's heart is waxed gross, and *their* ears are dull of hearing, and their eyes they have closed; lest at any time they should see with *their* eyes, and hear with *their* ears, and should understand with *their* heart, and should be converted, and I should heal them.

16 But blessed *are* your eyes,

---

received in the same year a hundred fold. Gen. 26: 12. The young reader may be reminded that this occurred many hundred years before the time of Christ.

10. *Why . . . in parables?*—The question is evidence that this, though not in itself a new method, was then newly used by our Lord. The variety that characterized our Lord's teaching was not employed as an end, but as a means of effecting greater moral purposes.

11. *Because*—He answers their question. *Unto you*—The disciples, but not the apostles only, for there were others, also, who, following him in a higher sense than the multitude, received his instructions and trusted in him. These, his real disciples, he contrasts with the multitude who followed him with no deep, spiritual interest. By God's gracious interposition, the former understand the mysteries of the kingdom, but the latter do not. The reason why the latter do *not* understand them is that it is not given them; that is, they are not made in this respect the objects of God's gracious interposition. *Mysteries* — Not things which, from their very nature, are difficult to be understood, but things which had been kept concealed. Eph. 3: 3-6; Rom. 16: 25, 26.

12. *Whosoever hath—Hath* implies *activity in using.* He who receives and improves what I say shall receive and will improve still more. *Hath not*—This implies *inactivity* in using. He who receives not and improves not what I say, shall be deprived even of what little he may have heard.

13-15. *Therefore, . . . because*— We need not understand him as here giving *another* reason why he speaks to the multitude in parables, but as repeating in a fuller form the reason given in vs. 11. They *see* both him and his miracles with the natural eye, and hear his words with the natural ear, but they have no spiritual perception. He illustrates their state by that of the people in the times of Isaiah. What was true of the people in the prophet's day is true of the people to whom the Lord speaks. We understand Jesus to mean that the parable is his method of conferring and his method of withholding. In other words, the parable had both a revealing and a concealing power. It made truth plainer to those who were sincere seekers of truth, and obscurer to those who were in bond-

for they see: and your ears, for they hear.

17 For verily I say unto you, That many prophets and righteous *men* have desired to see *those things* which ye see, and have not seen *them;* and to hear *those things* which ye hear, and have not heard *them.*

18 ¶ Hear ye therefore the parable of the sower.

19 When any one heareth the word of the kingdom, and understandeth *it* not, then cometh the wicked one, and catcheth away that which was sown in his heart. This is he which received seed by the way side.

20 But he that received the seed into stony places, the same is he that heareth the word, and anon with joy receiveth it;

21 Yet hath he not root in himself, but dureth for a while: for when tribulation or perse-

---

age to prejudice and sensuality. In the course which Jesus pursued toward the latter, there was doubtless something of the nature of retributive justice. This is seen more clearly in Mark 4: 11, 12: *That* seeing they may see, etc. *That* expresses not mere result, but design. Jesus would not, however, have admitted the plea of fatalism. Extremes meet. The slave of sense and the worshipper of reason alike *have not, see not.* Judicial blindness falls upon many now. Spiritual knowledge in a docile heart is an ever-increasing capital. Docility itself is the result of grace. Creating men for the purpose of hardening their hearts, and then consigning them to punishment, is not taught by Jesus.

17. *Prophets and righteous men desired* — Therefore, in character, though not in opportunity, they are to be classed with those whose eyes were blessed with seeing Jesus himself.

18. *Hear*—Not merely listen to the words of the explanation, but receive the spiritual meaning.

19. *The word of the kingdom*— The facts, the doctrines, and the sentiments preached by the Lord, or by his servants. Of course *reading* the word in the Bible must be included. *Understandeth it not*—

Does not spiritually perceive it. It is more than a failure of the intellect to comprehend the meaning of the words. *The wicked one*— Mark (4: 15) uses the word Satan, and Luke (8: 12) the word devil. In using either of these terms in this unfigurative discourse, Jesus must have knowingly confirmed the current belief of his hearers in a personal devil. If Jesus knew that there is no such being, he was unfitted, by dishonesty, to be a teacher of men. *Catcheth*—Snatches. Satan's method is not always so violent. In the parable, fowls came. Satan employs a variety of agents, as wicked men and other evil spirits. *Received seed* is incorrect. It should be, *was sown:* This is he which was sown by the way-side. But this seems to liken the hearer instead of the word to the seed. This was not, however, the Lord's intention. "The meaning is, this is the one whose case is represented by seed sown by the way-side."

How apt is the representation in the parable itself! The heart that has no spiritual perception of the truth is like the way-side. It is hard. The word falls upon the surface of it; does not fall into it. This is true of thousands of persons who frequent the house of

CHAPTER XIII.

cution ariseth because of the word, by and by he is offended.

22 He also that received seed among the thorns is he that heareth the word; and the care of this world, and the deceitfulness of riches, choke the word, and he becometh unfruitful.

23 But he that received seed

God. The devil *snatches* it away,—a bad spirit, proving that he did not want it for his own good.

20, 21. *He that received the seed*, etc.—He that was sown; he whose case is represented by seed sown on rocky places. This hearer seems at first more likely to be permanently benefited by the word than the former. In the case of the other, the word made no impression whatever. This one not only receives it, but receives it with joy. It will not be correct to say that it was all joy and no faith; for Luke (8: 13) says, Which for a while *believe*. Observe particularly that Matthew, Mark, and Luke agree in this remarkable fact, that joy is the *first* state into which this second hearer comes. That makes him worthy of suspicion; for it is not the order in which the Holy Spirit works upon a sinful being. Conviction of sin followed by faith, and faith followed by peace, and in many cases by joy; or, if one prefers to say so, all at the same time,—this is the Spirit's method. That joy should come first as a genuine work of the Spirit is impossible. What Luke means by the *faith* which he represents this hearer as having, is evidently the same as Matthew and Mark mean by *dureth for a while*. In other words, had Luke, instead of saying, which *for a while believe*, said, *but dureth for a while*, he would have meant the same thing as he does mean. Here, then, is no such thing as a regenerate person becoming unregenerate; that is, "falling from grace." *By and by*, as now used, means some time in the future, which is here not the true sense. It should be *immediately*. *Offended*—Caused to stumble, that is, to fall away, to abandon even his profession of interest in the truth. *Not root in himself*—The little root that he has is in something outside of himself; it is in mere circumstances. The word has not become a principle.

Hearers of this sort are found in great number wherever the gospel is preached, even in the most genuine "revival," and especially in times when the impulses of men are excited by superficial preaching and artificial measures. Too much care cannot be taken lest such persons become members of churches. "In ten years," says the "Methodist," Oct., 1867, "namely, from 1856 to 1865 inclusive, there were received on probation throughout the bounds of our church, the vast number of one million two hundred and six thousand one hundred and forty-five! In 1856, we had six hundred and ninety-eight thousand three hundred and seventeen members; in 1866, we had eight hundred and seventy-one thousand one hundred and thirteen, showing a net increase in ten years of only one hundred and seventy-two thousand two hundred and ninety-six. . . . We confess to a feeling of utter astonishment at the revelation made in these statistics of the very small proportionate increase in the time named." This quotation is made for the purpose of suggesting that in all evangelical denominations more care should be used in discriminating between those who have no root in themselves, and those who receive the word into good ground.

22. *He also that received seed*—He that was sown. The explanation is similar to that of the corre-

into the good ground is he that heareth the word, and understandeth *it;* which also beareth fruit, and bringeth forth, some a hundredfold, some sixty, some thirty.

24 ¶ Another parable put he forth unto them, saying, The kingdom of heaven is likened unto a man which sowed good seed in his field:

25 But while men slept, his enemy came and sowed tares among the wheat, and went his way.

26 But when the blade was sprung up, and brought forth fruit, then appeared the tares also.

27 So the servants of the householder came and said unto him, Sir, didst not thou sow

---

sponding words in vv. 19 and 20. In the case of this third hearer, the seed is as good as in either of the former cases, and the soil is deep and rich. That is to say, it is *truth* that is preached, and he to whom it is spoken is not specially indifferent and hard (the way-side hearer), nor specially given to superficiality and impulse (the rocky hearer); yet he gets no permanent good from the truth. *The care of this world*—An anxious, divided mind relative to things temporal. See note on 6:25. *Deceitfulness of riches*—Both of riches obtained and riches sought. They are deceitful in either case as an end of life, since they allure the soul away from the only worthy end. See Heb. 3:13. *The deceitfulness of sin.* In the heart where these thorns are permitted to grow, the truth is outgrown and overshadowed, and therefore leads to no spiritual results.

23. *He that received seed into the good ground*—He that was sown, etc. See vv. 19 and 20 for the explanation. This hearer's heart is receptive. It is free from hardness (the first), from shallowness (the second), from solicitude about temporal things (the third). This greater receptivity is itself chiefly the result of divine aid; for, though there is doubtless a natural difference in men in respect to this quality, yet no man has naturally so much of it as to incline him without God's help to receive spiritual truth. Jesus does not mean to teach that any man's heart is in itself naturally good, that is, holy.

The first hearer may in process of time become what the second is, and the second what the third is, and the third what the fourth is. Jesus does not teach that either of the first three is "fated" to remain what he is. The first may become what the fourth is, as the fourth may have once been what the first is. "It has been noticed, also," says Alford, "that the first is more the fault of careless, inattentive *childhood;* the second of ardent, shallow *youth;* the third of worldly, self-seeking *age.*"

THE TARES.

24–26. In this parable is represented the conflict of good with evil. *The kingdom of heaven*—See note on 3:2. It is important to the correct understanding of this parable to bear in mind, that by kingdom of heaven is not meant the universal, visible, organized Church: for the existence of such a body is not recognized in any part of the New Testament. Of this we shall speak more hereafter. It is sufficient to remark here that the phrase is used to designate *the new dispensation. Likened unto a man* —The man and the circumstances about to be narrated. *While men slept*—The words are not intended

CHAPTER XIII.

good seed in thy field? from whence then hath it tares?

28 He said unto them, An enemy hath done this. The servants said unto him, Wilt thou then that we go and gather them up?

29 But he said, Nay; lest while ye gather up the tares, ye root up also the wheat with them.

30 Let both grow together until the harvest: and in the time of harvest I will say to the reapers, Gather ye together first the tares, and bind them in bundles to burn them: but gather the wheat into my barn.

31 ¶ Another parable put he forth unto them, saying, The kingdom of heaven is like to a grain of mustard seed, which a man took, and sowed in his field:

32 Which indeed is the least of all seeds: but when it is

---

to express blame. It is only another way of saying that it was done *in the night;* or, possibly, as Dr. J. J. Owen suggests, at the time of the noon-nap. *Tares*—The English reader has become so accustomed to this word that the use of any other in this connection is not pleasant; yet the tare, which is well known in Europe as good fodder for cattle, and is even considerably cultivated for that purpose, is not that to which Jesus refers. There is a weed called *darnel*, which is doubtless the weed referred to in the text. "It is a widely distributed grass, and the only species of the order that has deleterious properties." Its botanic name is *lolium temulentum*. It often produces nausea. "The whole of the inmates of the Sheffield workhouse were attacked some years ago with symptoms supposed to be produced by their oatmeal having been accidentally adulterated by *lolium*." "It is a strong soporific poison, and must be carefully winnowed and picked out of the wheat, grain by grain, before grinding, or the flour is not healthy. Of course the farmers are very anxious to exterminate it, but this is nearly impossible." The farmers in the East believe that wheat in unfavorable seasons turns into the weed; but the opinion has no foundation in fact. *His*

enemy sowed tares—Thomson says that such an act is altogether unknown at the present day, though he has no doubt that it was done in the time of our Saviour. It may be unknown in Palestine, but it is done in some other countries. "Thus, in Ireland," says Trench, "I have known an outgoing tenant, in spite at his ejection, to sow wild oats in the fields which he was leaving." Roberts says that in the East *pandinellu*, that is, pig-paddy, is sometimes cast in the night into the soil of the ploughed field in revenge upon a neighbor. Springing up before the good seed, it gives great trouble to the owner. Alford says that a field belonging to himself, in Leicestershire, was maliciously sown with charlock over the wheat.

29, 30. The tares were so much like the wheat, that there was great danger of pulling up the wheat in the effort to get out the tares. "I have collected," says Dr. Hackett, "some specimens of this deceitful weed, and have found, on showing them to friends, that they have mistaken them quite invariably for some species of grain, such as wheat or barley." Thomson says that the farmers are not only in danger of mistaking good grain for "the tares," but very commonly the roots of the two are so inter-

grown, it is the greatest among herbs, and becometh a tree, so that the birds of the air come and lodge in the branches thereof.

33 ¶ Another parable spake

twined that it is impossible to separate them without plucking up both. Both, therefore, must be left to *grow together* until the time of harvest. When both are fully grown, they are more easily distinguished.

THE MUSTARD SEED.

31, 32. The object of this parable is to illustrate the progress of the kingdom of heaven in the heart and through the world. There is no need of supposing that any other than the well-known mustard plant is referred to. "Of the mustard plants which I saw on the banks of the Jordan," says Dr. Hooker, in Smith's Dictionary, "one was ten feet high." Thomson saw the wild mustard plant as tall as the horse and his rider. The following beautiful description is by Dr. Hackett: "Some days after this, as I was riding across the Plain of Akka, on the way to Carmel, I perceived, at some distance from the path, what seemed to be a little forest or nursery of trees. I turned aside to examine them. On coming nearer, they proved to be an extensive field of the plant which I was so anxious to see. It was then in blossom, full grown, in some cases six, seven, and nine feet high, with a stem or trunk an inch or more in thickness, throwing out branches on every side. I was now satisfied in part. I felt that such a plant might well be called a tree, and, in comparison with the seed producing it, a great tree. But still the branches, or stems of the branches, were not very large, or apparently very strong. Can the birds, I said to myself, rest upon them? Are they not too slight and flexible? Will they bend or break beneath the superadded weight? At that very instant, as I stood and revolved the thought, lo! one of the fowls of heaven stopped in its flight through the air, alighted down on one of the branches, which hardly moved beneath the shock, and then began to warble forth a strain of the richest music. All my doubts were now charmed away. I was delighted at the incident. It seemed to me at the moment as if I enjoyed enough to repay me for all the trouble of the whole journey." All further doubt respecting the matter may well be dismissed. Every condition is here fulfilled except the smallness of the seed, and the seed may have been the smallest of all seeds known to the Jews; or the expression may be rhetorical for *very small.*

Likening the progress of the kingdom of heaven to the growth of a tree from the seed is very beautiful and instructive. Compare Dan. 4: 10–12; Ezek. 31: 3–9. One little seed planted in Bethlehem has become a great tree, with roots striking deeply into the soil of all lands, and with foliage spreading widely over all nations! Let the Sabbath-school teacher illustrate the thought by speaking to his class of the obscurity of the Saviour's human origin, and of the splendid victories which Christianity has achieved, and of the yet more splendid victories which it will achieve in the future. Let him contrast with this the decay of false systems of religion, whether Christian, as Romanism, or pagan. How much like the least of all seeds is the beginning of Christ's life in the soul! How different after many years of growth, as in John, Paul, Augustine, Luther, Judson! *Birds of the air—* This should not be regarded as intended to convey any particular spiritual thought; as, for example (Trench), that the "church should

he unto them; The kingdom of heaven is like unto leaven, which a woman took, and hid in three measures of meal, till the whole was leavened.

34 All these things spake Jesus unto the multitude in parables; and without a parable spake he not unto them:

35 That it might be fulfilled which was spoken by the proph-

---

become a resort for multitudes for protection from worldly oppression, as well as the satisfaction for all the needs and wants of their souls." For, 1. The idea of a great church capable of affording such protection has no foundation in the Scriptures; 2. The multitudes who obtain "satisfaction," etc., will become, it is to be presumed, members, and so they become a part of the tree itself, instead of being birds, and lodging in it for a night or two. The words seem to be intended merely to indicate the size to which the tree has attained.

THE LEAVEN.

33. This parable seems intended to teach the inward, pervasive force of the kingdom of heaven. *Leaven*, as generally used, "consisted of a lump of dough in a high state of fermentation, which was inserted into the mass of dough prepared for baking." *Corruption* is the idea which, in the Scriptures, leaven most frequently expresses. "A multitude of small, oval, organized bodies, which do not exceed one two hundred and fiftieth of an inch in diameter, and which, when viewed under the microscope, are seen to consist of nucleated cells, form the essential constituent of *yeast*." The doctrine of the Pharisees was called by our Lord *leaven* (16: 6, 12). Paul says (1 Cor. 5: 7), Purge out therefore the *old leaven* that ye may be a *new lump*, as ye are *unleavened*; and in vs. 8 he speaks of *the leaven of malice and wickedness*, and the *unleavened bread of sincerity and truth*. How sin has spread from Eden through the habitab'e earth! How it diffuses itself through the race; through the entire mental nature of the individual! But the *diffusiveness* of leaven, irrespective of quality, may fitly represent the pervasive power of the kingdom of righteousness; and this is the use which Jesus makes of it in the parable. Illustrations may be brought from the history of primitive missions (see The Acts of the Apostles), from that of modern missions, and from the history of each renewed heart. *And hid*—The secret, unobservable working of truth by the Holy Spirit may be intended. *Three measures*—One measure, nearly a peck and a half. Sarah was told by Abraham to make ready three measures of fine meal, knead it, and make cakes upon the hearth. Gen. 18: 6. To suppose that the number three indicates "the three sons of Noah," or "body, soul, and spirit," or "the Jews, the Samaritans, and the Greeks," or "the three grand forms in our Christian world,—individuals (catechumens), Church and State, and the physical Cosmos" [universe], is fanciful. Three measures was probably about the quantity commonly taken when bread was to be made. *Till the whole was leavened*—The regenerated soul will at length be completely delivered from evil, and the race will be very greatly permeated by the spirit of Christ. We are forbidden by innumerable other passages to regard it as teaching that all men will be saved.

34, 35. *Spake he not*—Spoke he nothing, is the meaning of the correct text,—nothing on the present occasion, and generally during the remainder of his ministry. *By the prophet*—Psalm 78: 2. Asaph

et, saying, I will open my mouth in parables; I will utter things which have been kept secret from the foundation of the world.

36 Then Jesus sent the multitude away, and went into the house: and his disciples came unto him, saying, Declare unto us the parable of the tares of the field.

37 He answered and said unto them, He that soweth the good seed is the Son of man;

38 The field is the world; the good seed are the children of the kingdom; but the tares are the children of the wicked one;

39 The enemy that sowed them is the devil; the harvest is the end of the world; and the reapers are the angels.

40 As therefore the tares

---

was the writer, and is here called a prophet in the more general sense. *Will utter things . . . secret*—Jesus is the great truth-revealer. Rationalism affirms that he *revealed nothing;* that "the men of science are God's true prophets;" that "we must get wholly rid of belief in any old thing or in any new thing of either the Old Testament or the New;" that "truth is the only Redeemer we should acknowledge;" that "religion is the affirmation of spirit in the mind of man;" that "if we call ourselves by the name of Christ, we lose the true expression of truth." The human mind gets its most valuable truth from Jesus Christ, not from its intuitions or its reasonings.

THE TARES EXPLAINED.

36. *Sent . . . away*—Dismissed, let them go. *Into the house*—The house where he commonly dwelt, perhaps the house of Andrew and Peter, which, it must be remembered, was in Capernaum. *Declare*—Explain.

37, 38. *Son of man*—See note on 12: 8, second paragraph. Jesus here speaks of himself as if he were the only sower; yet Paul (1 Cor. 3: 6) says, *I have planted.* But Paul adds, *Neither is he that planteth anything.* All other sowers get their seed from Christ, and sow with strength ministered by Christ. To say, therefore, that Christ is the *chief* sower does not exhaust the meaning. He is actually the only sower, in the sense of furnishing all the seed and all the strength.

38. *Is the world*—Is the inhabited earth. It expresses *the extent of territory* in which the wheat and the darnel were sown. Nothing can be plainer than that it does not mean "The Church." It will be noticed that *seed* here does not have the same meaning as in the parable of the sower. There it is the word; here it is men. *Children of the kingdom*—Not, as in 8: 12, members of the Jewish theocracy, not many of whom were regenerated persons, but sons by adoption, true disciples of Christ. *Children of the wicked one*—Those who are like the wicked one. The distinction made by the evangelical pulpit between the righteous and the wicked is authorized by the divine Teacher. It is not error, but errorists, not wickedness, but the wicked, that Jesus represents as *the devil's darnel.*

39. *The devil*—Being not the words of the parable but of the Lord's interpretation, these words are another striking proof that Jesus *intended* to teach the existence of a personal Satan. Satan began to sow in Eden, and has been a busy sower ever since. If he *went his way* (vs. 25), it was not that he

CHAPTER XIII.

are gathered and burned in the fire; so shall it be in the end of this world.

41 The Son of man shall send forth his angels, and they shall gather out of his kingdom all things that offend, and them which do iniquity;

42 And shall cast them into a furnace of fire: there shall be wailing and gnashing of teeth.

---

might settle down in inactivity, but that he might sow elsewhere. *The enemy*—Nothing that Satan does is the work of a friend. He works secretly: While men slept. *The end of the world*—The end of this probationary state.

41. *His angels*—Compare 25:31. *Out of his kingdom*—Not, out of "The Church." Church and kingdom are not synonymous. We have already defined kingdom as *the new dispensation*, conceived as extending over the entire inhabited earth. *To gather*, then, *out of his kingdom all things that offend* is a figurative way of saying that all the wicked—whether they are in organized churches or not is not at all the question—shall be separated from the righteous and be consigned to punishment. As a matter of fact, some of the wicked will be found in true Christian churches, many in those heterogeneous bodies called, each, "The Church," married to the State, and many outside of all churches, the true and the false. Dr. Whedon's view of the parable seems to us to be much more nearly correct than that of most of the commentators; for most of them commit the great mistake of supposing the Saviour to refer to "The Church," as if that were the body in which the wheat and the tares (the regenerate and the known unregenerate) are to be permitted to grow together. "It is not so much," says Dr. Whedon, "a parable of the *church* as of the *world and the church under the Messiah; for the field is the world*."

The true ideal of a Christian church, according to the New Testament, is that of a company of persons living in one city or village, all of whom have been regenerated by the Holy Spirit, not through baptism or in baptism; and, after regeneration, have been baptized, and have agreed to associate together for the maintenance of spiritual life in their own souls, and the conversion of others to the same kind of life. Of course this ideal can never be fully realized in this world; but does this justify us in opening the doors of "The Church," or of Christian churches, so widely, by infant membership or infant baptism, as very nearly to transform the field of wheat into a field of darnel? The churches will be far enough from perfection, even if we adhere to the apostolic example. Besides, the duty of excommunicating members who give no evidence of regeneration is expressly enjoined. See on 16:18, concerning the distinction between "The Church" and churches, last paragraph but one.

42. *Furnace of fire*—Conscious suffering as a punishment for their sins. On the subject of future punishment, see notes on 25:41, 46 As to the *figure* here employed, it may be remarked that the Jewish mind had become familiar with the fact that the furnace was used as a means of inflicting capital punishment. Whoso falleth not down and worshippeth, shall the same hour be cast into the midst of a *burning fiery furnace*. Dan. 3:6. "A parallel case" [in Persia] "is mentioned by Chardin, two ovens having been kept ready heated for a whole month to throw in any corn-dealers who raised the price of corn."

43 Then shall the righteous shine forth as the sun in the kingdom of their Father. Who hath ears to hear, let him hear.

44 ¶ Again, the kingdom of heaven is like unto treasure hid in a field; the which when a man hath found, he hideth,

---

43. *Shine forth* — This beautiful verse is still more beautiful in the original: *Shine out!* There it is one word. The righteous will shine forth with the glory reflected from Christ. *The kingdom of their Father*—The kingdom is conceived as in heaven in its completed state.

The Hidden Treasure.

44. Here is illustrated the fact that the blessings of the new dispensation, though they may not have been *sought*, may yet be joyfully taken when they are unexpectedly put within one's reach. It has always been more common in the East than in the West to hide treasures in the earth, and that because the rights of property have there been less respected. Hence the hiding of treasure is often spoken of in the Bible. Prov. 2: 4; Job 3: 21; Jer. 41: 8. A few years ago about eight thousand gold coins of Alexander and his father Philip were found in or near the city of Sidon. They were contained in several copper pots, and are estimated as worth, at the price of gold in the time of Alexander, forty thousand pounds. Thomson, who speaks of the discovery, suspects "it was royal treasure, which one of Alexander's officers concealed when he heard of his unexpected death in Babylon, intending to appropriate it to himself, but being apprehended, slain, or driven away by some of the revolutions which followed that event, the coin remained where he had hid it."

Men may differ concerning the morality of the act of purchasing such a field of the owner without informing him of the increased value of the land. Some say boldly that it would not be loving his neighbor as himself, and would, therefore, be wrong. Perhaps so; but the purpose for which the Saviour constructed the parable required no expression of opinion relative to the character of the act, that purpose being simply this, to show the joyful activity of the man to whom the blessings of the gospel have been presented, even without his searching. This proves that the preceding parables give no countenance to fatalism. No man may say, One is wheat, and another is darnel, and nothing can make darnel wheat. This parable and the next one teach the duty and the necessity of human activity. *In a field*—So many of the most distinguished interpreters are, or, when living, were, members of a State Church, or of some other great, visible organization called "The Church," that they incline to see "The Church" where others cannot see it. But the leading thought of the parable does not require that any special idea should be considered as intended to be expressed in the term *field*, as Church, or a "worldly ecclesiasticism," or even the Bible. That true Christianity has been hidden at times in a worldly organization arrogating the name of Church may serve well enough as an *illustration*, but it cannot have been the thought which Jesus intended to teach. Eph. 3: 9 is here important. And to make *all men see* what is the fellowship of the mystery, which, from the beginning of the world, *hath been hid in God*. *He hideth*—Merely a pictorial feature of the parable to aid

CHAPTER XIII. 175

and for joy thereof goeth and selleth all that he hath, and buyeth that field.

45 ¶ Again, the kingdom of heaven is like unto a merchant-man, seeking goodly pearls:

46 Who, when he had found one pearl of great price, went and sold all that he had, and bought it.

47 ¶ Again, the kingdom of heaven is like unto a net, that

---

in impressing the idea that the man is bent upon securing the treasure, which is the main thought conveyed in going, selling all, and buying the field.

THE PEARL MERCHANT.

45, 46. In the last parable, men are represented as active in receiving the blessings of the gospel when Providence puts them *in their way;* in this, as active in *seeking* them. *Merchant-man*—Merchant. The former is the common name of a trading vessel. This is a wholesale merchant in distinction from retail. The latter confines himself to the store; this man travels. *Pearl*—"A small, silvery, white, hard, smooth, lustrous substance, globular, oval, or pear-shaped, found in the interior of the shells of many species of mollusks, particularly of the pearl-oyster, apparently resulting from the deposit of the nacreous substance around some nucleus." Pearls are found in Ceylon, California, etc. Many of them are found by a class of men called pearl-divers,—in California, *Busos.* These, "armed with pointed staves, plunge into water four or five fathoms deep, and when they find a pearl-bearing oyster rise to the surface, and deposit their prize in a sack hung to the vessel's side. This they continue to do until they are exhausted, or their time of labor is over." In 1831, one vessel "brought home in two months forty ounces of pearls, worth six thousand dollars; another twenty-one ounces, worth three thousand dollars."—*Annual of Scientific Discovery,* 1851.

Goodly pearls—There is much difference of value even in real pearls. But there are pearls that are not real. 1. The cocoa-nut pearl, a specimen of which was once laid before the Boston Society of Natural History. That came from Singapore. Though much prized by the rajahs, yet a distinction is made between this kind and the oyster-pearl, the latter being distinguished as real pearl.—*An. Sci. Dis.,* 1861. 2. Pearls which are hastened in their growth in the oyster, by the people of two Chinese villages near the city of Tchtsing, by the introduction of irritating "moulds." When the moulds are removed, they are cut away from the nacre, and "melted resin is poured into the cavity, and the orifice artfully covered by a piece of mother-of-pearl." They are sold *at a cheap rate.* 3. Imitation pearls. These are made in Paris, being lined with fish-scales and wax, the scales being stripped from the fish while living that the hue of the real pearl may not fail to be imitated.—*An. Sci. Dis.,* 1854. 4. Another kind of imitation pearls, invented in the fifteenth century. "These are small beads of thin glass, lined in the interior with a substance obtained by rubbing up the scales of a fish, 'the *ablette,*' very common in the rivers of continental Europe."—*An. Sci. Dis.,* 1862. None of these pearls can be called "goodly" in the higher sense, for they are not real pearls.

Seeking goodly pearls—He who has become conscious of his ignorance and sinfulness goes about searching for something to supply his wants. Neither sensual pleasure, nor riches, nor philosophy, can satisfy him. He longs for some-

was cast into the sea, and gathered of every kind:

48 Which, when it was full, they drew to shore, and sat down, and gathered the good into vessels, but cast the bad away.

49 So shall it be at the end of the world: the angels shall come forth, and sever the wicked from among the just,

50 And shall cast them into the furnace of fire: there shall be wailing and gnashing of teeth.

51 Jesus saith unto them,

---

thing nobler. But like pearls even the noblest thing can be so closely counterfeited as to deceive him. *One pearl of great price*—Of such uncommon size and beauty that he was willing to sell all the other pearls he had collected and everything besides for the sake of obtaining it. *Salvation* is the pearl of great price. Compare Heb. 2:3: How shall we escape, if we neglect *so great salvation?* Salvation from the penalty of God's violated law and from sin is the invaluable pearl; not a mere "hope," not membership in the church, not even the Bible. *Sold all that he had*—Everything must be relinquished that comes in competition with the attainment of eternal life. Personal virtues, however real, must not be put into the scale with the boundless value of Christ's righteousness. *Bought it*— But eternal life is to be bought *without money and without price*. The pearl of great price may be imitated. The imitation may be very bad; but multitudes take it, and think they have the best pearl in the market. For these mock pearls a *very high price* is asked, and many are willing to pay it. The Chinese villagers above named sometimes deposit a "mould" of Buddha, and so are able to offer for sale gods of pearl *filled with melted resin!* The lining of the imitation pearls (4) is called by the "pompous name" *Essence d'Orient*, to conceal "the true nature of the material from which it was prepared," and it has been "discovered that it is identical with a principle extracted directly from guano."

The application of these facts to the assumptions of rationalism is not difficult.

The Net.

47-50. Here is taught the final separation of the bad from the good. *Net*—Drag-net. "Then," says Thomson, "there is the great dragnet, the working of which teaches the value of united effort. Some must row the boat, some cast out the net, some on the shore pull the rope with all their strength, others throw stones and beat the water round the ends, to frighten the fish from escaping there, and as it approaches the shore every one is active in holding up the edges, drawing it to land, and seizing the fish. This is that net which gathered of every kind, and, when drawn to the shore, the fishermen sit down and gather the good into vessels, but cast the bad away. I have watched this operation throughout a hundred times along the shore of the Mediterranean." *Every kind*—Of fishes. *Drew to shore*—Drew up on the beach.

This parable, also, has been interpreted (Lange, Trench, and others) under the influence of erroneous views of the nature of a Christian church. By *net* they understand "The Church;" by *sea*, the nations; by *fishes*, men; by *good fishes*, believers. Alford (Episcopalian) says, "This net is *the church gathering from the sea . . . of the world all kinds.*" To this interpretation is the insurmountable objec-

CHAPTER XIII. 177

Have ye understood all these things? They say unto him, Yea, Lord.

52 Then said he unto them, Therefore every scribe *which is* instructed unto the kingdom of heaven, is like unto a man *that is* a householder, which bringeth forth out of his treasure *things* new and old.

53 ¶ And it came to pass, *that* when Jesus had finished

---

tion that members of "The Church" were once fishes themselves. How, then, can they be considered as the net? The explanation seems to proceed from the mistake of regarding "The Church" as an ideal organization apart from the members who constitute it. It is the *kingdom of heaven* which the Lord represents as a net, and that, as in the parable of the tares, is the Christian dispensation. Within the limits over which that dispensation extends are the bad and the good, believers and unbelievers, who, at the end of the world, will be separated from each other. No doubt the purest Christian churches—those that endeavor to conform to the apostolic model by receiving to baptism and membership none but confessing believers—will be found to have received, though unintentionally, persons that were never renewed. Such unrenewed members of Christian churches are of course included in "the bad." But this is nothing in support of a *system*, like infant church-membership, which, according to Rev. Dr. Stearns, President of Amherst College, is the real basis of infant baptism,—a system that facilitates the introduction of unrenewed persons into a Christian church.

51, 52. *Have ye understood?*—What tender and eager interest does the Great Teacher manifest in his pupils! The light in which this simple question places our Lord is of wonderful brightness. Here is a rich lesson for Sabbath-school teachers and ministers. *Scribe*—See note on 5: 20 concerning the Jewish scribes. These disciples of Christ are to be the scribes of the world. Witness the four Gospels, their oral discourses, and their epistles. *As a householder*, the head of a family, brings forth for the support of those who are dependent on him provisions both new and old, since both may be good in their season, so these men, thus instructed *in* (not *unto*) the kingdom, must bring forth for the benefit of others all that Christ has taught them, whether it is the older class of truths, such as good men of former times had, or the newer class, such as he has given to themselves. "Great sermons" are those which are full of thought,—the old and the new. Physical energy in preaching is of great importance, but it is a miserable substitute for thought. Not all truth is suitable for the pulpit. Not all religious truth is distinctively Christian. Not all Christian truth is equally instructive. The lighter Christian truth is more adapted to immediate effect; the more solid is needful for the development of Christian character and for continuous usefulness. The *instructed* scribe will use both.

53-56. *Departed thence*—From Capernaum. *Come into his own country*—Not in the wide sense in which the word *country* is now used. His paternal city, Nazareth, is meant. It is not necessary to suppose that he went directly from Capernaum to Nazareth. According to Mark (4: 35), he went the same day, at evening, over the Sea of Tiberias. Only a few days, however, could have elapsed before he went to his former home. *Synagogue*—See note on 4: 23. *Carpenter's son*—This was not said in reproach; for such a trade was not held by the

these parables, he departed thence.

54 And when he was come into his own country, he taught them in their synagogue, insomuch that they were astonished, and said, Whence hath this *man* this wisdom, and *these* mighty works?

55 Is not this the carpenter's son? is not his mother called Mary? and his brethren, James, and Joses, and Simon, and Judas?

56 And his sisters, are they not all with us? Whence then hath this *man* all these things?

57 And they were offended in him. But Jesus said unto them, A prophet is not without honour, save in his own country, and in his own house.

Jews in disesteem. The Son of God made himself of no reputation; but not by working, if he did work, at the trade of a carpenter. The question relative to his being the son of the carpenter is equivalent to the question, Is not this the son of Joseph, who is known among us as Joseph the carpenter? It was prompted by the same spirit as the questions concerning his relations to his mother, his brothers, and his sisters. In all these questions alike they only mean to deny that he is superior to themselves; mean to affirm that they know him as having such persons as parents, and such persons as brothers and sisters. Thus they would invalidate his claims; or, possibly, they are only surprised, confounded, by what seems to them a difficult problem; namely, his works and words viewed in the light of his earthly relations; yet they are guilty of the sin of unbelief.

His brethren—Brothers in the usual sense? or cousins?—questions the discussion of which would be too long and uninteresting for the general student. The writer accepts as the more probable opinion that they were real brothers, children of Joseph and Mary, or of Joseph by a former marriage. As has been shown by Alford, (*a*.) They are mentioned, with a single exception (John 7:3), in connection with his mother; (*b*.) They are not spoken of as of the number of the twelve: by Schaff, (*a*.) They are never called cousins, though that term is found in the New Testament; (*b*.) They are represented as unbelievers long after the call of the apostles. Difficulties attend this theory, but not greater, to say the least, than are found in the other. The question has excited intense interest in the Roman Catholic Church in consequence of its relation to the subject of the perpetual virginity of Mary.

57, 58. *Offended in him*—Took offence at his professions. Compare, as of much interest in this connection, 11:6. *A prophet . . . not without honor*—A proverb rich in suggestiveness, but so easy to be understood as to need no comment. *Because of their unbelief*—An important statement, showing the relation of faith to the exercise of the Lord's healing power. It is also important, because showing how clearly Christ recognized the freedom of the human will.

CHAPTER XIV.

NEWS OF JOHN'S DEATH; FEEDING OF A GREAT MULTITUDE; RESCUE OF PETER.

782 U.C. April, A.D. 29.

1. *At that time*—It has been calculated that John was beheaded not far from the beginning of April, in the year of Rome 782, A.D. 29. The news must have been carried to

CHAPTER XIV.

58 And he did not many mighty works there because of their unbelief.

CHAPTER XIV.

AT that time Herod the tetrarch heard of the fame of Jesus,

2 And said unto his servants, This is John the Baptist; he is risen from the dead; and therefore mighty works do shew forth themselves in him.

3 ¶ For Herod had laid hold on John, and bound him, and put *him* in prison for Herodias' sake, his brother Philip's wife.

4 For John said unto him, It is not lawful for thee to have her.

5 And when he would have

Jesus (vs. 12) not many days after; and not till after he had put John to death did Herod hear of the popularity of Jesus. He may have been in Rome, or been engaged in war; or, which is quite as probable, was so engrossed in the administration of affairs and in pleasure that the new movement had not arrested his attention. *Herod the tetrarch*—See the genealogical table of the Herod family in the notes on 2:1. This was Herod Antipas, son of Herod the Great. His mother's name was Malthace. His first wife was a daughter of Aretas, King of Arabia Petræa. While she was still living he became enamored with Herodias, the wife of his half-brother, Herod Philip. Aretas, in revenge, waged war against Herod, and defeated him. According to Josephus, many believed that the defeat was a punishment for the murder of John. He died in exile. If he was less cruel than his father, it was rather because he had less intellect than because he had more compassion. He was sensual, ambitious, cunning. Sensual pleasures close the heart against merciful deeds.

2. Under the sudden working of conscience, which neither his pleasures nor his troubles could prevent, Herod imagined that John had actually *risen from the dead*. It has been hastily assumed that he was a Sadducee; but whether he was or was not, his fears were the natural result of consciousness of guilt. *Mighty works*—Not miracles, but *the powers* by which miracles were wrought. *Show forth themselves*—Energize. *Therefore do the powers*—that is, those powers of which I have heard, *energize or work in him*. He could not keep his fears to himself. He uttered them to his *servants*,—slaves, courtiers,—"an oriental expression." Bad men seek relief by disclosing their fears to those who are like them. From good men they generally conceal them.

3. We are now taken back to the time when John was beheaded. The circumstances of his death are narrated in parenthesis (3-12), for the purpose of explaining the state of Herod's mind. *In prison*—The castle of Machaerus, near the Dead Sea. *For Herodias' sake*—History has many mortifying illustrations of the influence which bad women have exerted over kings as well as over persons in private life.

4. *Not lawful*—Why not? "She first married Herod, surnamed Philip, . . . her full uncle; then she eloped from him . . . to marry Herod Antipas, her step-uncle, who had been long married to, and was living with, the daughter of Æneas or Aretas,—his assumed name,—King of Arabia. Thus she left her husband, who was still alive, to connect herself with a man whose wife was still alive. Her paramour was indeed less of a blood relation than her original husband; but being

put him to death, he feared the multitude, because they counted him as a prophet.

6 But when Herod's birthday was kept, the daughter of Herodias danced before them, and pleased Herod.

7 Whereupon he promised

---

likewise the half-brother of that husband, he was already connected with her by affinity,—so close that there was only one case contemplated in the law of Moses where it could be set aside, namely, when the married brother had died childless. Now Herodias had already one child—Salome—by Philip, and, as he was still alive, might have had more. Well, therefore, may she be charged by Josephus with the intention of confounding her country's institutions; and well may St. John the Baptist have remonstrated against the enormity of such a connection with the tetrarch."

In such matters, it has been very common for kings to act in defiance of all law, human and divine. Henry VIII., King of England, is a noted example, though a recent historian has set his case, *in some respects*, in a more favorable light. His case, however, even yet is far enough from that of a saint. John was a bold preacher. He was not "a reed shaken with the wind." See a similar case of boldness in Paul. *He* reproved the licentiousness of Felix, when Felix' mistress, Drusilla, herself one of the Herod family, was sitting by his side. See Acts 24: 24, 25. Violators of the seventh commandment are painfully numerous, and that not merely in the lower classes. They should be rebuked whatever their social position.

6. *The daughter of Herodias*—Salome. "She married in the first place Philip, the tetrarch of Trachonitis, her paternal uncle, and secondly Aristobulus, King of Chalcis." *Herod's birthday was kept*—As a feast-day. Where? Probably in Tiberias. This city was built by Herod, and became the seat of his residence. It stood on the western shore of the Sea of Tiberias, "about two-thirds of the way between the northern and southern end of the sea." On the same spot is the modern town of Tubarieh. It has been thought, by some, that the feast must have been held nearer the prison where John was confined. In favor of this, is the distance (two days' travel) from the capital to the prison; but against it is Mark's statement that there were present at the feast chief men of *Galilee*. On so distinguished an occasion, however, the chief men of Galilee may have had no hesitancy to go a two days' journey. "The Jews abhorred keeping birthdays, as a pagan custom." Has Matthew, then, made either a mistake, or a misrepresentation, in speaking of Herod's birthday feast? See how Matthew is confirmed by Josephus. "Herod the Great kept the day of his accession; Antipas . . . and Agrippa I., as Josephus tells us, . . . their birthday, with such magnificence, that the 'birthdays of Herod' had passed into a proverb when Persius wrote." This is what a Jew says concerning a Jew, neither having belief in Christianity, and, though Jews by religion, "the Herods may be said to have gone beyond Rome in the observance of all that was Roman," and with the Romans birthday feasts were a custom. Thus is the inspired report confirmed by profane history, even where it seems to clash with known Jewish prejudices. *Danced before them*—From what is known of the state of morals in oriental courts, and especially the morals of many of the Herods, it may be inferred that the dancing of Salome

CHAPTER XIV.

with an oath to give her whatsoever she would ask.

8 And she, being before instructed of her mother, said, Give me here John Baptist's head in a charger.

9 And the king was sorry: nevertheless for the oath's sake, and them which sat with him at meat, he commanded *it* to be given *her*.

10 And he sent, and beheaded John in the prison.

11 And his head was brought in a charger, and given to the damsel: and she brought *it* to her mother.

12 And his disciples came, and took up the body, and buried it, and went and told Jesus.

13 ¶ When Jesus heard *of it*,

---

was not greatly distinguished for propriety. *She danced alone* before all the court, which speaks poorly for her modesty. Herod is sensual enough to be pleased with it.

8. *Before instructed*—Urged on. Doubtless Salome was *instructed* in the details; but instructed is not strong enough to express the thought. Herodias was the moving spirit. Hating the bold reprover of her paramour, she stimulates her daughter to demand his head. A lustful and murderous mother, and a lustful, murderous daughter! Herod gave the order, doubtless, under the influence of wine. Few murders are committed without the stimulus of alcohol. Before such a revelling company, John's case could have had little chance of receiving justice. *Charger* — Platter.

9, 10. *Was sorry* — Not sorry enough to break the oath; he will sooner murder one who he knows is a just man and holy. Mark 6: 20. *Which sat at meat*—He feared his drunken courtiers more than God; desired to put him to death, yet sorry. Such was his vacillating state of mind. He shrunk from the precipice to which his oath had led him, and then shrunk from displeasing Herodias and his courtiers. So, after about eleven months' imprisonment, God takes the good man up to heaven, and lets Herod and his mistress go down to hell.

11. *Brought it to her mother*—Here again is proof that the mother had been the chief actor. The painter Guercino has represented the scene upon canvas. Even the steel engraving by Egleton is worthy of study. The executioner, stripped to his loins, the muscles of the back and arms wonderfully developed, stands with the right arm drawn back, as if not yet fully relaxed from its unnatural work, the hand still clenching the sword; and, holding in his left hand, by a lock of the hair, the head of the martyred preacher, is letting it drop into the platter held by Salome, who looks down upon it with ineffable contempt. Behind the daughter stands, by the license of art, the mother, with contempt even more satanic than the daughter's.

12. *Took up the body*—The castle, the place of which was identified, in 1806, with ruins found on a lofty crag, was "surrounded by ravines, at some points not less than one hundred and seventy-five feet deep." It was perhaps in one of those ravines that the body was found. We see the tenderness of John's disciples toward their master, and their conviction that Jesus will sympathize in their grief. All *our* sorrows should be laid before Jesus.

13. The news of John's death was brought to Jesus at or near Capernaum. *Into a desert place*—Crossing the Sea of Galilee, he

he departed thence by ship into a desert place apart: and when the people had heard *thereof*, they followed him on foot out of the cities.

14 And Jesus went forth, and saw a great multitude, and was moved with compassion toward them, and he healed their sick.

15 ¶ And when it was evening, his disciples came to him, saying, This is a desert place, and the time is now past; send

---

lands upon the eastern shore. It was doubtless the desert of Bethsaida. "Upon the east side lies the rich level plain of Butaiha (Batihah), forming a triangle, of which the eastern mountains make one side, and the river bank and the lake shore the other two. This plain, with its bordering hills, probably belonged to Bethsaida." The region was thinly inhabited. Here, in the southern corner, where the mountain met the sea, it is believed the miracle of feeding the five thousand was wrought. "In this little cove," says Thomson, "the ships (boats) were anchored. On this beautiful sward, at the base of the rocky hill, the people were seated." How strong the Lord's hold upon the people! How affecting that one who knew so well how to prize a few hours of spiritual companionship with those who loved him should not be permitted to have it! "The whole distance which the people had to travel was not more than six or eight miles, and, from the conformation of the coast, could be as rapidly passed by those on the shore as those in the boat." Concerning the location of Bethsaida, see note on 11: 21. *Ship*—By *ship* is now meant, strictly speaking, "a vessel with three masts, each of which is composed of a lower mast, a top-mast, and top-gallant mast, and square-rigged," though the term is much used by persons not familiar with nautical affairs for any kind of vessel employed in navigation, and even by English statute law "the term *ship* is declared to comprehend every description of vessel navigating the sea." The ships, as they are correctly enough called in our English Bibles, which were used on the Sea of Galilee, were much smaller than the ships that navigated the Mediterranean. Some of these carried several hundred persons, as the one in which Josephus was wrecked. Paul was wrecked in a ship that carried two hundred and seventy-six, "besides a cargo of wheat." There are data for believing that ancient ships were from five hundred to one thousand tons each. The ship in which Jesus now embarked was probably not much larger than a modern sail-boat. *Departed*—Withdrew from the more public region that lay on the western side of the sea. His motive may have been twofold,—to avoid all intercourse with Herod (not, however, in fear of him, for he very soon returned to the western side, to the region of Herod's capital), and (Mark 6: 31) to secure rest, and, doubtless, greater spiritual improvement to the disciples, who had been separated from him in their missionary work.

14. *Went forth*—From retirement on the mountains? or from the ship? Mark (6: 33) says that the people outwent them, and came together unto him. The going forth was, therefore, from the ship.

15, 16. *When it was evening*—And yet, in vs. 23, Jesus is represented as being alone in the mountain after the crowds had all been fed, *when the evening was come*. With the Jews, every day had two evenings, the former and the latter, the time of each depending on the

CHAPTER XIV.

the multitude away, that they may go into the villages, and buy themselves victuals.

16 But Jesus said unto them, They need not depart; give ye them to eat.

17 And they say unto him, We have here but five loaves, and two fishes.

18 He said, Bring them hither to me.

19 And he commanded the multitude to sit down on the grass, and took the five loaves, and the two fishes, and looking up to heaven, he blessed, and brake, and gave the loaves to *his* disciples, and the disciples to the multitude.

20 And they did all eat, and were filled: and they took up of the fragments that remained twelve baskets full.

21 And they that had eaten were about five thousand men, beside women and children.

---

season of the year. This was the early evening; that mentioned in vs. 23 was the later. *The time*—The hour; and so the entire phrase, *the time is now past*, expresses *the lateness of the hour*. The Jews divided the day into twelve hours, reckoning from sunrise to sunset. The hours were unequal in length except when the days and nights were equal. In popular language, the *third* hour, for example, was at nine o'clock, but it was so only at the equinoxes. The sixth hour was of course at noon at all seasons of the year. To determine when any given hour began and how long it was, we must determine at what hour the sun rose. The Jewish hour was "the twelfth part of the natural day, or of the time between sunrise and sunset." *Need not depart*—The power of Jesus was not dependent on locality.

17. "A boy carries the rations of more than five thousand persons."—*Dr. Whedon.* See John 6: 9: *There is a lad here*, which hath five barley loaves and two small fishes.

19. *To sit down*—To recline. *On the grass*--It was spring. Jesus was not uninterested in whatever would add to their comfort. Concerning the order in which they sat, nothing is here said, but see Mark 6: 40; Luke 9: 14. *He* *blessed*—That is, the loaves; Luke 9: 16. He asked God's blessing upon them as means of continuing life, and this implied praise of the infinite goodness which supplies the wants of men. Horace Mann was accustomed to ask a blessing upon the family meal. Theodore Parker pronounced the act as "savoring of hypocrisy." The Christian that neglects the duty might blush in the presence of an unchristian Jew; for craving the blessing of God upon the daily meal was a Jewish custom. Ministers of Christ are not to be mere receivers; the knowledge which they obtain from the Bible should be imparted to the multitude. Ministers of scholarly habits are in danger of selfishness in the prosecution of their studies.

20, 21. *They did all eat*—That is a singular inference which was drawn from these words by one of the most sententious of commentators (Bengel, born in 1687): "How much more can *all* partake of the Lord's one body in his supper." According to the New Testament, only those are expected to partake of the Lord's supper who have been regenerated and baptized. See the latter part of the notes on 28: 19, concerning the relation of the Lord's Supper to baptism. *Twelve baskets full*—The fragments exceeded, perhaps, the original amount.

MATTHEW.

22 ¶ And straightway Jesus constrained his disciples to get into a ship, and to go before him unto the other side, while he sent the multitudes away.

23 And when he had sent the multitudes away, he went up into a mountain apart to pray: and when the evening was come, he was there alone.

24 But the ship was now in the midst of the sea, tossed with waves: for the wind was contrary.

Took up—Of course the apostles carried them away. These fragments they must have eaten as their future wants required. Thus their memory and their gratitude would be quickened. The fragments might have been left, but that would not have been to the disciples a lesson of economy. The entire number fed could not have been far from eight thousand.

The primary object of this miracle, like that of all the miracles, is to convince men that Jesus was authorized to come as the Saviour of the world. But, like all the others, it teaches us many important lessons besides, as the compassion and the power of Christ. It suggests rich thoughts relative to Christ as *the bread of spiritual life.* All attempts to comprehend the process are useless. It was not a creation out of nothing. He who is curious to know at what point of time the change occurred, should consider that we have no information on the subject.

22. Jesus makes another effort to secure retirement. He is the more desirous to be alone, in consequence of the effect which the miracle has produced upon the people. Their enthusiasm rises into a purpose to seize him, however unwilling, and proclaim him king. John 6: 15. *Constrained* — The disciples had been so unwilling to leave him, that more than a mere request was necessary. *The other side*—The western side of the lake. The people would more willingly depart after the disciples had been sent away. Spiritual union is possible without bodily association.

23. *A mountain*—The mountain, that is, one of the mountains referred to in the note on vs. 13, as constituting one side of the plain. *The evening*—The later evening. *To pray*—Not to confess sin, though confession is a very important part of prayer when offered by us. To conceive of Jesus as praying only, or chiefly, to set us an example, misses the great truth that prayer, as communion with the Infinite Spirit, is felt even by a sinless being to be the normal state of the soul. Neither secret communion with God nor vigorous out-door work should be neglected. Let him who desires to be always in society, consider how different is his choice from that of Jesus. Solitude is needful to prevent the bad effects of necessary intercourse with the world. He who, like Isaac, meditates alone, will soon, like Isaac, find a friend to whom he can be joined in heart,—the marriage of spirit with spirit; Christ the husband, himself the bride. Solitude may be the hot-house of·sin. One may go into the mountain to pray, but take the multitude with him.

24. The obedience of the disciples brings them into peril. *In the midst*—They had rowed about five and twenty or thirty furlongs. John 6: 19. They seemed to have aimed for Bethsaida, near the entrance of the Jordan, where, perhaps, they hoped to take in Jesus, but were driven south-westerly toward the centre of the lake. *Tossed*—Vexed, as in 2 Peter 2: 8; for that righteous man . . . *vexed* his righteous soul, etc.

25. *Fourth watch*—"The Jews,

CHAPTER XIV.

25 And in the fourth watch of the night Jesus went unto them, walking on the sea.

26 And when the disciples saw him walking on the sea, they were troubled, saying, It is a spirit; and they cried out for fear.

27 But straightway Jesus spake unto them, saying, Be of good cheer; it is I; be not afraid.

28 And Peter answered him and said, Lord, if it be thou, bid me come unto thee on the water.

29 And he said, Come. And when Peter was come down out of the ship, he walked on the water, to go to Jesus.

---

like the Greeks and Romans, divided the night into military watches instead of hours, each watch representing the period for which sentinels or pickets remained on duty. The proper Jewish reckoning recognized only three such watches, entitled the first or 'beginning of the watches,' the middle watch, and the morning watch. These would last respectively from sunset to 10 P. M., from 10 P. M. to 2 A. M., and from 2 A. M. to sunrise. . . . Subsequently to the establishment of the Roman supremacy, the number of watches was increased to four, which were described either according to their numerical order, as in the case of the fourth watch, or by the terms 'even, midnight, cock-crowing, and morning.' These terminated respectively at 9 P. M., midnight, 3 A. M., and 6 A. M." *Walking on the sea*—By the sea, says rationalism. But in that case would the disciples have been so troubled? and, since the ship was more than half way across, must not Peter have had supernatural strength of voice to be heard by Jesus three miles or more; or Jesus have had supernatural power of hearing to hear Peter, on either of which suppositions we have a miracle? Besides, the rationalistic interpretation implies that Peter undertook to walk on the water three miles, which is a bolder thing than even Peter ever undertook to do. We cannot think, with some evangelical interpreters, that "the walking on the sea was a momentary manifestation of a spiritual power inherent in the body of Christ." We see no reason for supposing that the body of Jesus, before his resurrection, was different from that of any other human being. The miracle shows that Jesus could control matter by the exercise of his will.

26. *It is a spirit*—A ghost. Under the tuition of Jesus, these men will yet become free from the degree of superstition which still cleaves to them. When Jesus appears to *us* in any uncommon manner, as sickness, loss of a friend, or failure in business, we are in danger of mistaking him for an evil spirit. Faith keeps the vision clear. *All things work together for good to them that love God.* Rom. 8: 28.

27, 28. *Straightway*—Immediately. Jesus does not permit his people to continue long in doubt respecting himself. *It is I*—Infinite consolation in the smallest compass. *If it be thou*—That rings like genuine coin, but notice that Peter *asks the Lord to bid* him come. It is better to stay in the ship till Jesus, without any of our hinting, says Come. Faith lets Christ speak the first word.

29. *Come*—When this word falls from the lips of infinite love, it is such a foundation for faith that the vilest need not hesitate to build thereon. One may do what to the reason may seem the most absurd

16 *

30 But when he saw the wind boisterous, he was afraid; and beginning to sink, he cried, saying, Lord, save me.

31 And immediately Jesus stretched forth *his* hand, and caught him, and said unto him, O thou of little faith, wherefore didst thou doubt?

32 And when they were come into the ship, the wind ceased.

33 Then they that were in the ship came and worshipped him, saying, Of a truth thou art the Son of God.

34 ¶ And when they were gone over, they came into the land of Gennesaret.

35 And when the men of that place had knowledge of him, they sent out into all that country round about, and

---

of all things, if one has heard the voice of Jesus, saying, *Come! To go to Jesus*—Though Peter's spirit was defective, the direction was right.

30. *He was afraid*—Then faith is more than an act of the understanding. Peter's intellect assented as strongly to his Master's word when he was sinking as when he was walking. The difficulty was not in his intellect, but in his heart. He assented, but he did not trust. Faith, then, is the reliance of the heart as well as the assent of the intellect. *Beginning to sink*— Christ withdraws his strength that Peter may be weaned from self-reliance. He must learn to pray. He had set off on his perilous walk without prayer. *Lord, save me*— Now he prays from a deeper place in more senses than one than he had ever prayed from before. It is the cry of a soul struggling to give birth to faith; but he does not trust even in his faith. When rising to the divinest height, faith loses the consciousness of its own existence in its grasp of the strength of Christ. *The wind boisterous*—See note on 8: 24, first paragraph. Peter was a swimmer (John 21: 7), but swimming back to the ship, or calling upon his fellow-disciples for help, seems not to have been thought of. He must rely wholly on Christ.

31, 32. *Of little faith*—This was better than none, yet more would have been better. *The wind ceased* — Perhaps a miracle. But compare it with the case already examined, 8: 26: Then he arose and *rebuked* the winds and the sea; and there was a great calm. George Borrow, in his "Bible in Spain," speaks of a remarkable and instantaneous change of wind off Cape Finisterre, by which the ship that was just striking against the rocks was driven out into the open sea and saved from destruction. That, however, was natural; this was supernatural. *Were come — Had* come, or had entered.

33. Here the reference is probably to the sailors. *Worshipped*— More than an act of reverence, in this case. So impressed are the men that they exclaim, Of a truth thou art the Son of God. How much these sailors meant by the words, *Son of God*, it is difficult to say. In the Greek there is no article. *Thou art God's Son* is the true rendering. It is probable that they conceived of him not as the Messiah, but as a being of more than human power. See note on 16: 15-17. There Peter confesses, *Thou art the Son of the living God.*

34. *Were gone*—Having passed. *The land of Gennesaret*—A beautiful plain on the western side of the Sea of Galilee, about four miles long and two and a half broad. Josephus gives a very glowing and probably exaggerated description of the region. "No less than four

brought unto him all that were diseased;

36 And besought him that they might only touch the hem of his garment: and as many as touched were made perfectly whole.

CHAPTER XV.

THEN came to Jesus scribes and Pharisees, which were of Jerusalem, saying,

2 Why do thy disciples transgress the tradition of the el-

---

springs," says Stanley, "pour forth their almost full-grown rivers through the plain; the richness of the soil displays itself in magnificent cornfields; whilst along the shore rises a thick jungle of thorn and oleander, abounding in birds of brilliant colors and various forms; the whole producing an impression such as to the traveller of modern days recalls instantly the valley of the Nile. . . . The plain of Gennesareth became the home of Christ. . . . Few scenes have undergone a greater change. Of all the numerous towns and villages in what must have been the most thickly peopled district of Palestine, only one remains."

35, 36. *Had knowledge of him—* But they must have known him before. They now know of his *return.* The effect of his return shows that he had attained very strong hold of the people. As has been remarked by others, he is now at the height of his popularity. From Capernaum the people send *to all the country round about,* and the sick are brought in great number. *The hem of his garment—*Compare 9: 20, 21, and see the notes.

CHAPTER XV.

DEBATE WITH PHARISEES FROM THE CAPITAL; HEALS A GENTILE IN THE GENTILE WORLD; FEEDS FOUR THOUSAND.

782 U.C. Summer, A.D. 29.

1. The Passover had probably been held. Those who had gone from Galilee to attend it had doubtless made the Lord's works and words the subject of conversation in the capital. The Pharisees must have been alarmed at the evidences of his hold upon the people. As he had not attended the feast, a deputation is sent by the scribes and Pharisees to the north to watch him and procure evidence against him. The men selected go with that peculiar intensity of spirit which is apt to characterize partisans in the great centres of population. Some think the allusion is to Pharisees who had returned home from Jerusalem. *Scribes*—See note on 5: 20. *Pharisees*—See note on 3: 7.

2. They find him in Capernaum, and soon have an opportunity to assail him at what they consider a vulnerable point. *Elders—* This term was at first used to designate persons of considerable age, and as such persons would naturally be selected for an important office, it was afterwards used in an official sense. "Wherever a patriarchal system is in force, the *office* of the *elder* will be found as the keystone of the social and political fabric; it is so at the present day among the Arabs, where the sheikh (= the *old man*) is the highest authority in the tribe." In the earlier period of Jewish history, "their authority was undefined, and extended to all matters concerning the public weal." Some of the members of the Sanhedrim, in the time of Christ, were selected from the elders, but as a body the elders were distinct from the Sanhedrim. In *spirit,* they were one with the scribes and Pharisees. In this verse, the word has reference both to time and office;

ders? for they wash not their hands when they eat bread.

3 But he answered and said unto them, Why do ye also transgress the commandment of God by your tradition?

4 For God commanded, saying, Honor thy father and mother: and, He that curseth father or mother, let him die the death.

5 But ye say, Whosoever shall say to *his* father or *his* mother, *It is* a gift, by whatsoever thou mightest be profited by me;

---

that is, it refers to elders of former times. *Tradition*—See note on Pharisees, 3: 7, to which may be added: The Talmud is a book in the Hebrew language, consisting of two parts, The Mishna and the Gemara. The Mishna consists of Jewish traditions, and was written by a wealthy and influential Jew of the second century. The Gemara is a Commentary on the Mishna. Many of the traditions were believed to have been given by God to Moses, and from Moses to have descended *orally* to others. Some were traceable to the decisions of wise men. The Talmud is proof of the depth to which the Pharisees had fallen in their ritualism. That the oil for lighting the Sabbath might not be boiled suet, that it might be oil of radish seed; that if a bird which was neither to be eaten nor killed laid an egg on a festival, the egg was not to be eaten; that an animal ought not to be eaten unless slaughtered by a Jew; that eating and drinking with "people of the land" was defiling; that a Jew ought not to pay a debt to one who was not a Jew, "three days before any heathen festival, just as if a debtor had any business to meddle with the question of how his creditor might spend his own money,"—were among the cherished traditions of the Pharisees.

Wash not their hands— "As knives and forks were dispensed with in eating, it was absolutely necessary that the hand, which was thrust into the common dish, should be scrupulously clean." The frequent washing which was therefore necessary became through the morbid scrupulousness of the Pharisees a ritualistic act, "and special rules were laid down as to the times and manner of its performance." For aught we know the disciples were as cleanly in their habits as the Pharisees, but in part, at least, through the influence of Jesus, they had ceased to wash their hands *as an act of religious importance.* Of this these hypocrites from Jerusalem complain. It is doubtless a criticism upon Jesus rather than upon the disciples. Unlike a well-known commentator, we believe they were "designedly lying in wait for him." No such practice was required, but "so rigidly did the Jews observe it, that Rabba Akiba, being imprisoned, and having water scarcely sufficient to sustain life given him, preferred dying of thirst to eating without washing his hands." How intense is the bigotry of ritualism!

3. *You also*—He does not deny the charge, but makes a heavier charge against them, the nature of it implying the complete exoneration of the disciples. *By* your tradition—For the sake of. It refers to motive, not to means.

4. *God commanded, saying*—In Ex. 20: 12; 21: 17. Men who affect to despise the Old Testament may here see that Jesus regarded it as the authoritative word of God. *Die the death*—Equivalent to, *Let him surely die.*

5, 6. *But ye say*—Notice how our Lord *contrasts* what they say with what God says. *Gift*—Mark (7: 11) uses the word Corban, which he explains to his readers by this word gift. The Mosaic law allowed the

CHAPTER XV.

6 And honor not his father or his mother, *he shall be free.* Thus have ye made the commandment of God of none effect by your tradition.

7 *Ye* hypocrites, well did Esaias prophesy of you, saying,

8 This people draweth nigh unto me with their mouth, and honoreth me with *their* lips; but their heart is far from me.

9 But in vain they do worship me, teaching *for* doctrines the commandments of men.

10 ¶ And he called the multitude, and said unto them, Hear, and understand:

11 Not that which goeth into the mouth defileth a man; but

---

consecration of things to sacred uses, but the Pharisees, as in so many other cases, carried the practice to a very culpable degree. Corban implied a vow not to use the devoted thing *for one's self;* the Pharisees taught that the consecration of a thing to a sacred purpose forbade using it for the benefit of *any other* person. Should one in a fit of anger indulge in "incomplete exclamations," by which one, so to speak, should unintentionally consecrate an article of property, even these were held to be binding, and were called *yathoth*, or *handles*. He, then, who wished to get rid of helping a needy parent could take refuge under the hypocritical guise of piety. The two verses may be rendered thus: But ye say, Whoever says to his father or his mother, It is a gift, whatever thou mightest be profited with from me, shall not honor his father or his mother; and ye have made the word of God of no effect for the sake of your tradition. It may be expressed freely thus: But ye say, Whosoever says to his father or his mother, That by which I might relieve your wants has been consecrated to religion,—such a man is released from the obligation to relieve them. This is what Jesus charges the Pharisees as saying. The words which our English version supplies, *he shall be free*, are not needed. A tradition may express a truth; but it can be of no authority, for it is not a part of the inspired word. Few traditions express truth; most of them are falsehoods. Traditions abound most in those bodies which, under the name of churches, are built upon the doctrine of mixed membership. Some may be found lurking in the purest churches.

7-9. *Hypocrites*—Concerning the origin and meaning of the word, see note on 6: 2, latter part of the last paragraph. The italicised *ye* in our version might have been spared, which would have made it more forcible. *Esaias*—The words are quoted from 29: 13. *Draweth nigh unto me with their mouth and,* though genuine in Isaiah, are not supported here by ancient manuscripts and versions. *Prophesy of you*—Isaiah said this of his hypocritical contemporaries; the Holy Spirit, speaking through the prophet, intended they should be applied to hypocrites of all times.

10, 11. He now discourses of moral uncleanness, turning from the hypocritical few to the ignorant many. *Not that*—But Moses had been authorized by God himself to make a distinction between different sorts of food. The swine, the owl, the eagle, etc., were forbidden. Lev. 11. Does Jesus, then, aim to bring these divine regulations into disfavor? Not at all. He would teach the multitude their spiritual import. That import had been almost wholly overlooked by the people as well as by the Pharisees.

12. *Then came his disciples*—From Mark (7: 17) we learn that Jesus

that which cometh out of the mouth, this defileth a man.

12 Then came his disciples, and said unto him, Knowest thou that the Pharisees were offended, after they heard this saying?

13 But he answered and said, Every plant, which my heavenly Father hath not planted, shall be rooted up.

14 Let them alone: they be blind leaders of the blind. And if the blind lead the blind, both shall fall into the ditch.

15 Then answered Peter and said unto him, Declare unto us this parable.

16 And Jesus said, Are ye also yet without understanding?

17 Do not ye yet understand, that whatsoever entereth in at the mouth goeth into the belly, and is cast out into the draught?

18 But those things which proceed out of the mouth come forth from the heart; and they defile the man.

19 For out of the heart proceed evil thoughts, murders, adulteries, fornications, thefts, false witness, blasphemies:

20 These are *the things* which defile a man: but to eat with unwashen hands defileth not a man.

21 ¶ Then Jesus went thence, and departed into the coasts of Tyre and Sidon.

---

and the disciples had withdrawn from the people into a house. It was there the question was asked. Christians, especially ministers, should beware of the danger, in these times of boastful and spurious liberality, of withholding or diluting the offensive truths of the gospel. Thorough preaching, though with less striking immediate results, should be the motto.

13, 14. Our Lord's reply is twofold: 1. He assures his disciples, in figurative language, that all false doctrine shall be destroyed. Errors do not contain in themselves the elements of self-destruction. Like sin they are self-perpetuating. Both sin and error are like witch-grass. But God has decreed that error shall at last be rooted out of the earth. 2. He affirms that it is unnecessary for the disciples to engage in active, personal hostility against the men themselves. The people are blind, and their spiritual guides are blind. Retributive justice will overtake them. *Both shall fall*—Similarity in the *nature*, not in the degree, of the punishment that shall overtake both, is taught.

15, 16. *Declare*—Explain. What parable? That which is in vs. 11. It is not correct, though some affirm it, that the language in vs. 11 is plain. It is figurative, and that is the reason why Peter, using the word with more than usual latitude, calls it a parable. Dulness of understanding should not be unwilling to expose itself,—a condition necessary to its removal.

17–20. By a wise provision, even the unnourishing portion of what is eaten passes away without in the least defiling the soul. But there is such a thing as *moral* pollution. Its seat is in the *heart*, the *disposition*, and it proves its existence there by *acts*. *Thoughts* are acts of the soul. *To eat with unwashen hands* —That is, with hands which have not been washed *as a religious act*, has no demoralizing effect upon the man. It is implied throughout the discourse that the converse is true, —washing the hands as a religious rite pollutes the soul.

22. And, behold, a woman of Canaan came out of the same coasts, and cried unto him, saying, Have mercy on me, O Lord, *thou* Son of David; my daughter is grievously vexed with a devil.

23 But he answered her not a word. And his disciples came and besought him, say-

---

21. The Lord had attained very strong hold upon the people; but the plot to destroy him was ripening, and according to John (6 : 59, 66), even many of those who had followed him were so displeased with his discourse at Capernaum, that they ceased to follow him longer. He knew that he must yet visit Jerusalem. He had desired retirement and rest, but had failed to obtain them. He withdraws therefore from the populous and exposed region on the western side of the sea, not through *fear* of his enemies, but, as seems probable, for the twofold purpose of checking for a time the execution of their murderous designs and securing rest. See Mark 7 : 24. *Went thence*—Probably from the city of Capernaum, certainly from that region. *Coasts* —Region. *Tyre and Sidon*—See notes on 11 : 21, third paragraph. Let the student keep in mind that Jesus has now entered the *pagan* world.

22. *Behold*—An unusual event, for she was not a descendant of Abraham; and, besides, Jesus having withdrawn from the populous part of Galilee, Matthew would call special attention to the fact that he is so soon accosted by an applicant for aid. *Of Canaan*—Canaan was the fourth son of Ham. His descendants occupied the territory between the Mediterranean and the Jordan. But the term Canaanite was used in a narrower sense to indicate those who held the lower lands, the *plains* of that territory, among which was the maritime plain of Phœnicia, in which stood Tyre and Sidon. *Out of the same coast*—Out from those borders. *O Lord, thou son of David*—His fame had gone forth into all Syria. She had never seen him, but she had such confidence in his power and love, that she should be regarded as using these titles, though with little knowledge of their higher spiritual meaning, yet with more than mere respect. *Grievously vexed*—Possessed. On the subject of possession see note on 4 : 24. *On me*—But it was not herself that was possessed, but the daughter. It is a beautiful remark of a commentator of the seventeenth century, that the mother made her daughter's malady her own. See the power of maternal sympathy. The Sabbath-school teacher should cherish such Christian sympathy with the impenitent members of his class as to be able to cry, Have mercy *on me!* In this respect this woman of Canaan may serve as an example to us all.

23. *Not a word*—Yet he has words for her behind his lips which will wing joy to her heart. The silence of Jesus may be worth infinitely more than the loudest promises of men. *Send her away*—Dismiss her, whether by hearing her request or rejecting it is not expressed, but it seems probable that they expected Jesus would send her away with the blessing implored. *For she crieth after us*—There is nothing in these words which should expose the disciples to unfavorable judgment. The disciples may have felt that by this woman's cries their Master's desire for retirement was in danger of being frustrated. Dr. Schaff says: "Jesus, who penetrated into the heart of the disciples, interprets their request as an intercession in behalf of the poor woman (vs. 24), which agrees better, also, with their natural sympathy and charity.'

ing, Send her away; for she crieth after us.

24 But he answered and said, I am not sent but unto the lost sheep of the house of Israel.

25 Then came she and worshipped him, saying, Lord, help me.

26 But he answered and said, It is not meet to take the children's bread, and to cast *it* to dogs.

27 And she said, Truth, Lord: yet the dogs eat of the crumbs which fall from their masters' table.

28 Then Jesus answered and said unto her, O woman, great *is* thy faith: be it unto thee

---

24. So far as pertains to the effect upon the woman, it is all the same whether these words were addressed to her or to the disciples. *She overheard them*, and they would have been the knell of her hopes, had she not had Abraham's faith. *Sheep*—A beautiful metaphor, concerning the meaning of which the Sabbath-school teacher ought to speak to his scholars with tender interest. *Lost*—Before their captivity in Babylon the Jews had strayed from their Shepherd into the "great and terrible wilderness" of idolatry. The trials of the captivity reclaimed them to the doctrine of the unity of God, and to the established forms of the Mosaic economy; but with a few exceptions they had fallen into such a spirit of ritualism as proved them to be as thoroughly lost as when they were worshipping Baal and Astarte. It was in compassion that Jesus was moved to confine his personal efforts chiefly to those lost Jews, that thus, in part, the way might be prepared for the recovery of lost Gentiles.

25, 26. Not upon any encouraging *word* is her prayer based, but upon what she knows of his *character*. In the reply the Lord's object is to draw out the woman's faith, and to hold it up to the view of the disciples for their further enlightenment relative to the comprehensiveness of his merciful purpose, and to the view of all his disciples in all future ages. *Dogs*—The little dogs, that is, the household dogs. It is a singular fact that while the dog is considered one of the noblest of the irrational animals, the term is used, as it was in the days of our Lord, as a term of contempt. "Throughout the whole East 'dog' is a term of reproach for impure and profane persons, and in this sense is used by the Jews respecting the Gentiles, and by Muhammedans respecting Christians." It is used as a term "of humility in speaking of one's self. Knox relates a story of a nobleman of Ceylon, who, being asked by the king how many children he had, replied: 'Your majesty's dog has three puppies.'" As Jesus used the term, it doubtless *in form expressed severity*, but it was spoken in love. He means to say to the woman that privileges which belong peculiarly to Jews cannot be conferred upon Gentiles.

27. *Truth*—Yea. She admits it all. She knows too much, is too humble, to exalt herself to a level with the chosen people. Every word of her reply from first to last is a crushing blow of the logic wrought in her heart by the apparently repelling words of Jesus himself: *For* (yet), thou permittest me to draw this conclusion from thine own premises; *Dog*, I am one; *Eat*, then I may eat; *Crumbs*, that is all I want; *Which fall*, I am willing to take them as if they *chanced* to come to me; *Masters' table*, God is *my* master, and so I may believe the crumbs were intended for me. Faith makes good reasoners con-

CHAPTER XV.

even as thou wilt. And her daughter was made whole from that very hour.

29 And Jesus departed from thence, and came nigh unto the sea of Galilee; and went up into a mountain, and sat down there.

30 And great multitudes came unto him, having with them *those that were* lame, blind, dumb, maimed, and many others, and cast them down at Jesus' feet; and he healed them:

31 Insomuch that the multitude wondered, when they saw the dumb to speak, the maimed to be whole, the lame to walk, and the blind to see: and they glorified the God of Israel.

32 ¶ Then Jesus called his disciples *unto him*, and said, I have compassion on the multitude, because they continue with me now three days, and have nothing to eat: and I will not send them away fasting, lest they faint in the way.

33 And his disciples say unto him, Whence should we have so much bread in the wilderness, as to fill so great a multitude?

34 And Jesus saith unto them, How many loaves have ye? And they said, Seven, and a few little fishes.

35 And he commanded the multitude to sit down on the ground.

36 And he took the seven loaves and the fishes, and gave thanks, and brake *them*, and gave to his disciples, and the disciples to the multitude.

37 And they did all eat, and were filled: and they took up of the broken *meat* that was left seven baskets full.

38 And they that did eat were four thousand men, beside women and children.

---

cerning divine subjects. A humble heart makes a clear head. The logic of infidelity is always at fault.

28. *Great is thy faith*—O thou of *little* faith, to a son of Abraham a few days before, and that son of Abraham an apostle, and that apostle Peter! Parents persevering in intercession for their children pleasing to Christ.

29. *From thence*—From Phœnicia. *Came nigh unto the Sea of Galilee*—He went to the sea *through the midst of Decapolis* (Mark 7: 31), which, as we have already seen, lay on the eastern side of the Jordan. But he could have reached Decapolis by a northern route, crossing the river above the Sea of Galilee, or by a southern route, crossing below the sea. It is, on the whole, probable that he took the former. The mountain into which he went is not known.

30, 31. *Great multitudes*—Chiefly, it is probable, from the mountainous regions on this eastern side of the sea, rather than from cities and villages on the western side. *Maimed* —Crippled in the hands, though the word is sometimes used with reference to the limbs.

32-38. The student should carefully compare this account with that in 14: 15-21; for it has been said that Matthew has made the blunder of reporting the same thing twice, his memory failing to serve him in some of the details. It has also been affirmed that this is a forgery.

39 And he sent away the multitude, and took ship, and came into the coasts of Magdala.

CHAPTER XVI.

THE Pharisees also with the Sadducees came, and tempting desired him that he would shew them a sign from heaven. 2 He answered and said unto them, When it is evening, ye say, *It will be* fair weather: for the sky is red. 3 And in the morning, *It will be* foul weather to day: for the sky is red and lowering. O

But it has been well asked, "What could any one gain by inventing the account of Christ's having fed four thousand, when he had already fed five thousand? It is not thus that the fictions of tradition run. If we had read here of Christ having fed ten thousand with one loaf, the probability of forgery had been greater." It has been thought improbable that the disciples could so soon, after the feeding of the five thousand, have doubted whether the wants of so great a multitude could be supplied; but it should be considered that these men were yet babes in knowledge and faith. Many a Christian in our own days fears lest bread will not be given him to the end of life, though God has given it to him every day for fifty years. But it is by no means certain that the question in vs. 33 should be considered as expressive of doubt. It may be an indirect expression of expectation that Jesus will himself supply their wants by a miracle. Notice especially vv. 9 and 10 of the next chapter, in which Jesus distinguishes between the two miracles. Scholars have also remarked that in the account of the feeding of five thousand, the word used by all the four evangelists for *baskets* is different from the word used by Matthew and Mark in the account of the four thousand; and, what is very striking, Jesus makes exactly the same distinction when referring to the two miracles in 16: 9, 10. In vs. 9 he says, of the *five thousand*, and how many *cophini* (baskets) ye took up. In vs. 10 he says, of the *four thousand*, and how many *spurides* (baskets) ye took up. Matthew, it is clear, reports two different miracles.

39. *Magdala*—It lay, doubtless, on the western side of the sea, and to that side he now returns.

CHAPTER XVI.

A SIGN ASKED; PETER AND HIS FELLOW-APOSTLES CONFESS CHRIST AS THE MESSIAH; JESUS FORETELLS HIS OWN DEATH.

782 U.C. Summer, A.D. 29.

1. The leaders of Jewish thought cannot suffer Jesus to remain unmolested. A combination of the Pharisees and the Sadducees, who (see notes on 3 : 7) in some respects are the opposite of each other, is formed against him. These representatives of rival sects found him probably at Capernaum,—his home. They seem to have gone from Jerusalem, though the Pharisees of Galilee may have been united in the plot. Combinations *in form against* Christ, of parties who are at odds with each other, is a stimulating example to evangelical denominations to combine in *spirit*, even if they cannot in form, *for* Christ. *Tempting him*—Not merely putting him to the test, which is the sense which the word sometimes has, but laying a plan to entrap him. They wish to bring his claim as a divine teacher into disrepute. Demanding a sign from heaven was *their way of affirm-*

CHAPTER XVI.

ye hypocrites, ye can discern the face of the sky; but can ye not *discern* the signs of the times?

4 A wicked and adulterous generation seeketh after a sign; and there shall no sign be given unto it, but the sign of the prophet Jonas. And he left them, and departed.

5 And when his disciples were come to the other side, they had forgotten to take bread.

6 ¶ Then Jesus said unto them, Take heed and beware of the leaven of the Pharisees and of the Sadducees.

7 And they reasoned among themselves, saying, It is because we have taken no bread.

8 *Which* when Jesus per-

---

ing that his claims had no foundation in truth. *A sign from heaven*—A sign wrought further off, in the heavens, in distinction from one wrought near at hand, upon the earth. See 1 Cor. 1:22. They seem to have held that while an impostor might work miracles near to himself, he could not work them far off in the skies. Faith accepts the signs which God has seen fit to give in Christ.

2, 3. *Fair weather! foul weather!* is more vivacious than, *It will be fair . . . foul. Can discern*—Know how to discern. *The signs of the times*—Some say, "of times generally. The Jews had been, and were, most blind to the signs of the times at all the great crises of their history; and also particularly to the times in which they were then living. The sceptre had departed from Judah, the lawgiver no longer came forth from between his feet, the prophetic weeks of Daniel were just at their end: yet they discerned none of these things." *Evening . . . fair weather . . . sky red*—It is fanciful to consider these expressions as symbolizing the ending of the old dispensation; and *foul weather . . . the sky red and lowering*, though the beginning of the new era, as indicating the storm that was about to descend upon Israel. The thought is this, that persons who are so accustomed to notice weather-signs ought to be able to see the spiritual signs of the times.

4. See note on 12:39, 40. *Left them*—They would have protracted their attempt, had he permitted it. As has been suggested, there may have been something retributive in the sudden manner in which he seems to have left them. He is perfectly aware that the plot laid for his death is thickening. *Departed*—To the other side of the Sea of Galilee. He went in a ship. Mark 8:13.

5. *Had forgotten to take bread*—The original does not enable us to determine whether they forgot to take bread before they sailed, or after they landed before proceeding further. Mark (8:14) says, Neither had they *in the ship with them more than one loaf. Forgotten*—This implies that they generally took bread. The Lord was not prodigal in the use of his miraculous powers.

6. Being now alone with the disciples, he embraces the opportunity to fortify them against the influence of the Pharisees and Sadducees. *Leaven*—See note on the parable of the leaven, 13:33. In Luke 12:1 the leaven of the Pharisees is defined as hypocrisy; but see note on vs. 12.

7, 8. *Among themselves*—Implying that they *conversed with* one another. *Little faith*—Their failure to understand him was not so much through dulness of intellect as through weakness of faith. Strong faith is the mother of quick under-

ceived, he said unto them, O ye of little faith, why reason ye among yourselves, because ye have brought no bread?

9 Do ye not yet understand, neither remember the five loaves of the five thousand, and how many baskets ye took up?

10 Neither the seven loaves of the four thousand, and how many baskets ye took up?

11 How is it that ye do not understand that I spake *it* not to you concerning bread, that ye should beware of the leaven of the Pharisees and of the Sadducees?

12 Then understood they how that he bade *them* not beware of the leaven of bread, but of the doctrine of the Pharisees and of the Sadducees.

13 ¶ When Jesus came into the coasts of Cesarea Philippi,

---

standing. How little anxiety the Lord showed concerning his physical wants, but how much solicitude that these men, who were to be the founders of his kingdom, should be men of faith and knowledge!

9, 10. He reminds them of the two great miracles of feeding, to show them how easily their wants can be supplied. *Baskets*—See the latter part of the note on vv. 32-38 of chap. 15. It was not uncommon for a Jew when about to travel to take a basket with him.

12. *Doctrine*—Teaching. Jesus did not condemn *all* that the Pharisees and Sadducees taught. He condemned all that they taught contrary to Moses or himself. It was leaven: it was corrupting.

We have arrived at a very important turn in our Lord's life. Hitherto he has displayed the evidence of his Messiahship by his miracles and teachings, but has not distinctly avowed his Messiahship even to his disciples. That he is to suffer and die he has not clearly intimated even to the most confidential of his followers. He has been perfectly aware, however, of the increasing prejudice and hostility against him at the capital, and knows that the time is not far distant when, in accordance with the eternal plan, he will be called to surrender his life. In his infinite wisdom, he deems the time to have arrived when he may put the disciples fully in possession of the fact of his Messiahship and of the fact that he must die, though, as we shall see, they are even now poorly prepared to receive the announcement of the latter. Henceforth we must follow him as emphatically *the man of sorrows*, beginning to be *wounded, more deeply, for our transgressions*.

13. *Into the coasts of Cesarea Philippi*—From Bethsaida (Mark 8: 22). There was another Cesarea, which was in the western part of Palestine, on the Mediterranean shore, and which is often mentioned in the Acts. The city near which our Lord now comes is very beautifully situated at the foot of the mountains of Hermon, at the easternmost of the streams which have been usually considered as constituting the source of the Jordan. Here were the palaces of Philip the tetrarch. Here was the "beautiful temple of white marble" which was built by his father Herod in honor of Augustus Cæsar. The city was once called Paneas, in honor of the heathen god Pan, and the modern village bears the name *Banias*. "The situation," says Robinson, "is unique; combining in an unusual degree the elements of grandeur and beauty. It nestles in its recess at the southern base of the mighty Hermon, which towers in majesty to an

he asked his disciples, saying, Whom do men say that I, the Son of man, am?

14 And they said, Some *say that thou art* John the Baptist; some, Elias; and others, Jeremias, or one of the prophets.

15 He saith unto them, But whom say ye that I am?

16 And Simon Peter answered and said, Thou art the Christ, the Son of the living God.

17 And Jesus answered and

---

elevation of seven or eight thousand feet above." It is not certain that Jesus entered into the city itself, but he at least came near to it. He went into *the coasts* of it,—into the parts adjacent to it. Whether he went directly from Bethsaida to Cesarea Philippi cannot be known. *Whom do men say?* etc.—Proposed, not because he did not know, but because he would prepare them for the important words which are to follow. *The Son of man*—See note on 12 : 6, 8, second paragraph.

14. In their reply they give the current opinions. *Some, John the Baptist*—See 14 : 2. *Elias*—Elijah. See note on 11 : 14, 15. All these classes seem to have adopted the opinion that Jesus sustained some peculiar relation to the expected Messiah, that of a forerunner or herald, for example, but they had not attained to the conviction that he was the Messiah himself.

15–17. The answer to the important question of vs. 15 shows what has been the result of the tuition under which the disciples have been. Ignorant though they still are in comparison with what they will become, it shows what spiritual elevation they have attained in comparison with either the people generally, or the professional teachers of religion. *Peter answered and said*— He answered for his fellow-disciples as well as for himself; if not, we must regard the others as showing their Master the disrespect of not answering at all. It cannot be doubted that they considered themselves as having answered through Peter. This is important; for Romanists insist that he answered only

for himself. *Thou art the Christ*— The Messiah. See note on 1 : 1. This is the first, yet lower part of their confession. It is a distinct avowal of their conviction that Jesus is the Messiah whose coming in human flesh the prophets had foretold. *The Son of God*—This is the second and higher part of their confession. Ignorance of this great truth rested like a pall over the world. The Gentiles, of course, knew nothing of it. The Jews not only did not believe that this Jesus was the Son of God, but they did not believe that the Messiah, whoever should prove to be such, was to be the Son of God. They were criminal for not believing the latter, and, since Jesus was the Messiah, were criminal for not believing that Jesus was the Son of God. But what is the meaning of the words, Son of God? Whatever it is, the meaning did not become the possession of Peter and his fellow-apostles by human wisdom, either their own or any other man's; for (vs. 17) our Lord declares that *flesh and blood* — man, or, possibly, anything of a natural kind in contrast with the supernatural — has not revealed it to them. The meaning was revealed to them by God himself. Not only was the twofold *fact* that Jesus was the Christ and the Son of God revealed to them, but the *meaning* of the fact. The *fulness* of the meaning was not revealed: that is a study for eternity. It follows that the words, Son of God, are used in some sense that would not have occurred to the highest human intellect unilluminated from above. In what sense, then? We quote from a

said unto him, Blessed art thou Simon Bar-jona: for flesh and blood hath not revealed *it* unto thee, but my Father which is in heaven.

18. And I say also unto thee, That thou art Peter, and upon this rock I will build my church; and the gates of hell shall not prevail against it.

---

recent writer, Rev. Dr. Edward Meyrick Goulburn (Episcopalian): "Our Lord is the Son of God not only in respect of his birth of the virgin, not only in respect of his birth from the grave (or resurrection), not only in respect of his inheritance of all things, but also in respect of the communication (from all eternity) of the divine essence from the Father, which is far more truly and properly a generation than any natural generation of the creature.

"The scriptural texts which show this are:—

"God sent his only begotten Son into the world. John 4: 9. (He was the Son before he was sent.)

"God sent forth his Son, made of a woman. Gal. 4: 4. (He was the Son before he was born of a woman.)

"The first-born of every creature (or, as it might be rendered, Begotten prior to every creature). Col. 1: 17.

"The only begotten Son, which *is* in the bosom of the Father (evidently referring to our Lord's position in the Godhead, not to his birth in time). John 1: 18."

It has been proved, if any proposition whatever has been proved, that Christ, as the Son of God, is "co-equal and co-eternal" with the Father. *My Father*—Not *our* Father, as in the Lord's Prayer. He is the Father of Christ, as Christ is the Son of God, in a peculiar sense. See John 5: 18: But said also that God was his Father, making himself *equal with God;* John 10: 30: *I and my Father are one.* As son of man expresses the human nature of Christ, Son of God expresses the divine nature. *The living God*—Not dead like the gods of the heathen. Jesus approved the confession,—great arrogance if he was not the Messiah and was not God manifest in human flesh. Was Jesus revealed to them as the Messiah now for the first time? Long before this (John 1: 41) it had been said, *We have found the Messias.* But the confession which Peter has now made is the child of much deeper conviction, itself the offspring of much greater knowledge. It was almost like an original acknowledgment. *Bar-jona*—Son of Jonas.

18. Romanists use this verse and the following one as proof that "the Church is infallible in matters of faith," and that "St. Peter, by Christ's ordinance, was raised to the dignity of Pope or chief bishop." See Table of References at the end of the Douay Version, New York, 1848, and approved by "John Hughes, Bishop of New York." Protestants have been too much inclined to deny all reference in the words, *this rock*, to Peter, and have explained them as meaning either, 1. *Peter's confession,* Thou art the Christ, the Son of the living God, affirming that it is upon that great truth that Christ declares his purpose to build the Church; or, 2. *Christ himself.* The former explanation is forced and unnatural. The latter is more probable, since both in the Old Testament and the New, God or Christ is very often called a rock. It has been affirmed (*Alexander*) that the term is never applied, even by the strongest figure, to a merely human subject; and that this remarkable image is at least sufficient to create a strong presumption that the figure here is not applied to any mere man. We believe that the

CHAPTER XVI.   199

19 And I will give unto thee the keys of the kingdom of

---

reference is either to Christ or to Peter. So far as the pretensions of Rome are concerned, Protestants need not hesitate to explain them as referring to Peter. Admitting that Peter was the exclusive founder of the church in Rome,—though that can never be proved,—it by no means follows that the personages called Popes are *his divinely appointed successors*. That depends in part upon the question whether the Popes, all of them, or even most of them, have been essentially *like* Peter; and that is a question which the interests of Romanism require should not be pressed. A very little investigation of facts of history would reveal Popes wallowing in such licentiousness as to destroy every lineament of resemblance to Peter. Admitting again that Peter founded a Christian church in Rome, it does not at all follow that the present Church of Rome is that church continued. That depends in part upon the question whether the present Church of Rome is like the church which Peter founded, and that is a question which answers itself. For such a body as the Roman Catholic Church is and always has been, partly political, partly Jewish, partly Christian, partly pagan, to call itself the Church of Jesus Christ, a continuation of the original Christian church in Rome, is one of those monstrous assumptions which required the travail-pains of centuries to bring forth. *Peter may be the rock on which Christ promised to build his church*, and yet Romanism itself may be one of the forces which the gates of hell will employ in their vain resistance to Christ. We accept as more probably the true interpretation of our Lord's words, that he means *Peter* rather than *himself:* Peter, 1. In his own character. 2. As the representative of the apostolic body. More than any other apostle, *at first*, Peter was the means of introducing both Jews and Gentiles into the Christian church. But (*a.*) The other apostles as well as Peter are represented as being the foundation of the church. Eph. 2: 20; Rev. 21: 14. (*b.*) The powers conferred upon Peter were soon, even if not now, conferred upon the other apostles (John 20: 23), and indeed upon the entire church. 18: 18. (*c.*) Peter himself never assumed official authority over his fellow-apostles. (*d.*) Paul so conducted himself toward Peter as to show that he recognized in him no superiority of rank. (*e.*) On one important occasion (Acts 15), James towers quite above Peter in perception and influence. Gal. 2: 11-14. For these reasons it may be concluded that if in the words, Upon this rock I will build my church, Christ alludes to Peter, he alludes to him as the *representative* of the apostolic body.

Church—Not here an *organized* body, though generally so used in the New Testament, but all true believers, whether members of an organized church or not. In 18: 17, And if he shall neglect to hear them, *tell it unto the church*, it has the usual sense; that is, the church in an organized form. *Organization* can be affirmed only of *churches*, as the church in Corinth, the church in Pergamos, etc. There is no such body in the United States as The Baptist Church, though there are several thousand Baptist churches. See note on 13: 41, concerning the nature of a Christian church.

Hell—Hades, concerning which see note on 11: 23, under the same word. This is one of the cases in which *hades*, here translated *hell*, seems to be scarcely distinguishable from *Gehenna*, also translated hell, and expressing, as would be admitted by all evangelical scholars, the place of future punishment.

heaven and whatsoever thou shalt bind on earth shall be bound in heaven: and whatsoever thou shalt loose on earth shall be loosed in heaven.

20 Then charged he his disciples that they should tell no man that he was Jesus the Christ.

21 ¶ From that time forth began Jesus to shew unto his disciples, how that he must go unto Jerusalem, and suffer many things of the elders and chief priests and scribes, and be killed, and be raised again the third day.

22 Then Peter took him, and began to rebuke him, saying, Be it far from thee, Lord: this shall not be unto thee.

23 But he turned, and said unto Peter, Get thee behind me, Satan: thou art an offence unto me: for thou savourest not the

---

19. *Keys*—A figure expressing the idea that Jesus confers upon Peter and his brethren in the apostolate, authority in matters pertaining to the guardianship of the kingdom of heaven. They were hereby authorized to announce the conditions of membership, to receive persons as members, and to announce the reasons for which the membership of unworthy persons should cease. *Bind . . . loose*—These terms are substantially another method of stating what he has just stated under the figure of keys. The general idea in both forms of expression is that of government or control. *On earth . . . in heaven*—What the apostles do, under the guidance of the Holy Spirit, will be sanctioned in heaven. 20. *Tell no man*—The people were not prepared to receive it, and the disclosure might have prematurely hastened to a conclusion the conspiracy against his life.

21. Thus confirmed in respect to his nature and office, the disciples must be taught the great truth that he is to be put to death. *Must go unto Jerusalem*—1. The eternal plan requires it; 2. But between the execution of that plan and the freedom of the human will there is no clashing. If the doctrine that God *creates sinful volitions in the hearts of men* were true, God could have effected the death of Jesus in Capernaum or at the foot of Mount Hermon as well as in Jerusalem; but the doctrine is false. Both crime and virtue become more intense in the great centres of human life. That fact the eternal plan presupposed. Only in such a centre will the spirit of crime be virulent enough to accomplish the death of the Son of God. *Many things*—Let these be specified by the Sabbath-school teacher. *The elders, chief priests, and scribes* were the Sanhedrim. Concerning the first class see note on 15: 2, and the last two the note on 2: 4. *Be raised*—The active, *rise*, is the correct form. Observe that Jesus *knew* this; it was not a mere estimate of the possibilities of the case.

22. The two facts: 1. That Jesus is the Messiah, the Son of the living God; 2. That he is to suffer death, seem to Peter utterly irreconcilable; and, in the impulsiveness of his nature, strengthened by his comparative ignorance of spiritual things, he cries out, This shall not be unto thee. He makes no withdrawal of his noble confession. He still believes that Jesus is all that he has just confessed him to be, and it is because he believes it that he cannot admit that Jesus is to be put to death. It is contrary to all his conceptions of the Messiah. It is not to be supposed that the other disciples had juster views than Peter, but it is like Peter to do the talking. How

things that be of God, but those that be of men.

24 ¶ Then said Jesus unto his disciples, If any *man* will come after me, let him deny himself, and take up his cross, and follow me.

25 For whosoever will save his life shall lose it: and whosoever will lose his life for my sake shall find it.

26 For what is a man profited, if he shall gain the whole world, and lose his own soul?

---

many reject Christ on the cross who profess to receive Jesus in the manger! Many reject him both in the manger and on the cross. Conviction of a truth may become a source of temptation; and the profounder the truth and deeper the conviction, the more powerful may be the temptation. *Began*—" In the simplicity and particularity of the ancient manner, a person is often said *to begin* to do what he is to be understood as having actually done."

23. *Behind . . . Satan*—Severe but just; for who but Christ could comprehend all the issues involved in yielding to this new suggestion of the spirit of evil? *Satan* must not be taken in the sense of adversary. Jesus refers to "the wicked one," the prince of evil spirits, elsewhere called *diabolos*, devil. John Bunyan describes him with sufficient distinctness. The Lord applies the term to Peter, but with a vivid recollection of what he had suffered at Satan's hands in the wilderness. He rebukes Satan in Peter, as before he rebuked him to his face. *Offence unto me*—A ground of displeasure. *Savorest*—Savory food is food that *relishes*. But that is not the meaning here. As the word *savorest* is now used, it conveys to the English reader an erroneous idea. It has given rise in pulpits and vestries to many an exhortation which the original word does not justify. The meaning is: *Thou thinkest not the things of God, but the things of men;* that is, concerning the point of which he had spoken, Peter had not expressed the mind of God, but the uninformed and prejudiced mind of the Jews, who did not expect that the Messiah would be subjected to ignominy and death. Here John 12: 34 is very important.

24. *Will come*—It denotes purpose, which of course implies desire. *Come after*—Become my disciple. *Deny himself*—It refers not to some specific act, but to the entire being. One may live for self apart from God, may make his own will instead of God's the standard of all his actions. But this is what no one can do who purposes to be a disciple of Christ. *Take up his cross*—In allusion to the well-known custom of criminals carrying the cross on which they were to be crucified, and to the manner of his own death. Applying these words to a specific act, as speaking in a religious meeting, or being baptized, is a use which has no support whatever in the Scriptures, and ought wholly to cease. Ministers, whether pastors or evangelists, should not lend their countenance to such a perversion, and should teach young disciples that *taking up the cross* is a much more thorough and comprehensive thing.

25. Having taught his disciples that *he* must lose *his* life, he proceeds to teach them that they must be willing to lose theirs also. Thus he would educate them to see that Christian discipleship involves an entire elevation of soul above those semi-worldly views concerning the Messiah's kingdom, which had just found utterance through Peter. For the explanation of the verse see 10: 39, where the same words occur.

26. *His own soul*—The immortal,

or what shall a man give in exchange for his soul?

27 For the Son of man shall come in the glory of his Father with his angels; and then he shall reward every man according to his works.

28 Verily I say unto you, There be some standing here, which shall not taste of death, till they see the Son of man coming in his kingdom.

CHAPTER XVII.

AND after six days Jesus taketh Peter, James, and John his brother, and bringeth them up into a high mountain apart.

---

the spiritual nature, as in 10: 28; though in some instances the original word is used in the sense of *natural life*. *In exchange*—As an exchange, as a "counter-price." Here are two sums, the first of which is not difficult. A child can do it. One step will bring the true answer. The second sum cannot be done. The answer is infinitely remote. The value of *one* soul lies beyond the computation of all created beings. Teacher! be not insensible to this tremendous truth. Press it upon the attention of those committed to your care, and pray that the Holy Spirit may lodge it in their hearts. Jesus Christ teaches the possibility of losing the soul, which is a sufficient reply to all that men may say on the other side.

27. An argument to incite us to secure eternal life, and to cease striving to gain the world. He will come, at the end of the new dispensation, as the *Son of man;* that is, men will then see him as the being who, when in the world, bore the character represented in those words; a being of *voluntary humiliation;* but he will come in the *glory of his Father*—Invested with all the glory which he had with the Father from the beginning, not in the shame and weakness in which most men now view him; he will come to *reward every man according to his works*—To confer upon every man bliss, not as a thing merited, yet according to his entire course of life, from the consideration of which the question whether he has accepted the righteousness and death of Christ can no more be excluded, than the question whether he has been kind to the poor and faithful in paying the claims of his creditors.

28. *Till they see the Son of man coming*, etc.—To what time Jesus here refers is a question upon which there has been very great diversity of opinion. The time of the Transfiguration is most improbable of all. The time of the last advent is inadmissible, since the event was to occur before some present should die. Mark (9: 1) reports the same thing, without the words to which some are so inclined to attach a peculiar meaning,—*the Son of man coming*. His words are, Till they have seen *the kingdom of God come with power*. The kingdom of God was *at hand* when John preached in the wilderness. It *came with power* on the day of Pentecost, yet not to the exclusion of the subsequent apostolic period. That entire period, inclusive of the Pentecost and of the destruction of the Jewish polity at the downfall of Jerusalem, was the forming period of Christianity, both for that age and for future ages. There were some present who lived to see that powerful coming of the kingdom of God. We suppose, then, that there is an intended contrast between the statement in this verse and that in the preceding one. In vs. 27, Jesus speaks of his *final* coming; in this,

2 And was transfigured before them: and his face did shine as the sun, and his raiment was white as the light.

---

of that coming which some now living shall see.

CHAPTER XVII.

THE TRANSFIGURATION; A LUNATIC HEALED; CHRIST'S DEATH AGAIN ANNOUNCED.

782 U.C. Summer, A.D. 29.

Peter and the other apostles were so surprised and disappointed at the announcement that Jesus was to be put to death, that our Lord soon favored them with an uncommon means of illumination and faith. The event is not to be explained away as a dream or a trance. It was an actual occurrence, the word *vision*, in vs. 9, being no evidence to the contrary. The word sometimes denotes a supernatural appearance, and sometimes merely what is seen. That the latter is the meaning here is evident from Mark 9: 9, What things they had *seen;* and from Luke 9: 36, Those things which they had *seen.* In his second epistle (1: 16-18), Peter, many years after the event, referred to it in such terms as to put the reality of the occurrences beyond all question.

1. *Peter, James, and John*—Why were not the others taken also? Possibly because the wants of his own pure spirit would be more fully met by the presence of a smaller number, and perhaps because these were more qualified to be benefited by what was to occur. He selected these same men to accompany him into the house when he was about to raise the ruler's daughter from the dead, and into the garden of Gethsemane. So far as they are to be regarded in the light of witnesses, three were sufficient. How great the contrast between the glory of the transfiguration and the humiliation on the cross! But there was a connecting link, for, according to Luke 9: 30, the subject of conversation upon the mount was his decease. In periods of the highest spiritual elevation the death of Christ is a subject of transcendent interest. *A high mountain apart*—Apart refers to them, not to the mountain. There are no means of deciding what mountain it was. The popular idea that it was Mount Tabor is not well supported. Says Dr. Hackett, in Smith's Dictionary of the Bible: "If one might choose a place which he would deem peculiarly fitting for so sublime a transaction, there is none certainly which would so entirely satisfy our feelings in this respect as the lofty, majestic, beautiful Tabor. It is impossible, however, to acquiesce in the correctness of this opinion. . . . It is morally certain that Tabor must have been inhabited . . . in the days of Christ." It is more probable that one of the peaks of Hermon was the scene of the transfiguration, for that would be considerably nearer Cesarea Philippi.

2. *Transfigured*—Changed; in what respects is stated in the next two clauses. (*a.*) His face was supernaturally illuminated; (*b.*) Even his garments were, *became*, white as the light. See Ex. 34: 30 for a similar illumination of the face of Moses. In what the radiance of the Lord's face and raiment consisted is a useless inquiry. It is not stated either that the light proceeded from his body, or that it came upon him from without. It has been spoken of as the bursting forth of the inherent glory of Christ, but the same writer thinks this hardly sufficient to account for the brilliancy of his *garments.*

3 And, behold, there appeared unto them Moses and Elias talking with him.

4 Then answered Peter, and said unto Jesus, Lord, it is good for us to be here: if thou wilt, let us make here three tabernacles; one for thee, and one for Moses, and one for Elias.

5 While he yet spake, behold, a bright cloud overshadowed them: and behold a voice out of the cloud, which said, This is my beloved Son, in whom I am well pleased; hear ye him.

6 And when the disciples heard it, they fell on their face, and were sore afraid.

7 And Jesus came and touched them, and said, Arise, and be not afraid.

---

3. *Moses*—The representative of the law. *Elijah*—The representative of the prophets. Both were representatives of the entire old dispensation. The meeting shows the personal union of these glorified ones with each other and with the Son of God. It shows also the oneness of the spirit of the ancient economy with that of the new. The essential oneness of the law and the gospel, as taught in the Sermon on the Mount, is here, on the Mount of Transfiguration, illustrated in the meeting of Moses and Christ.

4. *Answered*—Not that any question had been asked. In the languages in which the Bible was written, this form is often used "where the words are occasioned by, or dependent on, something that precedes." *Lord*—In the epistles, this word, preceded by the definite article, expresses the exalted nature of Christ; here it is equivalent to Rabbi (teacher), which is the corresponding word in Mark. *Good to be here*—But there is no reason to suppose that Peter desired to remain there long. In this matter, Peter has been handled more roughly by interpreters than the record warrants. We cannot, with Lange, "understand Peter as willing to give up the prospect of that coming glory" [of Messiah's kingdom], "satisfied if, separated from the world, he could continue with the Lord and his companions, in spiritual communion with Moses and Elijah." We see in the account nothing like readiness to renounce the world by forming "an outward institution (such as monasticism)." This view implies too much deliberation. According to Mark, Peter *wist not what to say*. We prefer to regard him as having, in the excitement of the occasion, *no special aim* in the proposition, or as feeling that the heavenly visitants would probably remain a few days and nights, and that therefore some shelter on the mountain would be desirable. *Tabernacles*—Tents made of boughs, such as Peter had been accustomed to see at the Feast of Tabernacles. *Three*—None for himself and his fellow-disciples.

5. *A bright cloud*—Not a common cloud illuminated by the sun, but a supernatural brilliancy in the form of a cloud. It was similar, doubtless, to that which received him at his ascension (Acts 1: 9); to that in which the Lord went before the Israelites in their march through the wilderness; and to that which hovered over the mercy-seat in the tabernacle and the temple. In the old dispensation it was called the *Shekinah*, and was a symbol of God's presence. *Overshadowed them*—The apostles as well as the others. Luke 9: 34. Concerning the voice see on 3: 17. *Hear ye him*—Of great interest in this connection are the words in Hebrews 1: 1, 2; 2: 1-3. Thus God solemnly sets forth his Son, in the

CHAPTER XVII.

8 And when they had lifted up their eyes, they saw no man, save Jesus only.

9 And as they came down from the mountain, Jesus charged them, saying, Tell the vision to no man, until the Son of man be risen again from the dead.

10 And his disciples asked him, saying, Why then say the scribes that Elias must first come?

11 And Jesus answered and said unto them, Elias truly shall first come, and restore all things.

12 But I say unto you, That Elias is come already, and they knew him not, but have done unto him whatsoever they listed. Likewise shall also the Son of man suffer of them.

13 Then the disciples understood that he spake unto them of John the Baptist.

14 ¶ And when they were come to the multitude, there

---

very presence of Moses and Elijah, as the true Messiah of whom they themselves had spoken, and whom all men are henceforth under obligation to receive.

8. The object is accomplished. The apostles, more enlightened than ever by this wonderful display of divine glory, will be confirmed in their allegiance to Christ, and be prepared to work more effectually after their Master shall have returned to heaven; and therefore Moses and Elijah have departed.

9. *Vision*—See the remarks introductory to the notes upon the chapter. *Tell no man*—If, as is understood by most interpreters, this was a prohibition to tell it even to their fellow-apostles, which may be doubted, it is difficult to assign any other motive than that the others were not prepared to receive it. At any rate these three were doubtless in advance of the others in spiritual perception.

10. *Elias*—See on 11: 14, 15. "Within sight on a neighboring hill, was a pillar of stone, which the Jews said was Elijah's seat, because he was accustomed to rest there as he journeyed through this region. He will come again a second time, they remarked to me, and will then change the pillar into gold. Here we have a trace of the opinion in respect to which the Jews in Christ's time were so tenacious, that one of the antecedents of the Messianic age was that 'Elias must first come.' Their mistake was that they expected a literal return of the prophet, instead of the appearance of one who should manifest his 'spirit and power.'"—*Dr. Hackett* The question was probably prompted by the fact that Elijah did not now tarry and engage in the work which he was expected to do.

11-13. Jesus admits that the scribes are right in saying that Elijah must precede the Messiah, but exposes their blindness in that they do not see that he has already come. Elias *shall first come—Indeed comes*, is the correct rendering of the Greek. *Restore* — Shall restore. These words give no authority for the idea that Elijah's coming is yet future; for Christ says that he has already come; that is, that the words of Malachi (4: 5) have been fulfilled in the coming of John. He uses the future tense only because he would express the fact as conceived and proclaimed by the prophet. John came to take a preparatory part in the work of restoring to the Jewish mind the true ideal of the old covenant, which always included the coming of a purely spiritual king-

came to him a *certain* man, kneeling down to him, and saying,

15 Lord, have mercy on my son; for he is lunatic, and sore vexed: for ofttimes he falleth into the fire, and oft into the water.

16 And I brought him to thy disciples, and they could not cure him.

17 Then Jesus answered and said, O faithless and perverse generation, how long shall I be with you? how long shall I suffer you? bring him hither to me.

18 And Jesus rebuked the devil; and he departed out of him: and the child was cured from that very hour.

19 Then came the disciples to Jesus apart, and said, Why could not we cast him out?

20 And Jesus said unto them, Because of your unbelief: for verily I say unto you, If ye have faith as a grain of

---

dom through the Messiah. Observe that the Saviour, desirous of impressing it strongly on their hearts, repeats what he had so recently told them, that he is to suffer at the hands of the scribes.

15. This is one of the most instructive and affecting narratives of miraculous healing in the life of Christ. The details will be considered in the notes on Mark, who is very graphic in his delineation of the case. How striking the contrast between the scenes on the mount and the scenes which had been occurring in the plain!—on the mount, the forecasting of universal victory; in the plain, defeat suffered openly by the disciples in the presence of the scribes themselves! *Lunatic*—Another case of demoniacal possession. See note on 4: 24. *Sore vexed*—Sorely afflicted. *Fire . . . water*—Devils can drive men to extremes.

17. *O faithless and perverse generation*—By generation we understand the Jews of that period, but the rebuke has special reference to all—disciples, father, son, scribes, and people—whose unbelief has just been manifested. Many consider the word *unbelief*, as applied in vs. 20 to the disciples, too strong. They soften it by the translation, *want of faith*. Assuming this to be correct, the rebuke in this verse, in the full measure of its severity, cannot be regarded as intended for the disciples; that is, the apostles. These still believed that Jesus worked miracles by divine power, and therefore they tried to effect the boy's cure. This surely proves their unbelief to have been a state very different from that of the scribes. The scribes were *perverse;* in a thoroughly prejudiced, distorted spirit. *How long? . . . how long?*—Expressions of the Saviour's holy displeasure at their wickedness. *Suffer you*—Bear with you.

18, 19. *That very hour*—No stress should be laid upon the *very*. It expresses the thought more strongly than does the original. *Came . . . to Jesus apart*—How natural to be disinclined to ask him before those who had witnessed their failure! That their unbelief was the cause seems not to have occurred to them. He whose efforts to do good are not successful should prayerfully inquire, *Why not?*

20. *Unbelief*—See note on vs. 17. *Mustard-seed*—See on 13: 31, 32. *Faith*—See on 8: 8-10. If a man has faith that a given thing will be done, his faith is based upon some expression of God's will. Should a man have faith that he could remove a mountain, he could have it only because he has learned that

CHAPTER XVII.

mustard seed, ye shall say unto this mountain, Remove hence to yonder place: and it shall remove; and nothing shall be impossible unto you.

21 Howbeit this kind goeth not out but by prayer and fasting.

22 ¶ And while they abode in Galilee, Jesus said unto them, The Son of man shall be betrayed into the hands of men:

23 And they shall kill him, and the third day he shall be raised again. And they were exceeding sorry.

24 ¶ And when they were come to Capernaum, they that received tribute *money* came to Peter, and said, Doth not your master pay tribute?

25 He saith, Yes. And when he was come into the house, Jesus prevented him, saying, What thinkest thou, Simon?

---

it is God's will it should be removed. There is nothing, then, in the nature of faith which makes it impossible to secure the removal of a mountain. The Saviour's statement is therefore literally true that faith will remove a mountain; or, speaking generally, the nature of faith is such that, if exercised, it could effect changes in nature other than those effected through the course of natural law. This it often did when exercised by prophets and apostles, dividing rivers and raising the dead. If no instance of removing a mountain by faith has occurred, it is not because it would have been more difficult than to divide a river, but because there has been no necessity for doing it. Of course the faith to do it has not been given. *Mountain*, however, may here be used figuratively, which brings us to the same point. Anything, however difficult, which God has given us reason to believe it is his will should be done, through us, can be done, if we believe that he will give us the power to do it.

21. *This kind*—It is possible, as others have remarked, that this means, such faith as this; but it is probable that it refers to the peculiar severity of the case. There is difference in devils as well as in men. See 12: 45 for a devil that knew of seven others more wicked than himself.

Autumn, A.D. 29.

22, 23. After leaving the vicinity of the mountain, Jesus is supposed to have crossed the Jordan north of the Sea of Tiberias. He went again into Galilee, where he abode a little time, chiefly engaged in instructing the apostles. The principal subject of his teachings was his own death. *Betrayed*—Delivered. The original does not convey the idea of treachery. *Exceeding sorry* —It would be a total misconception of their state to suppose that they had any unwillingness to be saved by the death of Christ as an atonement for sin. That his death was necessary for such a purpose is a fact to the knowledge of which they had not attained. The possibility of such a painful, and, in the eyes of men, disgraceful, termination of his career, makes them *exceeding sorry*. All their misconceptions, however, will soon be removed, and Peter and all the apostles but Judas will stand forth as bold advocates of the necessity of Christ's death.

24. *Come to Capernaum*—After how many days or weeks it is impossible to tell. *Tribute money* —Literally translated, the *didrachma*, equivalent to the Jewish *half-shekel*. This latter is approved by Dr. Schaff and others as the better translation. A silver shekel, coined by Simon the Maccabee, has, on the

of whom do the kings of the earth take custom or tribute? of their own children, or of strangers?

26 Peter saith unto him, Of strangers. Jesus saith unto him, Then are the children free.

27 Notwithstanding, lest we should offend them, go thou to the sea, and cast a hook, and take up the fish that first com-

---

one side, the inscription *Shekel Israel*, with a vase over which was the first letter of the Hebrew alphabet. On the other side is a twig with three buds, and the inscription, *Jerusalem Kedushah ;* that is, Jerusalem the Holy. A silver half-shekel of the same period is stamped the same, with the word *chătsi,*— a half. The half-shekel "is differently estimated from fifty to seventy cents." It was required of every male Jew who was twenty years old, or more, toward the support of the temple service (Ex. 30 : 13-15), "in whatever part of the world he might be living. Large sums were thus collected in Babylon and other Eastern cities, and were sent to Jerusalem under a special escort." The collectors, meeting Peter, put the question, *Doth not your master pay tribute?* It is *possible* that the collectors were pushed forward with the question by the enemies of Jesus. The form of the question looks as if the demand were made for the first time.

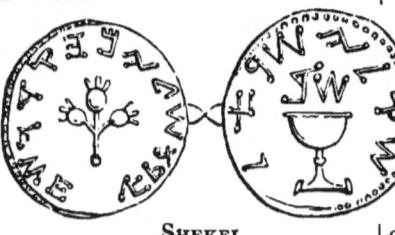

SHEKEL.

25. *He saith, Yes*—We cannot see, as some do, anything "hasty" in the affirmative character of Peter's answer. Nothing in our Lord's *life* could have justified Peter in answering otherwise. He had never known Jesus averse to any of the instituted services of the temple. It is very true that Peter saw but indistinctly that Christ was himself Lord of the temple, but had he seen this truth with clearness, how could he have been justified in committing his Master against the payment? Ought he to have regarded Jesus as not human because seeing him as more than human? *Prevented*—Anticipated him by speaking first.

26. *Of whom do the kings*—Kings do not take customs or tribute of their own sons,—the princes,—but of strangers; that is, of those who are their subjects. It is implied that he himself, being the Son of the King to whom the temple belongs, is, in his higher nature, not required to pay the customary sum. By using the plural, *children*, he seems to teach that in consequence of his spiritual relations to himself, Peter also is free from the obligation. Many hold, however, that he uses the plural merely to accord with the plural, *kings*. But may he not have used it in anticipation of the time, then very near, when, by the termination of the entire temple service, "the sons," that is, all his followers, would indeed be "free" from the obligation?

27. *Offend*—Lest the non-payment should be a ground of displeasure. Jesus never offended men uselessly; that is, when no moral end could be gained. *A piece of money*—A stater. "The stater must here mean a silver *tetradrachm ;* and the only tetradrachms then current in Palestine were of the same weight as the Hebrew shekel. And it is observable, in confirmation of the

eth up; and when thou hast opened his mouth, thou shalt find a piece of money: that take, and give unto them for me and thee.

CHAPTER XVIII.

AT the same time came the disciples unto Jesus, saying, Who is the greatest in the kingdom of heaven?

2 And Jesus called a little child unto him, and set him in the midst of them,

3 And said, Verily I say unto you, Except ye be converted, and become as little children, ye shall not enter into the kingdom of heaven.

4 Whosoever therefore shall humble himself as this little child, the same is greatest in the kingdom of heaven.

---

minute accuracy of the evangelist, that at this period the silver currency in Palestine consisted of Greek imperial tetradrachms, or staters, and Roman denarii of a quarter their value, didrachms having fallen into disuse. Had two didrachms been found by St. Peter, the receivers of tribute would scarcely have taken them; and, no doubt, the ordinary coin paid was that miraculously supplied." — *Reginald Stuart Poole*, of the British Museum. *For me and thee*—As the coin to be found was equal to two half-shekels, it would pay for both.

It will be observed that this miracle was wrought for the supply of the Saviour's personal want, and that in this respect it differs from all the other miracles reported. But as it is entirely improbable that so small a sum could not have been procured in some unmiraculous way, we must consider the miracle as wrought for the moral end of strengthening Peter's faith, and, through the record, our own also. That Peter caught several fish, and that the money was obtained by selling them, as the deniers of miracles have said, can be believed by none who study God's word in the spirit of Christ. That Jesus provided for the payment of only Peter's tax is none of our business. That all the other apostles were too young to be taxed is a supposition that nobody has authority to make.

CHAPTER XVIII.

JESUS' DISCOURSE TO THE DISCIPLES.

782 U.C. Autumn, A.D. 29.

Jesus is supposed to be yet in Capernaum. If the several parts of this discourse were not spoken upon the same occasion, most of them were doubtless spoken at times very near to each other, and while the occasion which led to the first part was still fresh in the memory of his disciples. Owing partly, perhaps, to the influence of the scribes and Pharisees, and partly to his avoidance of publicity, the people are less inclined to be with him. As he is soon to go up to Jerusalem, it is of special importance that still further instruction be given to the disciples.

1. Imperfect views of the nature of the Messiah's kingdom still lingered in the minds of the disciples. Jesus had shown a preference in some respects for Peter, James, and John, and in some respects for Peter alone. In their walk to Capernaum, they fell into a dispute on the question, who should have the highest place in the kind of king-

5 And whoso shall receive one such little child in my name receiveth me.

6 But whoso shall offend one of these little ones which believe in me, it were better for him that a millstone were hanged about his neck, and *that* he were drowned in the depth of the sea.

7 ¶ Woe unto the world because of offences! for it must needs be that offences come; but woe to that man by whom the offence cometh!

8 Wherefore if thy hand or thy foot offend thee, cut them off, and cast *them* from thee: it is better for thee to enter into life halt or maimed, rather

---

dom which they believed was about to be set up. Underneath was the conviction, with great confidence in his wisdom and love, that Jesus was the Messiah; but this unholy state of mind, ambition in some, envy in others, must be removed.

3. *Converted*—Not regenerated, but turned, that is, from their ambition and envy. *As little children*—It is not here implied that little children are sinless, but they are sufficiently free from such faults as the Saviour is rebuking to answer for an appropriate symbol. They feel their helplessness and dependence. These twelve men, grouped silently around this little child and their loved and loving Master, to learn the duty of humility, constitute one of the most touching pictures in the New Testament. *Enter* is emphatic. Without humility they cannot even *enter* the kingdom. Christ's is the only true standard of estimating greatness. Desire for greatness in the church may be strong when desire for greatness in the world has been conquered. Sensitiveness respecting position in the church or in the ministry may become so great as to mar one's usefulness and destroy one's comfort.

5. *A little child*—A little child as a symbol of one who is a little child in spirit, and therefore, chiefly the latter. Receiving such a one is loving him. If we love him, we shall do for him whatever his wants may require, even if it should be a menial service (John 13: 14). But it must be done *in my name*—To make such an act proof of qualification for the kingdom of heaven, it must be done *on the ground of the person's relation to Christ.* If it is done to secure merit, or if it is done in mere natural affection, it is no evidence that Christ has been received. So far as our own acts, however Christian in form, are wanting in reference to Christ, they are not Christian in spirit.

6. *Shall offend*—Shall cause one of these little ones to stumble. "Apostasy from the faith is not all that is meant. Whatever may be the influence by which the believer is turned aside from the right way, darkening his own spirit with error and sin, that is comprehended in this term, and is subject to the woe denounced in the next verse."—*Conant. Millstone*—See note on 24: 41. "The common millstone rarely exceeds two feet in diameter.... It was sometimes fastened to the necks of criminals who were to be drowned."—*Hackett.* Our Lord must not be understood as approving this or any other form of civil punishment for the sin referred to. It is his figurative way of saying that *God* will visit such a man with severe punishment.

7-9. *Because of offences*—On account of causes or grounds of sin. Be careful, therefore, says Christ, lest thy hand or thy foot cause thee to sin. See note on Matt. 5: 29, 30. *Everlasting fire*—See note on 5: 22,

than having two hands or two feet to be cast into everlasting fire.

9 And if thine eye offend thee, pluck it out, and cast *it* from thee: it is better for thee to enter into life with one eye, rather than having two eyes to be cast into hell fire.

10 Take heed that ye despise not one of these little ones; for I say unto you, That in heaven their angels do always behold the face of my Father which is in heaven.

11 For the Son of man is come to save that which was lost.

---

second and third paragraphs; 25: 46.

10. *Take heed . . . for I say unto you,* are forms of speech which show the high estimate which Jesus puts upon those of his people who are children in spirit, whether young or old, rich or poor, learned or unlearned. *Their angels*—Acts 12: 15, Then they said, *It is his angel,* is considered by some as clearly implying that every Christian has a particular guardian angel. We prefer the view held by Dr. Hackett in his Commentary on the Acts: "This idea appears here not as a doctrine of the Scriptures, but as a popular opinion which is neither affirmed nor denied." That there are beings in heaven who, in intellect and character, are superior to men, and that they are employed in some kind of service "on account of those who are to obtain salvation," is certain, but that Jesus intended to teach that each Christian is under the charge of a given angel is too hastily concluded from the passage before us; and as there is no other verse in the Bible that even *seems* to teach the doctrine, the least that we can do is to hold the question in suspense. The general idea may be this, that the children of God are objects of special interest with the angels.

That "the whole discourse is in deep and constant reference to *the covenant with infants*" (Alford) is impossible; for no covenant with infants, having reference to their salvation, was ever made. The covenant of circumcision ought not to be confounded with the covenant of grace. In the covenant of grace, God promises to make men his through *faith.* By the covenant of circumcision, Abraham was made the father of the Jews as a nation. In *that* covenant infants were included. By the covenant of grace he was made the head, not of believers and their infant, non-believing seed, but of believers only. If one asks, Who are the children of the covenant, the true reply is, The children of Abraham. If it is asked, Who are the children of Abraham, the true reply is, They that have Abraham's faith. As infants cannot believe, they cannot be, in the language of Paul, the children of Abraham; and as they are not the children of Abraham, *they cannot be the children of the covenant of grace,* whatever may be said of them as children of the covenant of circumcision.

11–14. Jesus here enforces the duty of refraining from whatever may injure his children. *Lost*— Under sin and exposed to eternal punishment, but the Son of man came to save them. *It is not the will of your Father,* etc. With this union of interest between the Father and the Son, the "little ones" will not be permitted to perish. Why, then, should you despise them? *Into the mountains—* Where the flock had been and where the lost one may yet be. Or, the arrangement of the words may be this: Does he not leave the ninety and nine upon the mountains, and

12 How think ye? If a man have a hundred sheep, and one of them be gone astray, doth he not leave the ninety and nine, and goeth into the mountains, and seeketh that which is gone astray?

13 And if so be that he find it, verily I say unto you, he rejoiceth more of that *sheep*, than of the ninety and nine which went not astray.

14 Even so it is not the will of your Father which is in heaven, that one of these little ones should perish.

15 ¶ Moreover if thy brother shall trespass against thee, go and tell him his fault between thee and him alone: if he shall hear thee, thou hast gained thy brother.

16 But if he will not hear *thee, then* take with thee one or two more, that in the mouth of two or three witnesses every word may be established.

17 And if he shall neglect to hear them, tell *it* unto the church: but if he neglect to hear the church, let him be unto thee as a heathen man and a publican.

18 Verily I say unto you, Whatsoever ye shall bind on earth shall be bound in heaven;

---

go and seek? But who are the ninety and nine that went not astray? Luke 15: 7: More than over ninety and nine *just persons which need no repentance.* We do not understand our Lord as teaching that there is such a difference in the character of men that some are by nature lost, and others not lost; some just and others not just. The difficulty of the parable may be met thus: Were it *supposable* that there are any who are not lost, yet I came to save the lost. The *point* of the illustration is in the words, *seeketh that which is gone astray.* The words, *ninety and nine which went not astray,* are not made by the divine Teacher himself *the* point or even *a* point. It should not be made a point by us. The allusion to the ninety and nine was of course indispensable in order to give any significancy whatever to *the one.* The Christian, whether a minister or not, that does not teach that men are lost, does not teach what Christ taught. Let us meditate much upon Christ as a shepherd seeking lost sheep. Let us sympathize in his joy at finding them. Let the Sabbath-school teacher explain to his class *how* Christ seeks the lost.

15-18. *Moreover*—But, turning us to the opposite possibility. He has spoken of my sinning against another. He now speaks of another as sinning against me. The law in such a case is this: *First.* I must go and tell him his fault alone. Christ thus forbids me to report it even to the church, and forbids the church to give it any consideration, and forbids my pastor to allow me to speak of it to the church. The reference is clearly to a personal wrong, not to an injury, committed against no one in particular. *Tell*—This fails to express the meaning, which is, to *show* him, *to try to convince* him, of the wrong done. *Gained*—Brought him back into union with God and therefore with yourself. Mark this, that you are not to wait for him to come to you. *Secondly.* If my brother refuses to acknowledge the wrong, I must take one or two more. If our united efforts effect the necessary change, that ends it; if they fail, the one is to serve with me as a witness, or, if I take two, the two

CHAPTER XVIII. 213

and whatsoever ye shall loose on earth shall be loosed in heaven.

19 Again I say unto you, That if two of you shall agree on earth as touching anything that they shall ask, it shall be done for them of my Father which is in heaven.

20 For where two or three are gathered together in my name, there am I in the midst of them.

21 ¶ Then came Peter to

---

are to act with me as witnesses, before the church, that *every word* which he may utter expressive of his unwillingness to confess the wrong may be established. See John 8: 17. *Thirdly. Tell it unto the church*—To that body of believers of which you are both members. It is remarkable that Mr. Wesley could explain it as meaning, Tell it to the elders of the church. Alford, however, though an Episcopalian, says, "It cannot mean *the Church as represented by her rulers*," and "Nothing can be further from the spirit of our Lord's command than proceedings in what are oddly enough called 'ecclesiastical courts.'" As to vs. 18, see on 16: 19 concerning *binding* and *loosing*.

"The decline of and the difficulties attending upon the exercise of scriptural discipline, constitute glaring evidence of the sad decay of our State Churches." Such is the testimony of one who, by his residence in Europe, could judge well of what he spoke. The evangelical churches of the United States should take warning. Discipline is here also so much neglected that we are shorn of half our strength. Discipline is the more needed in consequence of the unseemly haste with which many pastors and evangelists encourage professing converts to offer themselves for baptism.

19, 20. *If two . . . as touching anything*—Observe the smallness of the number, and the greatness of the range of objects promised. Notice also that even this small number is upon the earth, while he of whom the things are to be asked is in heaven. *In my name*—(*a*.) With confidence in Christ's character and work as they are regarded by the Father; (*b*.) With the mind of Christ; (*c*.) With acceptance of all the truth which Christ has revealed. See note on John 16: 23, 24. *Where . . . there*—Unlimited, then, as to place or time. See 28: 20: Lo, I am with you alway, even unto the end of the world. But is there *no* limitation in respect to objects of prayer? The true answer to this question may be seen in 1 John 5: 14. If we ask anything *according to his will*, he heareth us. He that prays *in the name of Christ*, as above explained, will not pray for anything which it is not God's will to grant. Two are enough to constitute a church of Christ. If in a church of one hundred there are only two who can agree to ask God for a given thing, the unbelief and remissness of the ninety-eight are not a necessary bar to the success of the two in prayer. "According to Jewish notions, there must at least ten persons be assembled in a synagogue, that they may have a well-founded hope that the Shekinah of the Divine Presence will be granted, and their prayer be heard and answered. The rabbinical writers say, 'A smaller number God despises.'"—*Dr. Nast*. The remarkable declaration contained in these verses demonstrates that the religion of Christ is infinitely superior to all the forms of natural religion. The most enlightened and virtuous heathen, Socrates, for example, had no such assurance.

21, 22. Jesus had virtually en-

him, and said, Lord, how oft shall my brother sin against me, and I forgive him? till seven times?

22 Jesus saith unto him, I say not unto thee, Until seven times: but, Until seventy times seven.

23 ¶ Therefore is the kingdom of heaven likened unto a certain king, which would take account of his servants.

24 And when he had begun to reckon, one was brought unto him, which owed him ten thousand talents.

25 But forasmuch as he had not to pay, his lord commanded him to be sold, and his wife, and children, and all that he had, and payment to be made.

26 The servant therefore fell down, and worshipped him, saying, Lord, have patience with me, and I will pay thee all.

27 Then the lord of that servant was moved with compassion, and loosed him, and forgave him the debt.

28 But the same servant went out, and found one of his

---

joined the duty of forgiveness. Peter inquires how *often* he ought to forgive. Penitence before each instance of forgiveness is of course implied. The question ought not to be regarded as indicative of peculiar narrowness of spirit. That Peter extended the number to *seven*, shows the advance which he had made under the teachings of Christ beyond the Jewish Rabbins; for these taught that forgiveness should be extended only to the *third* time. *Seventy times seven*—Either seventy-seven times, or, which is more probable, four hundred and ninety times. It was the same as to say, Do not forgive by weight and measure. Have no theory of limitation. As often as your brother does you a wrong and manifests penitence, forgive him. How can the Christian think this too great a demand? Will he not have been forgiven by his heavenly Father ten thousand times ten thousand?

23. *Therefore*—Since forgiveness should be extended, without limit, to the penitent. The object of the parable is, to enforce the duty of forgiveness by showing how God will deal with men of an unforgiving spirit. *Would take account*— Desired to make a reckoning with. *His servants*—His attendants, or, perhaps, tributary princes. They were not necessarily *slaves*, though, in some cases, in oriental courts, such officers were slaves. These men seem to have had charge of the king's financial affairs.

24, 25. *Ten thousand talents*— About ten millions of dollars. It well represents the vast indebtedness of sinful men to their Maker. Sins are debts. *Had not to pay*— Was not able to pay. How can man's indebtedness to God be paid? Who will pay it?

26. *Worshipped*—Bowed, prostrated himself. *Will pay all*—A daring avowal, but not so daring as that of the men who profess ability to square their account with God by honesty, generosity, and punctual attendance upon the services of religion.

27. *Forgave him*—This is no proof that sinners are forgiven by the mercy of God without an atonement; for Christ does not here profess to give an exhaustive view of the way of salvation. The different parts of the plan were revealed *progressively*, as the minds of the people were able to receive them.

28. *Went out*—Implying that

fellow servants, which owed him a hundred pence: and he laid hands on him, and took *him* by the throat, saying, Pay me that thou owest.

29 And his fellow servant fell down at his feet, and besought him, saying, Have patience with me, and I will pay thee all.

30 And he would not: but went and cast him into prison, till he should pay the debt.

31 So when his fellow servants saw what was done, they were very sorry, and came and told unto their lord all that was done.

32 Then his lord, after that he had called him, said unto him, O thou wicked servant, I forgave thee all that debt, because thou desiredst me:

33 Shouldest not thou also have had compassion on thy fellow servant, even as I had pity on thee?

34 And his lord was wroth, and delivered him to the tormentors, till he should pay all that was due unto him.

35 So likewise shall my heavenly Father do also unto you, if ye from your hearts forgive not every one his brother their trespasses.

CHAPTER XIX.

AND it came to pass, *that* when Jesus had finished these sayings, he departed from Galilee, and came into the coasts of Judea beyond Jordan;

2 And great multitudes followed him; and he healed them there.

---

little time elapsed between his forgiveness and his severity toward one of his own debtors. *Pence*—Denáries. A denáry was fifteen cents. Fifteen dollars were more to this man than the ten millions which he had owed to his king. How exact a representation of those who imperil their souls for money! Yet this does not express the point of the parable, which is not love of money, but, as above, the duty of forgiveness. *By the throat*—"According to Roman law, a creditor was allowed to drag his debtor by the throat before the tribunal." "Such is man, so harsh and hard, when he walks otherwise than in a constant sense of forgiveness from God."

30, 31. *He would not*—"Here is the climax of depravity, to be beggars with God and tyrants to our brethren." *Very sorry*—As we are all debtors to God, *anger* toward the wrong-doer is sinful. But indifference to wrong is also sinful.

34. *Wroth*—God's anger is the displeasure of an infinitely holy being. *Tormentors*—"Among the ancient Romans there were certain legal tortures, as a heavy chain and a system of half-starvation, which the creditor might apply to his debtor, for bringing him to terms." Says Prof. Bartlett, in his "Life and Death Eternal:" "It was invariably used in examining slaves. 'The parties interested either superintended the torture themselves, or chose certain persons for this purpose; hence called *tormentors.*'" The meaning, *prison-keeper*, is defended by some.

35. *So likewise*—How severe the punishment threatened to an unforgiving spirit! The nature and duration of the punishment should

3 ¶ The Pharisees also came unto him, tempting him, and saying unto him, Is it lawful for a man to put away his wife for every cause?

4 And he answered and said unto them, Have ye not read, that he which made *them* at the beginning made them male and female,

5 And said, For this cause shall a man leave father and mother, and shall cleave to his wife: and they twain shall be one flesh?

6 Wherefore they are no more twain, but one flesh. What therefore God hath joined together, let not man put asunder.

7 They say unto him, Why did Moses then command to

---

be viewed in the light of 25: 46, on which see note. *From your hearts* —Words alone will not answer.

CHAPTER XIX.

FINAL DEPARTURE FROM GALILEE; THE DIVORCE QUESTION; THE RICH YOUNG MAN.

782 U.C. November, A.D. 29.

1. *Departed from Galilee*—For the last time. His labors of love in that northern part of the land are closed. He goes to Jerusalem, but not directly. He labors here and there, but with his eye fixed (Luke 9:51) upon the city where he is to offer up his life for the salvation of men. But before this last journey, he did much which Matthew was not inspired to report. He had attended the Feast of Tabernacles at Jerusalem (John 7: 2, 10), where the Pharisees attempted to arrest him, and where he healed the man blind from his birth, *and had returned to Galilee*. There is, indeed, room for much difference of opinion concerning the order of events during the last five months of our Lord's life, but at least this seems probable, that Jesus returned to Galilee after the Feast of Tabernacles. *The coasts of Judea beyond Jordan*—The region referred to was Perea. See note on 4: 25, under the word Perea. "The direction of this journey is plain. Leaving Galilee, Jesus crosses the Jordan, and passing southward through Perea, thus comes to the borders of Judea, probably near Jericho."—*Andrews.*

783 U.C. February, A. D. 30.

3. Matthew, as the other evangelists lead us to suppose, omits *much* that occurred even upon this last journey. At precisely what point of it the event recorded in this verse occurred, it is impossible to determine, but there are reasons for placing it in the latter part. The date must therefore be regarded as only an approximation to the true one. Let the student still bear in mind that the journey, though directed toward Jerusalem, was circuitous. *Tempting*—See note on 16: 1. Compare what is here said upon divorce with what is said 5: 31, 32. These Pharisees, acting doubtless in the interest of the conspiracy against his life, mean to make him commit himself to the one or the other of the parties into which the scribes and Pharisees were divided on the subject of divorce, the one being strict and the other loose. It is possible, though there is no proof of it, that they had in mind the adultery of Herod Antipas (14: 3-10), and hoped to be able to report to Herod what would make Jesus as obnoxious as John the Baptist became.

4-6. *Have ye not read?*—See Gen. 1: 27; 2: 24. Without in the least

give a writing of divorcement, and to put her away?

8 He saith unto them, Moses because of the hardness of your hearts suffered you to put away your wives: but from the beginning it was not so.

9 And I say unto you, Whosoever shall put away his wife, except *it be* for fornication, and shall marry another, committeth adultery: and whoso marrieth her which is put away doth commit adultery.

---

compromising the divine law, he commits himself to neither party. The line of argument is well drawn by Dr. Conant: "The Saviour, in reply to the treacherous question of his enemies, argues first (in vs. 4) from what the Creator *did*, and secondly (in vs. 5) from what he *said*, stating his own conclusion in vs. 6. His brief statement of the case in this verse" [4] "contains the two following points:—

"*He who made them from the beginning* (from their first creation): that is, the original Author of their being, whose will is therefore its primary law;

"*Made them male and female:* showing by this his own purpose in their creation, namely, that they are made the one for the other; a relation to which all others must yield, and which, as being ordained by God, can be severed only by him.

"Such is the Saviour's argument from the original creation of man; and no moral truth can be more clearly demonstrated. . . . The argument turns on the relation of sex, and not on the *numerical* ratio of the two sexes at their creation. The latter consideration was not essential here; for the question was not, whether a man may have more wives than one, but whether he may put away the one wife he has."

7-9. *Writing of divorcement*—See note on 5: 31, 32. Moses had not commanded, instituted, originated, the sundering of the marriage tie. He found the practice existing. The hardness of the people's hearts relative to the matter was great. The evil had become deeply rooted. It could not be immediately removed. It must therefore be so hedged about that there should be great difficulty in securing separation. Such difficulty would be created by requiring a bill of divorcement. Such a bill "would in ancient times require the intervention of a Levite, not only to secure the formal correctness of the instrument, but because the art of writing was then generally unknown. This would bring the matter under legal authority, and tend to check the rash exercise of the right by the husband." Moses' law of marriage was a *civil* law. Under the peculiar difficulties by which Moses was beset, it was not intended to be a full expression of the *moral* law of marriage as originally promulgated by God. The Saviour teaches both here and in the Sermon on the Mount what that moral law is, and by that he expects his churches to be governed. The law as expressed in vs. 9 is plain. There is but one cause for which a man may put away his wife. Want of "spiritual affinity," intemperance, neglect to provide for the family, desertion, are not sufficient causes for divorce. Separation from "bed and board" is doubtless justifiable in cases of great and long protracted intemperance, and of neglect to provide. Whatever the law of Massachusetts or Illinois, or any other State, may permit, the churches of Christ must require their members to conform to the law of marriage as defined by Christ; and ministers of the gospel should not allow themselves to be *participants in the crime* by uniting in marriage persons the one or the other of whom, according to our

10 ¶ His disciples say unto him, If the case of the man be so with *his* wife, it is not good to marry.

11 But he said unto them, All *men* cannot receive this saying, save *they* to whom it is given.

Lord's interpretation of the original law, is already in the marriage relation.

"The Prussian laws on marriage, dating from the infidel reign of Frederic II., are scandalously lax and demoralizing, by increasing the causes, and facilitating the accomplishment, of divorce. With the revival of true Christianity in Prussia, a reform movement commenced, which aims at a return to the law of Christ."—*Dr. Schaff.* Similar laxness has marked and disgraced legislation in many of the States of our own country. "In Indianapolis, in 1866, there were eight hundred and twenty-two marriages, and two hundred and ten applications for divorce, which is more than one to four of the whole number of marriages. In Chicago, the same year, there were four thousand one hundred and eighty-two marriages, and three hundred and thirty-eight applications for divorce. The various courts of Chicago granted bills of divorce in 1865 to the number of two hundred and seventy-four; in 1866 the number was two hundred and nine; in 1867 the number reached three hundred and eleven." In 1868, the number of divorces was four hundred and forty-three. * Thus in the one city of Chicago there were in four years one thousand two hundred and thirty-seven divorces! In Vermont "there is one divorce to every two hundred and sixty-six marriageable persons, or one man in every one hundred and thirty-three men, and one woman in every one hundred and thirty-three women, with the enormous ratio of one divorce to every nineteen marriages." In Massachusetts,

* Not all were cases of residents.

"during the last five years, there has been one divorce to forty-four marriages (1868)." In Connecticut, during the same period, the divorces have been to the marriages as one to eleven. In Maine, the applications in the fall of 1868 numbered more than five hundred, and they are continually increasing "in consequence of the increased facilities that have of late years been afforded dissatisfied couples for release from matrimonial infelicities." The evils proceeding from the multiplication of divorces and from the marriage of persons divorced for some other reason than the one specified by our Lord, are so alarming that we hesitate not to say, that both churches and ministers should clear themselves of all responsibility in the matter. The churches should discipline members who become divorced for any other than the scriptural reason, members who marry with parties so divorced, and ministers who marry them. See President Alvah Hovey's excellent treatise on "The Scriptural Law of Divorce." It has been well remarked that "where the *legality* of marriage has been thoroughly undermined, and free love substituted in its place as the controlling principle of true marriage, the writing of divorcement is not, like that of Moses, intended to make separation more difficult, but, like that of Hillel" [a Jewish Rabbi], "to make it more easy." The following became the law of the Episcopal Church in the United States in 1868: "That no minister of this church shall solemnize matrimony in any case where there is a divorced wife or husband of either party still living; but this canon shall not be held to apply to the innocent party in a divorce for

CHAPTER XIX. 219

12 For there are some eunuchs, which were so born from *their* mother's womb: and there are some eunuchs, which were made eunuchs of men: and there be eunuchs which have made themselves eunuchs for the kingdom of heaven's sake.

He that is able to receive *it*, let him receive *it*.

13 ¶ Then were there brought unto him little children, that he should put *his* hands on them, and pray: and the disciples rebuked them.

14 But Jesus said, Suffer

---

the cause of adultery, or to parties once divorced seeking to be united again."

The modern Jews of course care nothing for our Lord's interpretation of the Mosaic law of divorce. In this they are more consistent than some Christians. "A divorce according to the Hebrew ecclesiastical law took place at Washington, May, 1869. A married couple, who had lived unhappily together, availed themselves of the ceremony in the presence of the rabbis and some other parties. The articles of divorcement having been agreed upon were transcribed on parchment. Certain passages of the Pentateuch were read, and the divorcement articles. The wife was then called forward, and her face uncovered, and her hands were placed together, the thumbs upward and extended. One of the rabbis asked certain questions of the husband, which were answered, and placed the parchment in his hands, and in turn the rabbi took it. Two persons attested their names as witnesses to file with the records of the church, the ceremony closed, and the parties separated. By this ceremony, founded on Deut. 24: 1, 2, 3, 4, the parties are separated and free,—the husband to marry another at any time, and the wife to marry after ninety-one days have passed, but not to a descendant of the tribe of Levi. Our civil laws, however, require a divorce granted by the courts before they can marry again."

10, 11. *If the case*—If such is the relation between man and woman.

His, in italics, was inserted by the translators, and *wife* is not here so accurate as *woman*. The disciples mean to say, If the relation between man and woman is such that the marriage tie is so nearly indissoluble, a man better not marry at all. But Jesus tells them that not all men can receive that saying; namely, that it is not good, even with such restriction, to marry. The disciples needed more light, and the Saviour gave them more. *To whom it is given*—Thus our Lord admitted that there are some who might with propriety lead an unmarried life, while nothing that he said gives countenance to celibacy *as a system*, such as has been adopted by the Romish Church. Such a system leads to gross immorality.

12. Our Lord divides those to whom he refers in the last verse into three classes: 1. Those who are incapacitated for the marriage state by natural defect; 2. Those who submit to mutilation by the cruel art of man; 3. Those who choose to live an unmarried life, with the conviction, which Paul himself had, that they can in that way be more useful in the kingdom of Christ. The plain implication is that most men ought not to live unmarried. The Romish priesthood would be a purer body had it not adopted celibacy as a system.

13–15. *Brought unto him little children*—Infants. Compare Luke 18: 15. *Rebuked them*—Why, we are not informed. *Of such* is not a perfect reproduction of the Saviour's thought. It should be, *To*

little children, and forbid them not, to come unto me; for of such is the kingdom of heaven.

15 And he laid *his* hands on them, and departed thence.

16 ¶ And, behold, one came and said unto him, Good Master, what good thing shall I do, that I may have eternal life?

17 And he said unto him, Why callest thou me good? *there is* none good but one, *that is*, God: but if thou wilt enter into life, keep the commandments.

---

such belongs the kingdom of heaven. But what does Jesus mean by *such?* Is it indicative of age, or of character? In 18: 6 he is represented as saying, these little ones *which believe in me*. It may be very true that infants will be saved,—the writer has no doubt they will be,—and in *that* sense, dying, become members of the kingdom of heaven; but what Christ teaches in 18: 6 is that the "little ones" are those *who believe*, whatever their age. If one has personal faith in Christ at the age of four years, and this, doubtless, is in some cases possible, he is a "little one;" and this is equally true of one who is eighty years of age. So in the verse before us. *Of such* indicates *character;* that is, character which is *symbolized* in the infant. "He does not say *of those infants*, but of such persons as *resembled* them."—*Barnes.* Even Lange, not a Baptist, says: "Of such, that is, of all those that have a childlike spirit and are like those little ones *that believe* in Christ. Compare 18: 2-6," though he insists that the children are included. "The ancient church," he adds, "have rightly regarded this passage as a proof in favor of the doctrine of infant baptism." On the other hand, Olshausen, himself also not a Baptist, says: "Of that reference to infant baptism which it is so common to seek in this narrative, there is clearly not the slightest trace to be found." Dr. Nast (Methodist) says: "In these words the Lord positively declares that all children that die while they are unaccountable are entitled to the bliss of heaven, and for the same reason while on earth, to *membership in his church*, in the same manner as children under the old dispensation were entitled to church membership." The doctrine that infants may be members of Christian churches has done incalculable injury to Christianity. There is no infant membership in these verses and no infant baptism, as many of the most distinguished writers in other denominations have admitted. The subject of infant baptism is more fully considered in the notes on 28: 19.

16-17. It is well for even the general student to know that the most approved Greek of vs. 17 yields a thought quite different from that which is here expressed, thus: *And he said to him, Why dost thou ask me concerning good? One is the Good.* This is the form approved by the most eminent scholars. But turning to the parallel verses in Mark (10: 18) and Luke (18: 19), we find substantially the same words as are found in Matthew in our common English Bibles, and the common Greek is also substantially alike in the three Gospels. In Mark and Luke, however, no change is required either in the English or the Greek. Matthew's report, then, of the Saviour's words in this case, as in some others, is different from that of Mark and Luke,—not contradictory, but different. Mark and Luke say: *Why callest thou me good? none is good save one, that is, God.* Matthew says, according to the true

CHAPTER XIX.

18 He saith unto him, Which? Jesus said, Thou shalt do no murder, Thou shalt not commit adultery, Thou shalt not steal, Thou shalt not bear false witness,

19 Honour thy father and *thy* mother: and, Thou shalt love thy neighbour as thyself.

20 The young man saith unto him, All these things have I kept from my youth up: what lack I yet?

21 Jesus said unto him, If thou wilt be perfect, go *and* sell that thou hast, and give to the poor, and thou shalt have treasure in heaven: and come *and* follow me.

22 But when the young man heard that saying, he went away sorrowful: for he had great possessions.

23 ¶ Then said Jesus unto his disciples, Verily I say unto you, That a rich man shall

---

Greek, *Why dost ask me concerning good? One is the Good.* Observe that in Mark and Luke the reply of our Lord turns on the fact that the man applied to Jesus the term *good*, concerning which see more in the notes on those Gospels. Here the Lord's reply turns on the fact that the man asked, What *good* shall I do? The jailer at Philippi cried, What shall I *do?* This man cries, What *good* shall I do? In his own opinion, he has left nothing undone that he ought to have done, yet he seems to think that possibly Jesus can tell him of some good thing more that he ought to do. He is evidently a Pharisee, but is free from the hostility and even from the prejudice which the Pharisees as a class have long manifested toward Christ. Jesus would turn his thoughts away from whatever *good thing he might suppose necessary to be done,* and direct them to him who is *The Good. Keep the commandments,* does not authorize the inference that it is possible for any human being to secure eternal life by the law. See Romans and Galatians, where the mind of Christ concerning this point is fully revealed. It is merely the Lord's method of leading this rich man to the consciousness of his deep poverty.

18-20. *Shalt do no murder,* etc. —Jesus quotes from the *second* ta-ble of the law; and that, perhaps, because the man's religion consisted chiefly of endeavors to obey that part of the law. Like many in our own times, the man thought he was in a fair way, because he aimed to conduct rightly *toward his fellow-men. What lack I yet?*—Here are confidence that he has done all, and sincere desire to know whether there is any other good thing which he may possibly have omitted. *Young man* —Not probably a mere youth; for, according to Luke, he was a *ruler.* Besides, the word here rendered *young man* was sometimes applied to men who were thirty and even forty years of age. It has been justly remarked that the words, *from my youth up,* harmonize better with the supposition that he had passed out of what *we* call youth.

21, 22. *Perfect*—If thou art determined to lack nothing, there is one thing more which thou must do. Jesus admits his claim to have done all these things, but only for the moment, that he may make it appear as it was—*groundless.* This he does by the two requirements: 1. Dispossess yourself of your property by distributing it to the poor; 2. Become my disciple. The former would test his profession of obedience to the second table of the law; the latter, to the first. *Sorrowful*—Some would have gone away

hardly enter into the kingdom of heaven.

24 And again I say unto you, It is easier for a camel to go through the eye of a needle, than for a rich man to enter into the kingdom of God.

25 When his disciples heard *it*, they were exceedingly amazed, saying, Who then can be saved?

26 But Jesus beheld *them*, and said unto them, With men this is impossible; but with God all things are possible.

27 ¶ Then answered Peter and said unto him, Behold, we have forsaken all, and followed thee; what shall we have therefore?

28 And Jesus said unto them, Verily I say unto you, That ye which have followed me, in the regeneration when the Son of man shall sit in the throne of his glory, ye also

---

angry. What Christ required in this case, he requires, substantially, in every case. Had human learning secured a stronger hold upon this man than riches, Jesus would have applied the test accordingly. Belief in the *doctrine* of eternal life does not secure the *gift* of eternal life.

23, 24. *Shall hardly enter*—Riches have great power to make men feel independent of God. Riches desired may prevent entrance into the kingdom of heaven as well as riches obtained. Some very pious men are rich, but, 1. The rich as a class are peculiarly averse to religion; 2. Rich Christians, with few exceptions, became Christians before they became rich. The words *camel* and *eye of a needle* should be taken literally. They express the *impossibility* of entrance into the kingdom of heaven by one who is rich, that is, by one who makes riches the end of life. "The same saying occurs in the Talmud about an elephant:" but, as has been remarked, "the camel was more familiar to the hearers of the Saviour than the elephant." To say that by the eye of a needle is meant a small gate through which a camel could not go, is an error.

25, 26. *Who then?*—How can *any* one be saved, not merely the rich. The disciples knew that most men make worldly good their chief object of pursuit. *This is impossible*—The salvation of men, including of course the rich. *With God . . . possible*—He can save *even the rich.*

27. *Forsaken all*—Some of them may have literally abandoned what little property they had. All of them had forsaken their occupation for the sake of following Christ. *What . . . therefore?*—Here are seen weakness and ambition, though in the preceding avowal, sincerity, love, and zeal. This mingling of good and evil was characteristic of all the disciples till after their special enlightenment upon the day of Pentecost, and especially of Peter.

28. Instead of rebuking his ambition, Jesus encourages his zeal. *Regeneration*—Renovation. It is nearly equivalent to *restitution of all things* in Acts 3: 21, which Dr. Hackett explains as referring to a state of "primeval order, purity, and happiness, such as will exist for those who have part in the kingdom of Christ at his second coming." The meaning is, ye who have followed me (this excludes Judas) shall be made partakers of my glory when my victories shall have been won, and I shall come a second time. *Regeneration* must be connected with the words which follow, thus: Ye which have followed me, *in the renovation when the Son of*

shall sit upon twelve thrones, judging the twelve tribes of Israel.

29 And every one that hath forsaken houses, or brethren, or sisters, or father, or mother, or wife, or children, or lands, for my name's sake, shall receive a hundredfold, and shall inherit everlasting life.

30 But many *that are* first shall be last; and the last *shall be* first.

CHAPTER XX.

FOR the kingdom of heaven is like unto a man *that is* a householder, which went out early in the morning to hire laborers into his vineyard.

2 And when he had agreed

---

man shall sit, etc. The manner of representing it, *twelve thrones*, etc., is figurative. The idea of *sharing* in the glory of Christ is expressed in the words, *ye also*. The followers of Christ are not without consolation and honor even in the present life, but, in the words of Dr. Hackett, it is "then" [at the second coming], that Christ "will raise the dead, invest the redeemed with an incorruptible body, and introduce them, for the first time and forever, into the state of perfect holiness and happiness prepared for them in his kingdom."

30. We regard these words chiefly as a caution to Peter and his fellow-apostles to cherish the right spirit relative to the rewards which Christ will see fit to confer. The Saviour would teach them that by indulging in a wrong spirit, they would be in danger, though first in time and first in personal relations to himself, of becoming last; that is, of losing that *high* spiritual position, and consequently that *great* favor in his eyes which they would otherwise have.

CHAPTER XX.

PARABLE OF THE LABORERS; HIS DEATH ONCE MORE ANNOUNCED; SALOME'S REQUEST; TWO BLIND MEN CURED.

783 U.C. March, A.D. 30.

It must be remembered that Jesus is still on the eastern side of the Jordan, in Perea, on his way to Jerusalem. It is unfortunate that this parable of the laborers was not made a part of the preceding chapter, as the object is to illustrate the sentiment with which that chapter closes. The *lessons* which this parable or any other *indirectly suggests* is one thing, and the *object* for which it was spoken is another. Here the object is to reprove the hireling spirit which spoke in Peter, saying, What shall we have therefore?

1. *The kingdom of heaven*—The new dispensation. *Householder*—God. *Early in the morning*—The apostles were called early into the service of their Lord. *Vineyard*—Not, as some say, "The Church." That explanation grows out of widely spread error relative to the nature of a Christian church. Dr. Whedon says, "The service of God on earth." Why not, then, as still better, *the world?* Go ye into all the *world* and preach the gospel to every creature.

2, 3. *A penny a day*—A denáry, a Roman silver coin, which, instead of being equal to one penny, "was about seven and one-half pence sterling, or about fifteen cents." Our translation, therefore, makes the pay much less than it was. We must not estimate the real value of the wages by a modern standard. A Roman soldier had about ten cents a day, and in Cisalpine Gaul hotel charges per day, to use the modern

with the labourers for a penny a day, he sent them into his vineyard.

3 And he went out about the third hour, and saw others standing idle in the market-place,

4 And said unto them; Go ye also into the vineyard, and whatsoever is right I will give you. And they went their way.

5 Again he went out about the sixth and ninth hour, and did likewise.

6 And about the eleventh hour he went out, and found others standing idle, and saith unto them, Why stand ye here all the day idle?

7 They say unto him, Be-cause no man hath hired us. He saith unto them, Go ye also into the vineyard; and whatsoever is right, *that* shall ye receive.

8 So when even was come, the lord of the vineyard saith unto his steward, Call the labourers, and give them *their* hire, beginning from the last unto the first.

9 And when they came that *were hired* about the eleventh hour, they received every man a penny.

10 But when the first came, they supposed that they should have received more; and they likewise received every man a penny.

11 And when they had re-

---

phrase, was only half an ass, ten of which made a denary. *Third hour . . . sixth and ninth* (vs. 5) *. . . eleventh* (vs. 6)—See note on 14: 15, under the words, *the time. Market-place*—See note on 11: 16, second paragraph, under the same word.

4. *Whatsoever is right*—Had Peter, instead of asking, What shall we have? been willing to leave the question of reward to the decision of infinite righteousness, it would have been better. He afterward learned to do so, partly, no doubt, through the influence of this very parable. Very beautifully does he say in his first epistle (4: 19), Let them that suffer according to the will of God, *commit the keeping of their souls to him in well doing, as unto a faithful Creator.*

7, 8. *No man hath hired us*—Any man to whom the gospel has been preached that says this is guilty of misrepresentation, not to say of downright falsehood. *Whatsoever is right, that shall ye receive*—These words are wanting in some of the best manuscripts and some of the oldest versions. With these men, no contract was made. Their case presents *the point* of the parable; for they were to serve as the model to Peter and the other apostles in respect to the spirit with which they should go to the work of their Master. *Steward*—The householder's agent or manager. Chuza was Herod's steward. Luke 8: 3.

10. *Supposed*—Because they had worked harder. Complaining because God gives us less than others, takes from the gift all its moral value.

11, 12. *Murmured* — Whether these men stand for genuine Christians has been much and needlessly debated. It has been thought impossible that Christ should represent any of his followers as complaining because others, for whatever reason, are rewarded as much as they. Such expounders lay much stress

CHAPTER XX.

ceived *it*, they murmured against the goodman of the house,

12 Saying, These last have wrought *but* one hour, and thou hast made them equal unto us, which have borne the burden and heat of the day.

13 But he answered one of them, and said, Friend, I do thee no wrong: didst not thou agree with me for a penny?

14 Take *that* thine *is*, and go thy way: I will give unto this last, even as unto thee.

15 Is it not lawful for me to do what I will with mine own? Is thine eye evil, because I am good?

16 So the last shall be first, and the first last: for many be called, but few chosen.

17 ¶ And Jesus going up to Jerusalem took the twelve disciples apart in the way, and said unto them,

18 Behold, we go up to Jerusalem; and the Son of man shall be betrayed unto the chief priests and unto the scribes, and they shall condemn him to death,

19 And shall deliver him to the Gentiles to mock, and to scourge, and to crucify *him:* and the third day he shall rise again.

20 ¶ Then came to him the mother of Zebedee's children with her sons, worshipping *him*,

---

upon the fact that the settlement is made at the close of the day; that is, as they affirm, at the close of life. This, however, is one of the unimportant details of the parable, —not one of its *points*. Peter's wrong spirit had just been shown; that is, it had been shown many years before the close of his life. Nor had Peter complained. He was only in danger of doing so, and therefore the Lord so constructed the parable that a warning should be given.

16. See 19: 30, and the remarks introducing this twentieth chapter.

17. *Going up to Jerusalem*—According to the other evangelists, we must suppose Jesus to have arrived at the city, through Perea, some time ago, to have attended the feast of Dedication, discoursed to the Jews, escaped from their murderous hands to Bethabara in Perea, to have gone to Bethany, near Jerusalem, where he raised Lazarus, and to have retired to Ephraim, after learning that the Sanhedrim had been summoned together in Jerusalem. The Passover is just at hand. He is now, therefore, returning to the city through Jericho and Bethany. *Apart*—Performed the journey with the disciples alone; or, at some point, separated himself and disciples from others.

18, 19. This is the third distinct announcement of his death. The first is reported 16: 21; the second, 17: 23. In the first instance, he told them that he must suffer many things and be killed, but he evidently felt that the time had not come for making a more particular statement. The second time he makes the additional and very important announcement that he will be delivered, but says nothing of the persons who were to deliver. He now repeats all that he had said before, with the addition that he will be delivered to the chief priests and scribes, and by them be delivered to the Gentiles. The still more important announcement is made that his death will be effected by *crucifixion*. According to Luke, they understood none of these things.

and desiring a certain thing of him.

21 And he said unto her, What wilt thou? She saith unto him, Grant that these my two sons may sit, the one on thy right hand, and the other on the left, in thy kingdom.

22 But Jesus answered and said, Ye know not what ye ask. Are ye able to drink of the cup that I shall drink of, and to be baptized with the baptism that I am baptized with? They say unto him, We are able.

20, 21. *The mother of Zebedee's children*—Salome. She was a good woman. She stood with other good women where she could see Jesus at the crucifixion, and went to the sepulchre. But she had faults. Believing that the Saviour was going to Jerusalem to set up his kingdom, she comes with her sons, James and John, and, in sincere, loving reverence, desires a certain thing of him,—*asks something* of him. *In thy kingdom*—Posts of honor next to Jesus in the *visible* kingdom, which she supposes Jesus is about to set up. Mark says that James and John asked the favor themselves. They asked it through their mother. An ancient writer says that they were ashamed to ask it themselves. That supposition is unnecessary, for though the scheme may have originated with the mother, the apostles, her sons included, had shown an interest in the matter before (18:1), and had even had disputes upon the question who should be greatest. We should not, however, do either the mother or the sons injustice. The ambitious request never would have been made, had they not come into possession of strong faith in the Messiahship of Jesus.

22. *Ye know not*, etc.—Ye do not realize how much is involved in the request. *Cup*—See 26:42; John 18:11. *To be baptized with the baptism that I am baptized with*—Says Dr. Whedon: "It utterly mistakes the force of this expression to make it mean immersed with the immersion that I am immersed with. To be baptized by suffering is to be puri- fied with suffering." But another Methodist commentator, Dr. William Nast, comes much nearer the truth when he says, "The word *baptize* is here used figuratively for being *overwhelmed with, immersed in,* or poured upon by sufferings." Dr. Lange says, "It may signify a festive *bath,* but also the baptism of blood which awaited the Lord." Rev. F. Myrick, M.A. (Episcopalian), says: "It is generally thought that baptism here means an *inundation* of sorrows; that, as the baptized *went down* into the waters, and water was to be poured" [?] "over him, so our Lord meant to indicate that he himself had to pass through 'the deep waters of affliction.'" Dr. Edward Robinson, not a Baptist, says on this passage, in his Lexicon on the New Testament, "Can ye endure to be *overwhelmed* with sufferings like those which I must endure?" Dr. George Campbell, not a Baptist, translates, "Can ye undergo an immersion like that which I must undergo?" "The metaphorical sense of *overwhelming suffering,*" as Dr. Conant justly remarks, "is founded on the idea of total submergence, as in floods of sorrow." That the Greek word means here, or anywhere else, *to purify,* is without the shadow of proof. This meaning was very elaborately advocated several years ago by Dr. Edward Beecher, but his theory failed to secure the confidence of scholars. See note on 28:19. The Greek language has a word which means *to pour,* and another which means *to sprinkle,* but neither of these words would have so clear-

CHAPTER XX. 227

23 And he saith unto them, Ye shall drink indeed of my cup, and be baptized with the baptism that I am baptized with: but to sit on my right hand, and on my left, is not mine to give, but *it shall be given to them* for whom it is prepared of my Father.

24 And when the ten heard *it*, they were moved with indignation against the two brethren.

25 But Jesus called them *unto him*, and said, Ye know that the princes of the Gentiles exercise dominion over them, and they that are great exercise authority upon them.

26 But it shall not be so among you: but whosoever will be great among you, let him be your minister;

27 And whosoever will be chief among you, let him be your servant:

28 Even as the Son of man came not to be ministered unto, but to minister, and to give his life a ransom for many.

---

ly and forcibly expressed the intensity of our Lord's sufferings. It should not, however, be left unsaid, that the Greek of the words, *and to be baptized with the baptism that I am baptized with*, and the related words in the next verse, are not found in the oldest manuscripts and versions. They are genuine, however, in Mark 10: 38, 39.

23. *Ye shall indeed drink*, etc.— They were to be called to great sufferings, infinitely less, indeed, than his, but as they are to be borne for him, he represents them as drinking *his* cup, etc. James was soon called to suffer death. Acts 12: 2. Though John died a natural death, he suffered much for Christ. John, according to some, was a martyr in spirit; James a martyr in spirit and act. "All Christians must be prepared for one or the other of them. Every one must be a James or a John." *It shall be given*, etc.—We are not to infer from these words that in his original, essential nature, Christ was inferior to the Father. The meaning may be this: It is not my special, exclusive prerogative, as you seem to think, to say who shall have positions of great honor in my kingdom, whether on earth or in heaven. That has already been decided by my Father. His arrangements in nature and grace with reference to that end have been made.

24. *Moved with indignation* is too strong. Better, *were displeased*. Here is a touch of the inspired pencil which is wonderfully lifelike. If one chooses to say they were *very much* displeased, one would not be going beyond the record. The two were ambitious: the ten were displeased. As Matthew was one of the ten, observe his honesty in reporting it. That does not look much like forgery.

25–28. He contrasts the spirit which they should cherish toward one another with that which prevails in the heathen world. There an ambitious, overbearing, place-loving spirit is the characteristic of rulers. In that is no true moral greatness. In Christ's kingdom greatness must be estimated by the willingness of the disciples to do one another *service*. *Even as the Son of man*—How tender the reproof! How high the Saviour's estimate of humility! *Ransom*—The price for any one's release. *For*—Not on behalf of, but *instead of*. Christ now reveals to them that the death which he is about to suffer is to be borne as a substitute for theirs. Though they could not then have understood him, yet their epistles,

29 And as they departed from Jericho, a great multitude followed him.

30 ¶ And, behold, two blind men sitting by the way side, when they heard that Jesus passed by, cried out, saying, Have mercy on us, O Lord, *thou* Son of David.

31 And the multitude rebuked them, because they should hold their peace: but they cried the more, saying, Have mercy on us, O Lord, *thou* Son of David.

32 And Jesus stood still, and called them, and said, What will ye that I shall do unto you?

33 They say unto him, Lord, that our eyes may be opened.

34 So Jesus had compassion on *them*, and touched their eyes: and immediately their eyes received sight, and they followed him.

---

and, so far as it is reported in the Acts, their preaching also, show that the Lord's instruction was not lost. Very rich are the sentiments in John's and Peter's epistles relative to the object of the Lord's death. Christ's sufferings as a substitute for the sinner's, accepted by the sinner himself, are the only ground of justification.

29. *Jericho*—A celebrated city lying in a plain east-north-east from Jerusalem. See more concerning it in the notes on Luke 10:30. Thus far, within seventeen or nineteen miles, had Jesus advanced toward the capital. A *great multitude*—On their way to one of the great annual festivals of the Jews,—the Passover.

30. *Two blind men*—See notes on the similar account, 9:27-31. Mark and Luke speak of *one* blind man. According to Matthew and Mark, the healing took place on departing from the city; according to Luke, on entering. Much needless effort to reconcile the little discrepancies has been made. "'The difference in the account of the evangelists is entirely unimportant, except as serving to show that they are independent historians; and it is idle to try to make them agree by the forced suppositions to which some commentators have resorted.' It is most probable that two were healed, though one only is mentioned by Mark and Luke."—*Prof. Norton, in Andrews' Life of our Lord.* As Alford remarks, "He must be indeed a slave to the *letter* who would stumble at such discrepancies, and not rather see in them the corroborating coincidence of testimonies to the fact itself."

31, 32. *Rebuked them, because*—Rebuked them *that*. The people may have thought it an indecorous interruption. Jesus thought otherwise. In a day or two the multitude were more vociferous in their cry of hosanna than the blind men had been in their cry for mercy, yet they would have deemed it a great impertinence had the blind men rebuked them. No man can estimate the criminality of interposing an obstacle in the way of the soul that is longing for spiritual light.

CHAPTER XXI.

CHRIST'S TRIUMPHAL ENTRY INTO JERUSALEM; CLEANSES THE TEMPLE; CURSES THE FIG TREE; UTTERS THE PARABLE OF THE TWO SONS, AND THE PARABLE OF THE WICKED HUSBANDMEN.

783 U.C. Sunday, April 2, A.D. 30.

1. Several events occurred between the healing of the blind men

CHAPTER XXI.

AND when they drew nigh unto Jerusalem, and were come to Bethphage, unto the mount of Olives, then sent Jesus two disciples,

2 Saying unto them, Go into the village over against you, and straightway ye shall find

---

near Jericho and the triumphal entry, but no mention is made of them by Matthew. According to Luke, it may be inferred that Jesus spent the night in Jericho with Zaccheus. The next morning he left Jericho, and arrived at Bethany, near Jerusalem, the same day, Friday, March 31. There he spent that night and the next day, which was the Jewish Sabbath, our Saturday. On Sunday, April 2, our Sabbath, he leaves Bethany for the city. *Come to Bethphage*—House of Figs. The spot has never been identified, but it was evidently very near to Bethany. *Mount of Olives*—A ridge of land on the east of Jerusalem, running north and south, consisting of three elevations, the middle one of which is regarded as the Mount of Ascension. It derived its name from the olive-trees which grew there. There are a few olive-trees upon the mount now. "The eight aged olive-trees, if only by their manifest difference from all others on the mountain, have always struck even the most indifferent observers. . . . They will remain, so long as their already protracted life is spared, the most venerable of their race on the surface of the earth; their gnarled trunks and scanty foliage will always be regarded as the most affecting of the sacred memorials in or about Jerusalem; the most nearly approaching to the everlasting hills themselves in the force with which they carry us back to the events of the Gospel history."—*Stanley*. Dr. Hackett thinks it "not impossible that the aged olive-trees may have sprung from the roots of those which grew there in the days of Christ." Such are the events which have occurred upon the Mount of Olives, that the Alps and the Andes dwindle into insignificance in the comparison. Over it, in tears, fled David from his rebellious son; on the eastern side the Son of God looked upon the unbelieving city and wept; at its western foot, in Gethsemane, he suffered his almost fatal agony; from its summit he ascended to his throne in heaven. "It took," says Thomson, "half an hour to walk over Olivet to Bethany this morning, and the distance from the city, therefore, must be about two miles. The village is small, and appears never to have been large, but it is pleasantly situated near the south-eastern base of the mount, and has many fine trees about and above it."

2. *The village over against you*—Bethphage. *Ass*—This animal was not chosen as a symbol of humiliation. "The most noble and honorable amongst the Jews were wont to be mounted on asses." "The most striking feature in the Biblical notices of the horse is the exclusive application of it to warlike operations; in no instance is that useful animal employed for the purposes of ordinary locomotion or agriculture, if we except Isaiah 28: 28, where we learn that horses (A. V." [authorized version] "horsemen) were employed in threshing; not, however, in that case put in the gears, but simply driven about wildly over the strewed grain." The ass was a symbol of peace. Much attention was paid to the cultivation of the breed. The contempt for the animal which is felt in the United States would have had little sympathy in Palestine. *Them*—As the

an ass tied, and a colt with her: loose *them*, and bring *them* unto me.

3 And if any *man* say aught unto you, ye shall say, The Lord hath need of them; and straightway he will send them.

4 All this was done, that it might be fulfilled which was spoken by the prophet, saying,

5 Tell ye the daughter of Sion, Behold, thy King cometh unto thee, meek, and sitting upon an ass, and a colt the foal of an ass.

6 And the disciples went, and did as Jesus commanded them,

7 And brought the ass, and the colt, and put on them their clothes, and they set *him* thereon.

8 And a very great multitude spread their garments in the way; others cut down branches from the trees, and strewed *them* in the way.

9 And the multitudes that went before, and that followed, cried, saying, Hosanna to the Son of David: Blessed *is* he that cometh in the name of the Lord; Hosanna in the highest.

---

colt had never been used (Mark 11:2), it was natural to take the mother too.

3. *He will send them*—There is no evidence of previous arrangement with the owner of the animal, but the owner was doubtless favorably disposed toward Jesus. Jesus knew *what was in man*. This man's willingness to trust an unused colt with Jesus is suggestive. The colt may be loaned, and the heart withheld. If the heart is given, all will be given.

4, 5. *That it might be fulfilled*— The words are taken from Isa. 62:11; Zech. 9:9. The prophet Zechariah foretold this very act of the coming Messiah. *Daughter of Zion*—Personification of Jerusalem as a woman. The figure is common in the Old Testament.

6, 7. In doing as Jesus commanded them, they were not aware that they were aiding in the fulfilment of the prophecy. See John 12:16: *These things understood not his disciples at the first,* etc. But did he sit on both animals? The infidel Strauss accuses the evangelist of so representing it in order to make Jesus "slavishly and unreasonably carry out the prophetic description." But in the words of Dr. Schaff, "Matthew knew as much Hebrew and had as much common sense as any modern critic of his Gospel." It was the *colt* that he rode: Mark, Luke. Popes, Christ's "vicegerents," have rode in gorgeous apparel on richly caparisoned horses led by kings.

8, 9. *Their garments*—Men put their garments down for Jehu to walk upon. 2 Kings 9:13. *Branches from the trees*—The palm-trees. There were many species of the palm. It is the date-palm for which Syria and Palestine were distinguished. Jericho so abounded in palm-trees that it was called the "city of palms." The tree was beautiful and straight. Hence, in Solomon's Song (7:9) it is used in the description of the form of a beautiful woman: *This thy stature is like to a palm-tree.* Hence, also, it is used as a symbol of the good man. *The righteous shall flourish as the palm-tree.* Ps. 92:12. In the Revelation of John (7:9) the saints are seen *before the Lamb, clothed with white robes, and palms in their hands.* "It is curious that this tree,

CHAPTER XXI.

10 And when he was come into Jerusalem, all the city was moved, saying, Who is this?

11 And the multitude said, This is Jesus the prophet of Nazareth of Galilee.

12 ¶ And Jesus went into the temple of God, and cast out all them that sold and bought in the temple, and overthrew the tables of the money changers, and the seats of them that sold doves,

13 And said unto them, It is

---

once so abundant in Judea, is now comparatively rare, except in the Philistine plain, and in the old Phœnicia about *Beyrout*. A few years ago there was just one palm-tree at Jericho, but that is now gone. Old trunks are washed up in the Dead Sea. It would almost seem as though we might take the history of this tree in Palestine as emblematical of the people whose home was once in that land." *Hosanna—Save now;* but it is here used as a thanksgiving rather than as a prayer. The people took these words from Ps. 118. They were familiar with them from being accustomed to recite vv. 25 and 26 at the Feast of Tabernacles.

The people were now evidently regarding Jesus as the Messiah, but were committing the mistake of supposing that he was now to set up his kingdom in the visible, semi-political form so commonly expected. In the graphic words of Stanley, "Two vast streams of people met on that day. . . . Half of the vast mass, turning round, preceded; the other half followed. Gradually the long procession swept up and over the ridge, where first begins 'the descent of the Mount of Olives' toward Jerusalem. At this point the first view is caught of the city. The temple and the more northern portions are hid by the slope of Olivet on the right; what is seen is only Mount Zion, now for the most part a rough field, crowned with the mosque of David, and the angle of the western walls, but then covered with houses to its base, surmounted by the castle of Herod, on the supposed site of the palace of David, from which that portion of Jerusalem, emphatically the 'City of David,' derived its name. It was at this precise point 'as he drew near, at the descent of the Mount of Olives,'—(may it not have been from the sight thus opening upon them?)—that the shout of triumph burst forth from the multitude, 'Hosanna to the Son of David.'" But amid these joyous outbursts Jesus weeps over the unbelieving inhabitants of the city. Luke 19:41.

10, 11. *All the city*—The excitement was universal and intense. The same Greek word is used in 27:51: The earth *did quake.* How absurd the theory that this entry of Jesus into Jerusalem was made for the purpose of setting up a political kingdom, the attempt proving a failure through the hostility of the Pharisees!

Monday, April 3.

12. Comparing Matthew with Mark 11:11, it would seem that the acts here recorded occurred on the *second* day of the Lord's arrival in the city, that is, on Monday, Matthew omitting to specify his visit to the temple on the day of the triumphal entry.

The temple—The Rabbins said: "The world is like to an eye; the white of the eye is the ocean surrounding the world; the black is the world itself; the pupil is Jerusalem, and the image in the pupil the temple." First was built the tabernacle, forty-five feet by fifteen, with its single court, one hundred and fifty feet by seventy-five. Then

written, My house shall be called the house of prayer; but ye have made it a den of thieves.

---

was built Solomon's temple, the dimensions of every part of which were exactly double those of the tabernacle. In plan it was only an enlarged copy of the tabernacle, but it was much more ornamental. That, too, had but one court, which was probably three hundred feet by one hundred and fifty,—twice the size of the tabernacle court. About five hundred and twenty years before Christ, was built the temple of Zerubbabel. Herod's temple was the temple of Zerubbabel greatly enlarged and embellished. A very particular description may be read in Josephus. The temple itself was in dimensions and arrangement very similar to that of Solomon, or rather that of Zerubbabel,—more like the latter; but this was surrounded by an inner enclosure of great strength and magnificence, measuring, as nearly as can be made out, one hundred and eighty cubits by two hundred and forty [two hundred and seventy feet by three hundred and sixty], and adorned by porches and ten gateways of great magnificence; and beyond this again was an outer enclosure, measuring externally four hundred cubits [six hundred feet] each way, which was adorned with porticos of greater splendor than any we know of attached to any temple of the ancient world. . . The most magnificent part of the temple, in an architectural point of view, seems certainly to have been the cloisters which were added to the outer court when it was enlarged by Herod. The royal porch which overhung the southern wall, a magnificent structure, was supported by one hundred and sixty-two Corinthian columns, arranged in four rows, forty in each row. At a short distance from the front of these cloisters was a marble screen or enclosure, three cubits in height, beautifully ornamented with carving, but bearing inscriptions in Greek and Roman characters forbidding any Gentile to pass within its boundaries. . . . The court of the temple was very nearly a square. . . . To the eastward of this was the court of the women. Outside of all the other courts was the court of the Gentiles. Both the altar and the temple were enclosed by a low parapet one cubit in height, placed so as to keep the people separate from the priests while the latter were performing their functions. Within this last enclosure toward the westward stood the temple itself. There is no reason whatever for doubting but that the *sanctuary* always stood on the same spot in which it had been placed by Solomon a thousand years before it was rebuilt by Herod.—*Condensed from Mr. James Fergusson, Smith's Dictionary.*

The temple itself, like all the sacred buildings that preceded it, was divided into two parts, the Holy Place, and the Most Holy Place. In the Holy Place of the tabernacle and of Solomon's temple was that most sacred chest called the Ark of the Covenant, three and three-fourths feet long and two and one-quarter broad and deep. On the upper side was the Mercy Seat, on which stood the cherubim, one at each end. This was the symbol of God's presence. "It was, however, never seen, save by the high priest, and resembled in this respect the Deity whom it symbolized, whose face none might look upon and live." What became of the ark when Solomon's temple was destroyed, is not known. Its absence from Herod's temple constitutes the most important difference between that and Solomon's.

And Jesus went into the temple— Not into the building itself, which only priests were permitted to enter, but into the *outer court.* It is quite

CHAPTER XXI.

14 And the blind and the lame came to him in the temple; and he healed them.

15 And when the chief priests and scribes saw the wonderful things that he did, and the children crying in the temple, and saying, Hosanna to the Son of David; they were sore displeased,

16 And said unto him, Hearest thou what these say? And Jesus saith unto them, Yea; have ye never read, Out of the mouth of babes and sucklings thou hast perfected praise?

17 ¶ And he left them, and went out of the city into Bethany, and he lodged there.

18 Now in the morning, as

---

certain that not even Jesus Christ, though this was his Father's house, was ever in the Most Holy Place. But he came from the place of which that was only a symbol. *Sold and bought*—Whatever was necessary in the services of the temple, as oxen, sheep, and doves; perhaps oil, incense, and wine. *Money-changers*—Brokers, men who accommodated the Jews that brought foreign money, by exchanging it for money that would be current at the temple, and enriched themselves by the exorbitant sum which they charged for the exchange. See note on 17: 24. The offering of a pair of *doves* was required of him who was too poor to offer a lamb. The court of the Gentiles had become a market. The abuse was great. God's house was not erected for brokerage and cattle-selling.

13. *Written*—In Isa. 56: 7; Jer. 7: 11. *Thieves*—Robbers. This is one of the cases in which the end did not justify the means. Those men were not there from pious regard to the wants of others, but from shameful love of gain. Consider the exceeding majesty of Jesus and the terrible power of conscious guilt. They quit the temple-court in impenitence. Had they been penitent, Jesus would have permitted them to go *further in*, that they might offer a sacrifice for their sin. The world is God's temple, but it needs cleansing. The Christian sanctuary needs cleansing. The heart of every man is a temple intended for the indwelling of God.

14. How boldly and rapidly here in the capital, before the eyes of his bitterest enemies, is he multiplying proofs of his Messiahship! 1. He has permitted himself to receive the acclamations of the people; 2. He has vindicated the honor of his Father's house; 3. He works miracles in a court of the temple itself. It is a mistake to regard these miracles, as most commentators do, chiefly as exhibitions of mercy. They were that, but they were intended, as were all his miracles, primarily, as evidence of his Messiahship.

15-17. The chief priests and scribes, far from being convinced that he is the Messiah, are indignant. They are committed against him, and no evidence can suffice. *Hearest thou what these say?*—The question was uttered in contempt. They probably intended to rebuke him for permitting himself to be so extolled by the children. The children may have been members of the temple choir, but it is more probable that they were attracted to the spot from the streets of the city by the report of his presence and miracles. They *may* have been very pious children, as many commentators take for granted, but their singing is no proof of it. The people sung the same words the day before, but they soon gave painful evidence of their unbelief. *Never read*—In Ps. 8: 2. *Perfected*—Prepared. Re-

he returned into the city, he hungered.

19 And when he saw a fig tree in the way, he came to it, and found nothing thereon, but leaves only, and said unto it, Let no fruit grow on thee henceforward for ever. And presently the fig tree withered away.

---

ferring the priests to these words of David is not to be considered as expressing himself concerning the spiritual state of the children. Dr. Whedon says: "Nor can there be a doubt that these children were moved by a divine impulse to utter these praises." Dr. J. J. Owen says better: "We do not mean that they had any special illumination or strengthening of their mental powers, above what was natural to their age. They cried *hosanna* with the spirit and understanding of little children, and we rob this incident of its power and moral beauty in attempting to explain it otherwise."

Bethany—It is not certain that the meaning generally given to this name, *house of dates*, is the true one. Some derive it from two words, meaning *house of the afflicted*. There were two villages of this name, the one on the eastern side of the Jordan (see John 1: 28), the other on the western side. The latter is the village here meant. "There never appears to have been any doubt as to the site of Bethany, which is now known by a name derived from Lazarus,—*el-'Azariyeh*. It lies on the eastern slope of the Mount of Olives, fully a mile beyond the summit, and not very far from the point at which the road to Jericho begins its more sudden descent toward the Jordan valley. The spot is a woody hollow, more or less planted with fruit-trees,—olives, almonds, pomegranates, as well as oaks and carobs; the whole lying below a secondary ridge or hump, of sufficient height to shut out the village from the summit of the mount." "Three pathways lead," says Stanley, "and probably always led, from Bethany to Jerusalem; one, a steep footpath over the summit of Mount Olivet; another, by a long circuit over its northern shoulder, down the valley which parts it from Scopus" ['the northern outlier']; "the third, the natural continuation of the road by which mounted travellers always approach the city from Jericho, over the southern shoulder, between the summit which contains the tombs of the Prophets and that called the Mount of Offence. There can be no doubt but that the last is the road of the entry of Christ." *Lodged there*—Bethany was the residence of Mary and Martha and their brother Lazarus. During the last of his ministry, and perhaps in the first, it was our Saviour's favorite resort. By comparison with Mark, it would appear that the lodging here mentioned is not related in the order of time. It is believed to have occurred on Sunday night. On the next day occurred what is related in vv. 12-16, but later in the day than that which is narrated in vv. 18, 19.

18, 19. *In the morning*—Of Monday, April 3. According to Mark (11: 12 compared with vs. 15) the cursing of the fig-tree and the cleansing of the temple occurred on the same day. But Matthew combines the cursing and the conversation in respect to the withering as if *they* occurred the same day. *He hungered*—Why he was hungry at that period of the day does not appear. He may have left the house of Mary and Martha before the family were astir, and this may show the intensity of his desire to be early at work again in the city. In his hunger we see his humanity, and in the miracle wrought upon the tree his deity.

CHAPTER XXI.

20 And when the disciples saw *it*, they marvelled, saying, How soon is the fig tree withered away!

21 Jesus answered and said unto them, Verily I say unto you, If ye have faith, and doubt not, ye shall not only do this *which is done* to the fig tree, but also if ye shall say unto this mountain, Be thou removed, and be thou cast into the sea; it shall be done.

22 And all things, whatsoever ye shall ask in prayer, believing, ye shall receive.

Fig-tree—The fig-tree was very common in Palestine, and it is found there still, though not in great abundance. *In the way*—On the roadside, and therefore, perhaps, common property, though this supposition is not necessary as a defence of the Saviour's purpose to pluck figs if he should find any there. By the laws of Moses great freedom in helping one's self to fruit was allowed, and Thomson says that the custom of plucking ripe figs as one passes by the orchards is still universal, . . especially from trees by the roadside, and from all that are not enclosed. *He came to it*—Came to it, expecting to find figs. But it is held that the season (the first of April) was too early to expect figs. Reply: 1. Thomson says: "There is a kind of tree which bears a large green-colored fig, that ripens very early. I have plucked them in May, from trees in Lebanon, a hundred and fifty miles north of Jerusalem, and where the trees are nearly a month later than in the south of Palestine; it does not, therefore, seem impossible but that the same kind *might* have had ripe figs at Easter, in the warm, sheltered ravines of Olivet." But this of course was exceptional. Thomson himself adds that the *ordinary* time for figs, it is true enough, had not yet arrived; 2. The fruit of the fig-tree comes as soon as the leaves, and often sooner. It matters not whether this was the ordinary time for figs or not. As leaves had appeared, Jesus did just what we should have done, went to see if it had figs. If the leaves had appeared before the ordinary time, it was not in the least unreasonable to turn a little out of the way and see whether figs, too, had not appeared before the ordinary time. It turned out that the tree was *precocious*. It was a *showy* tree. It made a boast of fruitfulness. It was a lying tree. It invited people to believe that it had figs. It promised, by its foliage, to give men figs. Christ, therefore, doomed it to perpetual barrenness. It is a great mistake to suppose that the act sprung from any feeling whatever on account of the fruitlessness of the tree. That, to such a being as Jesus Christ, was a matter of no consequence. But the apostles, who were looking on, needed more instruction and faith. The tree was cursed that the apostles might be blessed. The record of the miracle is full of solemn warning to churches and individuals. The leaves of a profession may exist where there is no fruit. A fruitless profession is a perpetual falsehood.

Tuesday, April 4.

20. Jesus is supposed to have returned to Bethany on Monday evening, and to have spent the night there. On Tuesday, he returns to Jerusalem, and on passing by the fig-tree, the disciples exclaim, *How soon is the fig-tree withered away! Is* should be dropped, for they speak not of the result, *is withered*, but of the act: How soon the fig-tree withered away! It may be read as a question: How did the fig-tree im-

23 ¶ And when he was come into the temple, the chief priests and the elders of the people came unto him as he was teaching, and said, By what authority doest thou these things? and who gave thee this authority?

24 And Jesus answered and said unto them, I also will ask you one thing, which if ye tell me, I in like wise will tell you by what authority I do these things.

25 The baptism of John, whence was it? from heaven, or of men? And they reasoned with themselves, saying, If we shall say, From heaven; he will say unto us, Why did ye not then believe him?

26 But if we shall say, Of men; we fear the people; for all hold John as a prophet.

27 And they answered Jesus and said, We cannot tell. And he said unto them, Neither tell I you by what authority I do these things.

28 ¶ But what think ye? A *certain* man had two sons; and he came to the first, and said, Son, go work to-day in my vineyard.

29 He answered and said, I will not; but afterward he repented, and went.

30 And he came to the second, and said likewise. And he answered and said, I *go*, sir; and went not.

31 Whether of them twain

---

mediately wither away? The disciples desire to know how it could have been done so quickly.

21, 22. See notes on 17:20; 18:19.

23-27. The conflict between Jesus and the rulers is now more fully developed. The chief priests and the elders (Mark and Luke mention scribes also) came probably as an official deputation from the highest Jewish tribunal in the land,—the Sanhedrim. That body had the right to sit in judgment upon men who claimed to be prophets. They had already exercised that right relative to John the Baptist. See John 1: 19-22. *By what authority* —The scribes who sat in Moses' seat considered that *they* were the only authorized expounders of religion. Ought not Jesus to have given them a decisive answer? Reply: In whatever forms of law they came clothed, their motive was essentially, intensely wicked. They wanted to get from his own lips avowals which would answer as evidence against him in the Sanhedrim. *The baptism of John*—The immersion of John, here standing for his entire work. *Reasoned with themselves*—Reasoned among themselves. It is not necessary to suppose that they returned to the Sanhedrim, and that the entire body entered into a formal consultation concerning the matter. The answer may have been given after the delegates had briefly consulted among themselves in an under tone. Their pride, combined with their hostility, would have induced them to make a quick answer. They are foiled, but will try again. *Cannot tell*—Jesus had silenced them by argument. He now exposes their wickedness. This he does in three parables: 1. The two sons; 2. The wicked husbandmen; 3. The marriage festival.

28-32. *Go work*—The Saviour's interpretation (vv. 31, 32) makes these words refer chiefly to that crisis in one's life,—*entering* into the

did the will of *his* father? They say unto him, The first. Jesus saith unto them, Verily I say unto you, That the publicans and the harlots go into the kingdom God before you.

32 For John came unto you in the way of righteousness, and ye believed him not; but the publicans and the harlots believed him: and ye, when ye had seen *it*, repented not afterward, that ye might believe him.

33 ¶ Hear another parable: There was a certain householder, which planted a vineyard, and hedged it round about, and digged a winepress in it, and bui't a tower, and let it out to husbandmen, and went into a far country:

34 And when the time of the fruit drew near, he sent his servants to the husbandmen, that they might receive the fruits of it.

35 And the husbandmen took his servants, and beat one, and killed another, and stoned another.

36 Again, he sent other servants more than the first: and they did unto them likewise.

---

kingdom of God; that is, becoming a disciple of Christ. Doing the Christian work which devolves upon one after that crisis has been passed is implied, but is not directly taught. *I will not*—The quick, blunt reply of the grosser class of sinners; the publicans and harlots. *I go, sir*—The equally prompt, more courteous, but boastful response of legalists and ritualists,—the very men whom he is addressing. But when did the Pharisees profess a willingness to go into the kingdom which Christ came to set up? Never; but they professed to be righteous. He exposes the hollowness of their professions, by showing that they had rejected John, who came preaching righteousness, while those who all their life had made no pretension to righteousness believed John. Concerning the publicans, see note on 5: 46. To be put, in respect to the point named, lower than publicans and harlots, must have been in the highest degree offensive to these "first-class" men. *Go before you* is regarded by some as indicating that their case was not hopeless; but see vs. 32: And ye, *when ye had seen it*—had seen the publicans and harlots believing—*repented not afterward*, that ye might believe him.

The parable is a perfect description of men of our own time; but it should be borne in mind that it is a description of the *extreme* men. Jesus does not teach that the case of grosser sinners is more hopeful than that of *all* others; he says nothing of that large class of persons who stand between the extreme classes. Observation teaches that moral and religiously educated persons, if not enslaved by the conviction that they are already so righteous as to need no change, will more probably come to a penitent acknowledgment of Christ as a vicarious sacrifice for sin than others; nor is there anything in this parable that teaches otherwise.

33–36. This parable is spoken "against" (Mark 12: 12) the Pharisees. It sets forth the success of their murderous purpose, and the consequent transfer of their privileges to others. *Vineyard*—The vine was so much cultivated in Palestine, and was such an emblem of peace, as to give rise to the saying, They shall sit every man under his vine. "The first parable," says Stanley, "that rises before the

MATTHEW.

37 But last of all he sent unto them his son, saying, They will reverence my son.

38 But when the husbandmen saw the son, they said among themselves, This is the heir; come, let us kill him, and let us seize on his inheritance.

---

mind of the traveller as he enters Judea from the desert, is that of the vineyard. . . . Here, more than elsewhere, are to be seen on the sides of the hills, the vineyards, marked by their watch-towers and walls, seated on their terraces,— the earliest and latest symbol of Judah. The elevation of the hills and table-lands of Judah is the true climate of the vine, and at Hebron, according to the Jewish tradition, was its primeval seat." *Hedge*—Of stones, or of thorns, or both. *Wine-*

WINE-PRESS.

press—"The wine-press of the Jews consisted of two receptacles or vats, placed at different elevations, in the upper one of which the grapes were trodden, while the lower one received the expressed juice. . . The two vats were usually dug or hewn out of the solid rock. Ancient wine-presses, so constructed, are still to be seen in Palestine, one of which is thus described by Dr. Robinson: 'Advantage had been taken of a ledge of rock; on the upper side a shallow vat had been dug, eight feet square, and fifteen inches deep. Two feet lower down, another smaller vat was excavated, four feet square by three feet deep. The grapes were trodden in the shallow upper vat, and the juice drawn off by a hole at the bottom (still remaining) into the lower vat.'"—*Smith's Dictionary*. *A tower*—"Such towers are still in use in Palestine in vineyards, especially near Hebron, and are used as lodges for the keepers of the vineyards. During the vintage, they are filled with persons employed in the work of gathering grapes." *Went into a far country*, should be *went into another country*, or, *went abroad*. The original expresses no such idea as that of distance. *Householder*—God. *Vineyard*—The nation of Israel. *Husbandmen* — The leading men, those on whom devolved the chief responsibility of keeping the nation in harmony with the spirit of the Mosaic economy. Applied to the Saviour's time, it refers to the Pharisees, scribes, and priests. *Servants*—Messengers commissioned at different periods to aid the people to attain to righteousness. In this sense they were to receive the husbandmen's fruit.

37. *His son*—The Pharisees could have had no difficulty in understanding this as referring to himself. *Last of all*—Afterward, say many; but

CHAPTER XXI.

39 And they caught him, and cast *him* out of the vineyard, and slew *him*.

40 When the lord therefore of the vineyard cometh, what will he do unto those husbandmen?

41 They say unto him, He will miserably destroy those wicked men, and will let out *his* vineyard unto other husbandmen, which shall render him the fruits in their seasons.

42 Jesus saith unto them, Did ye never read in the Scriptures, The stone which the builders rejected, the same is become the head of the corner: this is the Lord's doing, and it is marvellous in our eyes?

43 Therefore say I unto you, The kingdom of God shall be taken from you, and given to a nation bringing forth the fruits thereof.

44 And whosoever shall fall on this stone shall be broken:

---

it is not the less true that Jesus Christ is God's *last* messenger to the Jews, as he is the last to the world. Notice how distinct from the prophets is the Son of God, and how superior. Mark (12:6) makes it still clearer: *Having yet therefore one son, his well beloved.* "Christianity older than Christ," and "Christianity one of many religions, and, therefore, like others destined to fall," are sayings which, in the light of this verse, are seen to have originated with the father of lies.

38, 39. *Heir*—The Son of God was appointed heir of all things. Heb. 1:2. *Let us kill him*—See John 11:53, for proof that the priests and Pharisees had already resolved to put him to death. Who can describe their feelings as these words fell upon their ears? Their depravity, however, enables them to assume the appearance of ignorance of his meaning.

41. *Will . . . destroy those wicked men*—An answer made under the pretence of missing his meaning. *Miserably destroy*, is in the original so peculiar as scarcely to admit of adequate expression in English. "*He will wretchedly destroy those wretches,*" brings out the play of the words as well as can be done.

42. *Never read*—In Ps. 118:22,23. Christ is here represented as a stone, which the Jewish rulers, the builders of God's spiritual house, answering to the husbandmen in the parable, *rejected,*—disallowed. They did not allow his claims, and therefore rejected him. Yet he became the corner-stone. *The corner-stone*—That which serves both to build upon and to bind the two adjoining walls together. In the latter view, all the stones of each of the four corners of a building are cornerstones. Peter (Acts 4:10, 11) quotes some of the same words when arrested and brought before the Sanhedrim, applying them with great boldness to Jesus, whom they had so recently crucified. See also 1 Peter 2:4.

43. *Therefore*—Because you are rejecting me, as I have illustrated in the parable. *The kingdom of heaven*—The Christian dispensation, but with special reference to its privileges. *Be taken from you*—Not exclusively, or even chiefly, to the Jews as a people was the gospel preached. It began to be preached to them, but, as they rejected it, it was preached at last chiefly to Gentiles, and has been preached chiefly to Gentiles ever since. This view, however, should not be held as excluding reference to the true people

but on whomsoever it shall fall, it will grind him to powder.

45 And when the chief priests and Pharisees had heard his parables, they perceived that he spake of them.

46 But when they sought to lay hands on him, they feared the multitude, because they took him for a prophet.

CHAPTER XXII.

AND Jesus answered and spake unto them again by parables, and said,

2 The kingdom of heaven is

---

of God, whether Gentiles or Jews. Acts 15: 14, and especially Rom. 9: 30-33.

44. The popular interpretation of the first part of this verse is incorrect,—that those who fall upon Christ as their Saviour shall be blessed with brokenness of spirit. Christ here represents himself as a stone of *stumbling;* that is, as a stone against which one may stumble and be broken, *ruined.* This is precisely what Christ was to the scribes and the Pharisees. Hence Peter, in his first epistle (2: 8), speaks of Christ as being to the disobedient a stone of stumbling and a rock of offence, *even to them which stumble at the word.* According to Dr. Whedon, the meaning is that one may "get bruised, or have a *limb* broken, perhaps; but may recover himself and place himself upon *the corner-stone,*"—a view which is not easily suggested by the words, and one which seems to have no support in other parts of the Bible. *On whomsoever it shall fall*—See Dan. 2: 34, 35. Here the stone is conceived as loosened from its place, as a stone from a mountain, and crushing that upon which it falls. It is thus that Christ teaches that his displeasure shall fall with destructive weight upon those who reject him. Many are the ways in which Christ may become a stumbling-stone. The Pharisees denied his Messiahship. Some, in our own day, admitting that he was *a good man*, disbelieve his miracles and his supernatural conception. Some, accepting these, deny his deity and the vicariousness of his sufferings. Others, believing all this, are yet unwilling to lead the life of self-denial which he requires in order to be his disciples. Others, oppressed by a conscious load of sin, imagine that the spotless purity of his character is an obstacle to their pardon, and it would be were it not for that righteousness which arises from his atoning death.

45, 46. *Perceived that he spake of them*—Ministers and Sabbath-school teachers should so preach that a similar effect shall be produced upon *their* hearers. *Feared the multitude*—They were guilty, therefore, even then, of murder.

CHAPTER XXII.

THE PARABLE OF THE MARRIAGE FESTIVAL; THE PHARISEES, THE HERODIANS, AND THE SADDUCEES AIM TO ENSNARE JESUS WITH PERPLEXING QUESTIONS.

783 U.C. Tuesday, April 4, A.D. 30.

The supposition that the Pharisees departed after Jesus spoke the last parable is unnecessary. It is still Tuesday, and Jesus is still in the temple-court.

1-3. *A marriage*—Not merely the marriage strictly so called, but chiefly the marriage festival. It represents the privileges of the Christian dispensation. *King*—God. *Son* —Jesus Christ. *Servants*—God's

CHAPTER XXII. 241

like unto a certain king, which made a marriage for his son,

3 And sent forth his servants to call them that were bidden to the wedding: and they would not come.

4 Again, he sent forth other servants, saying, Tell them which are bidden, Behold, I have prepared my dinner: my oxen and *my* fatlings *are* killed, and all things *are* ready: come unto the marriage.

5 But they made light of *it*, and went their ways, one to his farm, another to his merchandise:

6 And the remnant took his servants, and entreated *them* spitefully, and slew *them*.

7 But when the king heard *thereof*, he was wroth: and he sent forth his armies, and destroyed those murderers, and burned up their city.

8 Then saith he to his servants, The wedding is ready, but they which were bidden were not worthy.

9 Go ye therefore into the

---

messengers to men, but not those of the old times. The last parable took us back into the days of the prophets. This begins very near where that ended. Observe that here it is the *kingdom of heaven,*—the *new* dispensation. John and Christ's apostles were sent to the Jews to invite them to come to the banquet of God's love. In oriental countries it was the practice to send two invitations to a feast, the first, *general;* the second, *particular,* in the sense of apprising the bidden that preparation had been made.

4-6. *Other servants*—There is no necessity for regarding this as meaning totally different messengers. They include both the apostles, *who often repeated* the invitation sent to the Jews, and any others who, sooner or later, before the destruction of Jerusalem, united in the work of calling the Jews to the blessings of Christ's kingdom. The *point* in this part of the parable is the *repetition* of the summons, whether by precisely the same messengers or not. In these repeated invitations we see evidence of God's sincere desire that the Jews might be saved. *Fatlings*—Animals that had been fatted for slaughter. *All things are ready*—A cheering word for those who are themselves ready.

Made light—Not made sport, but counted it an unimportant thing, neglected it, were easy concerning it. *The remnant*—The others. As these showed positive hostility, they may represent the more virulent of the scribes and Pharisees, and the others so many of those classes as were not hostile, but only indifferent and unbelieving, with those of the people also who were in a similar state. John the Baptist was not received, Stephen was stoned, Peter was imprisoned, Paul was stoned and beaten.

7. *Wroth*—Though of infinite tenderness, Jesus did not hesitate to represent God as showing anger toward the wicked. *His armies*—The soldiers of Rome under Titus, by whom *their city*, Jerusalem, was destroyed forty years afterward. That the Jewish rulers could have done so wickedly as to bring destruction to their city, and at the very same time have done so well as to bring everlasting life to themselves, is not very probable. The destruction, therefore, cannot refer merely to the city. If human governments will create and support armies, God will use them to punish the wicked. He sometimes uses armies to punish the very government that created them.

highways, and as many as ye shall find, bid to the marriage.

10 So those servants went out into the highways, and gathered together all as many as they found, both bad and good: and the wedding was furnished with guests.

11 ¶ And when the king came in to see the guests, he saw there a man which had not on a wedding garment:

12 And he saith unto him, Friend, how camest thou in hither not having a wedding garment? And he was speechless.

13 Then said the king to the servants, Bind him hand and foot, and take him away, and cast *him* into outer darkness; there shall be weeping and gnashing of teeth.

14 For many are called, but few *are* chosen.

15 ¶ Then went the Phari-

8, 9. *Not worthy*—Of the privilege offered. *Highways*—Not country roads, but thoroughfares in the city. *Both bad and good*—It is not implied that any are by nature not sinful. It is merely a comprehensive phrase including all sorts of persons in the great Gentile world, whether vicious or virtuous. The latter *need* the blessings of the gospel as well as the former. The very fact that the "good" are invited proves that they are not good in the sense of being pious,—above the necessity of regeneration. The spirit of the direction is like that of the commission, Go ye into all the world and preach the gospel to *every* creature.

11, 12. The scene changes, and we are carried forward to the day of judgment. *Not having a wedding garment*—To show the criminality of the man in appearing without a garment suitable for the occasion, the attempt has been made, but not with entire success, to prove that it was customary for kings to furnish such garments to invited guests. It is by no means certain that the custom did not exist, but even if it did not, this part of the parable is not to be considered as inconsistent. The man would not have been blamed for taking as much time to procure a garment as was necessary. The wedding garment is symbolical of the imputed righteousness of Christ, and that personal holiness to which faith in Christ's righteousness always leads. *Speechless*, notwithstanding the fact stated in vs. 14, that *few are chosen;* that is, he makes no attempt to justify himself on that ground.

13, 14. *The servants*—A different word in the Greek, and therefore not referring to those who had given the invitations. These servants may symbolize the angels, and the angels may be said figuratively to act as the executioners of God's will in the punishment of the wicked. See 25: 31. *Outer darkness*, etc.—See note on 8: 11, 12. *Many called, few chosen*—That all the saved will have been saved in consequence of God's purpose to save them, a purpose which God must have always had, and therefore properly called eternal, is very plainly taught in the Scriptures. This is undoubtedly the basis of the proverbial saying in vs. 14.

15. The Pharisees, greatly exasperated, doubtless, by these three parables, withdrew, and summoned all their skill in devising plans by which to bring him under accusation. *Took counsel*—As many do, with their minds thoroughly committed against him. *Entangle him in his talk*—More accurately, *ensnare him with a word*, such as is

CHAPTER XXII.   243

sees, and took counsel how they might entangle him in *his* talk.

16 And they sent out unto him their disciples with the Herodians, saying, Master, we know that thou art true, and teachest the way of God in truth, neither carest thou for any *man:* for thou regardest not the person of men.

17 Tell us therefore, What thinkest thou? Is it lawful to give tribute unto Cesar, or not?

18 But Jesus perceived their wickedness, and said, Why tempt ye me, ye hypocrites?

19 Shew me the tribute money. And they brought unto him a penny.

20 And he saith unto them, Whose *is* this image and superscription?

21 They say unto him, Cesar's. Then saith he unto

---

reported in vv. 17 and 28. Strauss, Theodore Parker, and many others, have undertaken a similar task. Mr. Parker dared to say that in some things Jesus "was fettered by the follies of his age." It is probable that there will be men enough for some time to come who will stultify themselves rather than admit the infinite superiority of Jesus Christ to all human beings.

16, 17. The Pharisees keep themselves in the background. They would make it appear that they have nothing further to say to him. But they send out to him *their disciples*, students, and therefore, perhaps, young men, who, possibly, were unknown to him. *The Herodians*—Partisans of Herod. They were probably a political, not a religious, party, supporting Herod as a representative of the Roman government, while the Pharisees and the people generally were exceedingly restive under the Roman yoke. One man, Judas the Galilean (Acts 5: 37), had several years before headed a party to resist the payment of the tax that had been levied on the Jews by the Emperor Augustus. It was felt by many that as God was their king, it was wrong to pay tribute to a foreign power. What they ought to pay should be paid to God. The two parties, thus differing from each other relative to the Roman government, now unite in an effort to secure testimony that can be used against Jesus. *Master*—Teacher. *We know*—The form of a truth, but the spirit of a lie. They knew it, but rejected the evidence. They did not *believe* what they professed to *know*. *The way of God*—The life which God approves. *Lawful*—Not, whether under all the circumstances it is expedient, but whether it is a violation of God's law to obey in this respect the law of Cæsar. Cæsar was the general name of the Roman emperors, as Augustus Cæsar, Tiberius Cæsar. "The New Testament history falls entirely within the reigns of the first five Roman Cæsars, namely, Augustus, Tiberius, Caligula, Claudius, and Nero; only the two former of whom and Claudius are mentioned by name." *Tribute* —The tribute coin, different from the tribute in 17: 24. That was to be paid toward the support of the Jewish temple.

18-21. *Perceiving*—Knowing, but how, whether through the senses or in some other way, cannot be affirmed. *Hypocrites*—See on 6: 2, last part of the note. He unmasks them, which is proof of the truth of their own words, *Neither carest thou for any man. A penny*—A denary. See note on 20: 2, 3. Specimens of Roman coin are still in existence, bearing both an *image*, likeness of

them, Render therefore unto Cesar the things which are Cesar's; and unto God the things that are God's.

22 When they had heard *these words*, they marvelled, and left him, and went their way.

23 ¶ The same day came to him the Sadducees, which say, that there is no resurrection, and asked him,

24 Saying, Master, Moses said, If a man die, having no children, his brother shall marry his wife, and raise up seed unto his brother.

25 Now there were with us seven brethren: and the first, when he had married a wife, deceased, and, having no issue, left his wife unto his brother:

26 Likewise the second also, and the third, unto the seventh.

27 And last of all the woman died also.

28 Therefore in the resurrection, whose wife shall she be

---

the emperor, and a *superscription*, his name or initials. *Cesar*—Tiberius Cæsar. The answer of Jesus was very different from what they expected. He wisely discriminated between allegiance to the civil power and allegiance to God, though his reply presents no opposition to the doctrine that *the powers that be are ordained of God;* and that *whosoever resisteth the power resisteth the ordinance of God.* Rom. 13: 1, 2. Loyalty to government is implied in loyalty to God; yet there is a sense in which the idea of loyalty to government is distinct from that of loyalty to God. Nor does his reply overlook the duty elsewhere taught (Acts 4: 19), of resisting "the powers that be," when they require us to do a sinful act. The reply amounts to this: You yourselves admit *the fact* of the existence of the Roman jurisdiction over you; for you use the currency of the government. Here, in the very image and superscription of the coin which you are using, is evidence of Cæsar's authority over the land. Pay back, then, to Cæsar from the money which you accept at his hands the required denáry. Whatever, also, God requires of you, render to God. Thus, if the Pharisees accused Jesus of forbidding to pay tribute to Cæsar, or of teaching in any sense disloyalty to God, they accused him falsely. *The union of church and state:* there is nothing here that sanctions it. *The right of revolution against an irretrievably oppressive government:* there is nothing here that denies it. *As to the right of Rome to rule over the Jews,* Jesus says nothing. He answers their question in the light of the admitted fact.

23, 24. *The Sadducees*—See note on 3: 7, third paragraph. *Moses said*—In Deut. 25: 5, 6. This law has been called the Levirate law, from the Latin word *Levir*, brother-in-law. It recognized a custom which Moses found existing. A similar custom existed in some other countries. In the case of the Jews the law was intended to prevent the extinction of a family. The first-born, after the second marriage, was considered as the first husband's son, inheriting his property, and, as some affirm, though this is not certain, taking his name.

25-28. *Seven brethren*—This may have been an imaginary case, though Dr. Whedon suggests that it had a foundation in the apocryphal book of Tobit, 3: 8. The words to which he refers, and those in the preceding verse, taken from the Roman

CHAPTER XXII.

of the seven? for they all had her.

29 Jesus answered and said unto them, Ye do err, not knowing the Scriptures, nor the power of God.

30 For in the resurrection they neither marry, nor are given in marriage, but are as the angels of God in heaven.

31 But as touching the resurrection of the dead, have ye not read that which was spoken unto you by God, saying,

32 I am the God of Abraham, and the God of Isaac, and the

Catholic version, are as follows: Now it happened on the same day, that Sara, daughter of Raguel, in Rages, a city of the Medes, received a reproach from one of her father's servant-maids, because she had been given to seven husbands. It is the aim of the Sadducees, who disbelieved the doctrine of the soul's immortality and the resurrection of the body, to ridicule both Jesus and the doctrine. Their case of seven brothers marrying one wife must have excited merriment in the bystanders, and possibly evoked a peal of laughter. If the question seems to us very easy to be answered, we should remember that then some of the most religious men (religious by profession) held such views relative to the nature of the future life, as to make the question in the judgment of the Sadducees extremely difficult to be answered in consistency with the doctrine of a future life. The Rabbinical doctrine was that if a woman had been married twice, she would revert to the first husband in the next world. *Whose wife*—What they *think* is this: It is impossible to tell whether she would be the first man's, or the last man's. As they all had her, either all must have her there, or only one. The former cannot be, and if only one has her, the other six will have been dealt hardly by. They think the perplexity may be avoided by their doctrine that there is no future life for either party.

29, 30. *The Scriptures*—Jesus assumes, as he had often assumed before, that the Old Testament is the authoritative word of God. He charges them with *not knowing*, not understanding its spiritual meaning, and so failing (the Sadducees, not the Pharisees) to see that it teaches among other things the doctrine of a future life. He also charges them with ignorance of the truth that God is a being of sufficient *power* to raise the dead. This implies the *weakness* of all philosophical objections to the doctrine of the resurrection. *As the angels of God*—As the angels in respect to what is now under consideration. He does not mean to say that they are like the angels in other respects. As no such distinction exists among the angels as that which is implied in the marriage relation on the earth, so no such distinction will exist among the saints in heaven. Jesus states this on the basis of his personal knowledge, not quoting from the Scriptures to prove it.

32. *I am the God of Abraham*, etc.—Jesus quotes from Ex. 3: 6. The words were spoken to Moses out of the burning bush. They are quoted by the Saviour as proof *that men will live after death*. The reasoning is this: God said to Moses, I am the God of Abraham, and the God of Isaac, and the God of Jacob. But God is not the God of one who has no existence. Therefore, Abraham, and Isaac, and Jacob are still alive. Admitting that this proves the existence of men after death as spirits, how does it prove the resurrection of their bodies? Reply: The Scriptures regard the separate existence of the soul as an unnatural condition; and therefore regard the renewed life of the body as im-

21*

God of Jacob? God is not the God of the dead, but of the living.

33 And when the multitude heard *this*, they were astonished at his doctrine.

34 ¶ But when the Pharisees had heard that he had put the Sadducees to silence, they were gathered together.

35 Then one of them, *which was* a lawyer, asked *him a question*, tempting him, and saying,

36 Master, which *is* the great commandment in the law?

---

plied in the continued life of the soul. It may be objected that the words, *I am the God of Abraham*, mean only this: I am the God who *was* the God of Abraham *during Abraham's life*, and that therefore they are not proof that Abraham was alive when they were uttered by Christ, or even when spoken by Jehovah to Moses, and that therefore they are not proof of the soul's immortality. The objection is of no weight; for, 1. Jesus knew much better than the objector the true meaning of the words, and *he* teaches that the meaning is, or, at least, that a valid inference from the meaning is, that Abraham was still alive; 2. The words seem to have reference to covenant relations. God encourages Moses by saying, that *he holds covenant relations* with Abraham, Isaac, and Jacob. But this was impossible if Abraham, Isaac, and Jacob were dead.

Many commentators teach that the reference is only to the righteous. It is certain, as we learn from other parts of the Bible, that the wicked are to be raised as well as the righteous. Even if it could be shown that both here and in Luke the reference is only to the resurrection of the good, it would not follow that the wicked are annihilated. *The resurrection of all mankind, without respect to character*, was a doctrine firmly held by the Jews of our Lord's time, the small sect of the Sadducees excepted. The annihilation of the *wicked* was not the distinguishing doctrine of the Sadducees, but the annihilation of both the wicked and the righteous.

33. *Astonished at his doctrine*—Not, of a future life, but of the *nature* of it; for even the people, though believing in the soul's immortality, had gross conceptions of its nature.

34, 35. The bluntness of the tools which the Pharisees had used leads them to try again. *A lawyer*—This may be synonymous with *scribe*, but it has been suggested as "more probable that the title *scribe* was a legal and official designation, but that the name *lawyer* was properly a mere epithet, signifying one 'learned in the law,' and only used as a title in common parlance." This man seems to have been put forward by the Pharisees, who stand where they can listen to the conversation. Their design was only bad; his was not wholly bad. He consented to be used as their tool, yet was of a better spirit. See Mark 12: 28, 32, 34. *Tempting*—Not here in a very bad sense, but rather in the sense of putting his knowledge to the test.

36. *The great commandment*—"The Jewish Talmud reckons the positive laws of Moses at two hundred and forty-eight, and the negative at three hundred and sixty-five, the sum being six hundred and thirteen. To keep so many laws, said the Jews, is an angel's work, and so they had much question which was *the great commandment*, so that they might keep *that* in lieu of keeping the *whole*."—*Dr. Whedon*. True piety does not care to ask, which, or, as some would render it, what kind of, commandment is great? No command can be otherwise than great that came from the infinite

37 Jesus said unto him, Thou shalt love the Lord thy God with all thy heart, and with all thy soul, and with all thy mind.
38 This is the first and great commandment.
39 And the second *is* like unto it, Thou shalt love thy neighbour as thyself.
40 On these two commandments hang all the law and the prophets.
41 ¶ While the Pharisees were gathered together, Jesus asked them,
42 Saying, What think ye of Christ? Whose son is he? They say unto him, *The son* of David.

God. Thinking any commandment of God unimportant is a bad sign.

37–39. *Heart . . . soul . . . mind*—It is not probable that these words are used with any nice philosophical distinction. It is sufficient to say that they express the duty of loving God with all our power of love. This implies the choice of God, by the will, as a continuous act in preference to all created beings. It also implies the illumination of the intellect, and the consecration of it to the Creator. It is observable, however, that the command pertains directly to the affections, and only indirectly to the intellect or to the will. It is not, *Choose*, though that must be done; it is not, *Reason*, though reasoning is a duty; but *Love*. *First and great commandment*—Not that any commandment is otherwise than great viewed in respect to comprehensiveness. The command to love God with all our powers is the most comprehensive of all. Love is the fulfilling, the filling up, the completion, of the law. *The second is like unto it*—Like it in nature. *As thyself*—Self-love, then, is not wrong: it is a duty. Self-love may become selfishness. He who loves himself as the work of God will love his neighbor, since his neighbor, too, is the work of God.

40. The meaning of this verse is well expressed by Dr. Conant: "*In these* (is the idea) lies the energy that sustains all; and hence *on* them all are suspended." Loving one's neighbor in the sense in which the words are often used, is possible without loving God. Loving God without loving one's neighbor is impossible.

41, 42. They are still in the court of the temple. Pharisees, Sadducees, and Herodians have all been baffled. Jesus can put questions which they cannot answer, as well as answer questions which they can put; but how different the spirit in which he puts them! He calls their attention to an apparent difficulty arising from the words of David in Psalm 110: 1. *What think ye of Christ?*—What think ye concerning the Messiah? is the more correct rendering. In consequence of the omission of the article before *Christ*, and of the present universal application of the term Christ to Jesus as a name, there is danger of failing to see the point. He is not asking what they think of himself, *Jesus*, but what they think of the Messiah whom they admit to be the subject of the Psalm. Whether he himself is the Messiah is an important question, but it is now only indirectly involved in the question he asks. He catechises them, not to ensnare them, but to convict them, before the bystanders and before all coming ages, of ignorance of spiritual things, and thus to aid in confirming the conviction of the apostles and ourselves that he is the Messiah. *The son of David*—So far all was plain. No Jew would have given any other answer.

43 He saith unto them, How then doth David in spirit call him Lord, saying,

44 The LORD said unto my Lord, Sit thou on my right hand, till I make thine enemies thy footstool?

45 If David then call him Lord, how is he his son?

46 And no man was able to answer him a word, neither durst any *man* from that day forth ask him any more *questions.*

CHAPTER XXIII.

THEN spake Jesus to the multitude, and to his disciples,

43–45. *David in spirit*—Not his own spirit, but *the* Spirit, the Holy Spirit. David, though a king, and the most distinguished king in the world, calls *his son* his *Lord.* What, then, becomes of your opinion that the Messiah is his *son? How*— In what sense? See Rom. 1: 3, 4. Those who say that the Psalms were written by the same kind of inspiration as Homer's "Iliad," or Milton's "Paradise Lost," contradict Jesus Christ.

46. Why were they unable to answer? Because they had no clear conception of the Messiah's *divine* nature. They saw that the Messiah was to be a descendant of David, but they did not see that he was to be of a nature higher than David's. Thus closed the oral conflict between Jesus and his enemies. But the conspiracy was not subdued. Jesus did not aim to subdue it. By the determinate counsel and foreknowledge of God it was allowed to gather strength. Jesus, on the other hand, became more direct and withering in his exposure of the hypocrisy of the ruling powers. Logic may shut an opposer's lips, but only the Holy Spirit can open his heart.

CHAPTER XXIII.

JESUS DENOUNCES THE SCRIBES AND PHARISEES.

783 U.C. Tuesday, April 4, A.D. 30.

1, 2. He who uttered this severest of all discourses was the meekest and lowliest of men. *To the multitude, and to his disciples,*—bu in the hearing of the scribes and Pharisees. They are not reported as interrupting him: they dared not; but the denunciations must have exasperated them in the highest degree. *Sit in Moses' seat*—Have sat down, or, sat down; strictly, have seated themselves, as interpreters of Moses' law. It does not necessarily express blame, as if they had usurped the position, though many so understand it. This is evident from the *therefore* in the next verse. If Christ meant to say that they were holding their office wrongfully, how could he say, Therefore observe what they bid? It may be added that Dr. Nast thinks the reference is to the highest court,—the Sanhedrim. He says: "*Divinely authorized teachers of religion were, after Moses, only the prophets,* not the priests and scribes. All that Christ enjoins in this passage, therefore, is obedience to their judicial decisions."

3. *Not after their works*—Jesus makes a broad distinction between the teaching and the life of the scribes and Pharisees. The discourse itself shows that a distinction was also to be made in their teachings. It shows us how we are to understand the *all* of this verse, all that Moses taught; not, however, to the exclusion of whatever explanations the scribes might be able to make in harmony with Moses. This direction, even with the limitations

CHAPTER XXIII.

2 Saying, The scribes and the Pharisees sit in Moses' seat:

3 All therefore whatsoever they bid you observe, *that* observe and do; but do not ye after their works: for they say, and do not.

4 For they bind heavy burdens and grievous to be borne, and lay *them* on men's shoulders; but they *themselves* will not move them with one of their fingers.

5 But all their works they do for to be seen of men: they

---

which must be given it, is a remarkable illustration of *true liberality*. Jesus utters not a word adapted to excite the people to eject the scribes from their office. Not preaching the truth in the life, while preaching it in words, exposes to the severest condemnation. These words of Jesus, though illustrating his liberality, are greatly perverted by those who affirm that men should be sustained in promulgating truth even if their lives are godless. This scandalous doctrine has done vast evil in the world.

4. *Heavy burdens*—Alford says, "Not, as so often misinterpreted, *traditions* and observances, but *the severity of the law.*" Yet he proceeds to say: "The irksomeness and unbearableness of these rites did not belong to the law *in itself*, as rightly explained, but were created by the rigor and ritualism of these men, who followed the letter and lost the spirit." Precisely so. It was not the law, then, to which Jesus referred, so much as the *additions* to the law which had been made by the scribes and Pharisees through their unreasonable interpretations. Yet the divinely authorized ceremonies of the law itself may be included, so far as the Jews used them for the purpose of self-justification. Hence Peter says (Acts 15: 10), Now, therefore, why tempt ye God, to put a yoke upon the neck of the disciples, *which neither our fathers nor we were able to bear?* "By this yoke," says Neander, in Hackett on the Acts, ". . . he certainly did not mean the external observance of ceremonies as such, since he would by no means persuade the Jewish Christians to renounce them. But he meant the external observance of the law, in so far as this proceeded from an internal subjection of the conscience to its power, such as exists when justification and salvation are made to depend on the performances of legal requirements." As to false interpretations of the law, see the Sermon on the Mount. *Not . . . with one of their fingers*—There are many parallels with this in the Romish Church. He who requires people to refrain from eating meat on Friday ought not to be caught eating meat himself.

5. *To be seen*—See 6: 1. *Phylacteries*—"Strips of parchment, on which were written four passages of Scripture (Ex. 13: 2-10, 11-17; Deut. 6: 4-9, 13-22) in an ink prepared for the purpose. They were then rolled up in a case of black calf-skin, which was attached to a stiffer piece of leather, having a thong one finger broad and one and a half cubits long. 'They were placed at the bend of the left arm, and after the thong had made a little knot in the shape of the letter '"' [*Yodh*, the tenth letter in the Hebrew alphabet] "'it was wound round the arm in a spiral line, which ended at the top of the middle finger.'" . . . They were also worn on the forehead. They are called phylacteries, "either because they tended to promote the observance of the law, . . . or from the use of them as amulets;" that is, as

make broad their phylacteries, and enlarge the borders of their garments,

6 And love the uppermost rooms at feasts, and the chief seats in the synagogues,

charms against evils. "The expression, 'they make broad their phylacteries,' refers not so much to the phylactery itself, which seems to have been of a prescribed breadth, as to the case in which the parchment was kept, which the Pharisees (among their other pretentious customs) made as conspicuous as they could. . . . It is said that the Pharisees wore them always, whereas the common people only used them at prayers. . . . The modern Jews only wear them at morning prayers, and sometimes at noon."

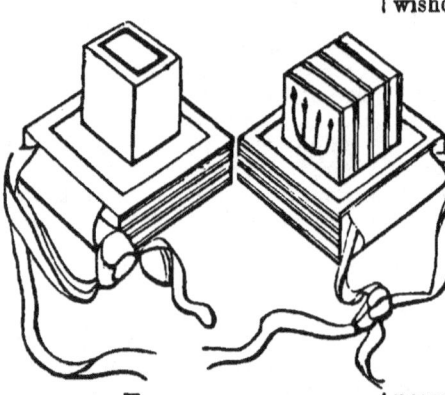

FRONTLETS.

Was the practice of wearing phylacteries required by the words in Ex. 13: 9, etc.? or are the words to be understood figuratively; that is, as intended to teach them the duty of keeping the commands of God continually in mind? Which view is correct is uncertain. Considerations of weight have been urged in favor of each. We incline to the former as more in accordance with the general character of the Mosaic system, and regard our Lord as inveighing against the *abuse* of the command. We are told that one Jewish writer, in commenting on Ps.

1: 2, starting the objection that it is impossible to meditate in God's law day and night, because of sleep, domestic cares, etc., answers that for the fulfilment of the text it is sufficient to wear *Tephillin* [Phylacteries].

*The borders of their garments—*Fringes. These were required (Num. 15: 38-40), and our Saviour himself wore one. 9: 20. They were intended to aid them in remembering the commandments of God, but, like the phylacteries, came to be worn in spiritual pride. He who wished to be considered as specially religious *enlarged* the fringe. Endeavoring by outward signs to make men believe that one has more piety than others proves that one has less.

6. *Uppermost rooms—*Not rooms as the word is now understood, that is, apartments of a dwelling-house, but *the first place at table*. See note on 9: 10, 11. *The chief seats in the synagogues* were those near the upper end; that is, the end which stood nearest Jerusalem, and in which was the chest containing a copy of the law. It was the place of honor. James 2: 2, 3. Jesus spoke not against such internal arrangements in themselves considered, but against choosing them for the sake of getting honor from men. Such places might have been avoided in pride, as well as sought. Madame Guyon, an eminent Christian woman of France, member of the Papal Church, refused the means which a friend offered her for reducing the scars which the small-pox made in her face, and, after recovering, conceived it to be her duty to walk in one of the most fashionable streets

CHAPTER XXIII.

7 And greetings in the markets, and to be called of men, Rabbi, Rabbi.

8 But be not ye called Rabbi: for one is your Master, *even* Christ; and all ye are brethren.

9 And call no *man* your father upon the earth; for one is your Father, which is in heaven.

10 Neither be ye called masters: for one is your Master, *even* Christ.

11 But he that is greatest among you shall be your servant.

12 And whosoever shall exalt himself shall be abased; and he that shall humble himself shall be exalted.

13 ¶ But woe unto you

---

of Paris, to humble herself. She had been considered as uncommonly beautiful.

7, 8. *Rabbi* is interpreted by John himself (1 : 38) to mean master, or, more properly translated. teacher. But how could a title which means teacher, a title which Jesus never refused, be condemned when permitted by the scribes to be applied to themselves? We do not understand Jesus to condemn the use of the word, but the vanity and ostentation which led them to love it. Rab, Rabbi, and Rabboni indicated degrees of honor, the last being the most distinguished. The titles were not of divine authority. "The title Rabbi is not known to have been used before the reign of Herod the Great, and is thought to have taken its rise about the time of the disputes between the rival schools of Hillel and Shammai. Before that period the prophets and the men of the great synagogue were simply called by their proper names, and the first who had a title is said to be Simeon the son of Hillel, . . . and from his time such titles came to be in fashion. . . . It was said in the Jewish books that greater was he who was called by his own name than even he who was called Rabban" [Rabboni]. *Master*—According to the true reading of the Greek this should be *teacher*. *Brethren*— Equal in rank, not in abilities. What, then, becomes of the doctrine of Peter's primacy? What becomes of that system of church government which makes the distinction in the ministry indicated in the words bishop and archbishop? Some excellent men, as Albert Barnes in his "Notes on the Gospels," consider the modern title of Doctor of Divinity as condemned by the spirit of these words. It is certain that the minister who schemes for the purpose of obtaining it gives humiliating proof of having, in that respect, the spirit of the men who *loved* to be called Rabbi.

9, 10. *Call no man your father* —Since children may call him that begat them *father*, since Paul calls himself the father of the Corinthian Christians (1 Cor. 4 : 14, 15), since Peter represents himself as the father of Mark (1 Peter 5 : 13), the meaning must be, Acknowledge no man as having *spiritual authority over you*. Aged ministers are called father, without violation of our Saviour's precept. It is simply an expression of affectionate respect. The *pope* of Rome assumes to be the *papa*, the father, of the whole Christian world in the sense of having divinely authorized supremacy, which is a stupendous imposition. *Masters*—Leaders. The original word is different from that in vs. 8. Christ is the only leader. Sadly have these precepts been violated by bodies of men each assuming to call itself *The Church*.

13. *Woe*—This is the first of *eight woes* denounced against the men

scribes and Pharisees, hypocrites! for ye shut up the kingdom of heaven against men: for ye neither go in *yourselves,* neither suffer ye them that are entering to go in.

14 Woe unto you, scribes and Pharisees, hypocrites! for ye devour widows' houses, and for a pretence make long prayer: therefore ye shall receive the greater damnation.

15 Woe unto you scribes and Pharisees, hypocrites! for ye compass sea and land to make one proselyte; and when he

---

who thought they had a better title to membership in the kingdom of heaven than Christ himself. These woes are terribly severe, but they were richly deserved. *For* gives the reason why the woe is denounced. *Shut up*—This they did by giving false interpretations of the law, and then attaching more importance to them than to the law itself. Thus they kept themselves out of the Messiah's kingdom, and others also, as, for example, the people, who often showed indications of desire to enter.

14. This verse is genuine in Mark 12: 40 and in Luke 20: 47, but it is not found in the oldest manuscripts and versions of Matthew.

15. *Proselytes* were converts from heathenism to Judaism. Some of them, dissatisfied with the errors and immorality of paganism, were sincere worshippers of Jehovah. Many of them gave no evidence of piety, or even of common sincerity, in the adoption of the Jewish religion. Some of the heathen became proselytes by compulsion. Josephus informs us that after John Hyrcanus had subdued the Idumeans, he permitted them to "stay in their country, if they would adopt the rite of circumcision, and make use of the laws of the Jews." Circumcision or exile was the alternative. At one time, the Jews "compelled a Roman centurion, whom they had taken prisoner, to purchase his life by accepting the sign of the covenant,"—circumcision. Such methods, however, of making proselytes, were probably as rare as they were extreme. Fraud was often used. Many of the proselytes became such voluntarily. In the reign of Ferdinand and Isabella, Cardinal Ximenes undertook to make Christians of the Moors by compulsion. *Proselytes of the gate* were not required to be circumcised, or to observe the Mosaic ritual in general, but they were under obligation to renounce idolatry. *Proselytes of righteousness* adopted the Jewish religion as such. They were circumcised, "special prayer" being offered on the occasion, and were baptized, that is, immersed. The baptism was held to be as important as the circumcision. The distinction between these two classes of proselytes has been often erroneously used (Barnes and even Dr. Nast) to illustrate the passage before us, as if the distinction existed in our Lord's time. The germ of the distinction may perhaps be seen, but nothing more.

Compass sea and land—Show the most fanatical zeal, or, as we sometimes say, leave no stone unturned. There is no decisive proof that the Pharisees made missionary tours for the purpose of converting heathen to Judaism, but a Jewish merchant who was travelling in a foreign land on business might attempt it. *Hell*—The place of future punishment. See on 5: 22; 25: 46. *Child of hell*—Depraved, and therefore worthy of the punishment of hell. *Twofold more*—How was this possible, since the Pharisees themselves were such children of hell as to deserve these terrible

CHAPTER XXIII.

is made, ye make him twofold more the child of hell than yourselves.

16 Woe unto you, *ye* blind guides, which say, Whosoever shall swear by the temple, it is nothing; but whosoever shall swear by the gold of the temple, he is a debtor!

17 *Ye* fools and blind: for whether is greater, the gold, or the temple that sanctifieth the gold?

18 And, Whosoever shall swear by the altar, it is nothing; but whosoever sweareth by the gift that is upon it, he is guilty.

19 *Ye* fools and blind: for whether *is* greater, the gift, or the altar that sanctifieth the gift?

20 Whoso therefore shall swear by the altar, sweareth by it, and by all things thereon.

21 And whoso shall swear by the temple, sweareth by it, and by him that dwelleth therein.

22 And he that shall swear by heaven, sweareth by the throne of God, and by him that sitteth thereon.

23 Woe unto you, scribes and Pharisees, hypocrites! for ye pay tithe of mint and anise and cummin, and have omitted the weightier *matters* of the law, judgment, mercy, and

---

woes? Proselytes of course became no better than their teachers, and besides this they brought along with them the vices peculiar to heathenism. "At Rome and in other large cities, they became the butts of popular scurrility. . . . An opprobrious proverb coupled them with the vilest profligates. . . . It became a recognized maxim, that no wise man would trust a proselyte even to the twenty-fourth generation."

16–22. Jesus here denounces them for their lax morality relative to oaths. See notes on the same subject, 5: 33–37. They taught, — this was a part of their theology, — that he who should swear by the temple, or by the altar, or by heaven, might consider himself as under no obligation to keep the oath; but if he should swear by the *gold* of the temple, that is, the golden offerings that were kept in the temple, or by the *gift* that had been laid upon the altar, or by *God*, he was under obligation to keep it. The force of his exposure of their hypocrisy lies in this, that all oaths have necessary reference to God himself, and are therefore binding. Notice his application of the term *fool*, and see 5: 22, with the remark in the last paragraph of the notes.

23. *Tithe*—A tenth. For the tithe-law, see Lev. 27: 30–32. By this law, the Jews were required to pay for the support of the Levites (concerning whom see note on John 1: 19), one-tenth of the produce of the soil and one-tenth of their flocks and cattle. *These ought ye to have done*—The tithe of the small herbs would seem, then, to have been required, though the terms of the law have been thought to make it doubtful. *Mint*—An herb used, doubtless, by the Jews as a condiment in cookery. *Anise*—The herb is "similar to the dill in properties, but is an entirely distinct plant. . . Both the plant and the seed were used by the ancients as a condiment, the latter having a warm, aromatic flavor resembling that of caraway seed." *Cummin*—"An umbelliferous plant," that is, a plant the flowers of which were shaped

faith: these ought ye to have done, and not to leave the other undone.

24 Ye blind guides, which strain at a gnat, and swallow a camel.

25 Woe unto you, scribes and Pharisees, hypocrites! for ye make clean the outside of the cup and of the platter, but within they are full of extortion and excess.

26 *Thou* blind Pharisee, cleanse first that *which is* within the cup and platter, that the outside of them may be clean also.

27 Woe unto you, scribes and Pharisees, hypocrites! for ye are like unto whited sepulchres, which indeed appear beautiful outward, but are within full of dead *men's* bones, and of all uncleanness.

28 Even so ye also outwardly appear righteous unto men, but within ye are full of hypocrisy and iniquity.

29 Woe unto you, scribes and

---

like an umbrella. "The seeds have a bitterish, warm taste, with an aromatic flavor." *Judgment*—Not justice, but the practice of what the principles of justice or righteousness require. The scrupulosity with which the Pharisees paid tithes of little garden herbs, and their inward unrighteousness, proved them to be hypocrites. Such hypocrisy has been shown in every age. The neglect of the few, simple, outward rites of Christianity, as the public worship of God, baptism, and the Lord's Supper, under the pretence of having inward righteousness, is itself also condemned in these words of our Lord: *Leave not the other undone.*

24. *Strain at a gnat*—Strain *out* a gnat, *at* being, probably, a typographical error in the very first edition of King James' translation (1611). Nearly all the previous English translations had it right. The scribes and Pharisees, in the great nicety of their outward righteousness, did undoubtedly, like the Buddhists of Hindostan, strain off their wine lest they should mar their claim to heaven by drinking a gnat. They were afraid of violating the law (Lev. 11 : 41): *And every creeping thing that creepeth upon the earth shall be an abomination: it shall not be eaten. Swallow a camel* —Commit the greatest sins without compunction.

25, 26. Figurative language, in which they are charged with *extortion*, rapacity, and with *excess*, licentiousness, while endeavoring to maintain the appearance of piety by attention to the outward forms of religion. Members of Christian churches who are guilty of dishonesty, and members who are living in secret impurity, may here see how they are regarded by Him whom they profess to serve.

27, 28. The denunciation becomes still more severe. He charges them with being full of *hypocrisy* and *iniquity*. For the meaning of the former, see note on 6 : 2, under the word *hypocrites*, last paragraph. Iniquity here means *lawlessness*. They were *lawless legalists*, and therefore profound hypocrites. The denunciation rests upon a comparison with sepulchres. These were full of the bones of dead men and of the impurity which would result from the decomposition of human bodies, the annual "whiting" of the sepulchres after the rains making of course no sort of difference with their inward state.

29-31. He here advances a step further, inasmuch as he makes the

CHAPTER XXIII.

Pharisees, hypocrites! because ye build the tombs of the prophets, and garnish the sepulchres of the righteous,

30 And say, If we had been in the days of our fathers, we would not have been partakers with them in the blood of the prophets.

31 Wherefore ye be witnesses unto yourselves, that ye are the children of them which killed the prophets.

32 Fill ye up then the measure of your fathers.

33 *Ye* serpents, *ye* generation of vipers, how can ye escape the damnation of hell?

34 ¶ Wherefore, behold, I send unto you prophets, and wise men, and scribes: and *some* of them ye shall kill and crucify; and *some* of them shall ye scourge in your synagogues, and persecute *them* from city to city:

35 That upon you may come all the righteous blood shed upon the earth, from the blood of righteous Abel unto

---

bold assertion that they are *themselves conscious* of hypocrisy. They build tombs for the prophets whom their fathers slew, and *garnish*, adorn, the sepulchres of the righteous, and think it a thing of great merit. They even boast that had they lived in the time of their fathers, they would not have imbrued their hands in the blood of the prophets. *Wherefore*—So that. As you go contrary to the teachings of the prophets by your persecutions of me, you are yourselves conscious of hypocrisy in your ostentatious honoring of their character by building monumental tombs. So you prove that you are *the children of*, like, the murderers of the prophets, instead of being like the prophets themselves.

32. *Fill ye up, then*—The imperative form of the verb should create no difficulty. It is not an authorization of their murderous purpose relative to himself, but is a rhetorical statement of what he knows they will do. When they shall have put him to death and shall have rejected the offer of pardon that will be made through the apostles, the measure of their fathers' guilt will be full. This of course contemplates them as constituting with their fathers the nation, but not to the exclusion of the guilt that rests upon them as individuals.

33. Compare with this the words which John addressed to the Pharisees and Sadducees who came to his baptism: O generation of vipers, who hath warned you to flee from the wrath to come? See note on 3: 7, last paragraph, and on 12: 34. Their case is now well-nigh hopeless. *The damnation of hell*—"The sentence which condemns to hell." There are not many, it is probable, of whom Christ would say so many years before the end of life, *How can ye escape?*

34. *Wherefore*—In consequence of your character. The two things which he announces as flowing from the fact of their terrible depravity are: 1. That he will send them *prophets, wise men, and scribes*,—that is, Christian teachers,—apostles and others; 2. That they will persecute those teachers, putting some of them to death. Stephen, James, and others were killed, and, doubtless, many of whom no report has reached us were crucified.

35. As a retribution for their national wickedness (the guilt of individuals still being included), they will be visited with the consequences of all the guilt incurred in shedding righteous blood from that of Abel,

the blood of Zacharias son of Barachias, whom ye slew between the temple and the altar.

36 Verily I say unto you, All these things shall come upon this generation.

37 O Jerusalem, Jerusalem, *thou* that killest the prophets, and stonest them which are sent unto thee, how often would I have gathered thy children together, even as a

---

the first martyr, to that of Zacharias. By the latter is probably meant the Zacharias of 2 Chron. 24 : 20–22. But that man is called the son of Jehoiada. Why he is here called the son of Barachias, it is impossible to say. Some would solve the difficulty by saying that Jehoiada was the grandfather and Barachias the father; some by supposing that an early copyist entered the name Barachias in the margin, under the impression that Jesus referred to Zechariah the prophet, and that afterward it crept into the text; for (Zech. 1 : 1) the name of the prophet's father was Barachiah. Where, however, we have no means of removing a difficulty, theories are of little value. There is nothing at all serious involved in the matter. *Between the temple and the altar*—Between the temple, strictly so called, and the altar of burnt offerings which stood in the court next surrounding the building; that is, in the priests' court. Zacharias was slain for preaching against the idolatry of the nation, and being son of a priest, being murdered in such a place, and for such a reason, the crime was peculiarly heinous. It is partly for that reason, and partly because, in the Jewish arrangement of the books of the Old Testament, the account of his death stood in the last book, that Jesus refers to it in connection with the *first* murder that ever occurred.

Jesus does not mean to teach that the Pharisees of his time were, as *individuals*, strictly speaking, guilty of the murder of Abel and Zacharias. He spoke chiefly of them as a nation, which is very evident from the use of the word *ye*,—*whom ye slew*,—an act which was done hundreds of years before these men were born. Yet it should be borne in mind that they had the murderous spirit of their fathers.

36. *Upon this generation*—Jerusalem was destroyed about forty years after. "Not the then living generation, but the Jewish people as such."—*Dr. Nast*. The time was so near, and so many of the people would be living at the destruction of the city, that such an interpretation is unnecessary.

37. *O Jerusalem, Jerusalem*—After the severity of the judge comes tenderness surpassing that of the most affectionate mother yearning over her wicked son. How wonderful the change! Ministers who presume to imitate the severity of Jesus forget that they are not omniscient. Let them aim to imitate his tenderness. Our Lord, personifying the city, views it in its entire history. It has been *accustomed* to kill the prophets and stone the messengers that Heaven has sent, and therefore he uses the present tense. *How often*—In former times by the prophets, and now also. *Would I have gathered*—Implying that it is now too late. *As a hen*—How both the power and the love of Christ shine in the beautiful comparison! Hens are now very common in Palestine, and, according to Rabbinical writers, must have been very common in the days of our Saviour. Dr. Hackett reminds us that "the eggs of the hen are no doubt meant in the Saviour's illustration (Luke 11 : 12), which implies that they were very abundant." But the hen is mentioned in the Bible only here and in the parallel passage in Luke 13 : 34.

nen gathereth her chickens under *her* wings, and ye would not!

38 Behold, your house is left unto you desolate.

39 For I say unto you, Ye shall not see me henceforth, till ye shall say, Blessed *is* he that cometh in the name of the Lord.

If this is remarkable, it is not more remarkable than that the hen "is nowhere represented in the paintings of ancient Egypt." *Ye would not*—Thus Jesus recognizes the freedom of the human will,—a fact which should be recognized by all preachers and by all systems of theology, not less than man's entire dependence on the execution of God's purpose for the renewal of the heart.

38. *Your house*—The temple, as the representative of the city and of the nation, or, perhaps, the city likened to a house.

39. So true is it that their house is left unto them desolate, that they shall not see him henceforth till they, that is, their descendants, shall say, Blessed is he that cometh in the name of the Lord,—shall acknowledge his Messiahship. This time is yet future. The Jews are still ungathered. The house is still desolate. *Henceforth*—Not, as many commentators teach, that the men whom he is addressing will literally never see his face again, for doubtless many of them were present at his trial and at his crucifixion. There is no probability that they saw him after his resurrection. If the Jews are yet to acknowledge Jesus Christ, the second advent cannot be so near as some are even now teaching.

CHAPTER XXIV.

JESUS DISCOURSES TO HIS DISCIPLES.

783 U.C. Tuesday Evening, April 4, A.D. 30.

1. *Departed*—Toward the evening of Tuesday, and probably for the last time. In verse 38 of the preceding chapter, he is reported as having prophesied that the temple should be destroyed. Under the influence of that remarkable announcement, the disciples called his attention to the stability of the building. According to Mark they say, Master, see what manner of stones and what buildings are here! They were unable to appreciate the prophecy, but we need not suppose, with some, that they were positively sceptical concerning it. *Buildings of the temple*—The Greek has two words for temple; the one meaning the sacred building itself, the other the entire premises,—the building and the courts. *Temple* is here used in the wider sense. Josephus says that some of the stones were sixty-seven feet long, seven feet high, and nine feet broad. This is not in the least incredible, for in the ruins of Baalbec, Syria, are stones of similar dimensions. Dr. Robinson measured three of the latter, and found them severally sixty-four feet, sixty-three feet, and sixty-three feet eight inches long. Referring to the stones of Baalbec, Thomson says: "How such blocks could be transported a mile over uneven ground to the temple, and elevated to their position on its platform, is yet an unsolved problem in the science of mechanical forces."

2. *Not one stone upon another*—This does not refer, let it be borne in mind, to the stones of the *city* walls, many courses of which are still lying in place, but to those of the temple. The prophecy was made in a time of profound peace, but was fulfilled to the letter, notwithstanding the efforts of Titus, the Roman general, to save the building, even after it had been set

CHAPTER XXIV.

AND Jesus went out, and departed from the temple: and his disciples came to *him* for to shew him the buildings of the temple.

2 And Jesus said unto them, See ye not all these things? verily I say unto you, There shall not be left here one stone upon another, that shall not be thrown down.

3 ¶ And as he sat upon the mount of Olives, the disciples came unto him privately, saying, Tell us, when shall these things be? and what *shall be* the sign of thy coming, and of the end of the world?

---

on fire. No human structures are proof against God's power, whether exerted through the forces of nature, or, as in this case, through the human will.

3. He was retiring to Bethany (26: 6), and stopping as he passed over the Mount of Olives, he sat down, and doubtless looked back over the doomed city. *The disciples*—Mark represents the questions as asked by Peter, James, John, and Andrew, but it is unnecessary to suppose that the others had passed on before him to Bethany. These four may have been nearer to him, and may be said, therefore, to have asked him *privately* so far as respects the other disciples.

In *form* three distinct questions are reported; but in the spirit in which they are put they are substantially one. How so? The disciples blended in their conceptions the destruction of Jerusalem, the coming of Christ, and the end of the world. Had they known more, they would have regarded the end of the Jewish polity as quite distinct from the end of the world. In attempting to understand our Lord's reply, we must be careful not to consider it as *exactly matching* the questions of the disciples. Such a method would lead us astray. The error of the disciples, however, is corrected.

The great question relative to the chapter is this: Is Jesus speaking only of the destruction of Jerusalem? If we must answer no, then the question will be, Does Jesus speak of the destruction of Jerusalem and of his coming at the end of the world, in distinct, consecutive portions? or, does he so blend them as to refer to both in the same words? If the last question must be answered in the affirmative, it will follow that we have here a specimen of *twofold* meaning, which is generally admitted to be a characteristic of several of the Psalms, in which both David and Christ are the object.

Through the courtesy of its author, Rev. William F. Snow, pastor of the Eliot Congregational Church in Lawrence, Mass., the writer has been permitted to examine a manuscript analysis of the chapter, read before the Andover Association of Congregational ministers, and to present for the consideration of his readers the substance of the view. It is of course impossible to do the author's interpretation justice in the little space that can be spared. Mr. Snow considers that the key of the whole discourse, ending with vs. 36, is found in its opening words, Take heed that *no man deceive you.* The disciples committed the mistake of supposing that the calamities of Jerusalem, culminating in the destruction of the temple, would be the result of the revelation of the Son of man, and as a prominent feature of the end of the world. The discourse is largely occupied with the correction of their mistake. It is not intended to impart information, but is entirely of a cautionary

4 And Jesus answered and said unto them, Take heed that no man deceive you.

5 For many shall come in my name, saying, I am Christ; and shall deceive many.

6 And ye shall hear of wars and rumours of wars: see that

---

character, and is not prophetic in the strict sense of that word, for it does not stimulate but allays expectation, does not invite but repels inquiry. It answers the question, When and what sign? only so far as is needful to prevent error. The discourse separates into four divisions: I. The first (5–14) suggests *the probable sources of deception* in regard to the coming of the Son of man; II. The second (15–28) considers *the calamities of Jerusalem*, as a *special* source of deception; III. *A description of the coming of the Son of man* with special reference to the question of the disciples; IV. The discourse is summed up (32–36), and is *the answer to the question of the disciples*, so far as any answer can be given. Here our Lord distinguishes between "these things" (33, 34) and "that day and hour" (36). By the former, which the disciples had used in their question, he means the calamities of Jerusalem; by the latter, his coming at the end of the world.

This analysis is suggested by its author as "avoiding the difficulty attending the double reference to the destruction of Jerusalem and the end of the world." While there seem to be difficulties in the interpretation to which this analysis is intended to open the way, it is worthy of examination by all who wish to understand this very difficult portion of the Gospel. It is doubtful whether the true meaning of the chapter will ever be satisfactorily determined. The interpretation now to be given, which is that of a large number of the best biblical scholars, will proceed upon the supposition that the primary reference, as far as vs. 43, is to the destruction of Jerusalem, with a possible reference,

also, to the coming of Christ at the end of the Christian dispensation.

4. *Deceive you*—Cause you to err, or, lead you astray,—*perhaps*, relative to Christ's coming at the end of the world. Freedom of will is not inconsistent with liability to be led astray by *men*. Devils, then, may lead one astray without destroying one's freedom.

5. *Many shall come*—Whether such men as Theudas, Dositheus, and Simon Magus are intended, as some think, is not quite certain. It is at any rate true that many impostors arose who professed ability to deliver the Jews from their troubles, and thousands were deceived by them. Some in our own times are deceived by men who profess to know even more concerning religion than Christ himself knew. *In my name*—Not in the name of Jesus, but in the name of the Messiah. *I am Christ*—I am *the* Christ, that is, the Messiah foretold by the prophets.

6. *Wars and rumors of wars*—It is worthy of special notice that when these predictions were made, it was a time of profound peace throughout the Roman empire. Three of the Roman emperors, Caligula, Claudius, and Nero, threatened the Jews with war; two Parthian kings were reported as declaring war against the Romans; and Palestine was often agitated with rumors of rebellion against Rome. *The end*—Of the Jewish State. Amid such civil commotions the disciples would be in danger of supposing that the end of the Jewish state was *very near*. He cautions them against the danger of the mistake; and, as they connected with the downfall of the state the end of the world, it would seem as if our

ye be not troubled: for all these *things* must come to pass, but the end is not yet.

7 For nation shall rise against nation, and kingdom against kingdom: and there shall be famines, and pestilences, and earthquakes, in divers places.

8 All these *are* the beginning of sorrows.

9 Then shall they deliver you up to be afflicted, and shall kill you: and ye shall be hated of all nations for my name's sake.

10 And then shall many be offended, and shall betray one another, and shall hate one another.

11 And many false prophets shall rise, and shall deceive many.

Lord must have also intended to caution them against the mistake of supposing that such civil agitations would foretoken the end of the world.

7. *Nation . . . kingdom*—It is unnecessary to suppose that any special distinction is intended by the use of these different terms. It is merely a specimen of that fulness of description which prevails in common speech. Many facts are reported by Josephus and Philo, not disciples of Jesus, which illustrate this part of the prophecy; as disturbances at Alexandria, the slaughter of fifty thousand Jews in Seleucia, and in a city near Joppa on the coast of the Mediterranean. *Famines*, etc.—See Acts 11: 28. "Ancient writers . . . speak of several local famines which were severe in particular countries. Josephus mentions one which prevailed at that time in Judea, and swept away many of the inhabitants. Helena, Queen of Adiabene, a Jewish proselyte, who was then at Jerusalem, imported provisions from Egypt and Cyprus, which she distributed among the people to save them from starvation."—*Hackett on the Acts*. *Pestilences*—Roman classical writers speak of a pestilence in Rome, A.D. 65, in which thirty thousand perished. Pestilences generally accompany famines. *Earthquakes*—Several of these are known to have taken place. They are specified by Alford as follows: *a*. In Crete, A. D. 46 or 47; *b*. One at Rome, A.D. 51; *c*. One at Apamea, in Phrygia, A.D. 53; *d*. One at Laodicea, A.D. 60; *e*. One in Campania. Thus our Lord's prophecy, earthquakes *in divers places*, was literally fulfilled.

8. *Sorrows*—Birth-pangs. See Paul's remarkable use of the same figure in Rom. 8: 22: For we know that the whole creation groaneth and *travaileth in pain together* until now. In this world of sin there can be no joy that is not born of sorrow.

9. *Shall kill you*—James the elder, James the younger, and probably Paul and Peter, were put to death before Jerusalem fell. *Hated* —Arraying themselves so manfully and persistently against the wickedness of the world and in favor of the Lord Jesus Christ, Christ's disciples could not but bring down upon themselves the wrath of men. Consider the entire life of Paul from the time of his conversion. Consider also the life of Peter. Consult Acts 28: 22: For as concerning this sect, we know that *everywhere it is spoken against*. In Tacitus, a Roman classical writer, Christians are spoken of as hated on account of their crimes. No fact is better attested than that the early disciples were the objects of bitter persecution both by Jews and Gentiles. Christians of the present day are the objects of much sly hatred and ridicule in social life.

10, 11. *Many be offended*—Dis-

12 And because iniquity shall abound, the love of many shall wax cold.

13 But he that shall endure unto the end, the same shall be saved.

14 And this gospel of the kingdom shall be preached in all the world for a witness unto all nations; and then shall the end come.

15 When ye therefore shall see the abomination of desolation, spoken of by Daniel

---

pleased, and so will renounce allegiance to Christ. The words *one another* imply that the reference is to professors of Christianity. *Betray*—Proof of the *meanness* of their depravity. Of course such depravity would lead to mutual hatred. *False prophets*—Teachers of error were then, probably, quite as numerous in proportion to the teachers of truth as they are now, and quite as daring. Proof of it may be seen in nearly every one of the epistles. See especially Acts 20: 30; Gal. 1: 7-9; 2 Cor. 11: 13. Those who are inclined to despond because there are now so many teachers of error will do well to consider this prophecy of our Lord.

12. *Iniquity*—Lawlessness, which may exist where there is no outward immorality. He who withdraws his *mind* from the control of God's will is lawless. This internal lawlessness is of course ever in danger of breaking over the bounds of external decency and of becoming *vice*. In proportion to the prevalence of this form of sin, whether subtile or gross, the love of *many*, or, more exactly, of *the* many, that is, the majority, will *wax*, become, cold. The Saviour means to say that so general will be the disregard of God's law, that even the majority of his own disciples will relapse, under its influence, into coldness.

13. *Saved*—This may refer in part to temporal deliverance, but the chief reference must be to spiritual, for there is contrast with the statement made in vs. 12, and that clearly refers to things spiritual. *Endure*—Notice that, as on so many other occasions, Jesus assumes with a divine. independence the freedom of the human will. He manifests no anxiety to save the doctrine from perversion, or from apparent contradiction with the doctrine of God's sovereignty. *To the end*—To the end of his life, whether that shall be at the end of the calamities that are to come upon Jerusalem, or many years after. The saints' perseverance implies the saints' activity, and this implies God's activity. Professions of loyalty to Christ that terminate before the end of life are worthless.

14. Here, as in nearly all the leading verses of the discourse, there is room for two widely different views. The reference must of course be either to the very general preaching of the gospel in the primitive age before the destruction of Jerusalem, or to the general preaching of the gospel in the latest times before the last advent of Christ. The writer inclines to the former view. *In all the world*—As then known. The gospel *was preached* from Spain to India. Paul says (Col. 1: 6), Which is come unto you, *as it is in all the world*. Consult the entire history of apostolic labor. *For a witness*—Of the Light, of God's love in Christ. John (1: 7) says, The same came for a witness, *to bear witness of the Light, that all men through him might believe. Then . . . the end*—Of the Jewish State, including the fall of Jerusalem. The city was not destroyed till after the gospel had been preached throughout the known world.

15. *When, therefore*—When, in view of the fact that the end of the Jewish State must come. *The holy*

the prophet, stand in the holy place, (whoso readeth, let him understand,)

16 Then let them which be in Judea flee into the mountains:

17 Let him which is on the housetop not come down to take anything out of his house:

18 Neither let him which is in the field return back to take his clothes.

19 And woe unto them that are with child, and to them that give suck in those days!

20 But pray ye that your flight be not in the winter, neither on the sabbath day:

---

place—The temple, or perhaps the city including the temple. *The abomination of desolation*—Not the erection of the statue of Titus or Hadrian "on the site of the desolated temple," not "the Roman cagles as military ensigns," not "the idol statue of Jupiter set up in the temple by Antiochus Epiphanes," not the desecration of the temple by the Zealots, but the Roman armies; and in proof see Luke 21: 20. *By Daniel*—9: 27; 11: 31; 12: 11. Here we have our Lord's authority for regarding Daniel as inspired to foretell events. *Whoso readeth*, etc.— Let the reader mark it! let him think of it! It is probable that these are the words, not of Jesus, but of the evangelist, calling special attention *to what is here said.*

16. The Christians obeyed the direction here given. An ancient historian affirms that they fled to Pella, a city supposed to be in Peræa, on the eastern side of the Jordan. It is believed that not one Christian fell in the siege. The siege was raised not long after it was begun, Cestius Gallus, the commander, recalling the troops. This gave opportunity, before the final siege by Titus, for the Christians to flee. Compare Lot fleeing from Sodom with Christ's disciples fleeing from Jerusalem. Wicked cities may become too bad for the righteous to dwell in. Until God bids the good depart from a wicked city, they better stay and help improve it.

17, 18. Strong expressions to awaken the disciples to promptness and even haste in the crisis that will come. They should not be taken too literally; yet, if at the approach of the Roman armies one chanced to be on the roof of his house—the roofs were flat—he might and probably would have found literal compliance with the command necessary. As houses were then built, one could have escaped without being under the necessity of going down into and through the house. One might have run over *many* roofs till he came near to a gate of the city. *Anything*—Not a single article, but things generally. Better lose all for the sake of escaping.

19, 20. *Woe*—Not like the woes denounced against the Pharisees. This is the woe of pity. How remarkable the words of vs. 19 as an expression of the Redeemer's holy sympathy! *Not in the winter*—Because of the greater suffering. "During January and February snow often falls to the depth of a foot or more, though it may not make its appearance for several years together. In 1854–5 it remained on the ground for a fortnight. Nor is this of late occurrence only, but is reported by Shaw in 1722. In 1818 it was between two and three feet deep. In 1754 a heavy fall took place, and twenty-five persons are said to have been frozen to death at Nazareth."—*Smith's Dictionary. On the Sabbath day*—Because the Jews might impede their flight by insisting that they should not travel more than a Sabbath day's journey, which was about a mile. *Pray*, etc.

21 For then shall be great tribulation, such as was not since the beginning of the world to this time, no, nor ever shall be.

22 And except those days should be shortened, there should no flesh be saved: but for the elect's sake those days shall be shortened.

—Another remarkable illustration of *our Lord's* perception, though not expressed, of the harmony between God's purposes and man's freedom. Observe, however, that Jesus makes no attempt to impart his knowledge of that harmony to us. He either saw. it is probable, that such knowledge was unnecessary, or that our minds are not endowed with capacity to receive it. The prayers which the disciples were to offer were a part of God's plan; but whether that fact or some other is the ground of the harmony, we have no means of knowing. Not even in heaven may we be able to see *the ground* of the harmony between the actings of the human will and the actings of the divine will. As Jesus saw not only the fact of the harmony, but the ground of the fact, we need not indulge in anxiety concerning the matter, and should be very careful how we speculate concerning it.

21. *For*—The reason why they should be in such haste to escape. *Great tribulation*—See Dan. 12:1, and the remarkable prophecy in Deut. 28:49-57. The strong statement of this verse would be admitted as literally true so far as respects the *Jewish* people. The sufferings which came upon the Jews during the siege are depicted by Josephus in fearful colors. The student should be apprised, however, that Josephus is believed by some to have greatly exaggerated the *number* of the sufferers. He affirms that one million one hundred thousand perished, and that ninety-seven thousand were carried into captivity. It has been estimated (*Jerusalem*, Smith's Dictionary), by Mr. James Fergusson, "that the population of Jerusalem, in its days of greatest prosperity, may have amounted to from thirty thousand to forty-five thousand souls, but could hardly ever have reached fifty thousand; and assuming that in times of festival one-half were added to this amount, which is an extreme estimate, there may have been sixty thousand or seventy thousand in the city when Titus came up against it." Mr. Fergusson suggests, however, that, in consequence of the flight of women and children, the population was probably not larger than usual. If Josephus has exaggerated, the probability is that Mr. Fergusson's estimate is quite too low. It is to be regretted that Mr. Barnes has done so much toward perpetuating the popular error, that there were more than three millions of human beings in the city at the time of the siege. There is no reason to suppose that Josephus exaggerated the *degree of suffering.* The number, he says, of those who perished by famine was prodigious, and their miseries were unspeakable, — a woman, named Mary, putting to death, and eating part of her infant son.

22. *Days ... shortened*—As to number, not as to length. The following causes have been enumerated as contributing to shorten the siege: 1. Claudius, A.D. 42 or 43, ordered Herod Agrippa to stop strengthening the walls; 2. In consequence of their divisions, the Jews had made no preparation to withstand a siege; 3. The corn and provisions had been burnt just before the arrival of Titus; 4. Titus arrived suddenly and the Jews voluntarily abandoned some part of the

23 Then if any man shall say unto you, Lo, here *is* Christ, or there; believe *it* not.

24 For there shall arise false Christs, and false prophets, and shall shew great signs and wonders; insomuch that, if *it* were possible, they shall deceive the very elect.

25 Behold, I have told you before.

26 Wherefore if they shall say unto you, Behold, he is in the desert; go not forth: behold, *he is* in the secret chambers; believe *it* not.

27 For as the lightning cometh out of the east, and shineth even unto the west; so shall also the coming of the Son of man be.

28 For wheresoever the carcass is, there will the eagles be gathered together.

---

fortification; 5. According to Josephus, Titus acknowledged that it was by God's power he had succeeded in capturing the city. *No flesh*—So many more would perish, that it might be said in the strong language of common life that not a man would be saved. *Elect's sake* —For the sake of the Lord's chosen people. According as *he hath chosen us in him, before the foundation of the world.* Eph. 1:4. Even wicked men may get some temporal good in consequence of God's love for his people. Compare God's forbearance toward Jerusalem, with that which he would have shown toward Sodom, had there been in that city ten righteous men.

23-26. *Then*—At the time of the siege. *Christ*—The Christ, *the Messiah*. He intimates that some impostor will cry out, Here is the Messiah! and that the words will hardly have escaped from his lips before another will exclaim, *Here* is the Messiah! It should be *here* in both cases, for the word is the same in the original. *Shall show signs*, etc.—Not necessarily miracles, but the appearance of them. Their signs will be as false as themselves. *If . . . possible*—The impossibility of leading the chosen astray was owing to the special provision which God had made for keeping them. *My sheep shall never perish.* John 10:28 Apart from that special provision, the chosen are as liable to fall as Adam, as liable to perish as Judas. *Behold*, etc.—This is said for the purpose of impressing upon their minds the duty of using their freedom in resisting the false Christs and the false teachers,—a rebuke to those church-members, who, in mere curiosity, give their presence and consequently their encouragement to spiritualists and other errorists. To say that they go merely *to look on*, is an insult to Christ. Would our Lord have justified the disciples in going into the desert, or into some *secret chamber*,—any private place,—where the false Christs were, merely to look on?

27, 28. *As the lightning*—Instead of having *time* to go forth into the desert, or into some private place, you will see Christ coming with such suddenness that, as I have already told you, it will be necessary to flee for your life. Many commentators have the utmost conviction that these words refer to the final coming of Christ. But see vs. 34. They may be regarded as *suggestive* of the second coming. *Wheresoever the carcass,* etc.—A proverbial saying applicable to any organization, religious, national, or political, or to any individual, whose sin has become so great as to call for special judgments. Here the reference is undoubtedly to the coming of the Roman armies to the city of Jerusalem. *Eagles*—

CHAPTER XXIV.

29 ¶ Immediately after the tribulation of those days shall the sun be darkened, and the moon shall not give her light,

It is assumed by Barnes, Owen, and even Lange, that it is *vultures* to which the Saviour refers; but in the American edition of Smith's "Dictionary of the Bible," it is affirmed, that "as eagles frequently prey upon dead bodies, there is no necessity to restrict the Greek word to *Vulturidæ;*" and in a note is the following: "It is necessary to remember that no true eagle will kill for himself, if he can find dead flesh."

29. At this verse, in the opinion of many, begins a distinct prophecy of the coming of Christ at the last judgment. In the opinion of others, equally learned and devout, the prophecy still pertains to Jerusalem, though suggestive, some would say symbolical, of Christ's last coming. We accept, as *the more probable*, the latter, and give the following as some of the reasons: 1. The statement (vs. 34), *This generation shall not pass till all these things be fulfilled*. The attempt to prove that the Greek here rendered *generation* means *race* has not been successful. It is very difficult to believe that by *this generation*—notice the force of *this*—the disciples could have understood Jesus as meaning any other than *the generation then living;* 2. The use of the word *immediately;* 3. The correspondence of the words, *the tribulation of those days*, with the words in vs. 21, *Then shall be great tribulation*, and in vs. 22, except *those days* should be shortened; 4. The evident connection, and that very close, of the parallel words in Luke 21: 25, with vv. 22-24; 5. The language of this 29th verse is used by prophets, figuratively, to denote great political changes. See Isa. 13: 9, 10. "Here," as we are reminded by Prof. Stuart, "vs. 10 contains the very same imagery which is employed in Matt. 24: 29." But the prophet is speaking of the destruction of Babylon. See also Isa. 24: 20, 23, for similar metaphors applied to former judgments of God upon Jerusalem. See Isa. 34: 4, describing judgments upon Idumea. See Acts 2: 19, 20, upon which we quote at length from Dr. Hackett's Commentary: "In the interpretation of the passage before us, I follow those who understand it as having primary reference to the calamities which God inflicted on the Jews in connection with the overthrow of Jerusalem, and the destruction of the Jewish State and nation. The reasons for these opinions are briefly these: 1. The law of correspondence would lead us to apply this part of the prophecy to the same period to which the other part has been applied, that is, to the early times of the gospel; 2. The expression, *the day of the Lord*, in vs. 20, according to a very common use in the Hebrew prophets, denotes a day when God comes to make known his power in the punishment of his enemies, a day of the signal display of his vengeance for the rejection of long-continued mercies, and the commission of aggravated sins. The subversion of the Jewish State was such an occasion. It appropriates fully every trait of that significant designation; 3. Part of the language here coincides almost verbally with that in Matthew 24: 29; and if the language there, as understood by most interpreters, describes the downfall of the Jewish State, we may infer from the similarity that the subject of the discourse is the same in both places; 4. The entire phraseology, when construed according to the laws of prophetic language, is strikingly appropriate to represent the unsurpassed horrors and distress which attended the siege and destruction of Jerusalem, and to announce the extinction

and the stars shall fall from heaven, and the powers of the heavens shall be shaken:

30 And then shall appear the sign of the Son of man in heaven: and then shall all the tribes of the earth mourn, and they shall see the Son of man coming in the clouds of heaven with power and great glory.

31 And he shall send his angels with a great sound of a trumpet, and they shall gather together his elect from the four winds, from one end of heaven to the other.

32 Now learn a parable of the fig tree; When his branch is yet tender, and putteth forth leaves, ye know that summer *is* nigh:

33 So likewise ye, when ye shall see all these things, know that it is near, *even* at the doors.

34 Verily I say unto you, This generation shall not pass, till all these things be fulfilled.

35 Heaven and earth shall pass away, but my words shall not pass away.

36 ¶ But of that day and hour knoweth no *man*, no, not the

---

of the Jewish power and glory of the Jewish worship which that catastrophe involved. Yet here too (see on vs. 18) we are to recognize the wider scope of the prophecy. The destruction of the Jews is held forth by the apostle as a type of the destruction which is to come upon every rejecter of the gospel." *Powers of the heavens*—Sun, moon, and stars.

30, 31. Most persons have been so accustomed to regard these words as descriptive of Christ's last coming, that it is not surprising that they find it difficult to believe them as descriptive of anything else; but let them weigh what is said concerning vs. 29, for most of it is as applicable to these verses as to that. Especially let them consider that, as stated in vs. 34, *all these things* were to be fulfilled *before that generation would pass away*. *The sign*—Not, as Alford, the sign of the cross, but the Son of man himself. *Coming in*—Coming *on*. How familiar to the Jewish mind of our Lord's day must have been this phraseology as a figurative description of *any striking judgment*, will appear by examination of Ps. 18: 11; 104: 3; Ezek. 1: 4; Isa. 19: 1; Dan. 7: 13. Christ was to come to take vengeance on Jerusalem. But it is admitted that his coming at the last judgment is elsewhere described in language similar to this; for example, in vs. 31 of the very next chapter, and 2 Thess. 1: 7. *His angels* —Comparing this with Luke 21: 28, we incline to the opinion that by angels is meant the ministering spirits, not necessarily visible, by whom the Christians were to be aided to escape. *Trumpet*—As it was by means of the trumpet that the ancient assemblies of the Jews were called together, the metaphor here used is very natural. *Shall gather*—" It was a summons," says Prof. Stuart ("Bibliotheca Sacra," April, 1852), "*to gather them together*, so to speak, that they might put themselves under the protection of the Son of man, while his judgments were abroad in the land. If, in the verse before us, it were a summons for the final judgment, why should not the *wicked* be gathered as well as the righteous?" *Four winds*—From every place where the chosen were.

32–35. Jesus now illustrates in a

angels of heaven, but my Father only.

37 But as the days of Noe were, so shall also the coming of the Son of man be.

38 For as in the days that were before the flood they were eating and drinking, marrying and giving in marriage, until the day that Noe entered into the ark,

39 And knew not until the flood came, and took them all away; so shall also the coming of the Son of man be.

40 Then shall two be in the field; the one shall be taken, and the other left.

41 Two *women shall be* grinding at the mill; the one shall be taken, and the other left.

42 ¶ Watch therefore; for ye

---

simple but impressive manner the certainty of his coming as indicated in the signs. As to the fig-tree, see notes on 21: 18, 19; Mark 11: 12-14. *A parable of*—The parable from: Learn the parable which may be constructed from the fig-tree. As the summer is known to be nigh when the branch of the fig-tree is *yet*, already, tender, and leaves are putting forth, so when *all these things*, the signs which I have given you, have appeared, know that the destruction which I have foretold is near. *This generation shall not pass*, etc.—In view of these words it is exceedingly difficult to see how Jesus can have hitherto referred to his final coming. *Heaven and earth*, etc.—See note on 5: 18. Many rationalists reverse this saying. Heaven and earth, they say, are eternal; Christ's words must give way to the teachings of science,—a sentiment distinctly avowed at a meeting of "The Free Religious Association."

36. Mark (13: 32) inserts: *Neither the Son.* Having made the general statement that his coming will occur before that generation has passed away, he now affirms, in answer to the inquiry of the disciples, *When?* that he does not know *exactly when.* He has proved himself to know but little less than infinitely more than men, and that little less pertains to the precise time. As to *this one point* he puts himself on a level with angels and men. How he *could* have been ignorant even of this, and have known so much as he did know, even affirming, and that, as the event showed, truthfully, that not one stone would be left on another, is indeed beyond our power to understand, but not in the least more so than that, if he was God, he could have *grown in wisdom.* Luke 2: 52. We must ever remember that Jesus Christ, when on earth, was not merely God, but that he was *God manifest in the flesh.* He avowed knowledge of so much of the future as to prove that as God he knew all the future; he knew enough less than all the future to prove that he was man. The harmony of the two facts is beyond our power to conceive.

37-41. *Noe*—The more proper form, *Noah.* He now illustrates the utter thoughtlessness of the Jews at the time of the crisis, and, secondly, the remarkable providential deliverance which many shall have. He illustrates the former from Old Testament history. As men and women continued their ordinary course of life, notwithstanding all the warnings they had received from Noah, and *knew not*, had no impressive conviction of the certainty of their destruction, but were all swept away, so it will be when the great crisis has come upon Jerusalem. Notwithstanding the distresses that the Jews shall have long endured in the siege, yet (this

MATTHEW.

know not what hour your Lord doth come.

43 But know this, that if the goodman of the house had

---

is the real point of the comparison) they will continue to flatter themselves to the last that they are free from all danger.

But to some there will be given such remarkable deliverance that it will be like taking the one and leaving the other of two men who are working together in the same field; like taking the one of the two women grinding at the mill and leaving the other. The history of disasters is full of equally striking contrasts. *Grinding at the mill*—See note on 18: 6, concerning millstones. "When at work with it" [the hand-mill] "*two women* sit at the mill facing each other; both have hold of the handle by which the upper is turned round on the 'nether' millstone. The one whose right hand is disengaged throws in the grain as occasion requires through the hole in the upper stone, which is called the rekkab (rider) in Arabic, as it was long ago in Hebrew. Both retain their hold, and pull to, or push from, as men do with the whip or cross-cut saw. The proverb of our Saviour is true to the life, for *women* only grind. I cannot recall an instance in which men were at the mill. It is tedious, fatiguing work, and slaves, or lowest servants, are set at it."—*Thomson.*

WOMEN GRINDING.

42. Here, or near this point, our Lord seems to pass to the higher subject of his final coming. Positiveness of opinion, however, concerning a matter so obscure is unseemly. Dogmatism is its offspring. It is clear that at a point not far in advance of this, Christ teaches the doctrine of the final judgment. As to this, nearly all the principal commentators in the Christian world are agreed.

43, 44. *Good man* — Master, house-keeper. *Broken up*—Broken through, or dug through. See on 6: 19-21, latter part of the notes. "As the vigilant householder does not wait to be informed of the approach of the thief, but is in a state of constant watchfulness against his at-

known in what watch the thief would come, he would have watched, and would not have suffered his house to be broken up.

44 Therefore be ye also ready: for in such an hour as ye think not the Son of man cometh.

45 Who then is a faithful and wise servant, whom his lord hath made ruler over his household, to give them meat in due season?

46 Blessed *is* that servant, whom his lord when he cometh shall find so doing.

47 Verily I say unto you, That he shall make him ruler over all his goods.

48 But and if that evil servant shall say in his heart, My lord delayeth his coming;

49 And shall begin to smite *his* fellow servants, and to eat and drink with the drunken;

50 The lord of that servant shall come in a day when he looketh not for *him*, and in an hour that he is not aware of,

51 And shall cut him asunder, and appoint *him* his portion with the hypocrites: there shall be weeping and gnashing of teeth.

---

tempts, so he who watches for the coming of his Lord needs not be informed of the particular time in which he may be expected, but will be in constant readiness to receive him."—*Dr. J. J. Owen.*

45–51. The Lord proceeds to utter *three parables* for the purpose of enforcing the duty of watching for his final coming. In this, the first, he supposes a man who is about to absent himself for a time, without disclosing how long, to set one over his household for the purpose of giving the food at the appointed hours of the day, or possibly once a month, to the members of the family. He represents this servant as so habitually faithful and wise in discharge of the duty, that, had the master of the house come at any hour, he would have been ready for him. He supposes another appointed to a similar service, who flatters himself that because his master has not come yet, he will not be likely to come for a long time; and so, instead of discharging with regularity and promptness the duties expected, falls both to beating his fellow-servants and to revelling with outsiders. The former is rewarded; the latter is punished.

Meat—Food. *That evil servant*—Another, and that an evil servant. *Smite*—Beat. Notice the difference between his conduct toward his fellow-servants, and his conduct toward others. Toward the former he plays the tyrant; with the latter the fool. One extreme follows another. *Cut him asunder*—See 1 Chron. 20: 3; Heb. 11: 37. "A case of sawing asunder, by placing the criminal between boards, and then beginning at the head, is mentioned by Shaw, Trav. p. 254."—*Smith's Dictionary. Weeping and gnashing*—See on 8: 12. *With the hypocrites*—He will deserve to be put with them, because he is a hypocrite himself. By holding his position as ruler over his master's household, he professed to be doing his master's will, but in fact he was doing exactly the opposite.

This entire parable, and not merely, as Alford thinks, the 45th verse, refers especially to ministers; and therefore the following references will be found to be of much

CHAPTER XXV.

THEN shall the kingdom of heaven be likened unto ten virgins, which took their lamps, and went forth to meet the bridegroom.

2 And five of them were wise, and five *were* foolish.

3 They that *were* foolish took

---

interest: 2 Tim. 2: 15; 1 Peter 5: 2-4.

CHAPTER XXV.

THE DUTY OF WATCHING FOR THE FINAL COMING FURTHER ENFORCED; THE LAST JUDGMENT.

1. The object of the second parable is well expressed by Dr. Alexander: "Having taught them the necessity of vigilance after his departure, he now shows them that the vigilance required is not mere watchfulness, but watchful preparation." *Then*—At the time of Christ's last coming. Alford and other pre-millenarians say: At his coming to reign, personally, on the earth a thousand years. *The kingdom of heaven*—Not the church, but the Messianic dispensation. It is not necessary, therefore, to regard the ten virgins as representing none but members of churches. They stand for *all* who profess to be waiting for the coming of Christ, whether members of churches or not. We should attach no importance to the number *ten*, though it was probably selected because for various reasons that number had become familiar to the Jewish mind. *Lamps*—Either "torches or flambeaux, consisting of small iron or brass bars inserted into a stick, to which pieces of linen dipped in oil were fastened;" or, "properly *lamps;* and the oil vessels were separate from the lamps."

Went forth—Ward's "View of the Hindoos" gives the following almost perfect illustration of the Jewish custom: "At a marriage the procession of which I saw some years ago, the bridegroom came from a distance, and the bride lived at Serampore, to which place the bride-groom was to come by water. After waiting two hours, at length, near midnight, it was announced, as if in the very words of Scripture, '*Behold the bridegroom cometh; go ye out to meet him!*' All the persons employed now lighted their lamps, and ran with them in their hands to fill up their stations in the procession; some of them had lost their lamps, and were unprepared, and it was then too late to seek them, and the cavalcade moved forward to the house of the bride, at which place the company entered a large and splendidly illuminated area before the house, covered with an awning, where a great multitude of friends, dressed in their best apparel, were seated upon mats. The bridegroom was carried in the arms of a friend, and placed upon a superb seat in the midst of the company, where he sat a short time and then went into the house, the door of which was immediately shut and guarded by Sepoys. I and others expostulated with the door-keeper, but in vain. Never was I so struck with our Lord's beautiful parable as at this moment. 'And the door was shut.' I was exceedingly anxious to be present while the marriage formulas were repeated, but was obliged to depart in disappointment." It is more probably the intention in the parable to represent the virgins as going forth to meet the bridegroom, when he is returning with the bride to his own house.

2. The equality of number has no special significance. The preacher not less than the interpreter should abstain from all unauthorized interpretations of this feature of the parable, and of all those features of other parables which have no

their lamps, and took no oil with them:

4 But the wise took oil in their vessels with their lamps.

5 While the bridegroom tarried, they all slumbered and slept.

6 And at midnight there was a cry made, Behold, the bridegroom cometh; go ye out to meet him.

7 Then all those virgins arose, and trimmed their lamps.

8 And the foolish said unto

---

bearing on the main points. In this respect the preacher should be a conscientious interpreter, saying nothing false for the purpose of rhetorical effect. *Wise . . . foolish*—In heart. It refers to moral qualities, not to intellectual.

3, 4. *No oil*—No supply in their vessels. But it would be a violation of the rule just named to infer from the fact that the foolish are represented as having *some* oil in the *lamp itself* (vs. 8), that they as well as the wise represent Christians. The point which the Saviour illustrates is simply this, that *at his coming* some who profess to have the forms of godliness will be found to have nothing more. *Oil*—We need not perplex ourselves, as many do, with the question whether this means *faith*, or *good works*, or *the anointing of the Holy Spirit*. If it means faith, it is that faith which is the gift of God. If it means good works, it is those good works which are born of faith. If it is the anointing of the Holy Spirit, *that* comes through grace. The important thing is to understand it as implying a state of heart which, through the merciful power of God, distinguishes the believer from the unbeliever.

5. *Slumbered and slept*—Slumbering, as here used, is that earlier stage of sleep which indicates itself by the nodding of the person. It is at least improbable that Jesus intended to teach here any spiritual lesson. The foolish are not called foolish because they slept, but because they had not provided themselves with a supply of oil. Nor are the wise blamed for sleeping, but they are commended for doing exactly that which the foolish did not do. The representation that they were *all asleep* is merely one of the little strokes of the divine pencil that are necessary to aid in bringing out the important points of the picture. Pulpit rhetoric relative to such features of a parable is worse than out of place,—it misleads. *Sleeping in death*, as was taught by many of the ancient interpreters, seems equally inadmissible.

6. *Midnight*—For the same reason that no significance should be attached to the sleeping, none should be attached to this. Both the *sleeping* and the *midnight* may be *suggestive* of important thoughts, but whether those thoughts are contained in the words themselves is another question. *Cry*—The final announcement, in whatever way made, that Christ is coming to judge the world. *Bridegroom*—Christ.

7. *All . . . arose . . . trimmed*—The foolish as well as the wise. *Trimming* was done "by pouring on fresh oil, and removing the fungi about the wick; for the latter purpose a sharp-pointed wire was attached to the lamp, which is still seen in the bronze lamps found in sepulchres." But trimming a lamp that has no oil in it will do no good. Giving a little more attention to externals is not getting ready to meet Christ.

8. *Are gone out*—Are going out. See the note on the words *no oil* (vv. 3, 4). Many who think they are prepared for the future life are never conscious of their want of

the wise, Give us of your oil; for our lamps are gone out.

9 But the wise answered, saying, *Not so;* lest there be not enough for us and you: but go ye rather to them that sell, and buy for yourselves.

10 And while they went to buy, the bridegroom came; and they that were ready went in with him to the marriage: and the door was shut.

11 Afterward came also the other virgins, saying, Lord, Lord, open to us.

12 But he answered and said, Verily I say unto you, I know you not.

13 Watch therefore; for ye know neither the day nor the hour wherein the Son of man cometh.

14 ¶ For *the kingdom of heaven is* as a man travelling

---

preparation (oil in the vessel) till death comes, and then it is too late to get it.

9. *Not so; lest there be not enough*—In our English Bibles *not so* is in italics, indicating that these words were inserted by the translators to help out the sense. A different reading, regarded by many as the correct one, would require the following translation: *Not so; there will not be enough for us and you.* It is by no means certain, however, that the common reading is incorrect. God has grace enough for all, but he never gives more to one than one needs for one's self. The Roman Catholic doctrine that a man can do works of supererogation, that is, can do more than God requires him to do, and that that can be passed over to the benefit of the less deserving, is therefore false. *Them that sell*— How this mere thread of the parable, which is woven in, it is probable, like the others, merely to aid in binding together the important parts, may be stretched even to breaking, may be seen in the interpretation which it received by some of "The Fathers," that "the sellers of oil signify *the poor*, who receive the *alms* (the oil) of the faithful, and sell the oil in return for the relief afforded to their wants." Even Alford says: "The sellers are the ordinary dispensers of the means of grace; a *particular class* of persons,—no mean argument for a set and appointed ministry,—and, moreover, for a *paid* ministry. If they *sell*, they receive for the thing sold." Such a method of handling the parables is unworthy even of a Sabbath-school teacher.

10, 11. *The door was shut*—Excluding them, not as Alford and other millenarians say, from the blessedness of "the first resurrection" and the Millennium, but from heaven. This verse answers to vs. 51 of the preceding chapter. *Lord, Lord*—Equivalent to our *sir, sir,* the repetition showing their earnestness. Many will say to Christ, Lord, Lord, who will give no evidence of *allegiance.* See 7: 22.

12. *I know you not*—See 7: 23. I *never* knew you. If these foolish virgins represent those that were shut out, as Alford says, "*only for that time,*" that is, from the Millennium, but are finally received to heaven, it is difficult to see why Jesus says, *I know you not.* It is infinitely better to be unknown by men in this world than to be unknown by Christ at the day of judgment.

13. *Watch therefore*—This is the point of the parable. While the reference is to the final coming of Christ, the door is in fact opened or shut with respect to each individual at the moment of his death. The doctrine of the final coming of Christ has too feeble a hold upon Christians of this day. Most of them seem to take it for granted as

CHAPTER XXV.

into a far country, *who* called his own servants, and delivered unto them his goods.

15 And unto one he gave five talents, to another two, and to another one; to every man according to his several ability; and straightway took his journey.

16 Then he that had received the five talents went and traded with the same, and made *them* other five talents.

17 And likewise he that *had received* two, he also gained other two.

18 But he that had received one went and digged in the earth, and hid his lord's money.

19 After a long time the lord of those servants cometh, and reckoneth with them.

---

settled that Christ's last advent is not to come for many years,—hundreds or thousands of years perhaps. But we know no better than the primitive disciples that it will not come the next hour. If we so far forget our Lord's words as to commit ourselves either for or against any given day, we lose the spiritual good which the uncertainty of the time is adapted to bring us.

14. The third parable teaches the duty of *wakeful activity in the service of the Lord. Travelling into a far country*—Going abroad, as in 21 : 33. *The kingdom of heaven* . . . *Who* need not have been supplied. The idea is, For as a man going abroad did, so the Son of man does. *Servants*—Slaves. That goods, or, as specified in the next verse, *talents*, should be intrusted to slaves as capital, is strictly in accordance with ancient custom. "Slaves carried on the whole business of the Athenians; even the poorer citizens depended on them. Many were skilful in the elegant arts, and versed in letters; while others were only qualified to toil in the mines."—*Manual of Classical Literature.*

15. *Five talents*—About five thousand dollars. *His several ability*—His own ability. *According to,* etc.—According to his natural capacity,—physical, but especially mental, the latter including, as the chief characteristics, reasoning power and power to feel. *Talents*—All the gifts which God grafts, so to speak, upon the natural capacity, as Christian character, education, that is, mental discipline, knowledge, property, reputation, religious and secular influence, opportunities of usefulness. *Natural capacity* also may be viewed as a gift, a talent, but the divine Teacher here chooses to consider it rather as a *measure of gifts. Five, two, one*—As natural capacity is given in different measure, talents are given in different number. Notice as a striking illustration the diversity of the apostles themselves; first, in "ability," that is, temperament and mental constitution; secondly, in "talents," that is, mental culture, knowledge, social position, and opportunities of usefulness.

16. *Traded with*—We are to put to use all the gifts which God confers upon us. *Made them other five talents*—Better, *made, or gained, other five.* No stress should be laid upon the fact that the number given was just doubled; though, when one is able to say, I doubled my money, one is supposed to feel that the increase was large. The lesson taught is this, that we are to use God's gifts so faithfully that they shall yield, according to our capacity, the largest possible increase both to ourselves and to our fellow-men.

18, 19. *Went* . . . *digged* . . . *hid*—Here see proof of the activity, strength, and persistency of his will. He was indeed slothful (v. 26), but only in doing right. Indolence in the Lord's service is activity in Sa-

20 And so he that had received five talents came and brought other five talents, saying, Lord, thou deliveredst unto me five talents: behold, I have gained beside them five talents more.

21 His lord said unto him, Well done, *thou* good and faithful servant: thou hast been faithful over a few things, I will make thee ruler over many things: enter thou into the joy of thy lord.

22 He also that had received two talents came and said, Lord, thou deliveredst unto me two talents: behold, I have gained two other talents beside them.

23 His lord said unto him, Well done, good and faithful servant: thou hast been faithful over a few things, I will make thee ruler over many things: enter thou into the joy of thy lord.

24 Then he which had received the one talent came and said, Lord, I knew thee that thou art a hard man, reaping where thou hast not sown, and gathering where thou hast not strewed:

25 And I was afraid, and went and hid thy talent in the

---

tan's. *His lord's money*—He was wicked (vs. 26), but if, like some, he had claimed the money as his own, he would have been still more wicked. *A long time*—This should not be so understood as to contradict the statement in vs. 13.

20. *Thou deliveredst unto me*— *Unto me* indicates a sense of personal responsibility which the faithful servant of Christ is ever ready to acknowledge, and *thou* indicates his cheerful acknowledgment of the fact that his talents are the gift of God. · No such words are put upon the lips of the unfaithful servant.

21–23. *Well done*—"An expression of commendation, often employed in the way of applause by the Greeks at their public games." *Few things*—Little. *Many things*—Much. *Will make thee ruler over*—Will set thee over,—will raise thee, say the millenarians, to higher posts of usefulness and honor in the Millennium; but it refers, we think, to the inheritance which will be given in heaven. *The joy of thy Lord*—That blessedness which the believer will have in possessing the inheritance with Christ. *Enter*—The Lord's welcome to that inheritance which will bring joy. Notice that the same form of approval is used relative to him that received two talents and to him that received five. According to some, his fidelity is rewarded, not his success. But his success cannot be separated from his fidelity. His success was as great in proportion to his "ability" as that of the other. In heaven, while the bliss of all will be perfect, there will doubtless be substantially the same difference of degree, according to capacity, as had been here.

24, 25. *A hard man*—The adjective is in such common use among men of business as to need no explanation. *Strewed*—Winnowed. See note on 3: 12. *Afraid* —That if he should trade with it, he should lose it. The fear was pretence. Weak as it was, the excuse was as strong as the excuses that men make for neglecting to improve the opportunities which God gives them. We incline to think that the hiding caused the fear, not the fear the hiding. *Lo, there thou hast that is thine* would have been sufficiently impudent, but the original might

earth: lo, *there* thou hast *that is* thine.

26 His lord answered and said unto him, *Thou* wicked and slothful servant, thou knewest that I reap where I sowed not, and gather where I have not strewed:

27 Thou oughtest therefore to have put my money to the exchangers, and *then* at my coming I should have received mine own with usury.

28 Take therefore the talent from him, and give *it* unto him which hath ten talents.

29 For unto every one that hath shall be given, and he shall have abundance: but from him that hath not shall be taken away even that which he hath.

30 And cast ye the unprofitable servant into outer darkness: there shall be weeping and gnashing of teeth.

31 ¶ When the Son of man shall come in his glory, and all the holy angels with him, then shall he sit upon the throne of his glory:

32 And before him shall be gathered all nations: and he shall separate them one from another, as a shepherd divideth *his* sheep from the goats:

---

have been more briefly rendered, *Lo, thou hast thine own.* He had not all, for he had the right to what the servant could have made. The servant was therefore in debt. That God requires those to love him who were born with depraved tendencies and are in a world of temptation, is no proof that he is *hard.*

26, 27. *Thou knewest*—Conceding, for the moment, that you are right in your opinion, and that your fear of losing in trade was well grounded, then you could at least have put my money to the exchangers. Exchanger was "a general term for banker or broker. Of this branch of business we find traces very early both in the oriental and classical literature." *Usury*—Here used in the milder sense of *interest.*

28-30. *Take . . . from him*—The first step in punishing him. Men who do not improve the gifts which God confers must at last lose them. See on 13: 12. *Outer darkness.*—See on 8: 12. This was the second step in punishing him. The man represents not those who *abuse* the gifts of God, but those who fail to improve them, whether they are members of a Christian church or not.

31, 32. There can be no possible doubt that the remainder of the chapter refers to the last judgment. This is held even by the millenarians. It can be made to apply to the destruction of Jerusalem only by the utmost violence. The most awfully solemn portion of the Bible, it should be studied with the prayer that we may feel that the truths disclosed are of infinite importance both to ourselves and to those to whom we may present them. *When*—This throws no light on the question, *How soon? Son of man*—See on 12: 8, second paragraph. It is a remarkable fact that in describing his coming to judge the world, he did not use the higher designation, *Son of God.* See the important words in John 5: 27. *Shall sit,* etc.—John 5: 22; Acts 17: 31. Keeping distinctly in mind that but a few hours after Jesus uttered these remarkable words, he was himself standing as an accused person before the highest court of the Jews and before Pilate, and was separated from the people as goats

33 And he shall set the sheep on his right hand, but the goats on the left.

34 Then shall the King say unto them on his right hand, Come, ye blessed of my Father, inherit the kingdom prepared for you from the foundation of the world:

35 For I was a hungered, and ye gave me meat: I was thirsty, and ye gave me drink:

---

were separated from sheep, we shall see that they show the most consummate conviction of final victory. It is impossible to believe that such faith could have been exercised by any other than a supernatural being. On the general subject, see 1 Thess. 4: 16, 17; Mark 8: 38; Jude 14 and 15; John 5: 25-29. *All nations*—Not, as Alford thinks, exclusive of the elect, but including them. It is to be a *universal* judgment, including both Christians and others; not, as millenarians say, a judgment of those only who are not saints. All nations include Gentiles as well as Jews, and these of every age of the world, yet not as nations, but as individuals. That the heathen—those who have not had the Bible—will be judged as certainly as others, is distinctly taught in Rom. 2: 9-12.

33. *Right hand . . . the left*—A figurative representation, based, perhaps, on the fact that the right hand is the place of honor. *Sheep*—The righteous, but in what sense must be learned further on. *Goats*—The wicked, and in what sense must also be learned further on. But why are the two classes called by these names? It cannot be said that goats were of no value. "Goats have, from the earliest ages, been considered important animals in rural economy, both on account of the milk they afford, and the excellence of the flesh of the young animals." The hair of goats was also useful. As sheep are an emblem of meekness (Isa. 53: 7), and for that reason stand here for the righteous, it may be supposed that Jesus applied the term *goats* to the wicked, because they are not meek; and the application would be natural, for the goat is not regarded as an emblem of meekness. The animal is rough, daring, independent.

34. *The king*—Even as the Son of man, Christ is endowed with *royal* prerogatives. *Blessed*—They had been lying under the curse of the law, but the curse has been removed. *Inherit*—This is one of the many expressive figures by which is stated the relation of believers to the bliss of the future world. See the very beautiful use which is made of the same figure by Paul in Rom. 8: 16, 17. See also Gal. 3: 29; Rev. 21: 7. *Kingdom prepared for you* —Therefore they were predestinated for the kingdom. Eph. 1: 4, 5; 2 Thess. 2: 13. *The kingdom* is here used in its essential idea as synonymous with *life eternal* in vs. 46. The kingdom which is consummated in the next world begins in this. Hence men are represented (Col. 1: 13) as translated in this life into the kingdom of God. Compare Rom. 14: 17; Luke 17: 21; Mark 12: 34. *From the foundation of the world*— In Eph. 1: 4 it is, *Before* the foundation. The meaning is essentially the same, it being the intention in both forms to express the thought that the event occurred before the material universe was created; that is, as we say, *from eternity*. Those whom Jesus Christ will call his Father's blessed ones will feel that it is a matter of infinitely little importance that their names were or were not known among men. A word for the pious poor,—*a kingdom is to be yours!* The rich Christian also should remember that his riches,

CHAPTER XXV.

I was a stranger, and ye took me in:

36 Naked, and ye clothed me: I was sick, and ye visited me: I was in prison, and ye came unto me.

37 Then shall the righteous answer him, saying, Lord,

---

compared with the kingdom which he is to inherit, are lighter than the dust of the balance.

35, 36. *For*—Our Lord represents himself as giving to the righteous *the reason why* they are welcomed to heaven. He who regards the reason as merely this, that the persons in question had practised kindness to the poor and the sick, and that therefore the reason is wholly *in themselves*, misses the meaning. That this cannot be the import of the Saviour's words is evident: 1. Other parts of the Bible teach that Christian character consists of *many* qualities. But here only *one* quality is named,—kindness to the suffering. Therefore this quality must here be put for all the qualities. He, therefore, who thinks he is an heir of the kingdom because he is kind to the suffering, should inquire whether his kindness is of that holy and comprehensive sort that implies the possession of all other qualities of Christian character; or whether it is that narrow and not necessarily holy quality which many mistake for that of which Jesus here speaks. 2. Christ represents even this comprehensive virtue as having direct reference to himself: Ye gave *me* meat; ye clothed *me*. See vs. 40, where he affirms that inasmuch as they have done it to one of the least of his brethren, they have done it to himself. The supposition that these acts of kindness had been done without *the intention* to do them to Christ, and that therefore the righteous were welcomed only on account of their personal excellences, is inadmissible. For the righteous are represented as showing kindness to *Christ's brethren*. The implication is that the kindness was shown *because* they were his brethren, which implies that they did it in love to Christ himself; and this implies *that they had faith in Christ*. See the important words, *in the name of a disciple* (10: 42), and the note. 3. It is elsewhere taught, even in Matthew—the narrative which presents the gospel more as the fulfilment of the law than either of the others—that we are saved not by our personal virtues as such, but by Christ. 1: 21; 9: 6; 11: 28-40. In Mark and John faith in Christ is clearly taught as indispensable to salvation. He that *believeth* shall be saved. Mark 16: 16. He that *believeth* on him is not condemned. John 3: 18. This is the work of God, that ye *believe* on him whom he hath sent. John 6: 29.

Our Lord, then, does not intend to teach that the righteous have in any true sense purchased their heavenly inheritance by works of merit. No helmsman undertakes to steer by the light on his own ship.

Took me in—To your house and heart. Taking the hungry man into one's house, and not at the same time into one's heart, is not a virtue: how much less is it piety! Many a man takes Christ into his creed, and commits the fatal mistake of supposing that therefore he has taken him into his heart. *Visited me*—The original word is very expressive: *To look upon, to look after.* Dr. Conant quotes the following from an ancient writer: "I should seem to be like the physician *going round visiting the sick.*" Christ means, then, not merely calling upon the sick, but calling for the purpose of doing something for their relief. *In prison, and ye came*—All that may be safely done for the physical, intellectual, and religious improvement even of criminals in prison

when saw we thee a hungered, and fed *thee?* or thirsty, and gave *thee* drink?

38 When saw we thee a stranger, and took *thee* in? or naked, and clothed *thee?*

39 Or when saw we thee sick, or in prison, and came unto thee?

40 And the King shall answer and say unto them, Verily I say unto you, Inasmuch as ye have done *it* unto one of the least of these my brethren, ye have done *it* unto me.

41 Then shall he say also unto them on the left hand, Depart from me, ye cursed, into everlasting fire, prepared for the devil and his angels:

42 For I was a hungered, and ye gave me no meat: I was thirsty, and ye gave me no drink:

43 I was a stranger, and ye took me not in: naked, and ye clothed me not: sick, and in prison, and ye visited me not.

44 Then shall they also answer him, saying, Lord, when

---

here finds its justification. Some of the apostles were thrown into prison for preaching Christ, and *many who boasted of their charities never visited them.*

37–39. *When saw we thee*—We must not suppose that any such reply will be made by the righteous. It is the divine Teacher's graphic method of representing *the state of mind* in which the righteous will be, —a state of such profound humility that they can scarcely see that they ever did anything of the kind. It is remarkable that Alford, who insists so strongly in his interpretation of many of the sayings in the Sermon on the Mount that we should not be slaves to the letter, but should endeavor to grasp the spirit of our Lord's words,—it is strange that he and some others should understand the righteous as here denying all knowledge of Christ himself, and as being, therefore, virtuous heathen that never knew Christ.

40. *My brethren*—Disciples. See the beautiful words in 12: 49, 50. With what moral dignity does Christ invest the simplest act of love done to the least of his disciples!

41. *Everlasting fire*—This should be preceded, as the original is, by the article,—*the* everlasting fire. Fire is doubtless a figurative word to express *intense punishment.* Concerning the general subject of future punishment, see note on vs. 46. Too much stress has sometimes been laid on the omission of the words *of my Father* after *cursed.* The punishment is to be inflicted by the Father, yet the omission may be designed to bring into greater prominence the *self-inflicting* power of sin. Perhaps more weight should be attached to the fact that the everlasting fire is not said to have been prepared for them, but for the devil and his angels. Respecting the *devil* see note on 4: 1, last paragraph. As to the *angels* of the devil, see 12: 24, where the devil, Beelzebub, is called the *prince of the devils*, of the *demons.* Demons, therefore, seem to be identical with the angels of the devil. Demons are called *angels* in the general sense of messengers to do the will of him who is their prince.

42, 43. *Gave me no meat . . . no drink*, etc.—It is worthy of special notice that *positive* sins are not alleged. If men are to be sentenced into the everlasting fire for sins of omission, as they may be called, how can those escape who are guilty of positive sin? A life of inactivity in the Master's cause is a damnable sin.

CHAPTER XXV.

saw we thee a hungered, or athirst, or a stranger, or naked, or sick, or in prison, and did not minister unto thee?

45 Then shall he answer them, saying, Verily I say unto you, Inasmuch as ye did *it* not to one of the least of these, ye did *it* not to me.

46 And these shall go away into everlasting punishment: but the righteous into life eternal.

---

44. Those who have done some good will yet feel that they have done so little that it amounts to nothing; but those that have done none will feel that they have done so much as to constitute a claim on the favor of the Judge.

46. This verse is one of great importance in its bearing upon questions pertaining to the destiny of men. Each of the three prominent words, *punishment, life,* and *everlasting* or *eternal,* has received extended examination. Universalists have striven hard to explain them in consistency with the theory that all men will be saved, Restorationists in consistency with the theory that the wicked will be restored, and Annihilationists in consistency with the theory that the wicked will be put wholly out of existence. We can indicate only the results to which most Christian scholars have been led. An able and exhaustive work upon the general subject, under the title, "Life and Death Eternal," has been written by Prof. Samuel C. Bartlett, D.D., of Chicago Theological Seminary. "The State of the Impenitent Dead" is the title of a valuable work on one branch of the subject, by President Alvah Hovey, D.D., of Newton Theological Institution. Both these works are commended to any who may need additional light. We are indebted to the former work for much that follows. It will be convenient to consider the term *death* in connection with the word *life,* though only its substantial equivalent, *punishment,* is found in the verse before us.

I. *Death, life*—1. Death does not *literally* mean cessation of existence; nor is life, in its lower sense, simply synonymous with existence. 2. These words have a higher sense by which the one (life) denotes a state of *true welfare;* and the other the reverse. 3. In common Scripture use, life is a state of *intimate union with God,* through the Lord Jesus Christ. John 17: 3. This state begins in this world (John 5: 24; 11: 26), but it is completed in the next. The Scriptures never represent life as mere happiness. Life is holiness and consequent felicity. Death is that separation from God in which all the higher faculties of human nature are working falsely and discordantly. It implies unhappiness. It is the extinction, not of the soul, but of the soul's well-being. 4. We can find no trace of any denial by the Jews in the time of Christ, of future punishment, except on the part of those who denied all future existence (the Sadducees). 5. Wicked men (vs. 41) are to become companions of devils. But there is no evidence that devils are to be either restored or annihilated. They (Jude 6) are reserved in everlasting chains under darkness unto the judgment of the great day. They shall be tormented (Rev. 20: 10) day and night forever and ever. 6. *Punishment.*—In vs. 41 this is called *fire.* It is conscious suffering. Annihilation is not conscious suffering. Annihilationists have affirmed that the original for punishment is derived from a word which means *to cut off, to extinguish,* that is, *to annihilate.* But the word has no such meaning anywhere in the Greek language as annihilation. If it is proper to call annihilation punish-

CHAPTER XXVI.

AND it came to pass, when Jesus had finished all these sayings, he said unto his disciples,

2 Ye know that after two days is *the feast of* the pass-

---

ment, which may be justly doubted, it is a punishment which has no duration beyond the instant of infliction.

II. *Everlasting . . . eternal*—Both words are alike in the original, and should have been rendered alike. 1. If the punishment of the wicked is to cease, no logic can prove that the life of the righteous is not also to cease. Common sense teaches that no other than the usual interpretation is possible. 2. As further evidence that the punishment is never to cease, consider that the sin against the Holy Spirit shall not be forgiven, neither in this world, *neither in the world to come* (12: 32); that the chaff is to be burnt up with *unquenchable* fire (3: 12); that Sodom and Gomorrah are set forth for an example, suffering the vengeance of *eternal* fire (Jude 7); that the beast and the false prophet (Rev. 20: 10) are to be tormented day and night *forever*. 3. If the word here rendered *everlasting* does not here mean *continuing without end*, the Greek language, with all its wonderful powers, had no word by which it was possible to express the idea. 4. If the Greek language had none, the English has none; *forever* being as incapable of expressing the idea of endless duration as the Greek word. It is admitted that the Greek word is sometimes applied with latitude to hills, etc., "everlasting hills;" but this no more disproves that the real meaning of the word is endless duration, than the occasional use of the English word *forever* in a limited sense proves that that does not denote endless duration.

The sentiments of this most solemn chapter should be more frequently and earnestly pressed upon men. They are a powerful means of arresting the attention of the impenitent and of strengthening the Christian's sensibility respecting spiritual things. No man can prove future endless punishment to be contrary to reason, but its reasonableness can be but dimly seen by men without the Scriptures. Jesus Christ teaches that the wicked shall go away into everlasting punishment. We can reject the teachings of Christ, if we will, and decide the question by what may seem to be reason, but what in truth is not reason; but in doing so we are guilty of great assumption, and incur fearful risk.

CHAPTER XXVI.

THE INSTITUTION OF THE SUPPER; THE LORD'S PASSION; PETER'S DENIAL.

783 U.C. Tuesday Evening, April 4, A.D. 30.

1. *All these sayings*—Those which Matthew has reported in the two preceding chapters. These "finished" our Lord's public instructions, but, according to John (chs. 14–17), he communicated many very precious thoughts to the apostles after this. While teaching publicly, he suffered privately; his teaching will henceforth be private, his sufferings public.

2. *After two days*—It is supposed to be still Tuesday evening, though some think the words were uttered on Wednesday. Not reckoning the day on which they were spoken, and assuming that Thursday was the 14th of Nisan (April 6), the day to which Jesus referred was Thursday.

Passover—The root of the He-

CHAPTER XXVI.

over, and the Son of man is betrayed to be crucified.

brew word means to *leap over*. "But since, when we jump or step over anything, we do not tread upon it, the word has a secondary meaning, 'to spare,' or to show mercy." The English word well expresses the meaning. See the account of the institution of this first of the three great annual Jewish festivals in Ex. 12. It commemorated the "sparing" of the first-born of the children of Israel when the destroying angel smote the first-born of the Egyptians. "On the tenth day of the month Abib[1] the head of each family was to select from the flock either a lamb or a kid, a male of the first year, without blemish. If his family was too small to eat the whole of the lamb, he was permitted to invite his nearest neighbor to join the party. On the fourteenth day of the month, he was to kill his lamb while the sun was setting. He was then to take the blood in a basin, and with a sprig of hyssop to sprinkle it on the two side-posts and the lintel of the door of the house. The lamb was then thoroughly roasted, whole. It was expressly forbidden that it should be boiled, or that a bone of it should be broken. Unleavened bread and bitter herbs were to be eaten with the flesh. No male who was uncircumcised was to join the company. Each one was to have his loins girt, to hold a staff in his hand, and to have shoes on his feet. He was to eat

[1] Abib was the earlier name of the month; Nisan the later. The opinion of the Talmudists that the word Nisan is of Babylonian origin is not now accepted. It is held that it was "probably borrowed from the Syrians," for the Syrian calendar has names of months "answering" to nearly all the later names of the Hebrew months. The later Jews had not two years, the sacred and the civil, but "two commencements of the year," with six months between them. The sacred commencement or "reckoning" began with Abib or Nisan, at the time of the exodus from Egypt.

3 Then assembled together the chief priests, and the

in haste, and it would seem that he was to stand during the meal. The number of the party was to be calculated as nearly as possible, so that all the flesh of the lamb might be eaten; but if any portion of it happened to remain, it was to be burned in the morning. No morsel of it was to be carried out of the house." Afterward, the lamb was required to be slain in the "national sanctuary," and the blood to be sprinkled on the altar. On the 14th of the month all leaven was put away from the houses. The festival continued seven days. The 15th and the 21st of the month were regarded as days of holy convocation. According to uninspired Jewish authority, when the lamb was to be roasted, a spit made of the wood of the pomegranate was thrust lengthwise through the lamb. Another spit was put transversely through the animal. This fact has been regarded by many preachers and some commentators as symbolical of the crucifixion of Jesus. But no such prominence should be given to the fact; for there is no proof that the Jews of earlier times used the cross-spit. The custom of using it is affirmed by Justin Martyr; but he was not born till ages after the institution of the Passover. "The modern Samaritans roast their paschal lambs in nearly the same manner at this day," and Mr. George Grove, in a letter to Rev. Samuel Clark, the writer of the article on the Passover in Smith's Dictionary, says: "Each lamb has a stake or spit run through him to draw him up by; and to prevent the spit from tearing away through the roast meat with the weight, a cross-piece is put through the lower end of it." It would seem more probable, therefore, as Mr. Clark remarks, that the transverse spit was a mere matter of convenience, and was per-

24*

scribes, and the elders of the people, unto the palace of the high priest, who was called Caiaphas,

'haps never in use among the Jews. "There is no mention of wine in connection with the Passover in the Pentateuch, but the Mishna strictly enjoins that there should never be less than four cups of it provided at the paschal meal even of the poorest Israelite. . . . It was mixed with water as it was drunk."

"The service of praise sung at the Passover is not mentioned in the law. The name" [Hallel] "is contracted from *Hallelujah.* It consisted of the series of Psalms from 113 to 118. The first portion, comprising 113 and 114, was sung in the early part of the meal, and the second part after the fourth cup of wine. This is supposed to be the hymn sung by our Lord and his apostles (Matt. 2: 30; Mark 14: 26)."

3. *Then*—This can scarcely be regarded as determining the exact time. The Sanhedrim, which is the body here meant, may have assembled that evening (Tuesday), or the meeting may not have been held till Wednesday. *Palace of the high priest*—The Sanhedrim had been accustomed to meet in a hall on the southern side of the temple. It is supposed by some that they had ceased to occupy it. It is not necessary to suppose that this was an illegal meeting, because held at the residence of the high priest. By *palace* is here meant the open court around which, according to custom, the house was built. See vs. 69: Now Peter sat *without in the palace;* that is, without in the court. See also Luke 22: 55: And when they had kindled a fire *in the midst of the hall;* that is, in the midst of the court. *The high priest*—The high priest differed from priests in the following particulars: He was anointed with the " precious

4 And consulted that they might take Jesus by subtilty, and kill *him.*

5 But they said, Not on the

ointment;" in addition to articles of apparel which he wore in common with the priests, he wore the breast-plate, the ephod, the robe of the ephod, and the mitre; his duties were different, the most solemn of which was entering the Holy of Holies once a year, on the great day of atonement, and sprinkling the blood of the sin-offering on the mercy-seat, and burning incense within the vail. According to Josephus, there had been from Aaron eighty-three high priests. The name of the last was Phannias, of whom Josephus says that he was such a mere rustic he scarcely knew what the high priesthood meant. The duties of the *priests* were numerous, the most important of which was the offering of the morning and the evening sacrifice. In some periods of Jewish history, the priests were sunk in the lowest immorality. In this connection it may be added, in the words of Rev. Edward Hayes Plumptre, A.M., Chaplain to the Bishop of Norwich, England: "It was the thought of a succeeding age" [succeeding the apostolic, and, therefore, without apostolic authority], "that the old classification of the high priest, priests, and Levites, was reproduced in the bishops, priests, and deacons, of the Christian Church." *Caiaphas*—He was the last high priest but fourteen.

4. *Consulted*—Consulted *together. By subtilty*—By craft. *Take* —Implying force. They had tried to catch him by means of his words; now they purpose to take him by hand-power. These leaders of public sentiment care nothing for the common rights of conscience, and are as ignorant of the true spirit of the old covenant, as the most ignorant of the people.

5. *Not on the feast-day*—Not at

CHAPTER XXVI.

feast *day*, lest there be an uproar among the people.

6 ¶ Now when Jesus was in Bethany, in the house of Simon the leper,

7 There came unto him a woman having an alabaster box of very precious ointment, and poured it on his head as he sat at meat.

---

any time during the festival. The city was full of people, and many of them were so much interested in him, that an arrest, at that time, would be very likely to create an *uproar*, tumult. Planning not to do, is as easily frustrated by God as planning to do. The Pharisees may work freely, but they must work. The wicked cannot always stay the hatching of their own plans.

6. This anointing is reported by John (12: 1) as occurring *six* days before the Passover. Some think that John's narrative anticipates it. We prefer, with others, to regard Matthew and Mark as reporting it later than the true time. There is really nothing in Matthew and Mark which proves these evangelists to have intended to say that it occurred only two days before. They seem to throw the narrative in, as Andrews has expressed it, "parenthetically." Simon *had* been a leper; he was not one then.

7. The incident which follows is a beautiful illustration of the faith that works by love. The woman was Mary, the sister of Martha. John 12: 2, 3. Lazarus, as well as the sisters, was present. *Alabaster*—" The *oriental alabaster* which is so much valued on account of its translucency, and for its variety of colored streakings, red, yellow. grey, etc., . . . is a fibrous carbonate of lime." This has been "long used for various ornamental purposes, such as the fabrication of vases, boxes, etc. The ancients considered alabaster (carbonate of lime) to be the best material in which to preserve their ointments. . . . Pliny tells us that the usual form of these alabaster vessels was long and slender at the top, and round and full at the bottom. He likens them to the long pearls, called *elenchi*, which the Roman ladies suspended from their fingers or dangled from their ears." Alabasters "may have been made, however, of any material suitable for keeping ointment in, glass, silver, gold, etc.," as the "term which originally was limited to boxes made of the box-wood, eventually extended to boxes generally; as we say, an *iron* box, a *gold* box, etc." *Ointment*—In Mark (14: 3) *ointment of spikenard*. "We are much indebted to the late lamented Dr. Royle, for helping clear up doubts that had long existed as to what particular plant furnished the aromatic substance known as 'spikenard.'" Dr. Royle obtained and planted in the East India Company's botanic garden, about thirty miles from the foot of the Himalayan Mountains, certain roots of the *jatamansee*, which was "annually brought from the mountains overhanging the Ganges and the Jumna rivers down to the plains." Upon growing, it proved to be identical with a plant called by the Arabs *Sunbul* (" spica"), and this name was used by Arabian authors as the equivalent of *nard*. It is described by an ancient writer as "having many shaggy spikes growing from one root," and as being found near the neighborhood of the Ganges. *Very precious*—It was worth, the disciples thought (Mark 14: 5), more than three hundred pence (about forty-five dollars); and there is evidence from an ancient writer that their estimate was not too high. John (12: 3) says there was a pound of it. *Poured it on his head*—How much was Mary indebted to Jesus! Her brother Lazarus had been restored

284 MATTHEW.

8 But when his disciples saw *it*, they had indignation, saying, To what purpose *is* this waste?

9 For this ointment might have been sold for much, and given to the poor.

10 When Jesus understood *it*, he said unto them, Why trouble ye the woman? for she hath wrought a good work upon me.

11 For ye have the poor always with you; but me ye have not always.

12 For in that she hath poured this ointment on my body, she did *it* for my burial.

13 Verily I say unto you, Wheresoever this gospel shall be preached in the whole world, *there* shall also this, that this woman hath done, be told for a memorial of her.

14 ¶ Then one of the twelve, called Judas Iscariot, went unto the chief priests,

15 And saith *unto them*, What will ye give me, and I will deliver him unto you? And they covenanted with him for thirty pieces of silver.

---

to life, and she herself had been led into a deep knowledge of spiritual things by the Lord's instructions. Simon, who may have been cured of the leprosy by Jesus, must have deeply sympathized, and Martha and Lazarus also, in Mary's act. It may have been done as an expression of *their* love also. *Sat at meat*—Reclined.

8, 9. Judas (John 12: 4-6) was the leader in showing this evil spirit. As manifested by him it was characteristic; as shown by the others, it was incidental. In him it was hypocrisy; in them it was weakness. All the money given for the Christian cause at home and abroad is wasted, say some; money given in support of foreign missions is wasted, say others. But those who shut the door of their hearts in the face of God's poor in heathen lands, do not open it very widely for his poor at home.

10, 11. *When Jesus understood it*—Conveys an erroneous impression. It should be, *And Jesus knowing it. Why trouble*, etc.—How lovingly he shields her! *A good work*—Not that he needed it, but he welcomed it as an expression of her piety. Christ is not in any inherent, essential need of the money of his people. He *can* accomplish the conversion of the world without it, but he welcomes their gifts as expressions of their love.

12. *Did it for my burial*—Not for his burial, but to prepare him for his burial. It was the custom of the Jews to prepare the dead body for burial by anointing it, or putting spices in the folds of the grave-clothes, or of the bandages with which the clothes were fastened. Does Jesus mean to say that Mary did this *intentionally, consciously*, with reference to his burial? It is difficult to decide whether that was his meaning or not. He may have meant only this, that her act admitted that interpretation by himself.

13. How literally is this prophecy continually fulfilling! *A memorial*—How much that little alabaster vase has done to perpetuate the fragrance of Mary's name! Judas' name will live as long as Mary's, but how different the ground of his fame! Fame, however, was not a part of Mary's motive.

14, 15. *Then*—Not immediately after the incident just related, for that incident, as has already been remarked, is probably introduced by Matthew later than the time of its

CHAPTER XXVI.

16 And from that time he sought opportunity to betray him.

17 ¶ Now the first *day* of the *feast of* unleavened bread the disciples came to Jesus, saying

---

actual occurrence; but soon after the assembling of the Sanhedrim on Tuesday evening, narrated with the consultation in vv. 3-5. *What will ye give?*— *What will you do it for?* would have been a very customary manner of replying. But they knew their man. They looked upon Jesus as no better than a slave, and so seem to have fixed their own price, which was the price at which slaves had in former times been valued. Ex. 21 : 32. Compare Zech. 11 : 12, 13. Joseph also was sold for twenty pieces of silver. Thus, as Dr. Schaff remarks, was committed by the Sanhedrim "a deliberate insult to our Lord, who died the death of a slave and a malefactor that he might redeem us from the slavery and eternal misery of sin." *Pieces of silver*—" Probably (though not certainly) the *sacred shekel*, heavier than the common shekel, and hence told out by weight."—*Conant*. *Covenanted*—Not, as Barnes and others, *agreed to give him*, but *weighed out*. It has been thought that fifteen dollars was too small a sum to make it possible to account for the terrible act of which Judas was guilty by referring it to his love of money. It is a matter of actual and reliable record that he did deliver the Lord to his enemies for just that sum; but avarice may not have been his only impulse. Conscious of wickedness, he must have become prejudiced against Jesus long before; for our Lord had frequently given utterance to thoughts which Judas must have believed to be aimed at himself. Prejudice quickened into indignation under the Lord's rebuke in the house of Simon, and love of money combined to force him to the fatal act. No apology should be made for him. Jesus made none; the apostles none.

16. *Sought opportunity*—Such as the absence of the people would give him.

Thursday, April 6, A.D. 30.

Concerning the manner in which our Lord spent Wednesday, we have no means of knowing. "We can well believe that some part of it was spent alone, that he might enjoy that full communion with God which he had so earnestly sought in the midst of his active labors, and which was now doubly dear to him in view of his speedy death. Some part of it, also, was doubtless devoted to his disciples, giving them such counsel and encouragement as was demanded by the very peculiar and trying circumstances in which they were placed."—*Andrews*.

17. *First day . . . unleavened bread*—Thursday, the 14th of Nisan (April 6), the day before our Lord was crucified. Whether Jesus celebrated the Passover at the usual time is a question concerning which there has not been entire agreement. The question could not have arisen had not John used expressions which "seem to imply that on Friday, the day of our Lord's crucifixion, the regular and legal passover had not yet been eaten, but was still to be celebrated on the evening after that day." It has been shown, however, we think, that all the expressions which John has used may be fairly understood as not in the least conflicting with the theory that the Lord ate the Passover at the legal time. The Jews began to *prepare* for the Passover on Thursday, Nisan 14, by removing from their houses all leaven, and, therefore, in popular language, *that* day was called the first day of unleavened bread, though strictly speaking the feast of unleavened bread did not begin till the time of the paschal

unto him, Where wilt thou that we prepare for thee to eat the passover?

18 And he said, Go into the city to such a man, and say unto him, The Master saith, My time is at hand; I will keep the passover at thy house with my disciples.

19 And the disciples did as Jesus had appointed them; and they made ready the passover.

20 Now when the even was come, he sat down with the twelve.

21 And as they did eat, he said, Verily I say unto you, that one of you shall betray me.

---

supper, that is, in the evening, at the beginning of the 15th. The attempt to throw discredit either upon John or upon the other evangelists by proving that they positively contradict each other in respect to the time of our Lord's crucifixion and the Passover is a failure. *That we prepare*—The reference is not, as some think, to the place *where*, for, according to Luke (22: 12, 13), the chamber would be found already prepared. They were to slay the lamb, procure the unleavened bread and the bitter herbs. The following striking description is by Starke, in "Lange's Commentary:" "A crowd of Israelites was received into the court, the gates were shut, the trumpets sounded. The householders slew their lambs. The priests formed a row which extended to the altar, received the blood in silver basins, which they passed on from one to another; and those who stood nearest the altar poured it out at its feet, whence it flowed subterraneously into the brook Kedron. The householder lifted the slain lamb to a hook on a pillar, took off its skin, and removed the fat. This last the priest burned on the altar. The householder uttered a prayer, and carried the lamb to his house bound in its skin. When the first crowd departed, another followed, and so forth."

18. *To such a man*—Various reasons have been assigned for silence relative to the man's name; it is useless to surmise when we have no possible means of knowing. *The city*—Jerusalem. They were then in Bethany. *My time*—Of suffering, not, as some say, of observing the Passover, making *my* emphatic, and therefore affording proof that he observed it before the usual time. The man was perhaps a friend to the Saviour, but accommodations were freely rendered to those who came to the city for such a purpose. It does not appear that Jesus had made arrangement with the man beforehand. His omniscience must be supposed, which is still more manifest when we examine the corresponding passages in Mark and Luke. Compare with this the account of sending two disciples for the ass (21: 2), and of sending Peter to the sea for "a piece of money" (17: 27).

20. *Sat down*—Reclined. It has been generally held that the law required the Jews to eat the Passover *standing*, Ex. 12: 11; and Lange considers it remarkable that the Jews ventured to modify the legal prescription. But Prof. Bush sees no evidence that the directions in Ex. 12: 11 were held to be binding in the subsequent observance. The directions were appropriate to the first observance, but not so afterward; and from the very fact that Jesus reclined, it may be inferred that he considered the standing posture as required only at the first observance. We, therefore, cannot see with Dr. Wordsworth in the Saviour's reclining posture "proof

CHAPTER XXVI.

22 And they were exceeding sorrowful, and began every one of them to say unto him, Lord, is it I?

23 And he answered and said, He that dippeth *his* hand with me in the dish, the same shall betray me.

24 The Son of man goeth as it is written of him: but woe unto that man by whom the Son of man is betrayed! it had

---

that positive commands of a *ceremonial kind*, even of divine origin, are not immutable if they are not in order to a *permanent* end," though it may be admitted, with Dr. Schaff, that Dr. Wordsworth's remark is "liberal," and "doubly to be appreciated as coming from a strict Episcopalian."

22. The additions by the other evangelists to Matthew's account of the Supper will be considered in their place. *Lord, is it I?*—Judas knows what he has already agreed to do, and therefore *his* question adds to the evidence of his hypocrisy. As asked by the others, it shows remarkable simplicity and sensitiveness of spirit, and entire ignorance of the purpose of Judas.

23. *That dippeth*—"That has dipped; that is, one who has been accustomed to do it, who has been admitted to the most intimate social relations with me. 'My own familiar friend, . . . that did eat of my bread.' Ps. 41:9."—*Conant*. But the Lord refers not to the general intercourse which Judas has had with him, but to the special act of eating with him at the Passover. As has been remarked, it would have been no answer whatever to the question, *Is it I?* for the other disciples had "been admitted to the most intimate social relations" with Jesus. See Mark 14:20: It is one of the twelve *that dippeth with me in the dish*. "What is meant here was the sop of *charoseth*, which was prepared of dates, figs, etc., and which was of a brick color (in remembrance of the Egyptian bricks)." "In ancient Egypt, and also in Judea, guests at the table handled their food with the fingers, but spoons were used for soup or other liquid food when required. . . . To pick out a delicate morsel and hand it to a friend is esteemed" [in modern Egypt] "a compliment, and to refuse such an offering is contrary to good manners. Judas dipping his hand in the same dish with our Lord was showing especial friendliness and intimacy."—*Smith's Dictionary*.

24. *Goeth*—To death. *As it is written*—That the Messiah was to die had been often foretold. Isa. 53: 4-9; Dan. 9: 26. Luke (22: 22) says: The Son of man goeth *as it was determined;* and Peter did not hesitate to say in his sermon on the Day of Pentecost (Acts 2: 23), that Jesus had been delivered by the *determinate* (established) *counsel and foreknowledge of God*. See also Acts 4: 28, which is very striking. Counsel is purpose. Purpose is the natural antecedent of foreknowledge. God does not purpose because he foreknows, but he foreknows because he purposes. But God's purposes do not imply the doctrine taught by Dr. Emmons and a very few others, that God creates sinful volitions in the hearts of men. That doctrine is neither taught in the Bible, nor approved by reason. Judas could have chosen *not* to betray the Lord. This is evidence that his choice to betray him was not compelled. "Foreknowledge," says Dr. Whedon, "does not force or compel an act, or make it less free than if it were wholly unforeknown." Certainly not; but the remark might have been more comprehensive; for the *purpose* of God must be taken into the account. It is equally true that God's *purpose*

been good for that man if he had not been born.

25 Then Judas, which betrayed him, answered and said, Master, Is it I? He said unto him, Thou hast said.

26 ¶ And as they were eating, Jesus took bread, and blessed *it*, and brake *it*, and gave *it* to the disciples, and said, Take, eat; this is my body.

---

does not make an act less free than if it were wholly unpurposed. God purposed to permit Judas to betray the Lord of life. Judas purposed to betray. But the purpose of Judas to betray, and the purpose of God to permit him to betray, were two perfectly distinct acts. The purpose of Judas was sinful. The purpose of God to permit the purpose of Judas was holy. It was born of infinite compassion toward a race of sinners. Dr. Nast (Methodist) makes an extended quotation from Stier in explanation of this verse, in which are the following words: "And the event signified by this emphatic *as*—the betrayal of Christ by one of his chosen ones—was recorded too, as it was ordained (compare Acts 2 : 23 ; 4 : 28)." *But woe*—God's purpose, then, did not lessen the guilt of Judas. The word is pregnant with compassion and with condemnation. *Good for that man*—Calling this a proverb makes nothing in support of Universalism or Annihilation. It cannot be that Jesus Christ would have used the words as a mere rhetorical exaggeration; for the hour was one of infinite moment.

25. *Is it I?*—Conscious guilt here aims by impudence to save itself from exposure. *Master*—Rabbi in the original. Its use by Judas indicates, perhaps, an assumption of reverence. *Thou hast said*—A Jewish form of affirming. "The day of salvation closed; the hour of the visitation of divine mercy expired; the angels of peace sorrowfully removed from his side, and Satan triumphantly entered into him. The saying of the Saviour, ' One of you is a devil,' was now verified." —*Krummacher*.

26. *As they were eating*—While the paschal meal was in progress. Up to this point Jesus must be supposed to have observed the Passover according to the usual forms, but here to have departed from them, and to have " elevated " the paschal supper into "the Lord's Supper." Briefly stated, the paschal service was as follows, the use of wine not being a requirement of the law. That part of the service had been introduced by the Jews without divine authority.

1. A blessing;
2. Wine (first cup);
3. Washing hands;
4. Eating bitter herbs;
5. Wine (second cup);
6. The feast explained;
7. Singing Ps. 113, 114;
8. Eating unleavened bread;
9. Eating the lamb;
10. Wine (third cup, " cup of blessing ");
11. Singing Ps. 115-118;
12. Wine (fourth cup);
13. Singing Ps. 120-138;
14. Wine (fifth cup, often omitted).

Took bread—This may be supposed to have been done between the acts which in the programme are numbered 9 and 10. *This is my body*—In the ninth century Paschasius Radbert, abbot of a monastery, began the advocacy of the doctrine "that by virtue of the consecration, by a miracle of almighty power, the substance of the bread and wine became converted into the substance of the body and blood of Christ." He insisted that in the bread and wine was the same body " as that in which Christ was born, suffered, arose, and ascended to heaven," the change being effected at the utterance by the priest of the

27 And he took the cup, and gave thanks, and gave *it* to them saying, Drink ye all of it;

---

words of consecration. The germ of this falsehood was of much earlier origin. Even Martin Luther taught that the communicant actually partakes of the body and blood of Christ in their "glorified state," though he rejected the Romish view that the bread and wine cease to be bread and wine. Luther's doctrine is called *consubstantiation*. According to Luther, even an unbeliever receives the real body of Christ in its spiritual state. Zwingle, a contemporary of Luther, taught "that the body and blood of Christ were not *really* present in the eucharist; and that the bread and wine were no more than external *signs*, or *symbols*, designed to excite in the minds of Christians the remembrance of the sufferings and death of the divine Saviour, and of the benefits which arise from it."—*Mosheim*. False views of the Lord's Supper still prevail very widely in the Christian world; in the Episcopal church as well as in the Romish, Greek and Lutheran. Dr. Pusey distinctly avows, in the preface of his once celebrated sermon on the Eucharist, his acceptance of the *literal* sense of the words, This is my body; that is, he believes the consecrated elements to become, by virtue of Christ's consecrating words, "truly and really, yet spiritually and in an ineffable way, his body and blood." But, *This is my body*, can no more mean, this bread has been *changed into* my body, than the words, *My body is bread*, can mean, My body has been *changed into* bread. Both logic and common sense teach that *is* here means *represents:* This represents my body; or, this symbolizes my body. *Take, eat*—They were not merely to *look* at the bread, even after it had been broken, and so had been made to represent the breaking, bruising, suffering, dying, of the Saviour's body, but they must *take it and eat it;* thus symbolically renewing that appropriation of the atonement which they are supposed to have made already, and without which they would have no right to the Supper. It is to be feared that many communicants, even in the most evangelical churches, are so feeble in Christian character, that in eating the bread and drinking the wine they do little more than to make an effort to remember the historical fact that Christ died for sinners.

27. *Took the cup*—This was probably in place of the third cup of the Passover. *All of it*—Not all the wine, but all ye disciples. *All* must not be restricted to the apostles, for (vs. 28) the blood was shed for *many*. As the Saviour's blood was shed for many, that which symbolized it was to be drunk by many. In this respect the apostles represent all the members of a scripturally organized Christian church. Yet the Church of Rome dared, A. D. 1418, in the Council of Constance, to enact that only the officiating priests should partake of the cup, endeavoring to reconcile the laity to the law by affirming that the blood of Christ was contained in bread! The Council of Trent decreed, July 16, 1562: "Whosoever shall affirm that the holy Catholic Church had not just grounds and reasons for restricting the laity and non-officiating clergy to communion in the species of bread only, or that she had erred therein: LET HIM BE ACCURSED." The object of denying the cup to the laity was, doubtless, to make greater distinction between the priests and the people, and so to add to the power of the priests. *Drink*—Looking at the symbol would not suffice. Drinking represents the appropriation of the blood of Christ, by faith, as the atonement for sin. The arti-

28 For this is my blood of the new testament, which is shed for many for the remission of sins.

---

cle to be drunk was wine (vs. 29). Whether the article in common use in Palestine in the days of our Lord was a fermented article, and whether in our own times, in oriental countries, by *wine* is meant, always, a fermented article, are questions which are discussed with scholarship and candor in the "Bibliotheca Sacra" of January, 1869, by Rev. Dr. T. Laurie, formerly a missionary of the American Board of Commissioners for Foreign Missions. Avowing himself, as practising on the principle of total abstinence from intoxicating liquors as a beverage, and as standing, both in the pulpit and at the ballot-box, among the friends of prohibitory law, Dr. Laurie maintains that "unfermented wine is unknown in the Bible or in Bible lands," and that fermentation is essential to the juice of the vine becoming wine. The churches ought to provide the purest article of wine possible, and not wine which, in the language of Dr. Laurie, "has been enforced by the addition of distilled liquors." Assuming that a church has done the best it can in this respect, the communicant who makes *a show* of obeying the dying command of Christ, *Drink ye all of it*, by applying the cup to his lips without partaking, offers, however unintentionally, an indignity to the King of heaven.

28. *This is*—This represents, or symbolizes. *The new testament*—new covenant. A covenant is an agreement between two parties, in which each pledges himself to do a given thing on a given condition. The difference between God and man is so great that this meaning of the word seems not to be strictly allowable as applied to God and man; for all that man may promise to do must proceed from what God has already promised to do for man. There are two great covenants; the Mosaic and the Christian. The former is the old, the latter the new. See Jer. 31: 31-34; Heb. 8: 6-13; Gal. 3: 17; 4: 24. They are not called the old and the new in consequence of difference in time. In this respect, the new is as old as the old. The new covenant was not distinctly and fully *developed* till about the time of our Lord's death. The fact stated in the verse may be expressed thus: For this wine represents my blood as the ratification of the blessings of the Christian dispensation, which blood is shed for *many*, for a great multitude. It is not the intention to express a definite number, whether all or less than all. *For the remission of sins*—How plainly is it taught that the death of Christ was *vicarious*, that is. borne in place of the death which our sins deserve!

The Romanists call the celebration of the Lord's Supper *Mass* and *High Mass*, the latter being more public and accompanied with music. The Council of Trent, Sept. 17, 1562, declared "that in the eucharist a true propitiatory sacrifice was offered for sin, in the same way as when Christ offered up himself as a sacrifice on the cross," and the Council consigned to damnation all who should deny it. According to Romish authors, the bread or wafer is turned into God, and so the priests, by using the words of consecration, can *create the Creator!* Raising the consecrated wafer, that is, God, at the celebration of the mass, so high that all the people can see it, and worshipping it as "*The Host*," that is, a victim, from the Latin *hostia*, was first ordered by the Pope Honorius. What "damnable heresies" has an apostate church not brought in! The epistle to the Hebrews (7: 27) says, *Who needeth not daily, as those high priests, to offer up sacrifice, first for his own*

CHAPTER XXVI. 291

29 But 1 say unto you, I will not drink henceforth of this fruit of the vine, until that day when I drink it new with you in my Father's kingdom.

30 And when they had sung a hymn, they went out into the mount of Olives.

31 Then saith Jesus unto them, All ye shall be offended because of me this night: for it is written, I will smite the Shepherd, and the sheep of the flock shall be scattered abroad.

32 But after I am risen again, I will go before you into Galilee.

33 Peter answered and said unto him, Though all *men* shall be offended because of thee, *yet* will I never be offended.

34 Jesus said unto him, Ver-

---

sins, and then for the people's: for this he did once, when he offered up himself. See also Heb. 9: 25-28. Whether Judas partook of the Lord's Supper will be considered in the notes on John. It will appear, we think, that he did not. This is the opinion of Andrews, Owen, Whedon, Ellicott, Barnes, Olshausen, Neander, Lange, and Nast. That unregenerate persons may partake of the Lord's Supper is still held by a very large majority of the Christian world; but it is an unscriptural and baneful doctrine. It grows very naturally, however, out of the doctrine of infant baptism.

29. *Until that day when I drink it new*, etc.—Too much mysteriousness has been attributed by some to these words. We understand our Lord as saying that he will not again unite with them in this world in the Holy Supper, but that he will unite with them in observing it in heaven; but of course in saying this last he speaks figuratively, meaning that he will participate with them there in spiritual joys. We proceed upon the supposition that Jesus partook of the Lord's Supper, and we see no more difficulty in his doing so than in his being baptized.

30. *Sung an hymn*—Probably Ps. 113-118. Meditate upon Jesus singing sinless songs in this sinful world. His lips, untouched by a breath of pollution, unite with lips that have uttered unseemly words of ambition and indignation. The songs which Jesus sung were not sorrowful songs, but were cheerful, exultant, expressive of trust. If there is a spot on earth where holy cheerfulness, thanksgiving, praise, should be poured forth with lavish fulness and richness, it is the spot where we celebrate the Redeemer's love. Our Lord sung *in the night*. "Joy wading in tears!" Jesus sung songs of joy when walking deliberately into the darkest cloud of sorrow that ever fell upon men. It is human to sing in the hour of joy; it is divine to sing in the hour of sorrow.

31. *Offended because of me*—Will be offended *in* me; I shall become a stumbling-block to you. *Written* —In Zech. 13: 7. The words seem to refer directly to the Messiah. The prophecy that he would meet them in Galilee was literally fulfilled.

33. *Though all men*—Though all his fellow-disciples. His self-confidence was great, yet it should not be forgotten that if Judas would not have said so, it would have been through *want of love* to his teacher.

34. *Thrice*—This word must have given terrible sharpness to the Saviour's affirmation. *Before the cock crow*—The Talmud, the Jewish Commentary, in praise of which so much has recently been said by those who have little regard for the New Testament, affirms "that the inhabitants of Jerusalem, and the priests everywhere, were forbidden to keep fowls, because they scratched

MATTHEW.

ily I say unto thee, That this night, before the cock crow, thou shalt deny me thrice.

55 Peter said unto him, Though I should die with thee, yet will I not deny thee. Likewise also said all the disciples.

36 ¶ Then cometh Jesus with them unto a place called Gethsemane, and saith unto the disciples, Sit ye here, while I go and pray yonder.

37 And he took with him Peter and the two sons of Zebedee, and began to be sorrowful and very heavy.

38 Then saith he unto them, My soul is exceeding sorrowful, even unto death: tarry ye here, and watch with me.

39 And he went a little further, and fell on his face, and prayed, saying, O my Father, if it be possible, let this cup

---

up unclean worms," but, as Dr. Hackett remarks, Lightfoot "has shown that the Talmud is not consistent with itself on this point." Besides, there were Romans in the city, and they could have kept owls in spite of the Jews. These domestic fowls are now very common in Palestine. *Deny*—That he knew him, which, of course, involved the idea of denying that he had faith in him.

36. *A place*—A field. The field was called *Gethsemane*. From John (18: 1) we learn that it was over the brook Kedron. It is called by John a garden, but by this we must not understand a garden in our sense of the word. Tradition places it on the western slope of the Mount of Olives, "about one-half or three-fourths of a mile English from the walls of Jerusalem." It is now surrounded by a "low wall, covered with stucco." Thomson would place the Gethsemane of the Scriptures "several hundred yards to the north-east of the present Gethsemane." Dr. Hackett considers the present inclosure as fulfilling all the conditions of the Scripture narrative. "We may sit down there," he says, "and read the narrative of what the Saviour endured for our redemption, and feel assured that we are near the place where he prayed, 'saying, Father, not my will, but thine be done,' and where, 'being in an agony, he sweat, as it were, great drops of blood, falling down to the ground.'" *Sit ye here*—The Redeemer requested eight of the disciples to remain behind, just inside the inclosure probably, that he might go further in and pray.

37–38. *Peter and the two sons*—The three whom he took with him upon the Mount of Transfiguration, must now be near him as he descends into the "valley of tears." *Exceeding sorrowful*—Girt round with sorrow. He was a man of sorrows; but sorrows such as even he had never felt now press upon him with almost fatal weight. *Unto death*—Doubtless, he would have died before he arrived at the cross, had he not been strengthened from above. Luke 22: 43. His sorrows are too heavy to be borne in the presence of even his three favorite disciples, and yet are too heavy to be borne unless they are near. He therefore requests them to tarry where they are, which will be sufficiently near to answer the demand of human nature. What a change from the Hallelujah of the Supper! *Watch with me*—The suffering Messiah could not ask his disciples to pray with him, much less for him.

39. *A little further*—Into the garden. It was meet that the God-man should suffer alone. Jesus separated himself first from the eight, then from the three, and on the cross he was separated in a profoundly mysterious sense from the

CHAPTER XXVI.

pass from me: nevertheless, not as I will, but as thou *wilt.*

40 And he cometh unto the disciples, and findeth them asleep, and saith unto Peter, What, could ye not watch with me one hour?

41 Watch and pray, that ye enter not into temptation: the spirit indeed *is* willing, but the flesh *is* weak.

42 He went away again the second time, and prayed, saying, O my Father, if this cup may not pass away from me, except I drink it, thy will be done.

43 And he came and found

Father. *Fell on his face*—Luke (22: 41) says that he *kneeled down.* —" The Saviour, habituated to the customary forms of worship, may have bowed his knees, and, without changing that position, may also have stooped forward, and inclined his face to the earth." Such changes, according to Dr. Hackett, would have been in accordance with the custom of worshippers in the East at the present day. *This cup*—Does he refer to the death of the cross? or only to the agonies which he is now suffering? There is a difference of opinion. Notice the word *this,* as if it were *the cup which he was then drinking.* But on the other hand should be considered the words in John 12: 27: Father, save me from *this hour; but for this cause came I unto this hour.* Here, the entire sufferings of Christ seem to be included. *Not as I will*—His soul is girt round with sorrow, but his will bends not. As his Father wills, so he wills. Omniscience itself saw not the least touch of disharmony between the will of even the man Jesus and the will of the Father. Some choose to say it was the *divine* will of Christ that remained firm, while his *human* will shrunk from suffering. But it was the *soul,* that is, the *sensibilities,* of Jesus that shrunk. If it is proper to distinguish between the human will and the divine will, the human will remained as firm as the divine, and so in this respect, as well as in others, he is an example to his followers. As to the cause of his sufferings, the only explanation is to be found in Isa. 53: 4, 5. He suffered as a substitute for sinners. The supposition that his agony in Gethsemane was caused by fear of the physical sufferings that awaited him on the cross is no explanation whatever. A being of his moral courage could have gone through the anticipation of those sufferings as calmly, to say the least, as his own followers, in subsequent ages, anticipated the bodily sufferings of martyrdom.

40. *Asleep*—This would show astounding insensibility, were it not that, according to Luke (22:45), they were sleeping for sorrow. It is remarkable that these very men slept, or were heavy with sleep, on the Mount of Transfiguration. Men less sorrowful, or more so, might not have slept. Men more interested, or less so, in what was taking place on the mount might not have slept. "Higher spiritual influences and transactions almost overpowered the feeble flesh. Yet the Lord expressly declares that the disciples were morally responsible for being in such a condition. An analogous influence we see under preaching. Sermons stimulate some, and send others to sleep, according to their dispositions and preparation."—*Lange.* *What!* This makes the rebuke too sharp. *So ye could not;* or, *ye could not then.* *One hour*—Definite time for indefinite. Observe that Peter, who had made the strongest professions, is the one addressed.

41. *Temptation*—God was apply-

them asleep again: for their eyes were heavy.

44 And he left them, and went away again, and prayed the third time, saying the same words.

45 Then cometh he to his disciples, and saith unto them, Sleep on now, and take *your* rest: behold, the hour is at hand, and the Son of man is betrayed into the hands of sinners.

46 Rise, let us be going: behold, he is at hand that doth betray me.

47 ¶ And while he yet spake, lo, Judas, one of the twelve, came, and with him a great multitude with swords and staves, from the chief priests and elders of the people.

---

ing to them a *test of character*. That test, should they fail to watch and pray, would become a temptation, an occasion of fall. There is enough within us, and enough without us, to make tests become temptations. See more concerning temptation in the note on 6: 13. *The spirit . . . the flesh*—Some say, *mind* and *body;* others, that higher spiritual nature which is the result of grace, and that lower nature which is ever struggling against the higher and aiming to secure the control. Neither view need be received exclusive of the other. The body has inherent weakness, which disqualifies it for long-continued exertion, and this natural difficulty is increased by sin. By its very constitution, the immaterial nature is qualified to do what the body cannot do, and this qualification is greatly strengthened when the spirit is brought under the power of grace. The words are a rebuke, but how tender! how much like a loving apology! *Willing*—This is not strong enough. Jesus means to say that the spirit is ready, eager.

45. *Sleep on*—The direction may be ironical, or it may be an actual permission to continue sleeping, yet, in a moment, he tells them to awake. *The hour*—The crisis which he had so often foretold to the disciples, and which is indicated in the next clause. *Of sinners*—Probably all that were concerned in the final tragedy, whether Jews or Romans.

46. *He is at hand*—"The best explanation of this language," says Dr. Hackett, "is that his watchful eye, at that moment, caught sight of Judas and his accomplices as they issued from one of the eastern gates, or turned round the northern or southern corner of the walls, in order to descend into the valley. The night, with its moon then near its full, and about the beginning of April, must have been clear, or if exceptionally dark, the torches (John 18: 3) would have left no doubt as to the object of such a movement at that unseasonable hour."

47. *While he yet spake*—Probably an hour or two after midnight. *One of the twelve*—From such a designation Judas can never escape. *One of the twelve!* Let the words ring in the ears of him, who, in our own times, turns away from his brethren in the ministry and from Christ! Judas needed no guide. Often had he been there. Says John (18: 2), *And Judas also, which betrayed him, knew the place: for Jesus ofttimes resorted thither with his disciples. A great multitude*—1. The band (John 18: 12); which Robinson believes to have been Levites who performed the menial offices of the temple and kept watch by night, and were under the command of a "captain." To the interpretation, "a band of Roman soldiers," he objects that these would have led Jesus to their own officers, and not to the chief priests. But would they have done that, had their officers

CHAPTER XXVI. 295

48 Now he that betrayed him gave them a sign, saying, Whomsoever I shall kiss, that same is he; hold him fast.

49 And forthwith he came to Jesus, and said, Hail, Master; and kissed him.

50 And Jesus said unto him, Friend, wherefore art thou come? Then came they, and laid hands on Jesus, and took him.

51 And, behold, one of them which were with Jesus stretched out *his* hand, and drew his sword, and struck a servant of the high priest, and smote off his ear.

---

been solicited by the priests to aid them by a detachment of soldiers under pretence of keeping down a tumult? If it was a band of soldiers, it was doubtless a detachment of the Roman cohort kept in the Tower of Antonia. 2. Assuming that by band is to be understood Roman soldiers, to this must be added the temple-watch. 3. Chief priests and servants. Luke 22: 50, 52. *Staves*—Clubs. How useless such a multitude, and that armed, to take the Lamb of God!

49. *Kissed him*—In the original the term is stronger than that used in vs. 48. The English has no word that exactly expresses it. It means that he kissed him *very tenderly*. To the priests and the soldiers the word would have been needlessly expressive. It was enough for their purpose and his too, to agree *to kiss* him; and, besides, expressing himself in the stronger manner would have made him in his own eyes, and in theirs, ridiculous. Judas was not a fool. His hypocrisy, however, is seen to be the more intensely diabolical, in that he showed greater affectionateness than was necessary to point out Jesus to the captors. It was thus that he attempted, notwithstanding what had passed at the paschal supper, to make the holy Redeemer believe that he was not privy to the designs of the armed band. In *this* he played the fool. Great crimes are woven into surprising inconsistencies. Jesus did not refuse the kiss. What an example to the man who refuses the hand of him who has offered him some real or imaginary slight! How void of passion is this inspired report of the treachery of Judas! Contrast it with the style in which it is spoken of by uninspired men: "Villain;" "diabolical betrayer;" "the basest of mankind;" "infamous purpose;" "nothing so detestable and vile;" "a masterpiece of the devil." The perfect freedom of the evangelists from all personal indignation in their narratives of the treatment of their Master is a strong proof that they were writing under the inspiration of the Holy Spirit.

50. *Friend*—Though this word may be a little stronger than the original, yet the use of even the original word is evidence of the Saviour's meekness and gentleness. *Wherefore*, etc. — The meaning which some have given, *Do that for which thou art here*, would not be generally admitted.

51. *One of them*—According to John (18: 10) it was Peter. Matthew, Mark, and Luke withhold the name. As their Gospels were written much earlier than John's, it has been supposed that they omitted the name through motives of prudence. It is not impossible that such was the fact, but it seems improbable, inasmuch as the man's ear was immediately healed, and many years elapsed between the act and the writing of Matthew's narrative, without Peter's arrest. *A servant*—The high priest's own servant, not one of the servants of the Sanhedrim, and therefore the original says, **the**

52 Then said Jesus unto him, Put up again thy sword into his place: for all they that take the sword shall perish with the sword.

53 Thinkest thou that I cannot now pray to my Father, and he shall presently give me more than twelve legions of angels?

54 But how then shall the Scriptures be fulfilled, that thus it must be?

55 In that same hour said Jesus to the multitudes, Are ye come out as against a thief with swords and staves for to take me? I sat daily with you teaching in the temple, and ye laid no hold on me.

56 But all this was done, that the Scriptures of the prophets

---

servant. Only John mentions his name (18: 10), which was Malchus. "This servant was probably stepping forward at the moment with others to handcuff or pinion Jesus, when the zealous Peter struck at him with the sword. The blow was undoubtedly meant to be more effective, but reached only the ear. It may be, as Stier remarks, that the man, seeing the danger, threw his head or body to the left, so as to expose the right ear more than the other."—*Dr. Hackett, in Smith's Dictionary.* Lange says: "Peter showed by his first stroke that he was no soldier." But if Stier is right, Peter was a better soldier just then than saint. Peter's act was inexcusable, but, as originating in an undercurrent of love, it stands in striking contrast with the act of Judas.

52. *Put up thy sword*—From these words it has been inferred, not unreasonably, that Peter still stood stretched for another blow. *That take . . . shall perish*—This is a general truth, but is intended primarily for this case. Had Peter continued to use the sword, he would undoubtedly have lost his life in the hand-to-hand fight which would have followed. It is true that in all times he who uses the sword must expect to perish by the sword; but we cannot see with some that this passage "justifies capital punishment as a measure of just retribution for murder in the hands of the civil magistrate." Capital punishment can be justified, but this passage is very slender proof in its support. The words, however, as Lange holds, condemn "the resort to all carnal measures on the part of the Church, which is a spiritual body, and should only use spiritual weapons."

53. There was before Jesus one of three courses: 1. He could have gone forward in suffering; 2. He could have resorted with his disciples to the sword; 3. He could have depended on help from his Father by means of angels. Had he avoided the first, it would not have been necessary to do the second; for prayer to his Father would have brought to his aid twelve legions (seventy-two thousand) of angels, which fact Peter had overlooked. Human help was not needed. The angels who had worshipped the Son (Heb. 1: 6) would not have hesitated to fly to his deliverance. *Legion*—Six thousand Roman soldiers.

54–56. God's eternal purpose, fragrant with love, lies at the basis of all the Old Testament prophecies relative to the sufferings of Christ. *Thief*—robber. *Teaching* —Very different from robbing. *Laid no hold*—But not for want of inclination. *All . . . forsook*—One of the most saddening features of the narrative. One betrays; one denies; all forsake. The first act was followed by suicide; the second by bitter weeping; the third by

CHAPTER XXVI.

might be fulfilled. Then all the disciples forsook him, and fled.

57 ¶ And they that had laid hold on Jesus led *him* away to Caiaphas the high priest, where the scribes and the elders were assembled.

58 But Peter followed him afar off unto the high priest's palace, and went in, and sat with the servants, to see the end.

59 Now the chief priests, and elders, and all the council sought false witness against Jesus, to put him to death;

60 But found none: yea, though many false witnesses came, *yet* found they none. At the last came two false witnesses,

61 And said, This *fellow* said, I am able to destroy the temple of God, and to build it in three days.

---

permanent, unconquerable fidelity.

57. *To Caiaphas*—Not to him first, but to Annas, father-in-law of Caiaphas. John 18: 13. The preliminary examination before Annas is omitted by all the evangelists but John. This verse records a night meeting of the Sanhedrim; another was held on the following morning (Friday). 27: 1.

58. *Afar off*—Yes, but he followed him, which is, more than many do who once professed to be his. *Afar off*—Too far, but not, like some, so far that he could not see him. *The high priest's palace* —The court, the interior, open space. "Besides the *mandarah*, some houses in Cairo have an apartment called *mak'ad*, open in front to the court, with two or more arches, and a railing, and a pillar to support the wall above. It was in a chamber of this kind, probably one of the largest to be found in a palace, that our Lord was being arraigned before the high priest."— *Smith's Dictionary*. *Sat*—"Unseasonable companionship," says Bengel. *To see the end*—Which he probably hoped would in some way be favorable, not even yet habituated to the teaching that Jesus "must" suffer death.

59. *All the council*—It is certain that Matthew could not have intended to include Nicodemus and Joseph of Arimathea among those who sought false witnesses, etc. Either these men had already ceased to meet with the council, or, which seems to be probable, *all* is here used in the general sense. *False*— Of course they did not seek false witnesses in preference to true, but witnesses they were determined to have, true or false. *To put him*— That they might put him. His death was a foregone conclusion; the important thing, in their judgment, was to give the conclusion a show of reasonableness. This deadly opposition of the leading religionists of the country was not a sudden outburst of passion. It began in the early part of the Lord's public life.

60. *Found none*—These priests and others of the council examining with breathless anxiety the "many" false witnesses, as their servants succeeded in drumming them up, is a scene surpassed by few which art has put upon canvas. Many a witness was sent off, because he did not answer their purpose. Either the testimony was too favorable, or two could not be found that told the same story. *At last*—After all previous efforts had failed. *Two*—The smallest number which the Jewish law allowed. Num. 35: 30; Deut. 17: 6; 19: 15.

61. *This fellow—Fellow* is need-

62 And the high priest arose, and said unto him, Answerest thou nothing? what *is it which* these witness against thee?

63 But Jesus held his peace. And the high priest answered and said unto him, I adjure thee by the living God, that thou tell us whether thou be the Christ, the Son of God.

64 Jesus saith unto him, Thou hast said: nevertheless I say unto you, Hereafter shall ye see the Son of man sitting

---

lessly supplied. *This man* is more correct. They probably pointed toward him with the hand. What Jesus had said *two years* before was this: *Destroy* this temple, and in three days I will raise it up. John 2: 19. What the witnesses testified that he had said was, *I am able* to destroy the temple of God. 1. Destroy *ye* this temple. and, *I* can destroy it, are very different. 2. The very substance of the thought which Jesus had expressed was totally different from that to which the witnesses testified. They made him refer to the temple of Jerusalem; but he referred in fact to the temple of his body. Their testimony was intended to show that he had spoken derogatorily, arrogantly, of God's house; but he had only said to the Jews, in figurative language, that if they should put him to death he would rise again in three days. Their testimony, then, was false. But did the witnesses *intend* to give false testimony? or had they merely misunderstood him? Did they really suppose that he meant their own sacred building? It is doubtful whether they gave the matter any serious thought whatever. They said (Mark 14: 58) that they had heard Jesus say it themselves; but Mark says their testimony did not agree. Matthew may have reported what the one said, and Mark what the other said. This need not be urged, however. It is enough to say that the witnesses destroyed the value of each other's testimony by telling different stories. They were evidently tools of the Sanhedrim. See Acts 6: 11-14 for the report of false testifying against Stephen.

In that case, the witnesses were suborned, that is, "secretly instructed" what to say. Had the testimony of the two witnesses against Jesus been true, would it have been sufficient to procure the death of Jesus? Some think it would have been sufficient by the Jewish law to convict him of blasphemy; and this was punishable by death. Deut. 13: 6-10. But Andrews says, "If the statements of the witnesses had been concordant and true, this language could be regarded at most as only a vainglorious boast; and if deserving of any punishment, certainly not of death." These false witnesses ought themselves to have been punished. Deut. 19: 16-19.

62-63. *Arose*—In excitement, assumed, *possibly*, that he might make an impression on the council. Some would read the two questions as one. Dost thou not answer what it is which these testify against thee? The difference results merely from a difference in pointing. *Two short* questions would indicate more fully the excited state of the speaker. *Held his peace*—It was useless to reply to testimony of that sort. The high priest himself distrusts it, and therefore resorts to another method. *I adjure thee*—By Jewish law the accused was put upon oath "to clear himself." The high priest, seeing it to be impossible to convict him by means of witnesses, and believing that Jesus had professed to be the Messiah, the Son of God, resolves to make him avow it on oath before the council. They evidently felt that it would be impossible to obtain *witnesses* that he had ever avowed himself as the Son of God,

on the right hand of power, and coming in the clouds of heaven.

65 Then the high priest rent his clothes, saying, He hath spoken blasphemy; what further need have we of witnesses? behold, now ye have heard his blasphemy.

66 What think ye? They answered and said, He is guilty of death.

67 Then did they spit in his

---

or as the Messiah. He had avowed his Messiahship to his disciples and to the woman of Samaria, but not to people generally. Hence the difficulty of getting proof.

64. *Thou hast said*—This was the Jewish method of answering affirmatively. It was equivalent to saying, *I am.* Thus Jesus allowed himself to be put on oath; or, to say the least, he did not resist the requisition of the high priest. To what extent this sanctions the system of civil oaths, see note on 5: 33-37. *Nevertheless*—Moreover, or but, in addition to what I have just said, I now add that hereafter ye shall see the Son of man, etc. *Sitting*, etc.—Clothed with omnipotence. *Hereafter*—Not, necessarily, from that moment, but, speaking generally, from the time of this crisis in his life. Speaking after the manner of the world, he is now in their power; but soon, at the time of his resurrection, his power will be manifested, and will continue to be manifested till his final coming. What a scene is this! Seventy of the leading men of the nation sitting in judgment upon this apparently friendless and helpless man—they emphatically the weak party, he the almighty one—and compelled to hear this bold announcement!

65. *Rent his clothes*—"'Not his high-priestly robe, which he wore only in the temple.' . . . 'The rent made in the garment was from the neck downward, and about a span in length.'" It was an official act, expressive of indignation at the greatness of the alleged crime. Notice the plural. He tore both his garments. *Hath spoken blasphemy*— That was true unless Jesus was what he professed to be. The Sanhedrim would have been loyal to the old covenant had it put any man to death who was proved guilty of blasphemy; but it was disloyal to the old covenant in condemning Jesus without a candid examination of the question whether *his* avowal of divine Sonship was not justified by the old covenant itself.

66. *Guilty of death*—The law making death the penalty of blasphemy is in Lev. 24: 16. Mr. Salvador and some others have maintained that the sentence was strictly just. It would seem that nothing but unbelief that Jesus was the Son of God could make one of that opinion.

67. *Did spit in his face*—Spitting in the face was not less an insult in very early times than now. Deut. 25: 9; Num. 12: 14. Job says (30: 10), *They spare not to spit in my face.* "Such is the enormity attached to this offence that it is seldom had recourse to except in extreme cases. A master, whose slave has deeply offended him, will not beat him (for that would defile him), but he spits in his face."—*Roberts.* "Seneca records that it was inflicted at Athens upon Aristides the Just, adding, at the same time, that with considerable difficulty one individual was at last found willing to do it."—*Browne, in Lange.* *Buffeted*—Struck a blow or blows with the fist. How many such blows were laid upon him is not said, but men who could have done it once could have done it many times. *Smote him*—The original word does not decide whether they smote him with the open hand or with rods. Many omit *with the palms of their hands.*

face, and buffeted him; and others smote *him* with the palms of their hands,

68 Saying, Prophesy unto us, thou Christ, Who is he that smote thee?

69 ¶ Now Peter sat without in the palace: and a damsel came unto him, saying, Thou also wast with Jesus of Galilee.

70 But he denied before *them* all, saying, I know not what thou sayest.

71 And when he was gone out into the porch, another *maid* saw him, and said unto them that were there, This

---

According to Mark (14: 65), it was the servants that struck him, and it would seem that some of the Sanhedrim participated in other parts of the abuse. *His visage was so marred more than any man, and his form more than the sons of men.* Isa. 52: 14.

68. *Prophesy*—They first blindfolded him (Mark 14: 65), and, by asking him to tell who smote him, ridiculed his claims as a prophet. It was a denial of the claim by direct insult.

69. *Without in the palace*—Without the room where Jesus was, and in the open court around which the house was built. See note on vs. 58. The following diagram may aid in obtaining the correct conception. When Peter *went in* (vs. 58), he went into the court from the street through the porch.

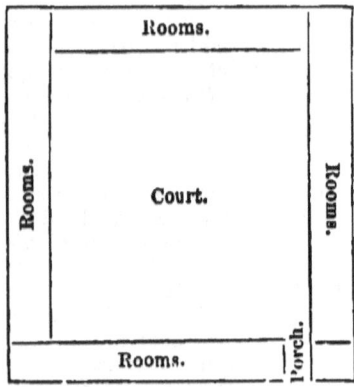

Of Galilee—The Galilean. This brings out the contempt which the damsel meant to express.

70. *He denied*—Concerning the variations of the other reports of the denial, see notes on the verses where they occur. *I know not*—A lie direct. It will give birth to worse sins. Satan would sift him as wheat. More denial of self would have saved him from denying Christ.

71. *Gone out into the porch*—He quails before the damsel, but more before the voice of conscious guilt. *Them that were there*—Servants and guards. *This fellow*—Here, also, the word *fellow* should give place to *man*. *Of Nazareth* should be *the Nazarene*. "Whenever men spoke of Jesus as the Nazarene, they either consciously or unconsciously pronounced one of the names of the predicted Messiah, a name indicative both of his royal descent and his humble condition."—*Prof. Day, in Smith's Dictionary*. See, in explanation of this view, the note on 2: 23, second paragraph.

72. *With an oath*—An offspring of the lie, the twin of the second falsehood. Thus cowardice puts on the mask of courage. Profane swearers are none the braver for their profanity. As Peter's passion burst out in profanity, it is not difficult to believe that he may have been a profane swearer before his conversion.

73. *Speech bewrayeth thee*—Betrays, discovers. The Galileans had some peculiarities of speech which seem to have been well known even among the common people of Jerusalem. They sounded three of the letters of the language so that they could not be distinguished from

fellow was also with Jesus of Nazareth.

72 And again he denied with an oath, I do not know the man.

73 And after a while came unto *him* they that stood by, and said to Peter, Surely thou also art *one* of them; for thy speech bewrayeth thee.

74 Then began he to curse and to swear, *saying*, I know not the man. And immediately the cock crew.

75 And Peter remembered the word of Jesus, which said unto him, Before the cock crow, thou shalt deny me thrice. And he went out, and wept bitterly.

CHAPTER XXVII.

WHEN the morning was come, all the chief priests and elders of the people took counsel against Jesus to put him to death:

---

each other, and still another letter they pronounced like the last in the alphabet. The color of a grain of sand has aided, through the microscope, in detecting a criminal; so may a letter of the alphabet. 74, 75. *To curse*—Not, to curse those who had just spoken, but *to invoke curses on himself* in confirmation of the words, I know not the man. He has become more passionate, and fills the court with his self-imprecations. *The cock crew*— How many things may combine to expose the wrong-doer! nay, let it rather be said, to lead him to repentance!—a damsel; a letter of the alphabet; the crowing of a cock: memory; reflection (Mark 14: 72); the eye of Christ (Luke 22: 61). Yet the Holy Spirit is the convicting agent (John 16: 8). *Went out* —It was quite time, for though he had been attracted to the spot by love to his teacher, he had been in bad company. Penitence seeks solitude. *Wept bitterly*—Thus we have an illustration of the Saviour's words. *My sheep shall never perish;* and in his intercessory prayer (John 17: 12), our Lord says to the Father: While I was with them in the world, *I kept them in thy name.* It is true, as the Methodist commentator, Dr. Whedon, says, that "Death, in his present impenitent condition, would have consigned him to remediless woe;" but Christ had prayed for him that his faith fail not. Judas did not deny Christ, and yet he was an unregenerate man. Peter did deny him, though regenerate. Judas' depravity was chronic; Peter's was acute. Chronic sinfulness can be cured only by regenerating power; acute sin may be conquered by a look. Whence the difference, if we must go to the bottom, between Peter and Judas? The prayers of Jesus were the link in the chain that bound Peter to eternal life. We have no right, therefore, to make the supposition that had Peter died with the burden of his new guilt upon him, he would have been lost, without at the same time making the supposition that Christ had not prayed for him. It is wiser to deal with facts than to speculate upon possibilities.

CHAPTER XXVII.

THE SUICIDE OF JUDAS; JESUS CRUCIFIED AND BURIED.

783 U.C. Friday Morning, April 7, A.D. 30.

1. *Morning*—Friday morning, between five and six o'clock. The Sanhedrim may have adjourned, leaving Jesus in the hands of the

2 And when they had bound him, they led *him* away, and delivered him to Pontius Pilate the governor.

3 ¶ Then Judas, which had betrayed him, when he saw that he was condemned, repented himself, and brought again the thirty pieces of silver to the chief priests and elders,

---

guard. It had adjudged him guilty of blasphemy and guilty (worthy) of death, but before Jesus could be crucified, their decision that he ought to die must be sanctioned by Pilate, as the representative of the Roman power, the Romans having taken from the Jews the right of capital punishment. This second meeting, therefore, is held for the purpose of maturing the plan of bringing him before Pilate. The members of the Sanhedrim must also have been perfectly aware that the judgment which had already been passed upon him was illegal, because taken in the night. Their action had been hasty and irregular, and the personal abuse which Jesus had suffered was in total violation of justice. It was barbarous. Whether this morning meeting was held in the high priest's palace, or in the council chamber near the temple, it is difficult to decide. The words in John (18: 28), Then led they Jesus *from Caiaphas*, look as if they held this session in the former place.

2. *Had bound him*—According to John (18: 12), the soldiers bound him when they took him in the garden. He may have been partly or wholly unbound; or he may have now been bound still more securely. *Led him away*—To the judgment-hall (John 18: 28), the Pretorium; but whether this was at Herod's former palace (the palace of the reigning Herod's *father*), or whether it was in the Tower of Antonia, is held by some to be doubtful. The tower adjoined the temple area on the north; the palace was on Mount Zion, in the western part of the city. It will be assumed that Pilate, when in the city, resided in Herod's palace.

Pontius Pilate the governor—Pilate was a Gentile, a Roman. He was governor, procurator, of Judea. He is the man of whom the well-known Roman historian, Tacitus, some of whose works are studied in American colleges, says: "Christ suffered death at the hands of the procurator Pontius Pilate in the reign of Tiberius." His was by no means the best specimen of Roman character, nor, irrespective of the part which he took in the condemnation of Jesus Christ, was it the worst. His administration was sometimes stained by acts of intolerance and severity, but many of the rulers of Roman provinces were in these respects worse than he. There were Romans, doubtless, who would on no account have given Jesus up to death. There were others who would have done that deed without hesitation. Pilate had more conscientiousness than these, more timidity and love of office than those, and so, with a vacillation which makes even a bad man mean, he stands associated with Judas—the one a Jew, the other a Gentile—in the blackest crime of history. He was accused by the Samaritans, and was sent to Rome for trial. It is *said* that, "'wearied with misfortunes,' he killed himself." One cannot but desire that the official report which he doubtless made to the Roman emperor of the trial and crucifixion of Jesus had been preserved. That which is now extant is spurious.

3. *When he saw*—He may have seen it as the procession of priests and elders were going with Jesus

CHAPTER XXVII.

4 Saying, I have sinned in that I have betrayed the innocent blood. And they said, What *is that* to us? see thou *to that.*

5 And he cast down the pieces of silver in the temple, and departed, and went and hanged himself.

6 And the chief priests took the silver pieces, and said, It is not lawful for to put them into the treasury, because it is the price of blood.

---

from the council chamber, or, if that was the point of departure, from the palace of the high priest. *Repented himself*—Godly sorrow would have saved him from self-destruction. The original word does not necessarily imply that kind of repentance which consists of sorrow showing itself in a change of life. Such sorrow is almost always expressed by another word. Judas was filled with remorse on account of the consequences. According to Barnes and others, this verse shows "that Judas did not suppose that the affair would have resulted in this calamitous manner." But as Judas must have known that the Pharisees had long been determined to kill Jesus, he could not have been wholly without expectation that death would be the result. It was as true of Judas as of other criminals that he did not stop to give the consequences of his act much thought; but that he was so startled at the result is no proof that the result was entirely unanticipated. The view from which we dissent, if correct, would compel us to deny to Shakespeare that knowledge of human nature, in some of his delineations of the workings of conscience, which all the world has believed him to have. See Macbeth.

4. *I have sinned*—Judas had none of that consciousness of sin which David had when he confessed, *Against thee, thee only, have I sinned; Wash me thoroughly from mine iniquity.* We need not, however, regard him as merely saying, *I erred* (Dr. Lange); or, *I did evil* (Luther).

5. *In the temple*—He did not toss the thirty pieces over into the court of the Gentiles, but he pressed his way to the *holy place*, and, possibly, entering it, threw them down at the feet of the priests. *Hanged himself* —A poor preparation for heaven. There is no contradiction between this and the statement in Acts 1: 18: *And falling headlong, he burst asunder in the midst, and all his bowels gushed out.* "Matthew," says Dr. Hackett, Commentary on the Acts, "does not say that Judas, after having hanged himself, *did not* fall to the ground and burst asunder; nor, on the contrary, does Luke say that Judas *did not* hang himself before he fell to the ground; and it is obvious that the matter should have been so stated, in order to warrant the charge of inconsistency... It has been thought not improbable that Judas may have hung himself from the limb of a tree, on the edge of a precipice near the valley of Hinnom, and that, the rope breaking by which he was suspended, he fell to the earth and was dashed to pieces." As he stood in the valley and looked up the rocky terraces, which he found by actual measurement to be in one place forty feet high, Dr. Hackett was more than ever "satisfied with the explanation." If Judas went at once to heaven, he fared better than his fellow-apostles, for most of them lived long, labored hard, and suffered much.

6. *Not lawful*, etc.—They probably based this opinion upon Deut. 23: 18. *The treasury*, or corban, was the receptacle for money given to the service of God in the temple. Josephus makes the following al-

7 And they took counsel, and bought with them the potter's field, to bury strangers in.

8 Wherefore that field was called, The field of blood, unto this day.

9 Then was fulfilled that which was spoken by Jeremy the prophet, saying, And they took the thirty pieces of silver, the price of him that was valued, whom they of the children of Israel did value;

10 And gave them for the potter's field, as the Lord appointed me.

lusion to it in speaking of the oppressive acts of Pilate: "After this he raised another disturbance by expending that sacred treasure which is called *corban* upon aqueducts." See Mark 7: 11, where *corban* means not treasury, but the gift itself. *The price of blood*—They ought to have prayed, with David, *Deliver me from bloodguiltiness*, O God. Their conscientiousness was dishonest.

7, 8. *The potter's field*—Where it was is not stated, though, as Dr. Hackett remarks, "It is not impossible that the potter's field which the Jews purchased may actually be the present Aceldama, which overlooks the valley of Hinnom. The receptacles for the dead which appear in the rocks in that quarter show that the ancient Jews were accustomed to bury there." It was on the southern side of Jerusalem. The pottery which is now in operation in the city is furnished with clay from that locality. *Strangers*—Persons who had come from a foreign country, whether Jews, or Gentile proselytes, or pagan Gentiles, does not appear. It is less probable that Jews are meant. - *They* bought. But in Acts (1: 18) it is said that *Judas* purchased the field. The difficulty may be removed by supposing that the Greek word in Acts has, what many Hebrew verbs have, a *causative* sense, that is, a sense implying that Judas was the cause or the occasion of the purchase. Many Greek verbs have this sense, and there can be no objection to admitting it here. According to some, tradition teaches that there were two Aceldamas, Luke, in Acts, referring to the one, and Matthew to the other; but it is affirmed that there are no traditions to that effect which are old enough to be traced to the apostolic age.

9, 10. *By Jeremy*—Jeremiah. But there are no such words in Jeremiah. The following, which are very similar, are in Zechariah 11: 12, 13: And I said unto them, If ye think good, give me my price; and if not, forbear. *So they weighed for my price thirty pieces of silver.* And the Lord said unto me, Cast it unto the potter: a goodly price that I was prized at of them. And I took the thirty pieces of silver, *and cast them to the potter in the house of the Lord.* No satisfactory solution of the difficulty has yet been reached, though many have been proposed. The name *Jeremiah* instead of *Zechariah* may be the error of a transcriber. To affirm that it is a mistake of the evangelist is a very bold thing. In the words of Dr. J. J. Owen, "As it regards the quotation itself, the prophet had demanded of the Jewish rulers his wages for feeding the flock. He received thirty pieces of silver. This paltry sum, sarcastically declared to be a goodly price, at which the prophet (that is, his services) had been prized of them, he is directed to cast to the potter, who was at work near the house of the Lord. This low estimation of the labors of Jehovah's servant, and his rejection of the wages, which was just the very sum paid by the priests to Judas, became a remarkable predic-

11 And Jesus stood before the governor: and the governor asked him, saying, Art thou the King of the Jews? And Jesus said unto him, Thou sayest.

12 And when he was accused of the chief priests and elders, he answered nothing.

13 Then said Pilate unto him, Hearest thou not how many things they witness against thee?

14 And he answered him to never a word; insomuch that the governor marvelled greatly.

15 Now at *that* feast the governor was wont to release unto the people a prisoner, whom they would.

16 And they had then a notable prisoner, called Barabbas.

17 Therefore when they were gathered together, Pilate said

---

tion of the valuation put upon Christ by the chief priests, and the rejection by Judas of the wages of iniquity. The two events were in these particulars so similar, that the last might be said to be the fulfilment of the former."

11. *Jesus stood*—In the judgment-hall. John 18: 28, 33. The Jews, lest they should be defiled by going into the judgment-hall of a Gentile (John 18: 28), stood outside. *Art thou the king*, etc.—According to Luke (23: 2), they charged him with the design of overturning the Roman power in Palestine, and of making himself king. He answers the question affirmatively in the usual Jewish form: *Thou sayest.* But here is no equivocation, for (John 18: 36, 37) he soon stated in what sense he was a king. Observe that they have already condemned him in their own council on the charge of blasphemy, but now, in accusing him before a Roman governor, they shift their ground, making his crime civil instead of ecclesiastical. In *this* accusation there is no sincerity; for, with fair prospect of success, they would undoubtedly have gladly followed Jesus as their chief in rebelling against the Roman government.

12. *Accused*—Not necessarily "to his face." The chief priests were the chief liars. They were fierce and clamorous (Luke 23: 5). The accused is inside the hall; the accusers are outside. Pilate (John 18: 29) went out to them.

13, 14. *Hearest thou not*—Jesus may have overheard their accusations, or Pilate, on returning, may have reported them. *How many*—The governor refers not to the number of the things charged, but to the character of the charges. It does not imply that Pilate believed the accusations. *To never a word*—Not even to one word. After this, according to Luke, Pilate sent Jesus to Herod, hoping thereby to escape the necessity of deciding the case himself.

15, 16. *At that feast*—It is a general statement, applying to the Passover as held from year to year. Of the custom scarcely anything is known. It is remarkable that such sticklers for the law allowed themselves to be participants in sustaining a custom which *to them* was a violation of the law of Moses. That law said (Ex. 21: 12), *He that smiteth a man, so that he die, shall surely be put to death;* and Barabbas, a *notable*, noted, prisoner, was guilty of insurrection, robbery, and murder, the first of which crimes was the very one of which they had accused Jesus, and of the last two of which they did not pretend that he was guilty.

unto them, Whom will ye that I release unto you? Barabbas, or Jesus which is called Christ?

18 For he knew that for envy they had delivered him.

19 ¶ When he was set down on the judgment seat, his wife sent unto him, saying, Have thou nothing to do with that just man: for I have suffered many things this day in a dream because of him.

20 But the chief priests and elders persuaded the multitude

17, 18. *Gathered together*—They, that is, the chief priests and scribes, went from the judgment-hall to accuse Jesus before Herod. This gathering together, therefore, is their reassembling before the judgment-hall, after Jesus had been sent back to Pilate. The governor, still vacillating, resorts to another expedient, which he evidently expects will succeed; for he takes for granted that they will not demand the release of such a notorious criminal as Barabbas. *For envy*—They envied his popularity. They, not the Sadducees, had led the people. They knew that he had gained wonderfully in influence over the popular mind, and that if he should be permitted to go on, *their* power would be lost. Pilate knew Jewish character well enough to feel assured that this was the real ground of their opposition.

19. *The judgment-seat*—The elevated seat on the pavement (John 19: 13) outside the judgment-hall. It was probably the regular tribunal of justice. Pilate had now taken the seat to pronounce judgment; and while he was sitting there, giving the Pharisees a moment to decide whether they would have Jesus or Barabbas, he received a remarkable message. The communication of the message must have been observed, though perhaps not overheard, by some of the Pharisees. The wife of a Roman governor could accompany her husband to the province over which he was to rule, though the practice had met with opposition. Nothing is known of Pilate's wife except what we learn here. Tradition says her name was Claudia Procula, or Procla. The Greek church has enrolled her among their saints, which makes the dead woman none the better, and makes some living women worse by making them more superstitious. *Just man*—Not merely innocent of the charges alleged, but a man of uncommon excellence. Pilate's wife may have been one of the very few heathen who had arrived at some knowledge of the true God, and had some reverence for his character. "It is a remarkable fact," says Dr. Schaff, "that a woman, and she a heathen, should be the only human being who had the courage to plead the cause of our Saviour during those dreadful hours when his own disciples forsook him, and when the fanatical multitude cried out, Crucify him! Crucify him!" There is much truth in the remark, but the courage necessary to send a private message to her own husband could not have been great. Had she gone in person and stood between the innocent sufferer and the bloodthirsty priests, the act would have commanded the admiration of the world. Let not injustice be done to such women as the Lord's mother, and Mary, and Martha. Their relations to Pilate were very different. Still, Pilate's wife defended Jesus. Let pious women who have irreligious husbands remember this. *Many things*—Much. The dream may have been natural, but even if it was, God is clearly to be seen in the event.

20. *Should ask*—Should ask *for*. The Pharisees now attempt to turn aside the course of justice. They bit and bridle the multitude, and

CHAPTER XXVII.

that they should ask Barabbas, and destroy Jesus.

21 The governor answered and said unto them, Whether of the twain will ye that I release unto you? They said, Barabbas.

22 Pilate saith unto them, What shall I do then with Jesus which is called Christ? *They* all say unto him, Let him be crucified.

23 And the governor said, Why, what evil hath he done? But they cried out the more, saying, Let him be crucified.

24 ¶ When Pilate saw that he could prevail nothing, but *that* rather a tumult was made, he took water, and washed his hands before the multitude, saying, I am innocent of the blood of this just person: see ye *to it.*

---

spur it on to trample Pilate in the dust. It has been considered by most commentators that the people here mentioned are the same as those that sung hosannas in the triumphal march. It is perhaps scarcely just to regard this as wholly a misconception; yet it may be hoped that not many who cried Hosanna were of those who demanded the death of Jesus. In proportion as the living power of Christianity controls the many will the many become in the best sense independent of the few.

21. *Whether of the twain*—Which of the two. *Barabbas*—Men are now asked to choose Christ, and many of them exclaim, *Not this man!* Sin is chosen in his place, who, like Barabbas, has been guilty of insurrection, murder, and robbery. O man! will you not reconsider your choice?

22. *Let him be crucified*—Surprise has been expressed that the people cried, *Crucify him,* instead of *Stone him.* But it would have been more surprising had the latter been their cry. For, (1.) The charge of blasphemy, which, under Jewish law, was punishable by stoning, had been shifted to the charge of sedition, and this, under Roman law, was punishable by crucifixion; (2.) Barabbas would have suffered death by crucifixion, and in demanding the release of Barabbas they naturally demand that Jesus shall be punished as Barabbas would have been. Some sayings of our Lord would never have been fulfilled had Jesus been stoned (Matt. 20: 19; John 18: 32), and the meaning of some portions of Scripture would have been lost. See Matt. 16: 24; Deut. 21: 23; Gal. 3: 13. In atoning for sin, it was needful that Jesus be made *a curse by crucifixion.*

23. *What evil*—Still reluctant to surrender him, yet still afraid to release him. *Cried out the more*—They had at length taken on the form and spirit of a mob. Luke 23: 23.

24. He yields to the popular clamor, but protests that the responsibility is not his. David says (Ps. 26: 6) *I will wash mine hands in innocency.* The Jewish law (Deut. 21: 1-9) required that in case a man was found slain, the elders of the nearest city should wash their hands over a slaughtered heifer, saying, *Our hands have not shed this blood.* *This just person*—Pilate does not even attempt to persuade himself that Jesus deserves punishment. To admit the perfect innocence of an accused person, and at the same time to surrender him to execution, is a most infamous crime. How much *the heart* of such a man needs washing!

25. How terribly has this self-imprecation been answered! So

25 Then answered all the people, and said, His blood *be* on us, and on our children.

26 ¶ Then released he Barabbas unto them: and when he had scourged Jesus, he delivered *him* to be crucified.

27 Then the soldiers of the governor took Jesus into the common hall, and gathered unto him the whole band *of soldiers*.

28 And they stripped him, and put on him a scarlet robe.

---

many of the Jews were crucified when the city was destroyed by the Romans, that, according to Josephus, it was difficult to find room for the crosses; and to this day the Jews have suffered as no other people on earth have suffered.

26. *Scourged*—Pilate scourged him at the hands of the soldiers. "It was usually lictors that scourged; but Pilate, being only sub-governor, had no command over lictors, and handed Jesus over to the soldiers. Hence it is probable that Jesus was not beaten with rods, but scourged with twisted thongs of leather." The Jewish law permitted only forty stripes, and thirty-nine was the common number, lest the legal number should be exceeded. No such limitation was made by the Roman law; and, besides, those Roman soldiers would not be likely to spare their strength. The thongs were sometimes loaded with pieces of bone, or iron, or lead. Jesus having been doubtless stripped of a part of his clothing, the blows were laid upon his back. Scourging by the Romans was exceedingly severe. Beyond all question the back of our Lord was greatly lacerated, the blood flowing in streams from the wounds. Death sometimes ensued from the scourging itself. *I gave my back to the smiters.* Isa. 50: 6. *The chastisement of our peace was upon him; and with his stripes we are healed.* Isa. 53: 5. "By delivering Jesus to the Sanhedrim," says Dr. Schaff, "Pilate sacrificed his lofty and independent position as a secular judge, and representative of the Roman law, to the religious fanaticism of the Jewish hierarchy. The State became a tool in the hands of an apostate and bloodthirsty church. How often has this fact been repeated in the history of religious persecution!"

27, 28. *The common hall*—In Mark (15: 16), the same word is translated *Pretorium*. See on vs. 2. The building was Herod's palace, but here the court is intended. *And gathered unto him*, etc.—Lange speaks strongly in saying that "this is conclusive for the palace being the fortress of Antonia." *But in mine adversity they rejoiced, and gathered themselves together: yea, the abjects gathered themselves together against me, and I knew it not; they did tear me, and ceased not. With hypocritical mockers in feasts, they gnashed upon me with their teeth.* Ps. 35: 15, 16. *The whole band*—The entire cohort, one-tenth of a Roman legion. The number of the cohort varied, however, from three hundred to a thousand. Calling this cohort five hundred, there could not have been, in the court and around the building, less than a thousand persons, all thirsting for the blood of their victim. It is not unreasonable to suppose that the number was much larger. *They stripped him*—As they had already stripped him for the scourging, they had either restored the clothing to his back, or they now take off still more. *A scarlet robe*—The scarlet dye "was produced from an insect, somewhat resembling the cochineal, which is found in considerable quantities in Armenia and other eastern countries. . . . . The tint produced was crimson rather than scarlet." In John (19:

29 ¶ And when they had platted a crown of thorns, they put *it* upon his head, and a reed in his right hand: and they bowed the knee before him, and mocked him, saying, Hail, King of the Jews!

30 And they spit upon him, and took the reed, and smote him on the head.

31 And after that they had mocked him, they took the robe off from him, and put his own raiment on him, and led him away to crucify *him*.

32 And as they came out,

---

2) the same robe is called purple. In Judges (8: 26), we read of "purple raiment that was on the kings of Midian," and purple robes were esteemed among the Greeks and Romans. The robe is put upon Jesus in mockery of his alleged pretensions to royalty. Perhaps it belonged to one of the military officers.

29. Still making themselves merry over the innocent one, the soldiers weave a *crown of thorns*, and put it on his head. It is impossible to decide which of the many kinds of thorn that grew in Palestine was used. One kind is called *Zizyphus Spina Christi*. "This plant," says a Swedish naturalist, "was very suitable for the purpose, as it has many sharp thorns, and its flexible, pliant, and round branches might easily be plaited in the form of a crown." The crown of thorns was put upon him partly to mock him, and partly to cause him pain. *A reed*—Ahasuerus, King of Persia, into whose presence Esther ventured, had a golden sceptre. The soldiers mock the King of kings by putting into his hand a hollow reed. *Bowed the knee*, etc.—This mock homage is an unconscious prophecy of the real homage of future ages. Here we see the spirit of paganism fired by the hate of ritualism; for it is difficult to believe that the Pharisees were not instigators of all this personal abuse. *He is despised and rejected of men*. Isa. 53: 3.

30. *Spit upon him*—See on 26: 67. The blow given by the reed, if not heavy, was insulting, and doubtless drove the thorns into his head and temples.

31. *Led him away*—Before this (John 19: 4, 5), Pilate brought him forth from the Pretorium, wearing the crown of thorns and the purple robe, and said to them, *Behold the man!*

32. *As they came out*—Not from the Pretorium, but from the city, for the man was coming out of the country. Luke 23: 26. *Cyrene* was a region of North Africa, lying between Egypt and the country about Carthage. Many Jews lived there. We read, in Acts 2: 10, of the parts of Libya, about Cyrene; in Acts 6: 9, of a synagogue of the Cyrenians in Jerusalem, and in Acts 13: 1, of a teacher in the church at Antioch,—Lucius of Cyrene. *Simon*—He was born at Cyrene, and was now either a resident in Jerusalem with other Jews of Cyrene, or was an attendant at the feast. He had, at least, two well-known sons, Alexander and Rufus. (Mark 15: 21). *Compelled*—The act may not have been an unauthorized compulsion of the man, but legal impressment, concerning which, see note on 5: 41. Plutarch, an ancient Greek writer, says in his work concerning "The Delay of Providence in the Punishment of the Wicked:" "Each of the criminals bears his own cross." John (19: 17) represents the cross as being laid upon Jesus. The opinion that Jesus was unable to bear it longer alone is reasonable. How much he had suffered both in body and mind since he left the sacramental table!

they found a man of Cyrene, Simon by name: him they compelled to bear his cross.

33 And when they were come unto a place called Golgotha, that is to say, a place of a skull,

34 ¶ They gave him vinegar to drink mingled with gall: and when he had tasted *thereof*, he would not drink.

35 And they crucified him, and parted his garments, cast-

Isaac carried the wood upon his shoulders. What Simon did by compulsion, we should do in love.

33. *When they were come*—The way over which tradition represents our Lord as having passed is now called *Via Dolorosa*, the sorrowful way. The tradition, which has not yet been traced back farther than to the fourteenth century, is doubtless without any foundation; for, as Andrews remarks, "If the trial of the Lord was at the palace of Herod on Mount Zion, he could not have passed along the Via Dolorosa." Recent excavations have settled the question, that even if the *direction* of the way over which our Lord passed was the same as that of the Via Dolorosa, the way must have been in many places "not less than thirty or forty feet" below the present level of the Via Dolorosa. "The latest excavations by Lieut. Warren near 'Robinson's Arch' have gone to a depth of fifty-five feet below the surface before coming to the bottom of the valley between Zion and Moriah. . . . In digging for the foundations of the house of the Prussian Deaconesses, a subterranean street of houses was found several feet below the street above it." *Golgotha*—A word meaning *skull*. Why was the place called so? is a question which has received different answers. Some say, because, being (as it doubtless was) the common place of execution, skulls must have abounded there. But the Jewish laws concerning cleanliness make this improbable. It is more probable that it was so called in consequence of the shape of the place. "A tradition at one time prevailed that Adam was buried on Golgotha; that from his skull it derived its name, and that at the crucifixion the drops of Christ's blood fell on the skull and raised Adam to life." The tradition is not worth naming, except as an explanation of the fact that some of the early artists introduced the skull into their pictures.

Golgotha was outside the city (Heb. 13: 12). It was near the city (John 19: 20). This is nearly all the Bible says concerning the location of the most remarkable spot on the face of the whole earth. It has been believed by the entire Christian world that it was outside the *western* wall. Very recently, however, an elaborate attempt has been made by Mr. James Fergusson, Fellow of the Royal Institute of British Architects, to prove that the topography of Jerusalem has been totally misunderstood. In accordance with his reasoning upon the general subject, he transfers the site of the crucifixion and burial from the western side of the city to the eastern. He puts it between the eastern wall and the valley of the Kidron. These "original" views, "unsupported by a single tradition," and contradicting "the previous impressions of the Christian world," have been shown by the Rev. Samuel Wolcott, D.D., of Cleveland, Ohio, to be without foundation.

34. *Vinegar*—Sour wine. *Gall*—Used, probably, to designate the *bitterness* of the article, which, as we learn from Mark, was myrrh. *Would not drink*—He would not permit his sensibilities to be deadened, but chose to suffer the whole possible weight of our sins.

ing lots: that it might be fulfilled which was spoken by the prophet, They parted my garments among them, and upon my vesture did they cast lots.

He would *taste death* in all its bitterness. To say that it was a refusal of *superficial means of comfort*, that he might have comfort from the highest source, shows that the meaning of this entire tragical scene is missed. A thousand years before, David, speaking by the Holy Spirit, said, *They gave me also gall for my meat; and in my thirst they gave me vinegar to drink.* Ps. 69: 21. Rare cases excepted, is it not better for the pious to suffer more in their last sickness than to take opiates? Our Lord died in full possession of his mental powers.

35. *Crucified him*—Nailed him, alive, to the cross. See Ps. 22: 16: *They pierced my hands and my feet.* It should be remarked, however, that scholars, without regard to their theological opinions, are not agreed that the Hebrew will bear this translation.

Crucifixion was very common and very barbarous. The Romans were not the only people that used it. The Jews, it is thought, borrowed it from the Romans. Its barbarity was such that the great Roman orator, Cicero, said that it ought to be removed from the sight, hearing, and thought of men. To be crucified was proof of special disgrace. Thieves, robbers, and slaves were crucified. The victim was entirely naked, with the exception, perhaps, of a cloth around the loins. In some cases he was nailed to the cross while it was lying on the ground, but more frequently after it had been sunk into the hole prepared for it. A nail was driven through each hand. That the feet were also nailed has been almost universally believed, but the German rationalist, Paulus, affirms that they were tied. If Jesus did not die on the cross, but only swooned, he might have walked after being taken down; but that would have been impossible had the feet been nailed. Hence it is for the interests of rationalism to prove that the feet were tied. Dr. Hovey, after carefully considering the question, concludes (Smith's Dictionary) thus: "The nailing of the feet of Jesus to the cross may therefore be said to rest on satisfactory evidence; but whether a single nail was driven through both feet, or they were fastened separately to the cross, cannot be ascertained with any degree of certainty." To prevent the hands from tearing away from the upper nails by the weight of the body, a little seat, or "peg," was prepared, on which the body rested. The following description of the physical sufferings of our Lord is by Dr. Richter, who, in the words of Dr. Schaff, in a note in Lange's Commentary, was "a pious physician of the Orphan House in Halle:" "1. On account of the unnatural and immovable position of the body and the violent extension of the arms, the least motion produced the most painful sensation all over the body, but especially on the lacerated back and the pierced members. 2. The nails caused constantly increasing pain on the most sensitive parts of the hands and feet. 3. Inflammation set in at the pierced members, and wherever the circulation of the blood was obstructed by the violent tension of the body, and increased the agony, and an intolerable thirst. 4. The blood rushed to the head, and produced the most violent headache. 5. The blood in the lungs accumulated, pressing the heart, swelling all the veins, and caused nameless anguish. Loss of blood through the open wounds would have

36 And sitting down, they watched him there:

37 And set up over his head his accusation written, THIS IS JESUS THE KING OF THE JEWS.

38 Then were there two thieves crucified with him; one on the right hand, and another on the left.

39 ¶ And they that passed by reviled him, wagging their heads,

40 And saying, Thou that destroyest the temple, and buildest *it* in three days, save

---

shortened the pain, but the blood clotted and ceased flowing. Death generally set in slowly, the muscles, veins, and nerves gradually growing stiff, and the vital powers sinking from exhaustion." We should ever remember, however, that the greatest sufferings of our Lord were mental. Crosses have been of different forms, as follows:—

ROMAN.   GREEK.   ROMAN.   ST. ANDREW'S.   NINEVEH (Sculptures.)

The first is probably the form of the cross on which Jesus died: it would have given room for the inscription over his head. *Casting lots*—The clothes of the crucified became the property of the executioners. The Saviour's *garments* consisted of the *coat*, or tunic worn next to the skin, and the *cloak*, which was "a large piece of woollen cloth, nearly square, which was wrapped around the body or fastened about the shoulders." The coat (John 19: 23) was without seam, woven from the top throughout. It was for this that lots were cast. The cloak was divided into four parts, and these were given to the four guards. Calling the soldiers "*gamblers*," because they cast lots, is unjust to the apostles; for these cast lots for one to take the place of Judas. All scholars are agreed that for the words in this verse following *lots*, there is no good manuscript authority. In John, however, they are genuine, where see notes.

36. *Watched*—This was customary, that the sufferer might not be released by friends.

37. *Set up*—Whether it was the soldiers just mentioned that set it up, or some one sent directly by Pilate after he had written it, is not stated. *This is Jesus*—An inscription to indicate the nature of the charge was generally placed above the head. Such an inscription, in Greek, is found in the writings of Eusebius, the translation of which is, This is Attalus the Christian. The inscription, The King of the Jews, was the title which, in the judgment of Pilate, would indicate the crime for which the Jews demanded the crucifixion of Jesus. He adopted the inscription, not as indicative of his own private opinion, but as sufficiently expressive of the view pretended to be held by the priests. It is not surprising that the priests were displeased with it, and asked that it be changed for another. See John 19: 21. In the narrow sense, the inscription was false, whether in the form in which it appeared, or in that which the priests desired him to substitute; in the wider sense, Pilate reproduced, unconsciously, the grand Old Testament truth that Jesus was indeed the King of the Jews.

38-40. *Two thieves*—Two robbers. They may have been tried by

thyself. If thou be the son of God, come down from the cross.

41 Likewise also the chief priests mocking *him*, with the scribes and elders, said,

42 He saved others; himself he cannot save. If he be the King of Israel, let him now come down from the cross, and we will believe him.

43 He trusted in God; let him deliver him now, if he will have him: for he said, I am the Son of God.

44 The thieves also, which were crucified with him, cast the same in his teeth.

45 Now from the sixth hour there was darkness over all the land unto the ninth hour.

46 And about the ninth hour

Pilate during this visit to Jerusalem. Jesus is put, not on a level with them, but below them, which is indicated in his being made the central sufferer. *Wagging . . saying*—Even now that the purpose to crucify him has been effected, they cannot refrain from insulting him. See Ps. 22: 7. They have now nothing to say of his *forbidding to give tribute to Cæsar.* That charge was intended to serve a purpose with Pilate; now they taunt him with the crime brought against him before the Sanhedrim. *Come down*—He *could* have come down from the cross, but that, instead of lessening the difficulties of the case, would have made them greater; for, on the one hand, had he released himself from the cross, it would have been proof of divine power, and, on the other hand, would have failed to do precisely that which the Old Testament affirms the Messiah was to do,—*to die.*

41–43. *The chief priests mocking* —The rabble *wagged their heads* and mocked: the priests *mocked.* The extremes of Jewish society are in Satanic union. *He saved others* —He pretended to do so is their meaning, but their scorn is condensed into such terms that the statement becomes an unconscious acknowledgment of that which is the crowning glory of his life. *Will believe in him*—Self-imposition, for the miracle of releasing himself from the cross might be wrought by "Beelzebub" as truly as releasing Lazarus from the dead. *Trusted in God*—How many truths fall from the lips of these children of him who was a liar from the beginning! *If he will have him*—If he desires him. See Ps. 22: 8. Quoting from their own Scriptures, and so unintentionally proving Jesus to be the Messiah!

44. *The thieves also*—Luke says that *one* of the malefactors railed on him, and represents the other as penitent and praying. There is not even apparent contradiction. Had Matthew stated that neither of the robbers died penitent, or had Luke reported that *only one* of the malefactors railed, the contradiction would have been palpable. They say no such thing. Here our responsibility in defending the evangelists against dishonesty or mistake ends. Yet it may be added that both the robbers may have reviled at first, and that afterwards, one of them, affected by the glory that shined from the Saviour even in the disgrace which the priests and the people attempted to cast upon him, was smitten with penitence. *Cast the same in his teeth*—Reproached him with the same thing.

45. *From the sixth hour*—Twelve o'clock at noon. *Darkness*—It was not an eclipse, for an eclipse cannot occur at the time of full moon; and it has been shown that at that time the moon *was full.* It was undoubtedly the result of that special exer-

Jesus cried with a loud voice, saying, Eli, Eli, lama sabachthani? that is to say, My God, my God, why hast thou forsaken me?

47 Some of them that stood

cise of divine power implied in the word *supernatural*. It was "God-made darkness." "When Christ was born," says Lange, "night became bright by the shining of the miraculous star, as though it would pass into a heavenly day; when he died, the day darkened at an hour when the sun shone in the fullest glory, as though it would sink into the awful night of Sheol." What profound silence must have reigned among the soldiers and people! Some doubtless withdrew from the spot. The Pharisees would have been the first to do so. *Over all the land*—Over Judea and the adjacent countries. Some say, over so much of the earth as was then illuminated by the sun. The former is to be preferred in absence of proof that the latter was intended. In the boldness of metaphor it may be said that nature sympathized with the suffering Son of God. The darkness was God's reproof to the Jews; a source of light to the disciples. But neither view exhausts the meaning of this amazing event. Consider its extent, —over all the land! its duration,—three hours! its intensity,—such that not one of the evangelists attempts to measure it!

Writers upon the sufferings of our Lord have been accustomed to call special attention to what they denominate *the seven words from the cross*. These are as follows:—

1. Father, forgive them, for they know not what they do (Luke 23:34).
2. Verily I say unto thee, To-day shalt thou be with me in paradise (Luke 23:43).
3. Woman, behold thy son! ... Behold thy mother! (John 19:26, 27.)
4. My God, my God, why hast thou forsaken me? (Matt. 27:46; Mark 15:34.)
5. I thirst (John 19:28).
6. It is finished (John 19:30).
7. Father, into thy hands I commend my spirit (Luke 23:46).

Men have discoursed upon these words, not only as individual utterances, but as a connected whole; and, in whichever method they are considered, very rich and very affecting are the thoughts which they contain. "What significance," says Stier, "is there in the individual words; how sharply definite is each single tone in the seven-toned symphony!" It will be noticed that Matthew reports one; Mark one; Luke three; John three. The one which Matthew and Mark report is indeed the most remarkable of the seven.

46. *Eloi, Eloi, lama sabachthani* —These words, the fourth of the seven utterances, are in the Syro-Chaldaic language, which, having displaced the Hebrew, was the language then in common use. Mark translated them into Greek for his readers. Through all the three hours of darkness our Lord suffered in silence. Not a word escaped his lips. Not after the sun shone out again, but near the end of the period of darkness, he exclaims, *My God, my God, why hast thou forsaken me?* These are the opening words of the twenty-second Psalm. The Psalm describes the sufferings of David, but it does more. It portrays sufferings such as David never was called to bear. Beyond all question, the Holy Spirit intended to represent, through David, the sufferings of the Messiah. These words from the cross are the words of the Psalmist; but the Saviour was plunged into too deep and awful darkness to permit him *deliberately and consciously to quote them.* Though familiar with them as the words of David, yet, in the intensity of his mental suffering, he appropriated them as completely as if they were originally his own. Let

there, when they heard *that*, said, This *man* calleth for Elias.

48 And straightway one of them ran, and took a sponge, and filled *it* with vinegar, and put *it* on a reed, and gave him to drink.

49 The rest said, Let be, let us see whether Elias will come to save him.

50 ¶ Jesus, when he had cried again with a loud voice, yielded up the ghost.

51 And, behold, the vail of the temple was rent in twain

---

the student here pause, and, before proceeding further, read the whole of that remarkable composition.

Forsaken me—The Son forsaken of the Father? The Messiah forsaken by him who had moved men by the Holy Spirit to speak of his coming? He who had said that he was one with God, that he could do nothing without the Father, that God loved him before the foundation of the world, now forsaken by God?—and not concealing the terrible thought in his own bosom, but uttering it aloud in the ear of the penitent robber, and in the ear of the men who are saying this very thing concerning him, he thus seeming to admit to the latter the truth of what they affirm! He has fallen to the lowest possible depth of mental suffering; the darkness that rests over the land is a symbol of the darkness that has come over his spirit; but he is not forsaken. He is permitted to *feel* that he is forsaken, and this is permitted that he may realize as deeply as is possible for such a sinless One to do, the eternal separation from God which lost men would have suffered. Thus *the Lord laid on him the iniquity of us all*, yet not by any means in the sense of *punishing* him. The few persons who take, if indeed there are any who take, that view of his sufferings, have adopted a theology for which there is no warrant in the Scriptures. *My God*—My Father is the form which Jesus had almost always used, but now the terrible sense of desertion does not permit him to say Father; yet his continued trust in God permits him still to say, My. Victory will soon restore to him the profounder appellation. See John 20: 17.

47. *Calleth for Elias*—Conscience-stricken, they make the mistake of supposing that he calls for the help of Elijah, and think that the day of vengeance is now to be ushered in by the old prophet; or, which is much more probable, it is "a blasphemous Jewish joke, by an awkward and godless pun upon Eli." As the darkness has passed away, their terror must have subsided.

48, 49. *Straightway*—Immediately, yet not necessarily implying that it was the very next act. He had just cried, *I thirst* (John 19: 28). *One*—Of the Roman soldiers. *Vinegar*—Undrugged sour wine, usually weakened with water. It was given him in sympathy. Would a priest have given it? *A reed*—Of hyssop (John 19: 29). *The rest*—The other Roman soldiers. *Let be*—This is not said to deter the man from giving the vinegar. It is equivalent to our English word, *Come*, used in an indefinite, hortatory sense; as, Come, let us see whether. This is clear from the fact that in Mark the man who gives the drink uses the same phrase, and he would not exhort himself not to do what he was doing. There is no end to the mockery of this solemn scene.

50. *Cried again*—Father, into thy hands I commend my spirit (Luke 23: 46). How many of the

from the top to the bottom; and the earth did quake, and the rocks rent;

52 And the graves were opened; and many bodies of the saints which slept arose,

53 And came out of the graves after his resurrection, and went into the holy city, and appeared unto many.

54 Now when the centurion, and they that were with him, watching Jesus, saw the earthquake, and those things that

---

followers of Christ have died with these words on their lips! *Yielded up the ghost*—Thus, by enduring what God accepts as if it were equivalent to all that men deserve to suffer forever—which is the true meaning of *vicarious sacrifice*—he made eternal life possible to every one that believes. The scribes and Pharisees have at last effected the purpose which they had cherished for two years, and, unwittingly, as God's instruments, have accomplished inconceivably more.

51. *The vail*—The innermost one, that is, the vail which separated the holy place from the most holy. See a description of the vail in Ex. 26: 31-33. Into the most holy place no one was permitted to go but the high priest, and he only once a year; that is, on the great day of atonement. The Jewish people and even the common priests were wholly shut out; how much more the Gentiles! To this fact the writer of the epistle to the Hebrews (9: 7) makes distinct allusion; and he states (vs. 8) the typical meaning. "In consequence of Christ's death, approach to God, with offerings of praise and prayer, is freely given to *every one*, at all times, who desires it."—*Dr. Ripley's Notes on Hebrews*. Rationalism asks how the evangelists could have known that the vail was rent. Reply: Many of the priests became disciples. See Acts 6: 7. *The earth did quake*—By supernatural power. Here was an earthquake without loss of life. This is a scene of mercy and of wrath, but mercy predominates.

52, 53. *The graves were opened*—The earthquake *restores* life. By graves is meant tombs. Whenever possible, the Jews buried in natural or artificial excavations of rock. *Saints*—Whether of recent times or of times long ago is not stated. In absence of proof it is more reasonable to suppose the former. *After his resurrection*—The rock *sepulchres* were opened at the time that the *rocks* were rent, but, unless we err in too strict an interpretation of the language, the bodies did not quit them till after Christ arose. *Holy city*—Unholy in consequence of this day's work of its priests and people, but holy in the sense of having long been the centre of God's government over the Jews. The resurrection of these saints was indeed a stupendous event, but no more to be disbelieved than any of the accompanying events. It is a pledge of the general resurrection. Whether those who were raised died again, or whether they ascended to heaven, would have been told us had it been important for us to know.

54. *Centurion*—As in the former part of the gospel, captain of a hundred men. *That were with him*—The guards. *Those things*—All the attending events, especially the expiring groans and dying words of Jesus. See Mark's way of reporting it: 15: 39. *The Son of God*—God's son, there being in the Greek, as in some previous cases, no article. The centurion had probably heard the words during the trial, and though, being a heathen, he may not have had a very definite conception of what the words imply, yet he doubtless felt that this being was more than human. Less than this can hardly be supposed.

were done, they feared greatly, saying, Truly this was the Son of God.

55 And many women were there beholding afar off, which followed Jesus from Galilee, ministering unto him:

56 Among which was Mary Magdalene, and Mary the mother of James and Joses, and the mother of Zebedee's children.

57 When the even was come, there came a rich man of Arimathea, named Joseph, who also himself was Jesus' disciple:

58 He went to Pilate, and begged the body of Jesus. Then Pilate commanded the body to be delivered.

Where were the scribes, the expounders of Moses and the prophets? There are a few *heathen*, who are so superior to the system under which they have been educated, that they are better guides than the whole army of ritualists and rationalists.

55. *Women were there*—A beautiful fact in contrast with the absence of all the apostles save John. *Afar off*—Not so far as to show little interest in the sufferer; not so near as to show insensibility to the gross conduct of the chief actors.

56. *Mary Magdalene*—A native, perhaps, of Magdala, on the western coast of the Sea of Galilee. By a singular and widely spread misunderstanding, she has been considered as identical with the "woman which was a sinner." Luke 7:37. Preachers, painters, poets, philanthropists, have all represented Mary Magdalene as having once been a woman of dissolute character. The Irish poet, Thomas Moore, has helped perpetuate the libel in the beautiful poem,—

"Were not the sinful Mary's tears."

As Rev. Charles C. Starbuck remarks, the common opinion is "little better than a posthumous slander." The opinion has no scriptural foundation. The Roman Catholic Church, especially in the person of Gregory the Great, has contributed largely toward the erroneous view. "Magdalen societies," formed for the purpose of reclaiming fallen women, ought to show respect for the memory of Mary Magdalene by taking some other name. The presence of these pious women at the cross reminds one of the scurrilous representation of Renan in his "Life of Jesus," in which he attempts to account for the sorrows of Jesus in the garden by the supposition that he was sighing for the society of the beautiful Jewish maidens of Galilee.

57, 58. *When the even was come*—By the Jewish law (Deut. 21:22, 23) dead bodies were to be removed before sunset. Joseph, knowing what the law is, feels that he must act promptly. This man is a native or a resident of Arimathea, concerning the location of which men are not agreed. The investigations hitherto made point, on the whole, to some locality north-west of Jerusalem, about half way from that city to the Mediterranean coast. Joseph was a disciple, but he had been wanting in decision (John 19:38). He is now a disciple openly. He has lost his "fear of the Jews." He was an honorable counsellor, that is, probably, a member of the Sanhedrim; and he was one of the truly pious Jews that were waiting for the kingdom of God (Mark 15:43). *Begged*—Asked for. The Jews had already besought Pilate that it might be taken away. The Romans were accustomed to let the bodies of the crucified remain on the cross till birds and beasts devoured them. Had Pilate given the body to the

27 *

MATTHEW.

59 And when Joseph had taken the body, he wrapped it in a clean linen cloth,

60 And laid it in his own new tomb, which he had hewn out in the rock: and he rolled a great stone to the door of the sepulchre, and departed.

61 And there was Mary Magdalene, and the other **Mary**, sitting over against the sepulchre.

62 ¶ Now the next day, that followed the day of the preparation, the chief priests and Pharisees came together unto Pilate,

63 Saying, Sir, we remem-

Jews, it would doubtless have been thrown into some receptacle of the dead with the bodies of the robbers.

59. *Linen cloth*—Linen, as young readers may not have learned, is made of flax. In ancient times, flax was much cultivated in India and Egypt. It was affirmed that "the mummy-cloths used by the Egyptians were cotton, and not linen. . . . But a more careful scrutiny by Mr. Bauer of about four hundred specimens of mummy-cloth has shown that they were universally linen." In accordance with the custom of the Jews, Joseph caused the body of Jesus—perhaps he did it with his own hands—to be wrapped up in the linen cloth. The cloth was wound several times round the body. Spices were used. John 19:40. The bodies of the robbers, of course, received no such tender care.

60, 61. *New tomb*—No man had ever been laid in it. John 19; 41.

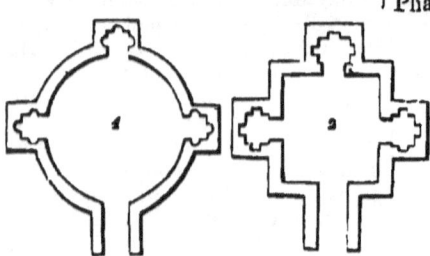

GROUND PLANS OF SEPULCHRES.

Artificial rock-tombs could not have been very numerous. "These tombs were sometimes very roomy, and provided with passages. The sep-ulchres were either made with steps downward, or placed horizontally; while the particular naves were hollowed out, either lengthwise or crosswise, in the walls of the tomb." *Sitting*—Not Peter, not John, but two women. It is admitted, without misgiving, that the majority of our Lord's disciples has thus far consisted of women. It is a fact often mentioned, but not the less deserving to be mentioned again, that woman was last at the sepulchre on the day of the crucifixion and first on the day of the resurrection.

62, 63. *The day of preparation*—More properly translated, *the preparation*. This was Friday. It was the day on which the Jews prepared for their Sabbath, which answers to our Saturday. *We remember*—As the disciples seem not to have remembered it, it has been deemed by some rationalistic interpreters difficult to believe that the priests and Pharisees could have even known it. But the disciples had not forgotten it, though the announcement that he was to rise had made only a feeble impression upon them, which is easily accounted for by the fact that they were exceedingly unwilling to think that he was to be put to death. The Pharisees could not have been ignorant of the fact that he had said he should rise from the dead; for he had once distinctly told them (12: 40) that the Son of man would be *three days and three nights in the heart of the earth.* Besides, such a

ber that that deceiver said, while he was yet alive, After three days I will rise again.

64 Command therefore that the sepulchre be made sure until the third day, lest his disciples come by night, and steal him away, and say unto the people, He is risen from the dead: so the last error shall be worse than the first.

65 Pilate said unto them, Ye have a watch: go your way, make it as sure as ye can.

66 So they went, and made the sepulchre sure, sealing the stone, and setting a watch.

CHAPTER XXVIII.

IN the end of the sabbath, as it began to dawn toward the

---

remarkable announcement as that he would rise from the dead could not have been kept from general circulation. Would not Judas have been likely to speak of it at last? It cannot be doubtful that the priests had some fearful forebodings lest he should again appear among men alive. They knew that Lazarus had been raised from the dead by this very man; and even if they believed that he had been raised by the help of Beelzebub, who could tell but that Beelzebub might help the man to raise himself?

64. *Be made sure*—Secure. *The last error*—That of the people believing that he had actually risen. In that case their influence over the people would be lost. We see in this request to Pilate, in a striking manner, the working of fear. No other body being in the tomb, they could not apprehend imposition of another sort.

65. *A watch*—Some think this implies that the four soldiers who watched him before the body had been taken down, were still on duty at the sepulchre, but this is without proof. He may have used the present in a hurried, colloquial manner; or, it may mean, You have a watch at your command; all you need to do is to go and employ it. Pilate shows no special desire to relieve them from their apprehensions.

66. *Sealing the stone*—Seals were much used in oriental countries for the purpose of making a document stronger. They were made of precious stones, common stones, and even of pottery. In the Alnwick Museum is a seal in the cylinder form, which "bears the date of Osirtasen I., or between 2000 and 3000 B.C. . . . In many cases the seal consisted of a lump of clay, impressed with the seal, and attached to the document, whether of papyrus or other material, by strings. . . One such found at Nimroud was the seal of Sebaco, King of Egypt, B.C. 711, and another is believed by Mr. Layard to have been the seal of Sennacherib, of nearly the same date. In a somewhat similar manner, doors of tombs or other places intended to be closed were sealed with lumps of clay." *How* secure the sepulchre was made by this twofold precaution, sealing and watching, will soon appear.

CHAPTER XXVIII.

RESURRECTION OF JESUS; THE LAST COMMISSION.

783 U.C. Sunday, April 9, A.D. 30.

God did not suffer his Holy One to see corruption. Jesus died, as truly died, as any human being whatever, but from the instant that his spirit departed the body was proof against decomposition. Hence it has been denied that the blood which came from his side, when

first *day* of the week, came Mary Magdalene and the other Mary to see the sepulchre.

2 And, behold, there was a great earthquake: for the angel of the Lord descended from heaven, and came and rolled back the stone from the door, and sat upon it.

3 His countenance was like lightning, and his raiment white as snow:

4 And for fear of him the keepers did shake, and became as dead *men*.

5 And the angel answered and said unto the women, Fear not ye: for I know that ye seek Jesus, which was crucified.

6 He is not here: for he is

---

pierced, was coagulated blood. Unless divine power interpose, the death of a sinful human being necessarily involves the total dissolution of the body. In the case of Jesus, death was only the temporary separation of the spirit from the body. *Whom God hath raised up, having loosed the pains of death: because it was not possible that he should be holden of it* (Acts 2: 24). To the narrative of this stupendous but thoroughly attested fact we are now to turn our attention. Matthew's report of what occurred between the resurrection and the ascension is brief. It omits much which is found in the other gospels. Except so far as is necessary to the correct understanding of Matthew's report, no attempt will here be made to remove apparent discrepancies with those which follow. Difficulties which may arise hereafter will be considered in the appropriate place.

1. *The end of the Sabbath*—The Jewish Sabbath, our Saturday. This closed at sunset, but the phrase, the end of the Sabbath, must not be too strictly interpreted. *After the Sabbath* is doubtless the meaning. It does not necessarily imply that they went *immediately* after sunset. The expression is evidently intended by Matthew himself to be limited by the next clause. They went as it was dawning into the first day of the week, our Sunday, now and long known as the Christian Sabbath. *The other Mary* —These two Marys are not the only women which went. See Mark 16: 1; Luke 23: 55, compared with 24: 1. *To see the sepulchre*—Their special object was to anoint the body (Mark 16: 1).

2. *The angel*—An angel. There are tens of thousands of angels; this was *one* of them. *Rolled back the stone*—Not to let the women in, but to let Jesus go out. The stone was rolled away before the women arrived. Some hold that Jesus left the sepulchre before the stone was removed; but this makes a miracle where the Bible makes none. Joseph of Arimathea rolling the stone *to* the door and the angel rolling it *from* the door are both God's agents. *Sat upon it*—It is not said that he was sitting upon it when the women arrived. The stone was under his control. One angel is more than a match for the entire military power of Rome and the entire ecclesiastical power of the Jews. The gospel of the rationalists: Jesus did not die; or, if he died, he is dead still.

4. *The keepers did shake*—And these are the men by whom the priests were to make the sepulchre secure!

5. *The angel*—If it is the angel referred to in vs. 2, it would appear that he must have gone into the sepulchre. Compare Mark 16: 5. *Fear not ye*—*Ye* may be emphatic. Let the Roman soldiers fear.

6. *As he said*—These pious women, and even the apostles, had strangely lost sight of this part of

CHAPTER XXVIII.

risen, as he said. Come, see the place where the Lord lay.

7 And go quickly, and tell his disciples that he is risen from the dead; and, behold, he goeth before you into Galilee; there shall ye see him: lo, I have told you.

8 And they departed quickly from the sepulchre, with fear and great joy; and did run to bring his disciples word.

9 ¶ And as they went to tell his disciples, behold, Jesus met them, saying, All hail! And they came and held him by the feet, and worshipped him.

10 Then said Jesus unto them, Be not afraid: go tell my brethren that they go into Galilee, and there shall they see me.

11 ¶ Now when they were going, behold, some of the watch came into the city, and shewed unto the chief priests all the things that were done.

12 And when they were assembled with the elders, and had taken counsel, they gave large money unto the soldiers,

13 Saying, Say ye, His disciples came by night, and stole him *away* while we slept.

---

our Lord's teachings. *Come, see*—With what sweet familiarity the angel addresses them! He seems to stoop and point them *to the niche in the tomb* where the body had lain.

7. *Into Galilee*—But after *I am risen again, I will go before you into Galilee* (26:32). *Go quickly*—Work for Christ should be done with promptness and dispatch.

8. *Fear and great joy*—The union of fear with great joy is as possible as the union of sorrow with joy; and Paul says, Sorrowful, yet always rejoicing. *Did run*—If Christians of our times would study more critically the narratives of the Saviour's life, especially those parts which pertain to his passion and his resurrection, their views of Christ would attain such freshness that they, too, would run to communicate to others what they have learned. The study of Christ's sufferings and resurrection is a tonic for weak disciples.

9. *Met them*—Women had the honor of seeing him first. Mary Magdalene is not included. See John 20:11-18. *Hail*—A term of salutation nearly equivalent to rejoice. *Held him by the feet*—They were so overcome with mingled awe and joy that they immediately prostrated themselves at his feet, and *worshipped him*, rendered him divine honor; that is, honored him as a divine being, as the Messiah.

10. *Go tell my brethren*—Jesus reveals himself to the women, and the women must tell the men, "but not on that account must the women exalt themselves into apostles." *Brethren*—The apostles and the disciples generally. Galilee must be the place of meeting after the passover-feast is ended. Some of them will see him before.

11. *Showed*—Reported. *All the things*—The guards may not have seen him rise, but they had seen the quaking of the earth and the rolling back of the stone by the angel; and what they reported awakened in Pharisees and priests the appalling conviction that Jesus had risen.

12, 13. *Assembled*—The facts were such that it would have been much more surprising if they had *not* called a meeting of the Sanhedrim than it is that they did call one. Two courses are possible: they may either deny that he died; or, they may give currency to the notion

29*

14 And if this come to the governor's ears, we will persuade him, and secure you.

15 So they took the money, and did as they were taught: and this saying is commonly reported among the Jews until this day.

16 Then the eleven disciples went away into Galilee, into a mountain where Jesus had appointed them.

17 And when they saw him, they worshipped him: but some doubted.

18 And Jesus came and

---

that his body had been stolen by his disciples while the guards were sleeping. If they do the former they will make themselves either fools or knaves,—*fools*, for making the mistake of supposing he was dead when he was not; *knaves*, for imposing on Pilate. If they do the latter, they will make themselves both *fools and knaves*,—*fools*, for not seeing the worthlessness of the testimony of sleeping men; *knaves*, for bribing men to tell a stupendous lie. They conclude to do the latter; that is, they decide to do what will make them both knaves and fools,—which very few human beings are at the same time.

14. *If this come*—The meaning is not, if he should happen to hear of it, but, if the affair should be brought before him for official investigation. *Will persuade*—Will satisfy. *Secure you*—Save you from all trouble.

15. *Took the money*—Fifteen dollars was paid to Judas for the sake of getting him; a "large" sum (vs. 12) to the soldiers for the purpose of saving themselves from the disgrace of losing their end. *Commonly reported . . . until this day*—About thirty years had passed.

16. *The eleven disciples*—This new phrase is mournfully suggestive. *A mountain*—*The* mountain. It is useless to speculate concerning what mountain it was. The eleven are not mentioned to the exclusion of the women and many others.

17. *Some doubted*—It is not necessary to suppose that it was any of the apostles that doubted. They had all seen him before. Even Thomas had seen him and believed. Paul (1 Cor. 15: 6) says that he was seen of above *five hundred* brethren at once; and there is no good reason to doubt that this is the occasion to which he refers. The news that he had come to Galilee must have spread very rapidly, and a great many of his disciples would desire to be present, most of whom, probably, had never seen him since his resurrection.

18. *And Jesus came*—Came nearer to them, that all might distinctly hear the important words which he was about to utter. *All power*—This is connected in sense with *in heaven and in earth:* All power in heaven and in earth, that is, throughout the universe. *Is given unto me*—The Word had all power before he was made flesh. He was God. John 1: 1. All things were made by him. John 1: 3. All power is *given* to him, therefore, as the Messiah. The words, *is given*, are not contradictory, then, to that class of texts which represent him as having all power before, as the Word, he was made flesh. Besides, as Dr. J. J. Owen remarks, "it might admit of some question whether such power as is here referred to could be conferred upon or exercised by a created being, inasmuch as in effect it raises him to an equality with God." It may also be represented as follows: Christ cannot exercise power to bring men into union with God, to found a church, and to bring men of all nations into it, independently of the Father. Between the Father and the Son there is co-op-

CHAPTER XXVIII.

spake unto them, saying, All power is given unto me in heaven and in earth.

19 ¶ Go ye therefore, and teach all nations, baptizing them in the name of the Fa-

eration. But between such a supposition and the supposition that Christ was God, there is no possible contradiction. Nay, such exalted and perfect co-operation implies the equality of the two. An admirable expression of the fact that all power is given him is found in Dan. 7: 14; Eph. 1: 20-22. In Col. 2: 10, Christ is called *the head of all principality and power*. How sublime the utterance! All power! A few days before he was apparently the most helpless of beings.

19. "Reluctant as we may feel to enter upon the discussion of controverted points,—on which the profoundest scholars, most acute thinkers, and Christians of unquestioned piety and sincerity have taken opposite sides, and on which volumes after volumes have been written without effecting, in general, a radical change of previous conviction on the subject,—nevertheless the doctrinal character of this Commentary imperatively demands an answer to two questions: 1. Is infant baptism scriptural? 2. Does the Greek word *baptizein* mean exclusively *to immerse*, or is the administration of baptism by other modes of applying the water in this ordinance consistent with the legitimate meaning of this Greek verb?"

Such is the opening of a "Dissertation on Christian Baptism" by Dr. William Nast (Methodist), at the close of his Commentary on Matthew. Mr. Barnes, Dr. J. J. Owen (Presbyterian), and Dr. Whedon (Methodist), all enter more or less deeply in their respective Commentaries into the same subject. As interpreters of the Bible it was their duty to do so. The writer of the present volume has no desire to be excused from doing likewise.

As preliminary to the examina-

tion, it should be remarked that *teach* (vs. 19) and *teaching* (vs. 20), though seeming to the English reader to represent the same Greek word, do in fact represent very different words. All scholars are agreed that *teach* is not the true rendering, while *teaching* in vs. 20 is correct. The Greek means *make disciples of*, or, in a shorter form, *disciple*.

First. Before touching the meaning of the Greek word rendered *baptizing*, the question arises, What is the relation of the three acts to one another,—*discipling, baptizing, teaching?* 1. Does this order of the *words* prove that there should be corresponding order in the *acts?* or, is the order of the acts immaterial? Supposing the three acts to have been expressed thus: Go ye, therefore, and *having baptized* all nations, *disciple* them, and *teach* them to observe, etc., it would have been perfectly clear that *baptizing* should be first in the series. That would have been authority enough for baptizing unregenerate persons. But such is not the order of the words, and if the order of the words is worth anything as a guide to the order of the acts, then the first act should be discipling, the second baptizing, the third teaching. 2. Notice the *tense of the participle*. It is not, *having baptized*, which might, perhaps, imply that the baptizing was to precede the *discipling*, but it is *baptizing*. All this is very clear in the Greek; and even if the reader is not acquainted with the original, it may be well to remark that a feeble effort has been made to show that the true reading of the Greek is in that tense which would have required the rendering, *having baptized*. Could this effort have been made successful, it might, per-

ther, and of the Son, and of the Holy Ghost:

20 Teaching them to observe all things whatsoever I

haps, have thrown baptism back of discipleship, and therefore have justified us in baptizing unregenerate persons. But, according to all recent critical editions of the Greek Testament, the point must be considered as settled that the *present*[1] participle is the true reading. Neither the order of the words, then, nor the tenses of the participle, permit us to regard our Lord as requiring us to baptize men before they have been made disciples. 3. If we now turn to John 4: 1, we find words which are in remarkable correspondence with those before us: When therefore the Lord knew how the Pharisees had heard that Jesus *made and baptized more disciples* than John. Here are two acts precisely corresponding with the first two of the series which we are examining: 1. Made; 2. Baptized. What did Jesus make? Disciples. Whom did he baptize? The disciples that he had made. Jesus, then, did not intentionally baptize unregenerate persons and then make them disciples. Not one case of the kind is recorded. His practice was first to make disciples and then to baptize them. In consigning to his disciples the work of extending his kingdom through the world, he commanded them to proceed in the same way: 1. Disciple; 2. Baptize. If this is not the order which he requires, he requires them to go directly contrary to his own practice. 4. That this order is the one intended by our Lord is also evident from Mark 16: 15, 16: Go ye into all the world, and preach the gospel to every creature. He that *believeth and is baptized* shall be saved. Here is the same order: 1. Preach;

2. Believe; 3. Be baptized. On this verse Dr. Lange (not a Baptist) says: "Baptism is not named along with faith as in itself an indispensable matter, but as the natural, certainly, also, necessary consequence of faith; because baptism indicates the entering of the believer into the communion of the believing church." Even Dr. Nast says upon the same verse: "It cannot be denied that we find, in the recorded practice of the apostles, faith uniformly preceding baptism," but he cannot think that this warrants "the conclusion of the Baptists, that only converted and regenerate persons may be received into the church by baptism."

INFERENCES FROM THE ABOVE.— 1. A church, consisting of both regenerate and unregenerate persons, the latter brought into the church, not, as was Simon Magus, through inability to discern the hypocrisy or the self-deception of the applicants, but systematically through deliberate intention to bring them in,—such a church is not formed after the model given in the New Testament; and it is difficult to see how such a body can with any propriety be called a *Christian church*. When the system is carried to its legitimate extreme, as in the Roman Catholic Church and the Greek Church, the departure from the primitive church is so great, that such bodies are utterly unworthy to be regarded as in any sense Christian churches. 2. Infants, of whom neither hypocrisy nor self-deception can be affirmed, are not fit subjects of baptism. They cannot believe, that is, they cannot be *discipled;* therefore they ought not to be baptized. Believing is exclusively the act of the person that believes; therefore just as the faith of a man cannot also be the faith of his wife,

---

[1] Tischendorf has given up the reading *baptisantes*—having baptized—and in his eighth edition, now going through the German press, has *baptizontes*.

CHAPTER XXVIII.

have commanded you: and, lo, I am with you alway, *even* unto the end of the world. Amen.

---

cannot become hers, can in no sense be reckoned to her benefit, so the faith of the parent can in no sense be passed over to the advantage of his infant child. The human being that dies in infancy will be saved, there is good reason to believe, but not through *faith*. He will be saved by virtue of the atonement; and the mere fact that Christ has made an atonement which may avail for dying infants is, not a reason why infants should be baptized. 3. That *male* infants were *circumcised* is, in view of the commission contained in these last two verses of Matthew, no proof that *female* infants or even *male* infants should be baptized. As the distinguished German scholar, J. Jacobi, "a dear friend" of the German historian, Neander, neither of whom was a Baptist, says, "There was no necessity for excluding them in plain words, since such exclusion was understood as a matter of course." That infants became by circumcision members of what has very improperly been called the "Jewish Church," and would therefore naturally be considered as entitled to the privilege of membership by baptism in the Christian Church, is with some an argument of great strength. This is the basis of Dr. Nast's defence of infant baptism, though many who defend the rite consider this line of defence as worthless. Noah, Abraham, Moses, Isaiah, Daniel, and other good men, belonged to the *invisible* church, which was wholly an *unorganized* body; but the idea that the Jewish people, the overwhelming majority of whom were so wicked as to call for the most signal rebukes and the severest chastisements, were a *church*, in any such sense that visible, organized Christian churches can be said to be a continuation of it, is an idea which has no foundation in the Scriptures. This is he that was in the *church* in the wilderness (Acts 7: 38), is the only passage in the entire New Testament in which King James' translators call the Jewish people a church; and here, as eminent critics hold, the Greek ought to have been rendered *congregation*. The *Hebrew nation* was indeed a peculiarly constituted nation, enjoying, for many years, God's special protection for a special end, and for that reason was called the people of God; but the Hebrew nation was not a church. "Circumcision," says Rev. T. T. Perowne (Episcopalian), "was made a necessary condition of Jewish nationality." On the other hand, a Christian church in the days of the apostles was "a body of baptized men and women who believed in Jesus as the Christ, and in the revelation made by him, who were united by having the same faith, hope, and animating spirit of love, the same sacraments, and the same invisible Head."—*Rev. F. Meyrick* (Episcopalian).

Secondly. Baptizing them— What is the act here enjoined? Baptize is a good English word, but was derived from the Greek word, *baptizein*. Assuming that in the earlier history of the word, *to baptize* meant *to immerse*, *to dip*, and meant nothing else, it is impossible to regard that as its only acknowledged meaning now. Webster defines it thus: "To administer the sacrament of baptism; to christen." To christen is defined, "To baptize, or rather to baptize and name." Worcester: "To administer baptism to; to immerse in water, or to sprinkle in water; to christen." The same lexicographer defines baptism as "a Christian rite performed by immersion, ablution, or sprinkling." To learn, then, what our Lord meant when he said, *baptizing them*, we must have recourse to whatever means of information we can obtain relative to the original word itself.

What, then, does the Greek word, *baptizein*, mean? But in what manner is the true answer to be obtained?

1. By examining all the passages in all the Greek books in which the word is used with no reference to the Christian rite. Until the present century this was never thoroughly done. The leader in this kind of investigation was Dr. Alexander Carson, a native of Ireland, once a Presbyterian and afterward a Baptist. "A complete historical exhibition of its use, both in pagan and Christian literature," has been made by Dr. T. J. Conant, of Brooklyn, N. Y. Not one known sentence containing the Greek word has been left out of consideration. The entire number of sentences examined in which the word is used with no reference to the Christian rite is one hundred and seventy-five. "These examples," says Dr. Conant, "are drawn from writers in almost every department of literature and science; from poets, rhetoricians, philosophers, critics, historians, geographers; from writers on husbandry, on medicine, on natural history, on grammar, on theology; from almost every form and style of composition, romances, epistles, orations, fables, odes, epigrams, sermons, narratives; from writers of various nations and religions, Pagan, Jew, and Christian, belonging to many different countries, and through a long succession of ages. In all, the word has retained its ground-meaning" [to immerse, to dip, to plunge, to imbathe, to whelm] "without change. From the earliest age of Greek literature down to its close (a period of about two thousand years), not an example has been found in which the word has any other meaning. There is no instance in which it signifies to make a partial application of water by affusion or sprinkling, or to cleanse, to *purify*,[1] apart from the literal act of immersion as the means of cleansing or purifying."

2. To ascertain what the Greek word *baptizein* means, one may also examine its use by the Church Fathers with reference to the Christian rite, including those who, writing in the Latin language, used such a *Latin* word (one meaning *to immerse*) as proves that they considered the Greek word as meaning *to immerse*. This examination has also been made by Dr. Conant,—sixty-one passages having passed under his review; and from this examination it "appears that the Christian Fathers" [men who wrote within a few hundred years after the apostles themselves] "understood this word in its ordinary, established signification in the Greek language,"—*to immerse*.

3. Nor ought the practice of the Greek Church, which extends over Greece and the vast empire of Russia, of the Roman Catholic Church, and the Church of England (Episcopalian), to be left out of the investigation. That practice shows that nearly the entire Christian world has understood *baptizein* as meaning *to immerse*.

The Church of England.—The Book of Common Prayer, published in London in the reign of Edward VI., 1549, *requires* the child to be dipped. It gives no authority to sprinkle, but grants permission, "if the child is weak," "*to pour* water upon it." Going back seven hundred years, we find that the Church of England forbade even *pouring*. The rule was as follows: "Let the presbyters also know, when they administer the holy baptism, that they may not pour the holy water over the infants' head, but let them always be immersed in the font; as

---

[1] The meaning assigned to it by Dr. Edward Beecher, the thing symbolized, *purification*, being confounded with the act, *immersion*, by which it is symbolized.

the Son of God furnished by himself an example to every believer when he was thrice immersed in the waves of the Jordan."—*Lingard's History*.

The Roman Catholic Church.—The former practice of this body leads to the same result. The Order of Sacraments composed by Pope Gregory I., in the sixth century, *required immersion*.

The practice of these two churches, as is well known, has changed, sprinkling having gradually usurped the place once held by immersion. The change is frankly acknowledged by eminent scholars in the Roman Catholic Church and in the Church of England, and by many of them is sincerely regretted.

The Greek Church.—The modern Greek language is essentially the same as the ancient Greek; and surely the Greeks know the meaning of *baptizo*, as well, to say the least, as others. But before we proceed to show what are the sentiments of the Greek Church relative to the mode of baptism, we present the following remarkable statement, made by Dr. Nast in his "Dissertation on Christian Baptism": "To this very day baptism is administered by pouring, not only in the whole Greek Church, but also in the churches of Asia Minor." In the Appendix of a volume[1] written by Rev. William Goodell, Missionary in Constantinople of The American Board of Commissioners for Foreign Missions, is the Order of Exercises at a Greek Baptism, as witnessed by Rev. Mr. Riggs, in Smyrna, April 21, 1851 (Easter Monday). The Order embraces seventeen articles, the eleventh of which is as follows:

"11. The baptism. The priest taking the infant, perfectly naked, into his hands, and holding it over the font, said, 'The Servant of God, Iphigenia, is baptized' (placing it in the water which reached up to its neck, and thrice taking up water with his right hand and pouring upon the child's head), 'in the name of the Father' (then lifting the child up, and again placing it in the water and repeating the affusion as before), 'and of the Son' (same movement repeated), 'and of the Holy Ghost, now and ever, even forever and ever. Amen.'"

"I have witnessed this ceremony," says Mr. Riggs in a note, "a number of times, and in no instance was the whole body of the person baptized immersed in the water."

Rev. Mr. Riggs is a credible witness. How much is proved by his testimony?

1. That the *creed* of the Greek Church is in favor of sprinkling and opposed to immersion? For the means of answering this question, the author is indebted partly to A. N. Arnold, D.D., Professor in the Theological Seminary of Chicago, who kindly communicated facts in reply to a letter of inquiry. Dr. Arnold resided in Greece as a Missionary more than eleven years.

a. In the Office for Baptism, in the Greek Service Book, or Euchologion, the rubric says, "and when the whole body has been anointed (ears, feet, and hands, besides the fore-mentioned parts) the priest baptizes him, holding him upright, and facing toward the East, saying, 'the servant of the Lord [naming him] is baptized in the name of the Father,' etc., etc., sinking him and raising him at the utterance of each name."

b. In the Commentary on Apostolical Canons XLVI. and XLVII. [Canons of the General Councils received by the Greek Church], pouring and sprinkling are repeatedly characterized as "pseudo-baptism," false baptism.

c. In 1848 there appeared in the modern Greek language an Encyclical Letter which was issued by a Synod of the Greek Church. The Synod, called by the Patriarch of

---

[1] The Old and the New; or, the Changes of Thirty Years in the East. 1853.

Constantinople, was composed of four Patriarchs, and about thirty archbishops and bishops. In this high official document, the most authoritative, perhaps, on the doctrine and practice of the Greek Church of any declaration that has been made in our day, the practice of the Romish Church in baptism is characterized as an *innovation*, a departure from the apostolic form, a substitution of sprinkling in place of baptism, a making superfluous the baptism which the Lord delivered to the Church.

d. On the eighth of October, 1851 (only six months, let it be observed, from the time Mr. Riggs witnessed the administration of baptism as described above, *and after it*), Rev. William Palmer appeared before the Patriarch of Constantinople, who was surrounded by a company of bishops, constituting what is called Lesser Synod or Council. The real question was whether he, who had only been *sprinkled*, could be admitted as a member of the Greek Church. The Patriarch spoke as follows: "There is only one baptism: if some others allow a different one we know nothing of it, we do not accept it. Our Church knows only one baptism, and this without any subtraction, or addition, or alteration whatever. To this the bishops gave assent.

e. Dr. Arnold affirms that during his residence among the Greeks he never heard the slightest intimation of any diversity of views among them relative to the mode of baptism, except on this one point: The National Greek Church of Russia has for two centuries received converts from the Catholic Church and Trinitarian Protestants, without re-baptism, only giving them the chrism, which corresponds to confirmation. This concession was made only after a long and stormy discussion.

These facts prove that Mr. Riggs' testimony is no evidence whatever that the *creed* of the Greek Church is in favor of sprinkling and opposed to immersion. What has so often been affirmed, that the Greek Church, in its written formularies, recognizes nothing as baptism but immersion, remains unshaken.

2. Does Mr. Riggs' testimony prove that the Greek Church *practises* sprinkling, or even pouring, thus violating its own canons? Mr. Riggs testifies that he has seen a Greek priest put a naked infant in the water up to its neck three times, saying in the first instance, The servant of God is baptized, and each time pouring water thrice from his hand upon the child's head. Here, plainly, was no sprinkling for baptism; no pouring for baptism. The baptism was the immersion of the child to its neck, and because the priest knew that that was not an exact compliance with the canons of his church, he "helped out the immersion, in respect to the defect, by an act more or less nearly resembling an affusion. To say that this was *baptism by affusion*, or was intended to be such by the administrator, is to pervert language and misrepresent facts."[1] As Dr. Arnold freely admits, the Greeks are not always punctilious about the absolute totality of the submersion in baptism, but that they either sprinkle or pour for baptism is not shown by the testimony of Mr. Riggs. Dr. Nast's statement that the whole Greek Church has to this very day administered baptism by pouring may have been based upon Mr. Riggs' and other similar representations.

"To this form" [immersion], says Dr. Stanley in his Lectures, "the Eastern Church still rigidly adheres; and the most illustrious and venerable portion of it, that of the Byzantine empire, absolutely repudiates and ignores any other mode of administration as essentially invalid." McClintock and

---

[1] Dr. Arnold, in reply to a letter calling his attention to Mr. Riggs' testimony.

Strong, in their new Cyclopædia, say: "The Greek Church requires trine immersion in its rubrics, but in Russia baptism by sprinkling or affusion is regarded as equally valid." No authority is given for the latter statement. In "Sketches of the Rites and Customs of the Greco-Russian Church," by H. C. Romanoff, the wife of a Russian officer, it is affirmed that "in cases of extreme sickness, sprinkling or pouring of water is considered sufficient." But, as a writer has remarked,[1] this is contradicted by what the author says on a subsequent page: "In the event of a child's being born in a hopeless state, or of its becoming ill so suddenly as to have no time for sending for the priest, the nurse, or any one else, may legally baptize it. A pure vessel is procured, and the infant is *immersed*, with the same words as those used by the priest." The author's representation proves that "baptism by sprinkling or affusion" is not regarded in the Russian Greek Church as "equally valid" with immersion.

"The invalidity of sprinkling," says Dr. Arnold, "is made a prominent point in the controversial writings (the latest no less than the earlier) of the Greeks against the Latins and the Protestants."

We add the testimony[2] of Dr. Galusha Anderson, Professor of Sacred Rhetoric in the Newton Theological Institution: "When I was at Mar Sabas, I visited the chapel of the baptistery. This baptistery was circular, about four feet in diameter and five feet in depth. I asked the monk who was our guide how they baptized infants. Suiting his action to his word, he said that they plunged them into the water all over. When I was in Athens, I heard that Dr. King, a Congregationalist, immersed infants, not venturing to repeat the formula of baptism before an Athenian audience without performing the act so evidently expressed to a Greek by the word *baptizo*; and that he had immersed a child of a Greek Congregational brother who has an American wife, only a few days before."

In accordance with both the canons and the practice of the Greek Church, Alexander de Stourdza, "one of the most learned of all the modern apologists for the Greek Church," affirms that the word *baptizo* has only one signification; that it means literally and always *to plunge*. "Baptism and immersion," he says, "are identical, and to say *baptism* by *sprinkling* is as though we should say immersion by sprinkling."

The practice, then, in former times, of the Church of England and of the Romish Church, and especially of the Greek Church even to the present day, shows that a large portion of the Christian world has understood Jesus Christ as meaning in the use of the word *baptizein* that disciples should be *immersed*.

4. That this is exactly what Christ intended is also evident from the connections in which the word is found. The word is *never* found in such connections as would be natural if it means *to sprinkle*, but always in such as are natural if it means *to immerse*. For example, it is used in connection with a *river* and with *much water*. It is of course not impossible that one was sprinkled who went to a river, or to a place of much water. It is not impossible that one was sprinkled who went as Jesus did and as the eunuch did down into the water. But is it probable? Is it natural? Is it at all common for men and women now to go to a river when they are to be only sprinkled? What *might possibly* have been done, is not the question which a sincere seeker of the will of Christ would ask. Again, in the words of Dr. Arnold, in the "Bibliotheca

---

[1] Baptist Quarterly, April.
[2] In a letter to the author, under date of Dec. 18, 1869.

Sacra," January, 1869, "*persons are always said to be baptized, the element never.* We never read, 'A baptized water upon B,' but always, 'A baptized B in water.' We never read, 'water was baptized upon them,' but always, 'they were baptized in water!'" Substitute in the first form of expression the word sprinkle or pour, and there is no unfitness: A sprinkled, poured, water upon B. Substitute these words in the second form: A sprinkled, poured, B in the water, and the unfitness is immediately seen. Substitute immerse in the first form, and the unfitness is equally great: A immersed water upon B. Substitute immerse in the second form, and there is no unfitness: A immersed B in water. Now it is in the *latter* form in which *baptizein* is found in the New Testament. The meaning *to immerse* is, therefore, entirely fitting in the connection in which the Greek word is used.

5. Baptism is symbolic of a great spiritual change; namely, death to sin and resurrection to holiness. This death to sin resembles Christ's burial, and this resurrection to holiness resembles Christ's resurrection. See Rom. 6: 3-5; Col. 2: 12. Is there appropriateness in sprinkling as a symbol of these great facts? But nothing can more appropriately represent these facts than immersion.

As baptism is to follow faith, so partaking of the Lord's Supper is to follow baptism. The Roman Catholic Church, the Greek Church, the Lutheran Church, the Church of England, the Presbyterian Churches, and the Methodist Churches, regard baptism as properly antecedent to the Lord's Supper. It is but a very small portion of the Christian world that denies that this is the true relation of the two ordinances. The unanimity of Christians in all ages respecting it is remarkable.

1. *Baptism is supposed to follow the act of faith immediately;* that is, assuming that a man has actually believed he is under obligation to be immediately baptized. If a man, in other words, has been buried by the Spirit of God to sin and been raised to holiness, it is his duty to submit at once to the rite which symbolizes those acts. This would leave no room for the observance of the other great rite of the Christian religion. The observance of that rite between the act of believing and the act of submitting to baptism is, so to speak, intentionally *crowded out* by our divine Lord himself through the requirement to be baptized as the next step after believing. The Supper must be observed, then, either before believing or after baptism. The former would be advocated by none. It follows that its only place is after baptism.

2. *The Lord's Supper as well as baptism is a symbol.* But the meaning of the two symbols is not the same. Expressed briefly, baptism symbolizes the soul's *entrance* into life; the Supper symbolizes the *fuller participation* of life. Put, then, the Supper before baptism, and you spoil the *natural relation* of the symbols, and of course destroy their meaning.

3. The *practice of the apostles and of the churches in apostolic times is in harmony with the above.* There is not a case in the book of Acts in which the Lord's Supper was administered to persons who had not been baptized. The primitive practice in this respect should be our guide. It is equivalent to divine appointment. It is equivalent to divine authority.

4. But it has already been proved that our Lord's command to be baptized is a command to be immersed. It follows that neither sprinkling nor pouring is the ritual qualification for the Lord's Supper. *Immersion is the ritual qualification.*

5. As neither baptism nor the

Lord's Supper is to be observed in heaven, the argument that unbaptized persons may commune together here at the Lord's table, because the saints will commune together in heaven, is worthless. Saints will not commune together in heaven in any such sense as we are considering. The question is one pertaining to the *visible, organized* bodies, which exist only in this world under the name of churches.

6. *There is nothing singular, therefore, in the position of Baptist churches respecting even ritual communion.* Like nearly all Protestant churches, they hold that though given spiritual qualifications entitle a man to given spiritual privileges in the *invisible, unorganized* church, a given ritual qualification, baptism, is necessary to entitle one to the privileges of a *visible, organized* church. At what point, then, do others separate from Baptist churches? At baptism,—something being introduced for baptism which is not baptism. The point of separation is not on the question of communion.

In the name of the Father, etc.— The popular understanding of these words is incorrect. It does not mean, *by authority of*. *Into* the name is the rendering now generally admitted, though some adhere to the common version. *Into the name* may mean into "professed subjection" to the Father, etc.; or, into the obligations due to the Father. *Name*—"All that belongs to the *manifestation*" of the Father, etc. Observe that the singular is used. It is not *names*, though the three persons of the Trinity are mentioned. We must not conceive of the Father, and the Son, and the Holy Spirit, as so distinct that they occupy *three distinct localities side by side*. Yet they are distinct, and equal in all the essential attributes of their nature. How arrogant, blasphemous, the assumption here made by Jesus Christ, if he was not in his higher nature the *Word* (Logos), that was with God and was God!

20. *Teaching them to observe all things*—As the baptized are supposed to have been made disciples, they are already taught what are the conditions of salvation,—repentance and faith. From the time of their baptism, which is supposed to follow immediately after their acceptance of Christ, they are to be instructed in all that Christ has revealed. This includes instruction in the Old Testament and in the New. Christ taught his disciples the meaning of the Old, and much of what he taught them besides is now included in the New. Here is a lesson of vast importance for ministers, Sabbath-school teachers, and all others who can teach, and for those who are to be taught. Converts to Christ must be taught, or they will have either no zeal, or "zeal not according to knowledge." They should be taught to *observe all things*, etc.—not to do more than Christ has commanded, not to do less. They should be taught that Christ's will is to be learned *through the teachings and the practice of the apostles*, as well as through his own teachings and practice. They should be taught to do exactly what Christ has enjoined, whether it pertain to the state of the heart or to a rite. They should be taught to attain all that faith, spirituality, devotedness, zeal, and meekness in the family, in business, in study, in the affairs of the nation, which Christ requires. *With you*— Apostles, ministers, teachers of the truth. *Alway*—Literally, all the days, that is, every day. *Unto the end of the world*—To the end of the Messianic dispensation, when Christ shall come the second and last time. The promise is made not only to apostles but to ministers of the gospel to the end of time. It is intended, substantially, for the universal Church of Christ. Here is divine authority for making known

he gospel to men of every nation, age, and color. How vast the responsibility! how rich the promise!

Praise God, from whom all blessings flow;
Praise him, all creatures here below;
Praise him above, ye heavenly host;
Praise Father, Son, and Holy Ghost.

www.ingramcontent.com/pod-product-compliance
Lightning Source LLC
Chambersburg PA
CBHW021203230426
43667CB00006B/529